Melodramatic Tactics

MELODRAMATIC TACTICS

Theatricalized Dissent in the English Marketplace, 1800–1885

Elaine Hadley

Stanford University Press
Stanford, California ▪ 1995

Stanford University Press
Stanford, California
© 1995 by the Board of Trustees of the
Leland Stanford Junior University
Printed in the United States of America

CIP data appear at the end of the book

Stanford University Press publications are
distributed exclusively by Stanford University Press
within the United States, Canada, Mexico, and Central America; they are
distributed exclusively by Cambridge University Press
throughout the rest of the world.

For Olive Reitz Hadley and Samuel Trevor Hadley

Acknowledgments

I would like to thank a variety of people for their guidance, knowledge, and support during the conception and execution of this book. Mary Poovey merits special gratitude for her intellectual acuity, sense of argument, and awareness of the stakes involved in this form of cultural criticism. Sarah Winter and Joe Sitterson have commented on some or all of this manuscript and made it better by having done so. Judith Walkowitz's own work and comments on an earlier version of this manuscript added historical depth, especially to the final chapter. Thanks also to Anna Clark, who responded generously to early queries and directed me to the melodramatic rhetoric of the anti–Poor Law movement. Advice in the later stages from Elizabeth Helsinger helped me to see clearly during my final revisions. Illuminating questions on an early version of the second chapter came from students and faculty at the University of California at Los Angeles and the University of California at San Diego, who attended presentations of that draft. The students of my senior seminar at Yale and my graduate seminar at the University of Chicago must be mentioned as well, for they both inspired and challenged me to work out the implications of some of my local readings, especially of

Acknowledgments

East Lynne. I am also grateful to my editor at Stanford University Press, Jan Spauschus Johnson, my copy editor, Evelyn Mercer Ward, and, for last-minute proofing, Lise Shapiro.

I would like to offer a broad gesture of thanks to the librarians of the Library of Congress and the staff of the Pusey Library at Harvard University, all of whom simplified my access to crucial historical documents that form the basis of my argument. The chapter on the Old Price Wars is an expansion of an article that appeared in *PMLA* 107, no. 3 (May 1992). It is reprinted by permission of the copyright owner, The Modern Language Association of America.

And in keeping with the dramaturgy of melodrama, I must people one of my last scenes with family. My parents, Trevor and Olive Hadley, evinced their heartfelt support of my endeavors not least through their remarkable willingness to proofread a messy version of this document; to them I am more than grateful.

Finally, I must thank Alexis Cain, whose constant encouragement, editorial assistance, and outrageous confidence in this book always made my work seem both a pleasure and a mission.

E. H.

Contents

Figures

Melodramatic Tactics

Melodrame Mad!

Staging the Melodramatic Mode

In the hope of selling large numbers of tickets to a Surrey Theatre production, the prolific Thomas John Dibden labeled one of his dramatic pieces "Melodrame Mad!" as if to enact in the title the sort of response he hoped to elicit in his audience. It was an early form of subliminal advertising. In the second decade of the nineteenth century, as indicated by Dibden's marketing ploy of 1819, the term *melodrame* or *melodrama* was presumed capable of soliciting popular curiosity, partly because of this still-emerging genre's novelty and its continuing status, at least in theory, as a form of "illegitimate" drama—neither tragedy nor comedy.[1] By midcentury, however, stage melodrama and its distinctive style of presentation had become so common in most London theaters that plays of a melodramatic cast no longer identified themselves as such; in most respects melodrama was drama.

Despite melodrama's pervasiveness on the stage during the Regency and Victorian eras in England, it has not been accorded proportional critical attention. Its derivative reliance on continental forms, its widespread popularity, and its reputed origins in illegitimate drama have usually discouraged scholarly analysis. Although in the middle decades of this century historians of the theater obligatorily documented the rise and dominance of melodrama on the nineteenth-century stage, and some more recent literary criticism has studied the translation of its theatrical style into canonical Victorian novels, melodrama has consistently suffered from the low expectations and unacknowledged biases of its critics.[2] For theatrical historians, the nineteenth century has always been supposed the nadir of the English drama, the decades when *Richard III* was performed entirely on horseback, when tanks of water replaced the stage, and when dogs sometimes had more lines to deliver than great tragedians; consequently, melodrama has routinely been relegated by them to a pejorative footnote in these surveys. Literary critics have shared this estimation and generally treat melodrama as a literary convention of vague definition that is situated beyond the boundaries of what has been deemed Literature. Moreover, modern critical theory's resistance to the emotive and gestural as qualities worthy of analysis has also forestalled consideration of melodrama's function in cultural formation, a function its pervasiveness seems to confirm.[3]

Nineteenth- and twentieth-century literary evaluation of melodrama has all too often measured the genre in terms of prejudicial assumptions about its audience, thereby introducing social and political values into a critical methodology often considered by its practitioners to operate objectively. In one of the early modern studies of English melodrama, William Dye demonstrates this critical move, typically aligning the genre with political and emotive misrule. Melodrama, he observes, "employs the methods of the mob orator, and of the ordinary type of evangelist."[4] Somewhat more recent studies prove incrementally more tolerant, but J. O. Bailey, as an example, nonetheless reads the impact of melodrama through stereotypical constructions of its early audiences that lead him into a contradictory but very familiar appraisal of the form. According to Bailey, melodramatic plots both reflect the gritty lives of common people and, through exciting spectacle, deliver those common people from the monotony of their existences.[5] Bailey exemplifies most twentieth-century critics and echoes many nineteenth-century observers who condescendingly define melodrama in terms of wish fulfillment and sensory excitement. Such terms are influenced by these commentators' infantilizing conceptions about the popular psyche. These conceptions are undoubtedly the heirs of high realism's strong critique of melodrama, which diagnosed it as one symptom of a widespread philistinism in the nineteenth century. In fact, melodrama was never immune from such condescension by association, perhaps especially during its infancy. In March 1818, one reviewer wrote: "The taste then, for melo-drama, must arise from an inertness in the minds of the spectators, and a wish to be amused without the slightest exertion on their own parts, or any exercise whatever in their intellectual powers."[6] As Dibden implied, consumers of popular theatrical fare were presumed to be, quite literally, "melodrame mad."

Given contemporary literary practice's more recent move away from questions of form and aesthetic value, the time seems auspicious for an alternative approach to the analysis of melodrama that encompasses its cultural and historical significance. In part because no one has problematized the assumptions of these older analyses, while many have continually cited them in footnotes, there has been as yet no systematic effort by a literary critic to place English stage melodrama in its social context or to account for what is generally conceded to be the nearly paradigmatic presence of its defining features throughout nineteenth-century English society.[7] Melodrama's familial narratives of dispersal and reunion, its emphatically visual renderings of bodily torture and criminal conduct, its atmospheric menace and providential plotting, its expressions of highly charged emotion, and its tendency to personify absolutes like good and evil were represented in a wide variety of social settings, not just on the stage.[8] Indeed, a version of the "melodramatic" seems to have served as a behavioral and expressive model for several generations of English people.

I

My object of study in this book will therefore not be a series of literary texts or even a specific literary genre. Instead, this book delineates and charts what I call a "melodramatic mode," which appeared in myriad social contexts during the nineteenth century. Comprised of the melodramatic features I briefly listed above, features that we now too exclusively associate with stage melodrama and certain literary texts, the melodramatic mode emerged in the early and mid–nineteenth century as a polemical response to the social, economic, and epistemological changes that characterized the consolidation of market society in the nineteenth century, especially the varied effects of the classificatory procedures instituted by English bureaucracies, such as the New Poor Law of 1834 or, later in the century, the Contagious Diseases Acts. Detectable in the convictions and practices of heterogeneous groups of people throughout the course of the nineteenth century—theatrical audiences, paupers, married women, and reformers—the melodramatic mode was a reactionary rejoinder to social change but not, it must be stressed, necessarily a politically reactionary response, for both the opinions it embodied and its objects of protest did not always fall neatly within the predefined categories of party. In the early decades of the nineteenth century, for example, London Radicals, rural Tories, and miscellaneous nonpartisans combined as an audience to stage their own melodrama of sorts to protest against altered theatrical practices, while a generation or two later, a Whig socialite lobbied for marriage reform in the style of a melodramatic heroine.

The melodramatic mode was manifest in texts and speeches but also, as the above instances indicate, crucially expressive in nonlinguistic forms of representation—physical gestures, political actions, and visual cues, such as clothing and other objects. Indeed, these last two terms should be replaced by *costumes* and *props*, for these terms more precisely articulate the melodramatic mode's adherence to theatrical representation and the cultural values of publicity and visibility formerly attached to such representation. By the latter half of the century, for example, the full resources of the traditional royal progression through England were deployed to express these particular cultural values in the costumes and gestures of Queen Victoria and her family. In the face of rapid industrialization, private capital accumulation, and bureaucratization, the melodramatic mode's distinctive theatricality insisted on the continued vitality of traditionally public, social formations, especially patriarchal status hierarchies, which constituted identity in terms of familial and communal relationships. By the overused term *patriarchy*, I refer to a specific political and cultural formation that governed England for several centuries. In a 1630 treatise, Sir Robert Filmer provided a succinct definition of patriarchy that remained descriptively accurate for at least two hundred more years: "The authority of the parent and the authority of the statesman were one and the same. All forms of social obedience were construed in terms of the patriarchal family . . . and, indeed, so were all forms of social organization."[9] Although the political edge of the melodramatic mode grew blunter as these patriarchal status hierarchies slowly collapsed over the course of the eighteenth and nineteenth centuries, and its conceptual cohesion slackened as it became entangled with the more modern commodity culture of leisure, the melodramatic mode retained sufficient definitional coherence to remain a prevalent behavioral and rhetorical paradigm to the end of the century.

In the central chapters of the book, I elaborate on the content and method of this melodramatic mode by charting four notable appearances of it that occur at intervals over the course of nine decades. In the second chapter, I chart the emergence of the melodramatic mode by examining the productive relationship between some typical early melodramas—Thomas Holcroft's *The Tale of Mystery* and *Deaf and Dumb*, William Dimond's *Adrian and Orrila*, and Theodore Hook's *Tekeli*—and the rioters who initiated the "Old Price Wars" in Covent Garden Theatre in 1809. The Old Price Wars, a protest against increased ticket prices and architectural renovations within the theater, were also an early and partially formulated expression of community insurgency against the reorganization of the theater and, by extension, society, in terms of antagonistic "class" relationships. These rioters sensed that the privatizing effects of the market, as manifested in the new private boxes, undermined status hierarchies and their patronage economies and so they retaliated by staging a melodrama in the pit. Necessarily dependent on its newly diverse consumers, theatrical melodrama responded in a similar fashion, dramatizing on the stage the revered symbols of a deference society for the benefit of its audiences.

Having delineated the features of the melodramatic mode by relating it to its stage version, I consider in my third chapter the popular opposition to the New Poor Law of 1834, a widespread reaction that included Charles Dickens's novel *Oliver Twist*. In this novel, Dickens, echoing members of various contemporary protest groups throughout England, adopted the melodramatic mode in order to resist the alienating and classifying effects of early Victorian England, especially those effects at work in the Poor Law Amendment Act of 1834, whose operations provide the explicit context for *Oliver Twist*'s initial chapters. Offering an analysis of the new law's wide-ranging effects on social exchange and the constitution of personhood, I also identify the structural issues that the melodramatic mode in *Oliver Twist* addresses throughout the entire novel. In arguing for this continuity in the novel, I thus differ with those who maintain that Dickens simply tacked the early workhouse scenes on to an escapist gothic romance. As a result, I clarify *Oliver Twist*'s relationship to its social setting, but additionally I reveal how the melodramatic techniques that create a familial and communal identity for Oliver not only respond to the new law's attempts to classify society and privatize the subject, but also defy similar modes of ideological discipline that, some current critics contend, characterize the novel as a genre.

In the fourth chapter, I examine Caroline Norton's polemical and fictional writing of the 1840's and 1850's in the context of the midcentury feminization of the melodramatic mode. In her works, Norton deployed the melodramatic mode and the persona of the melodramatic heroine to detect the modernizing impulse of classification even as it became complicatedly encoded by gender. Furthermore, Norton's writing proves that not all midcentury romances about family life should be deemed bourgeois repressions of economic and sexual injustices in the service of capitalist ideology. On the contrary, when staged as melodrama, polemical works like *English Laws for Women in the Nineteenth Century* and *A Letter to the Queen* could react against the new system's gender-based classificatory and commercial effects. Norton's melodramatic rhetoric of motherhood publicized a somewhat modernized version of the inclusive, hierarchical, and deferential family as the model for all social exchange. Central to this is her representation of the figure of Queen Victoria, who is depicted as both a mother to all England and Norton's patron. In a brief conclusion to the chapter, I discuss the ways in which Victoria herself ultimately deployed the melodramatic mode in her theatrical progressions through London in the latter part of her reign.

In these last decades of the nineteenth century, late Victorian market culture—a culture politically, socially, and artistically unlike the Regency period of theatrical riots and patent theaters—could nonetheless experience an eruption of the melodramatic mode into the public scene. And yet the passage of considerable time necessarily altered the meaning and impact of the melodramatic mode's intervention, which can be seen to have far more diverse and yet diffuse effects as the century comes to a close. By juxtaposing Josephine Butler's melodramatic speeches opposing the Contagious Diseases Acts with George Meredith's career and his 1885 novel, *Diana of the Crossways*, I argue in the fifth chapter that the melodramatic mode played paradoxical roles in late-nineteenth-century struggles over political and aesthetic value. I demonstrate in the instance of Butler's movement that the melodramatic mode could still provide a coherent polemical response to the classificatory and invasive procedures of state bureaucracy. Yet Butler's public protest, which celebrated the sovereign roles of wife, mother, and daughter presiding over a deferential moral culture, was explicitly engaged in a discursive and material battle with alternative behavioral models, especially the revised version of proprietary subjectivity espoused by the liberal cultural elite, men like George Meredith or his friend John Morley, who touted intellectual self-possession and the exchange of ideas. Given this context, Meredith's psychologized rendering of Mrs. Norton's story in *Diana of the Crossways* can be construed as an assertive attempt to appropriate and privatize the melodramatic mode and the public women often affiliated with its enactment in order to fortify his professional and aesthetic status as "man of letters." In the plots of his novels and in the plotting of his editorial decisions as a reader of manuscripts for Macmillan Books, Meredith helped to institutionalize the gendered classification of writing that came to organize the fiction market in the late nineteenth century by effectively casting romance writers as female speculators and novelists of psychological realism as male intellectuals.

II

Because I am identifying a participant in the formation of nineteenth-century culture that has not been identified before, I must take particular care in naming, defining, and researching my object of study. I have chosen the word *mode* both to distinguish my object from the term *discourse*, a distinction I will discuss shortly, and from more familiar linguistic terms, such as *rhetoric* or *genre*. These latter terms emerge from and are determined still by the formalist tradition of literary studies, and to use them would, I think, invoke formalist assumptions and the particular field of vision they induce. *Mode*, by contrast, implies a more heterogeneous perspective, one that enables us to see what lies beyond what has all too often become the self-reflexive "linguistic turn" of modern critical practice, a turn that has deflected attention from other media of representation.[10]

Since no traditional literary history can address this interdisciplinary object of study, an alternative approach becomes crucial. In this book, I will use the interpretive skills of a literary critic—a practiced sensitivity to rhetoric and figuration as well as an awareness of the structural organization of texts—but will apply these familiar skills to political, legal, and cultural documents while armed with a corresponding conception of the ways by which cultural meaning is represented. This interdisciplinary methodology is justified by and derives from two related assumptions. First, it surmises that issues of cultural representation are integral to any analysis of social formations and accounts of historical change. Second, it presumes that genres such as melodrama, as well as individual literary texts, did not exist in isolation from the larger ideological designs of nineteenth-century culture but were active participants in the discursive contests that resulted in that era's productions of meaning. During these discursive contests, the distinctions between melodrama and Literature, between Literature and other types of texts, between texts and historical events, and between melodrama and political practice, distinctions that still seem relatively timeless and essential in the late twentieth century, were unstable, engaged in the negotiations that would only later result in the categories we recognize today.

Insofar, then, as this project shifts attention away from the study of melodrama per se and redirects it toward a melodramatic mode that is considered both a product and producer of social contestation, not an aesthetic artifact, it takes to its logical end what John Guillory has called "objective structuration." Objective structuration "apprehend[s] the work of art as the objectification not of subjects or communities but of the relations between subjects, or the relations between groups."[11] Although deployed by identifiable subjects and communities, the melodramatic mode is therefore not merely an unmediated expression of them; it is the expression of their productive relation with others. In the following analysis of the melodramatic mode, it will be readily apparent that its relational content necessarily exceeds any individual or corporate intention as well as oversteps the traditional parameters of a "work of art." Those opposed to the New Poor Law of 1834, for instance, may have enacted the melodramatic mode, but their grasp and acceptance of its full significance is uncertain, for it necessarily and imperfectly embodied their beliefs through a constitutive relationship with the market culture they struggled to understand. Moreover, their opposition, a mixture of open-air speeches, pamphlets, riots, and petitions, is not ordinarily categorized as a work of art.

Within this broader and more flexible critical context, stage melodrama no longer epitomizes an embarrassing century in English drama's otherwise illustrious chronology, but comprises one crucial version of the melodramatic mode. Furthermore, this theatrical genre ceases to be a localized literary convention and can instead be seen to play a significant role, along with other appearances of the melodramatic mode (in politics, journalism, and the novel) in the formation of modern culture. Even though I will continue throughout this book to urge readers to suspend aesthetic evaluation of melodrama as a literary genre, I am not thereby denouncing such efforts or lobbying for the disappearance of the concept of aesthetic value, as if such a result were even possible in our culture, where all practices and products are measured in units of value. Indeed, much of what follows concerns itself in detail with the contested evaluations—aesthetic, political, and social—of both melodrama as genre and, more generally, the melodramatic mode, for these contested evaluations give voice to the relations among subcultures that determine the historically specific content of the melodramatic mode from one generation to the next. I am simply suggesting that to consider melodrama as a manifestation of the melodramatic mode momentarily brackets our customary aesthetic assessment of the melodrama and, in so doing, enables us to see a portion of the social conflicts from which emerged the very practice of aesthetic evaluation and even the derivation of the genre melodrama.[12]

Since this book's object of study is not the genre melodrama, it necessarily generates different sorts of arguments than a literary history would. Although I discuss stage melodrama in the second chapter, I do so in the context of stage melodrama's involvement in political disputes during a transition in the economy of the English theater. In later chapters, I will continue to consider stage melodrama and its incorporation into the novel at times, but entirely in terms of its congruence with other instances of the melodramatic mode as these respond to the discursive strategies of political economy, law, and liberalism. This study of the melodramatic mode thereby offers a revised, if only partial, historical record of the emergence of the nineteenth-century English state and the classificatory culture that it engendered. Moreover, by articulating the rhetoric and restaging the theatrical quality of the melodramatic mode, I provide a fuller account of the ideological contest from which derives what we now know as "class," "literature," "middle-class domesticity," and "Romantic subjectivity."

As should by now be evident, this historicist approach to melodrama differs markedly in method and content from the most well-known and most compelling book-length analysis to date of literary melodrama, Peter Brooks's psychoanalytically informed *The Melodramatic Imagination.*[13] Brooks's title articulates our fundamental differences, for in his attribution of melodrama to the imagination—what amounts to a melodrama of consciousness—he locates melodrama within the psyche of the individual. Thus, the rhetoric of melodrama becomes an aestheticized form of psychological expression and its tropes a series of psychic pressure points that move melodrama out of history and, occasionally, into pathology. This latter version of melodrama, as I will argue, is not a timeless literary convention but was formulated and then employed by writers like Morley and Meredith at a historically specific moment for the purpose, among others, of institutional advancement.

This professionalization of authorship and the various other processes of cultural formation that are charted in the following chapters evince historicist assumptions that partially rely on Michel Foucault's work on discursive networks and their production of knowledge as power within a culture. Discursive networks consist of historically specific formations of individual discourses. These individual discourses are distinctive configurations of language, with their own rules of operation, that establish the field of possibility for the representation of meaning through language and through gestures, actions, and institutions at a given historical moment. They are thus to some extent disciplinary—prescribing, rather than simply describing, "reality."[14] Such discourses have material impact on a culture and its people because they inform many of the places and practices that organize society. In nineteenth-century England, these discourses shaped the bureaucratized state, including its national welfare policies, its court procedures, and its regulations governing trade and commerce. The individual discourses involved in these networks vary from period to period; some of the more dominant discourses during the nineteenth century in England included the discourses of law, religion, politics, political economy, medicine, and science. What counted as knowledge at various moments throughout the nineteenth century was produced through the operation of discourses like these and, more specifically, through the contestation among their respective versions of the "real."

Despite my stated indebtedness to Foucault, this study also displays my disagreement with some often-criticized features of Foucault's methodology—for instance, its tendency to overgeneralize and thus overlook the evidence that renders events historically specific and distinctive and its failure within a rather static archeological model to account for change, movement, and resistance in its historical record of "power." Foucault seems to deny that local or human initiative exerts much influence on these totalizing discourses and their practices. In arguing for the existence of a melodramatic mode, I am suggesting that amid the conflict among various discourses, there also operated less extensive, less powerful, and less autonomous modes (the melodramatic, the Romantic) that nonetheless participated in these conflicts and exerted an impact on the production of cultural meaning. The melodramatic mode could thus often manifest itself within a particular discourse, for instance, political discourse.

By providing in this introduction a shorthand definition of the melodramatic mode that characterizes it as an antagonistic response to the consolidation of market practices throughout nineteenth-century English culture, I run the risk of simply substituting my own monolithic, totalizing terminology in place of Foucault's. The melodramatic mode should not be seen as some sort of essentialized or anthropomorphized force in pure opposition to market society. Always already entangled with the market practices it rejects, as evidenced by Dibden's explicit co-optation of melodrama for purposes of solicitation, the melodramatic mode should be seen instead as a productive friction, a creative disjunction within the dominating practices that were becoming most strongly associated with the capitalist system; the resistant energy of the melodramatic mode thus emerges from what Jonathan Dollimore calls the "inevitable incompleteness and surplus of control itself."[15] Also helping to dispel any suggestion of totalization in this book is the following chapters' historical account of the melodramatic mode's dialectical relation to market practices, its record of varied practitioners and even more varied outcomes.

Differing, therefore, from discourses or discursive practices in its degree of logical self-sufficiency and range of influence, modes like the melodramatic mode may not utterly change the course of history that discourse networks determine, but they do change the manner by which history proceeds along that course. For example, through its contention with class society, the melodramatic mode did not prevent the consolidation of that society, but, as I describe in the following chapters, it did contribute to the distinctive shape class society took. The melodramatic mode's absence from our historical record of cultural formation in the nineteenth century has therefore resulted in a distorted analysis of the period that has overemphasized the dominance and internal consistency of, for example, the private sphere, the free market, and the bourgeois nuclear family. Moreover, with the melodramatic mode erased from the historical record, English romanticism has long endured as a narrow and distorted lens through which we have viewed early-nineteenth-century English culture.

In Chapter 1 I thus describe the conditions out of which both the melodramatic mode and romantic poetry emerged in the cultural contention and social realignment that characterized the end of the eighteenth century. Invisible in historical and literary records of the late eighteenth century, the melodramatic mode played a constitutive, if agonistic, role, especially for romantic conceptions of subjectivity and community. Both discursive modes responded to that period's theatricalized style of governance in which spectacular displays of state power disguised the radical restructuring of hierarchical England. In this theatrical culture, such structural changes both engendered and acknowledged a common perception that the public roles that had traditionally distinguished the various ranks had become suspect, and the actors of these public roles, impostors. By analyzing Wordsworth's "The Old Cumberland Beggar," I maintain that much of romantic poetry's response to this material and representational crisis was transformative rather than preservative, sustaining the traditional values that had authorized social exchange by utterly revising them, figuring them as products of the private conscience operating within a subjective consciousness. In providing a literary and spiritual lexicon for individuality, much romantic poetry effectively facilitated the ongoing fragmentation of the public sphere and the rise of class culture and its model of social exchange. The melodramatic mode, therefore, in its always public and theatrical response to the classification of English society, also resisted romantic poetry's interiorization of the subject.

Hearkening back to a deferential society and its patriarchal grounds for identity, the melodramatic mode in its various manifestations was profoundly reactionary, if not precisely politically reactionary. It thoroughly idealized a passing deferential society and the status hierarchies such a society nurtured; it also shared many of its features with the nearly forgotten procedures of sentimentality—the fall of a tear, the sympathetic exchange. Melodrama was not, however, simply a throwback to a bygone era, despite these numerous signs of the past. Nostalgia, after all, is always a practice in the present. The melodramatic mode was as much a product as a participant in the history of nineteenth-century capitalist culture, and its features were more a result of contemporary pressures than an exact historical reproduction. The melodramatic mode's hyperbole and exaggeration, its suspicion and providential plotting, to cite only a handful of its features, attest to the combative conditions under which it struggled to represent deferential values during the nineteenth century. Continually complicated and compromised by the market in which it labored, and yet continually complicating and compromising that market, the melodramatic mode was, as its earliest critics detected, a truly heterogeneous form. It is tempting to dramatize the melodramatic mode either as a collaborator colluding with the monopolizing tendencies of the market or as a resistance fighter valiantly opposing its onslaught. The melodramatic mode, however, was not so easily categorized, for it could both cannily subvert and unwittingly adopt some of the emerging values of institutionalized capitalism, as the following account demonstrates.

ONE

Magyars and Michaels

Unromantic Melodrama

> Melodrama, like the poor, will no doubt always be with us.
> Allardyce Nicoll

I

Traditional exegesis of the earliest nineteenth-century stage melodramas identified a subgenre, often designated romantic melodrama, that derived its name from certain external characteristics these plays share with contiguously composed romantic poems. There is, for instance, their mutual predilection for an occasional oriental location and cast of characters—Magyars and Tartars battling outside exotic Asian castles—or, for startling contrast, their taste for humble peasants in rural settings—Luke and Michael toiling in the fields.[1] As evinced in the term *romantic melodrama*, these common thematic traits encourage one to interpret the overall significance of melodrama in terms of the more prominent and more exhaustively discussed doctrines of English romanticism, which include specific versions of subjectivity, community, and sublimity. Insofar, then, as a stage melodrama does not portray its characters in firm possession of a self-conscious individuality, it is deemed an artistic failure that only serves to emphasize the virtues of a more fully realized romantic lyric. Subordinating melodrama to romanticism, however, not only leads to such a misreading of the meanings of individual stage melodramas, but would inevitably block a reading of the melodramatic mode because it assesses the relationship between romantic poetry and melodrama within a static hierarchy of genres rather than as a constitutive relationship within the historical record. The mutual interest in oriental settings or peasant laborers should be seen, instead, as an indication of their shared historical moment and their common but crucially dissimilar engagement with the pressing contemporary concerns of poverty and early-nineteenth-century imperialism.

Despite the continuing, if no longer hegemonic, hold on literary criticism exerted by romantic doctrine, evidenced, for instance, in criticism's continuing reification of linguistic representation, these doctrines are not ahistorical truths, but emerged out of specific discursive contests, one of which was between the romantic and the melodramatic modes during the social upheaval and realignment that characterized the end of the eighteenth century. Both responded, in drastically different and largely irreconcilable ways, to that period's transitional style of governance in which the theatricalized displays of the state were widely seen to distract critical attention from the economic and bureaucratic reconstitution of England into what we now call a class society.

In order to define with precision early versions of the melodramatic mode, I must place it in relation to these more commanding romantic doctrines and resituate them both during the massive structural changes of the late eighteenth century. In so doing, I encounter a deeply contested field of inquiry. The social climate of eighteenth-century England has been especially subject to mystification by scholars who hope to see there either a lingering precapitalist, agrarian feudalism or a nascent egalitarian society of advanced capitalism, the choice depending on both these authors' political intents and whether or not the century is to play the role of apex or nadir in their historical narratives.[2] For my own purposes, it is enough to suggest that, while every historical period is always already in transition, English culture in the middle of the eighteenth century, especially in comparison to English culture in the middle of the nineteenth century, was a largely agrarian one, albeit an agrarian culture unevenly responding to the capitalist logic of competition and production. Even as late as 1802, 80 percent of the English population was still centered in villages and on farms.

While it is undeniable that capitalism had begun to change farming methods and that urban society, especially in London, had begun to influence traditional forms of kinship even in the countryside, until the middle decades of the nineteenth century most English people lived in the country and typically associated with one another according to the attitudinal and behavioral norms associated with paternalistic deference hierarchies. Howard Newby has provided a careful definition of *deference* as the *"form of social interaction which occurs in situations involving the exercise of traditional authority."*[3] This rendition of deference may sound overly benign, neutralizing the probability that the exercise of traditional authority involved coercion. Surely it would be foolish to deny the occurrence of physical and mental coercion on the one side and resentment on the other; nevertheless, there existed a relatively widespread impression among the participants that a reciprocal, if delicately balanced, relationship inhered among the ranks. Not without its share of cruelty and injustice, this reciprocal relationship was nonetheless perceived to contain its own logic.[4] In return for the benefits the humbler ranks derived from patriarchal obligation—shelter or poor relief, for example—they displayed respectful behavior toward their "betters." Furthermore, traditional sources of authority, be they lords or gentlemen farmers, were seen as legitimate elites, father figures within what was still pervasively considered to be a preordained and patriarchal hierarchy, a conviction expressed by frequent representations of the status hierarchy as an extended family, implicitly seen as the most inherently natural formation. The delicate balance between coercion and volition, between respect and contempt was maintained through the enactment of ritualized social exchanges during which deferential roles and their appropriate attitudes were both produced and dramatically represented. The bestowal of benevolence and the expression of gratitude were perhaps the most crucial of these public and highly theatrical transactions.

Much has been written about the theatricality of eighteenth-century English culture. In addition to Foucault, the historians E. P. Thompson and Douglas Hay, the sociologists Derek Sayer and Philip Corrigan, and the literary critic Terry Castle have portrayed various features of the culture's theatricalized self-presentation.[5] As they have demonstrated, social interaction was theatrical not only within the confines of the theater, but in public life as a whole.[6] As I have suggested, this theatricality was crucial to the maintenance of deference hierarchies. By the term *theatrical*, I especially intend to emphasize the visible, public, and performative quality of these physical interactions; in fact, I will argue further and suggest that one's individual sense of identity was actually constituted through the hierarchical relationships and mutual feelings created by these theatrical exchanges. In short, one's subjectivity took shape in a public and interactive space; it was simultaneously produced and represented through social ties and performed via deferential exchanges. Speaking of a French, aristocratic culture similar to

Britain's agrarian hierarchy in this manner only, Paul Connerton details the social work accomplished by these theatrical scenes. Whether they occur at a court of assizes or a royal court, whether they affirm social or specifically familial ties,

ceremonies of the body, . . . remind performers of a system of honour and hereditary transmission as the organising principle of social classification. Blood relations are signs cognitively known and recalled through the visibly elaborate display of privileges and avocations which make sense only by constant reference to that principle.[7]

An individual identity formed through such ritual is both radically public and static and displays through visible, audible, and easily interpretable cues its position in the status hierarchy, what Jean-Christophe Agnew has called an "elaborately coded conversation of dress, gesture, and speech."[8] In almost every way, individual identity was a public, performative matter.

In sum, what a twentieth-century critic might wish to call, somewhat inaccurately, "a consciousness of self" was located across one's patriarchal, social, and geographic affiliations, hierarchical affiliations that were continually reinforced by theatricalized public exchanges of deferential feeling. Moreover, these constitutive virtues and feelings do not emerge into the public from a private space, for the subject position does not exist a priori in a private space; rather, these virtues and feelings are social virtues and feelings. By "social feelings" I do not mean the feelings an individual possesses about society. Instead, social feelings are socially constructed feelings that, like subjectivity itself, do not exist "outside" or independently from social exchanges. Because of the conditions by which they are produced, such feelings and virtues are not private possessions, but public attributes, not personal idiosyncrasies, but universal qualities. In this regard, my argument approaches Clifford Siskin's thesis about personification in his book, *The Historicity of Romantic Discourse*. He suggests that the eighteenth-century poet's frequent use of personification was a measure of his or her culture's cohesiveness as a community:

The personification of abstract human faculties or attributes requires the transplantation of a part of the body of the individual (e.g., each man's reason) to the body of the community (e.g., Reason as a standard faculty shared by all). . . . In rhetorical terms, personifications of this sort function as a metonymic affirmation of community.[9]

Siskin's otherwise perceptive account, however, radically misrepresents the actual process of personification; personified faculties and attributes were not so much transplanted from an individual to the society at large, but were seen to be immanent in society and thus, in turn, present in any individual inhabiting that society. Benevolence and gratitude, condescension and esteem were common property that materialized in the theatricalized public exchange.

This theatricalized exchange could also, of course, take place in the theater. Fictional performances do not adversely affect the constitution of the feeling subject since it is the generation of the social virtue that counts, not the authenticity of the stimulus. Francis Hutcheson, in his *An Inquiry into the Origin of our Ideas of Beauty and Virtue* (1725), echoes many other contemporary aestheticians, philosophers, and essayists when he suggests that people should practice compassion by watching stories and plays.[10] Like real events, stories and plays represented a social exchange between actor and audience that was presumed to evoke social feeling through sympathetic recognition. It is no coincidence, then, that such a culture yielded sentimental drama and fiction. The exchanges exacted by sentimental fiction reflect those occurring generally in the larger culture. Robert Markley, in discussing the material operation of sentimentality, thus also demonstrates the active production through visual cues of this feeling subject I am describing: "Sentimentality, therefore, cannot be reified as an abstract system of values or disembodied as passive sympathy; it is manifest only in the concrete particularity of a noble or generous action or in physical symptoms: tears, blushes, and palpitating hearts."[11]

Sympathy superseded in importance all other social feelings. For many eighteenth-century commentators, in fact, sympathy was not a feeling at all but a faculty that denoted the process of human exchange itself—fellow feeling—through which particular social feelings, individual identities, and society were established. In effect, sympathetic identification with another, often if not always an other of distinct status, confirmed one's personal identity; for example, the sympathetic exchange of feeling between father and son or between landowner and tenant produced and represented one's patriarchal, deferential identity. In these scenarios, sympathy is what might be called the recognition of sameness in difference, the delicate, highly orchestrated, and rigidly predetermined procedure of "relating" to another who is always both like and unlike oneself.

Up to this point in my discussion, I have consciously depicted the eighteenth century in England as a static culture, supremely coherent and self-confidently functional. However, the very presence of innumerable treatises on sympathy, even the existence of sentimental rhetoric in itself, expresses a certain need on the part of eighteenth-century men and women to articulate and, further, to ratify a process that was always potentially tenuous, illusive, and uncertain. A deference system based on sympathetic exchange operates at its best in a culture where people are bound together by regional traditions and common economic interests, where people stay in one place most of their lives, and where, therefore, face-to-face exchange is customary and frequent.[12] The lord, for instance, literally recognizes his tenants and the tenants their lord as a result of constant interaction. And most important, people not only recognize each other in these exchanges, but know each other because the moral codes of reciprocity and obligation, the costumes of rank and station, and the deferential gestures, such as a tug of the forelock, constitute knowledge. During these theatricalized social exchanges, both the lord and the tenant are actors who share a common script.

Throughout the course of the eighteenth century, however, massive structural alterations in the society at large jeopardized this fragile interplay of deference. The very gradual economic reorganization of England into a market society, a reorganization that long predated the eighteenth century, was entering a new phase of capital accumulation and industrial expansion that would in time forever alter the relationships among the ranks and the identities formed by these relationships, thereby transforming a deferential culture into a market culture.[13]

Because "market culture" figures so prominently in my following argument as a conceptual and experiential entity in relation to which both the romantic and the melodramatic mode take shape, this concept requires careful elaboration if it is not to be in danger of becoming a reified object in a book that proclaims to be a study of relations. At the risk of tautologizing, however, it must be remarked that many of the features of market culture come into sharpest focus when they are seen in relation to the melodramatic mode, taking shape as they elicit a melodramatic response. More specific definitional criteria are, nonetheless, still necessary.

Admittedly, the very notion of a "culture" of the market is both too capacious conceptually and too inexact temporally, but this concept helpfully encompasses all manner of shifts in the historical record, both the material manifestations of those changes as well as the behavioral and perceptual changes among people. Among these structural shifts must be included the transition from one mode of land appropriation, what Ellen Meiksins Woods calls "extra-economic surplus-extraction based on direct coercive control of those who work the land—through the extraction of rents, dues and the fruits of jurisdiction" to what we recognize as "economic" modes of appropriation founded on competition in the marketplace and increases in the productivity of labor. This period also sees local management of production within the manor or town succumb to the logic of capital, national competition, and an autonomous economy. The vast array of customary rights and obligations, for so long central to rural society, gives way to enclosure and leaseholds. In short, kinship rights and responsibilities are replaced by contractual obligations among discrete and contending economic parties. And in the face of these changes, the traditional precedence of corporate bodies as the elemental unit of society yields to the dominance of individualism.[14]

These structural changes denote a market "culture" insofar as they are accompanied by some type of recognition by and response from the people experiencing them, a response that is not necessarily fully aware of itself or of its object. In the rapidly industrializing setting of the eighteenth century, for instance, the division of labor potentially prevented workers from perceiving their participation in a common pursuit, while it often, though not always, pitted them against their employers in confrontations that seemed of a new order.[15] Although industrial expansion has come to epitomize the alienation of market society, it was not the sole cause or instance of such alienation nor was it always the object of people's complaints. In agricultural regions, the widespread enclosure of commons land and the increase in day labor that separated the lord and his economic interests from his tenant and tenants from each other often figured as the most harrowing departure from tradition. Moreover, as growing numbers of rural laborers left the countryside for the city or for counties in which waste lands existed in greater acreage, many observers felt they were witnessing the death of rural England.

This commentary provides the most cursory rendition of the consolidation of a market culture in England, but it does highlight the means by which the ranks became increasingly like strangers to one another, both literally and figuratively. As the century came to a close, then, there were fewer opportunities to perform together the crucial theatrical exchange of sympathy that cemented the connection among the ranks, whose members now rarely looked on members of other ranks as fellow actors participating with them in an enactment of communal ties. A merely cursory glance at late-eighteenth-century and early-nineteenth-century texts will show that a wholly different sort of theatrical relationship developed. Instead of mutually participating in a public script, each rank perceived the other as actors and themselves as the spectating audience.

As early as the mid–eighteenth century, Adam Smith in *The Theory of Moral Sentiments* (1761) almost inadvertently reveals the operational breakdown of sympathy in a celebrated passage from this treatise. In attempting to describe the workings of sympathy, Smith cites the meeting between a spectator and a lunatic: "The compassion of the spectator must arise altogether from the consideration of what he himself would feel if he was reduced to the same unhappy situation, and, what perhaps is impossible, was at the same time able to regard it with his present reason and judgement."[16] Looking at the suffering individual from this mediated distance, the spectator, by definition, no longer submerges himself in the operations of the theatrical exchange, the sharing of a tear, but observes from a distance and at this distance can only relate to the lunatic in terms of an image of his own self as lunatic, and then only as a lunatic divided. The spectator thus stumbles over the near futility of simultaneously being a lunatic and a rational man. He vainly struggles to detect sameness in a difference that is quickly becoming its most extreme and incommensurable version—a binary opposition. Perhaps most striking in Smith's account of sympathy is the diversion from any discussion of a socially constituted knowledge of the other through the process of exchange and the emphasis instead on what takes place in the spectator, who therefore becomes the subject, a divided subject. This prefigurement of romantic self-consciousness seems more than predetermined by Smith's apparently arbitrary selection of a lunatic, the preeminent tortured self, as an exemplary instance of failed sympathetic exchange.

The theatrical relationship between spectator and lunatic is even more strained than this preliminary analysis suggests, however, for the participant has become at the same time increasingly aware of the theatricality of the scene he witnesses—hence his denomination as spectator—and experiences that theatricality as the cause of the isolation he feels. As a spectator, he begins to apprehend drama and reality differently, distinctively; it now matters if sympathy is elicited through fiction or fact. This gradual change in perception is revealingly captured in two central political texts of this period: Thomas Paine's *Rights of Man* (1791) and Edmund Burke's *Reflections on the Revolution in France* (1790). Burke, in many respects the quintessential eighteenth-century aristocrat, continues to use theatrical metaphor in his description of the French Revolution because, for him, history is a social stage and the people shaping it are public actors. Paine, however, interprets Burke's rhetorical theatricality as intentional evasion. Holding Burke to Paine's own rationalist standard, a revisionist denigration of the theatrical exchange that considers costume a disguise and scenic prose a facade, Paine accuses Burke of seeking refuge in theatricality from some alternative "reality" of sympathetic exchange. Paine bitterly remarks in *Rights of Man* that Burke "is not affected by the reality of distress touching his heart, but by the showy resemblance of it striking his imagination."[17] The radical polemicist not only asserts here a stark disparity between reality and theater, but also aligns them with the absolute values of objectivity and subjectivity, respectively. Theater's social valence has been neutralized and has become instead a trope—a "showy resemblance"—of the imagination. According to this change in perception, the theatrical exchange no longer stages the transmission of sympathy, but inhibits it by translating dramatic roles into metaphoric figures. This local shift, one might argue as an aside, reflects a larger cultural shift in the dominant, populist forms of cultural transmission from oral, public communication to written, private dissemination.[18] It should be noted before moving on that Burke's self-presentation in his own text as a spectator rather than as an actor renders him vulnerable to Paine's attack and perhaps signals, as did Smith's spectator in his *The Theory of Moral Sentiments*, the problems besetting sympathetic recognition in the last half of the eighteenth century.

Once theatrical representation is castigated as "showy resemblance," sharp distinctions arise between that resemblance and some stipulated reality, between public role and private integrity, between acting and sincerity. The career trajectory of Hannah More conveniently marks this transformation in cultural attitudes toward the theatrical that was occurring late in the eighteenth century. Formerly a playwright and close friend of the renowned actor Garrick, More became an evangelical Christian and author of various admonitory texts that carefully delineated and policed this division between artifice and reality, acting and sincerity.[19] As a result of the newly imagined corruption of the theatricalized exchange, a corruption so widely perceived that the evangelical More and the radical Paine could agree on its basic premises, the camouflaged object of sympathy frequently evolves into an unworthy object of sympathy and becomes the subject of moral castigation. Paine claims that the lowlier victims of the French Revolution become just this for Burke.[20]

In the following chapters I will show how the players on the public stage in nineteenth-century England—be they actual actors or aristocrats, paupers, or women—and the roles they played were perceived to be two distinctive entities, with the theatrical performance often seen to be a mere disguise for the players' private, hidden, and often suspiciously immoral identities. In these scenes of rapidly urbanizing England, where rural populations were largely dispersed, the actors on the stage were not only strangers, they were impostors. This representational dissonance between an inside and an outside was utterly unlike the performative public role of the previous era, whose lines and costumes were not a disguise, not even a perfect reflection of an inner identity, but identity itself. By the beginning of the nineteenth century, people often utilized the verb *to act* as an accusation rather than a description. "Sincerity" became a crucial concept even as it was necessarily more difficult to ascertain. Indeed, the distinctions between reality and theatrical representation, distinctions that had little impact on the exercise of sympathy just a generation or two earlier, were of utmost significance, as Thomas Paine shows.

Criticism of theatricalized rituals became more common as the enactment of these rituals became less common. Paine and his radical associates, however, were not unique in their criticisms, for just as they accused aristocrats like Burke of faking sentiment, men of conservative persuasion responded in kind. Pervasive theatricality had turned into fears of widespread imposture as English culture became increasingly caught in relationships of structural specularity, what we might wish anachronistically (and erroneously) to describe in psychological terms as rampant paranoia.[21]

A variety of responses to this crisis in social cohesion and individual identity emerged at this time. Throughout the nineteenth century, what I will call the modern principle of classification was perhaps the most influential and wide-ranging of these responses, though its pervasive and powerful emergence was certainly more than a response to this one crisis; one should, in fact, posit it as a contributory cause of the current situation. The modern principle of classification was therefore both produced by and productive of the rise of market culture and its structures of specularity.

In Victorian England, the principle's most privileged manifestation was the idea of economic class, but its organizational features also dominated public policy, economics (through accounting, for instance), social and natural sciences, and medicine. This classificatory principle operated as a heuristic device and was often instituted by dominant castes within society that saw their interests served by transformative effects they only partly understood or controlled. Some of the practitioners of this principle included commercial interests, such as the proprietors of the Covent Garden Theatre in 1809, that precipitated the Old Price riots; or bureaucratic organizations, like the Commission on the Poor Laws in the 1830's, which framed the 1834 Poor Law; or contemporary social commentators in the middle decades of the century who organized their object of study by imposing classificatory systems.

As I will explain more fully in the following chapters, the classificatory impulse's most explosive effect was to reorganize society along horizontal, class lines and to reconstitute individual identity within those classes in terms of private and intrinsic characteristics as opposed to public and inherited traits. As can be seen in retrospect, this particular conception of class society and class membership was excessively static and essentializing; each class was not perceived to be formed in relation to another, as a classical Marxist analysis would have it, but to obtain its definitional parameters from its own intrinsic nature. Clearly, then, the "classes" formed by commercial, bureaucratic, or discursive actions that were influenced by the modern principle of classification are not the same classes defined by a Marxist analysis, but the two are historically and genealogically related. In fact, a Marxist analysis can ultimately provide a penetrating critique of this principle of classification's essentialist assumptions, not least because it, too, emerged during this period of class thinking.

The enormous transformations initiated by classificatory procedures did not go unnoticed by the larger society, especially by those members of society who did not recognize themselves in the new designations or discern in these changes any appreciable advantage for themselves. Such people did not demonstrate a "class consciousness," as E. P. Thompson has defined the concept during this period, but rather were resisting the specific notion of class imposed by those conducting their business according to this modern principle of classification.[22] Despite the investment in communal grouping and social feeling that these varied groups of protesters displayed, they can be provisionally if not exactly distinguished from the radicals and socialists whom Thompson has identified. In reacting to the institutional, practical, and intimate effects of the modern principle of classification, these people enacted the melodramatic mode and in so doing acted in the name of conservation and modest reform, not radicalization and revolution.

II

It is at this period in the late eighteenth century, a period when the principles of classification were being first articulated, that what I will call somewhat loosely the romantic mode and the melodramatic mode emerged as distinctive replies to the crisis in individual identity and social cohesion that characterized market culture. As with the "melodramatic mode," I use the phrase "romantic mode" to differentiate my object of study from fully operational discourses at the time and, perhaps more important, to avoid any confusion with what would be, for my purposes, misleading modern literary historical or critical terms, especially, in this case, "romanticism." In order to articulate the common assumptions and, most crucially, the critical differences between the melodramatic and romantic modes—to describe the different roles they played and to specify their respective relationships to the principle of classification—I will compare the melodramatic mode to germane portions of William Wordsworth's rendition of the romantic mode. Although Wordsworth does not hold a monopoly on the romantic mode, his poetry has certainly exerted the most influence on the majority of nineteenth- and twentieth-century literary critics of the English romantic period. And it is this critical tradition that, in reifying in particular Wordsworth's principles of romantic subjectivity, has obscured the existence and impact of the melodramatic mode during these years.

In the confrontation I will stage between the melodramatic and romantic modes, I will concentrate principally on Wordsworth's "The Old Cumberland Beggar" (1798). I do so not because it is the privileged origin of Wordsworth's unique genius, but because it both exemplifies certain features that literary critics consider "romantic" and at the same time examines a central debate that emerged from the eighteenth-century crisis I have been outlining. The poem thus provides a thematic nexus for the collision of the romantic and melodramatic modes that did occur at this time.

During the years just around the turn into the nineteenth century, the poor, more than any other group, were most widely accused of imposture, an accusation that pervaded the debate about this population. Their fate during these years is perhaps most emblematic of the demise of deferential society and its vertical loyalties, for under its former operation the poor had been considered a natural and ordained component of the community, as eligible for benevolence and as obligated to express gratitude as any other member. Their degree of estrangement from this deferential community can be measured in proportion to the amount of literature published that regarded them as a "problem." In order to see the poor as a problem, people had first to see them as a discrete and, literally, self-sufficient population. At this point in history, the non-poor more frequently saw difference, rather than sameness, when it turned its attention to the poor. This conceptualization of the poor, then, was a constant reminder of the failure of sympathetic recognition, of the slackening of communal loyalties, and thus of the deceptive mask that public identity had become in civil society. In "The Old Cumberland Beggar," the old society's obsolete social practices and rhetorical figures are compensated for by a hybrid mix of tradition and innovation that makes the poem an exemplary instance of the romantic mode.

Wordsworth wrote "The Old Cumberland Beggar" in 1798 and published the poem in 1800. In it he expresses what proved to be his long-standing conviction about poverty and its function in the world. Rather than rounding up paupers and placing them in "Houses of Industry," the government, according to the poet, should allow them to wander through the countryside compelling charitable behavior. Over thirty-five years later, Wordsworth reiterated these views after the New Poor Law of 1834 was instituted.[23] He, like many others including Charles Dickens, abhorred the new law's reliance on workhouses, which, for Wordsworth, had always seemed miniature versions of the rapidly urbanizing cities of England, specifically their trademark factories. Such workhouses, as Wordsworth notes in "The Old Cumberland Beggar," are characterized by their "pent-up din" and "life-consuming sounds that clog the air."[24] According to the poet, paupers belong in the silence of the rural countryside.

Insofar as "The Old Cumberland Beggar" continues to imagine sympathetic exchanges among people and the recognition of community that results from those exchanges, the poem reveals its engagement with the eighteenth-century themes I have outlined above. Generally, with few exceptions, "The Old Cumberland Beggar" has been accordingly esteemed as proof of Wordsworth's belief in sympathetic recognition and compassion.[25] Although I do not intend to impugn Wordsworth's morals, I do think that Wordsworth's version of the sympathetic exchange needs to be closely scrutinized and more carefully delineated within the context of other approaches to poverty during his time. Wordsworth's apparent insistence on the rural setting, the face-to-face encounter, and the geographic particularity of the poem seem, at least initially, to confirm his investment in traditional forms of social organization. Undoubtedly, "The Old Cumberland Beggar" is one of many poems in his early years in which Wordsworth attempts to reaffirm the sympathetic connections among members of society. At times, such poems even seem to suggest a certain longing on Wordsworth's part for traditional patriarchal and deferential ties—for parental love, for love of the land, even for inheritable identities.[26]

After reading his "Preface to *Lyrical Ballads*," one is encouraged to think of Wordsworth as an eighteenth-century patriarch whose poetic output constitutes a public legacy for his extended family and for future generations, a legacy that seems destined to become the coin of benevolence in countless face-to-face exchanges. Whereas a scientist labors for "personal and individual acquisition" and imagines his object as a "remote and unknown benefactor," a poet's knowledge is a "natural and unalienable inheritance" that produces a "habitual and direct sympathy connecting us with our fellow-beings."[27] Prefiguring in these sentences the arguments later provided by opponents of the New Poor Law, Wordsworth bemoans the spread of impersonal exchange among strangers. Although generally affiliated with the disinterestedness that was by then intrinsic to conceptualizations of scientific procedure, this exchange among "remote and unknown" actors was fast becoming linked to the self-interestedness of economic exchange, as evidenced by Wordsworth's phrase "personal and individual acquisition." Wordsworth thus implicitly links the rational procedures of science with observable transformations occurring in the public sphere, which poets and poetry were intended to forestall. Such stark contrasts between economic and poetic exchange, however, obscure the equally observable transformations implicit in his role as poetical patriarch.

The publication of the *Lyrical Ballads*, combined with the contemporary status of copyright law and the government's lax enforcement, designates Wordsworth's poems as radically alienable commodities, not inalienable heirlooms. Wordsworth seems to admit as much when he describes in the "Preface" the relation between himself and his audience as "voluntarily contracted."[28] Although it is true that successive copyright restrictions implemented throughout the nineteenth century ultimately reified the author as a proprietary individual, at the turn of the century Wordsworth, try as he might, could exert little control either in the role of patriarch or proprietor over his published poems, which were, like other texts, vulnerable to piracy. Wordsworth's substitution of uncopyrighted poems for inheritable land is thus an unequal exchange. In sum, the "Preface" portrays the competing ideologies of exchange that characterized this period and the individual's formulation of an uneasy compromise among them.

Inevitably, despite Wordsworth's claim that the poet engages in unmediated, deferential exchange with his subject and subjects, these exchanges, as reproduced in the ballads, seem painfully compromised. In "The Old Cumberland Beggar," Wordsworth does indeed continue to represent those crucial exchanges of benevolence that were so vital to the social order of eighteenth-century England. The beggar's solicitations, like other scenes of benevolence, sustain moral feeling within the community and even represent to those charitable souls engaged in these exchanges a sense of their own identity. Nevertheless, the poem signals from its inception a structural feature that aligns it more with Adam Smith's speculation on sympathy than with a hypothetical tract on sentimentality, for "The Old Cumberland Beggar" is not a performance in which actors immerse themselves in their interchanges, oblivious to distinctions between participation and spectatorship. Indeed, Wordsworth's dissatisfaction with his early attempt at drama, "The Borderers" (1795–96), suggests that theatrical exchanges were difficult for him to stage. Rather than a performance, "The Old Cumberland Beggar" is what Wordsworth calls a "description." In place of the enactment of the social exchange, Wordsworth provides a first-person description of it from a third-person vantage point—the position of the spectator. Like his immediate predecessors, then, Wordsworth finds himself in the position of a spectator, potentially encountering that position's unique obstructions to the operation of sympathetic recognition.

Just a brief glance at Wordsworth's "description" reveals his dilemma. In the poem, Wordsworth documents a face-to-face exchange of social feeling, feeling so universal, so communal that it seems, in keeping with Clifford Siskin's account, almost capable of the socialization implicit in personification—"we have all of us one human heart" (line 146). Throughout the exchange, however, the beggar's own face is averted—"His eyes are turned" (line 46).

> Instead of common and habitual sight
> Of fields with rural works, of hill and dale,
> And the blue sky, one little span of earth
> Is all his prospect. (Lines 48–51)

Rather than actively participating in "common and habitual sight," the old man seems, from the distant perspective of the narrator, lost in his own little plot of earth, blind to the world at large and oblivious to those who might seek recognition in his eyes. He seems alienated, disengaged, antisocial, potentially like the deceitful poor with their hidden motives, as portrayed in many treatises on poverty then current. In fact, at one point, when describing the old man, Wordsworth refers to his "idle computation" (line 12), a phrase that seems to echo the suspicions that were often voiced by critics of the poor, especially the utilitarian political economists who would write their treatises on poverty a few decades later. Lacking the familiar visual cues that might make them recognizable to their social superiors, the poor were seen by such theorists to be secretive and "idle," hiding within themselves what was presumed to be a compulsive desire for unearned profit.

By contrast, of course, Wordsworth's beggar is benign, suggesting the more benevolent intentions of the poet and his poems. Even though the beggar idly computes what are in effect unearned profits, those computations seem more an indication of the absence of a hidden motive than the presence of one, thus affiliating the beggar with another of Wordsworth's frustratingly opaque objects of sympathy, the idiot boy in the poem of the same name. In "The Old Cumberland Beggar," the beggar's unsocial behavior and his absent intent, though remarked, are remarkably unimportant because the exchange of sympathetic recognition has been revised. Given a closer look, the poem does not even begin to stage the theatricalized public exchange that both produces and represents social feeling and hierarchized identity. Those engaged in this scene are all "humble" people; the poem shows no interest in elaborating the ties among the ranks. And furthermore, the actors in the exchange seem not to communicate with one another at all, at least in a face-to-face and public manner, for the beggar is both still in his movement and silent in his gestures. In fact, the poem skirts entirely the problem of the beggar's inaccessible experience and concentrates instead on the experience of his benefactors. The central events in this poem consist of unacknowledged acts of kindness—a traveler who makes sure his proffered alms reach the hand of the decrepit old man, a postboy who gives forewarning of his passage and then side-steps the oblivious beggar, and a tollgate woman who opens the latch for him prior to his arrival. The face-to-face social exchange, which in truth is neither face-to-face nor social in these instances, is merely the preliminary for another form of exchange.

Irreducibly strange and distant in the immediate encounter, the beggar cannot possibly participate in or elicit sympathetic recognition. But, it is this very otherness, which had proved such an obstacle to the deferential exchange of feeling, that becomes productive of revised versions of feeling, one of which is what Wordsworth's poem describes as "a transitory thought / Of self-congratulation" (lines 116–17). Although drastically limited in his impact, for the beggar may "to no one give the fortitude / And circumspection needful to preserve / His present blessings" (lines 120–22), the beggar serves as a contrast to "those present blessings" and in so doing generates social virtues and feelings. These social feelings, however, are not socially constituted feelings generated in the moment of exchange, but feelings about society that develop both afterward and elsewhere in memory and by reflection: "Habit does the work / Of reason, yet prepares that after joy / Which reason cherishes" (lines 92–94). And, most crucially, such social feelings emanate from a subject who perceives him- or herself as being in excess of society, as one who both precedes and succeeds the social event.[29] Presumably, it is in this appropriated space outside the social—his own "little span of earth"—that the subject possesses (or fails to possess) the fortitude and circumspection that the beggar cannot give.

Having conceded the incommensurable distance between the beggar and his benefactor, and yet still in need of a place that is free of estrangement and alienation, the poem opens up something other than a social space, other than a public one, and other than a stage where blind actors do not see one another. This space is a "mental theatre," to borrow Jerome McGann's phrase.[30] This newly imagined and imaginative space, entirely produced through and represented in language, is the self-sufficient, self-conscious spectator in nature. From this perspective, nature and subjectivity are not merely mutually dependent terms in Wordsworth's romantic vocabulary, but must occupy the same intellectualized space. As theorized, the romantic subject cannot exist in society, at least as I have described one eighteenth-century version of that existence; it must exist in terms of nature, which most eighteenth-century thinkers considered to be asocial. Hence Wordsworth's insistence on the beggar being and remaining a creature of nature.[31] Like nature, the old Cumberland beggar is unconscious, described as possessing a sort of blind vision—"seeing still, / And never knowing that he sees" (lines 53–54). No longer occupying social space, the beggar does not function as a subject of recognition, but as an object of otherness—a Solitary Man—within the space of the subject. Instead of engaging in social exchanges, the Solitary Man is an inhabitant of the mind—"A silent monitor, which on their minds / Must needs impress a transitory thought" (lines 115–16). He has become the difference in sameness that Peter de Bolla in *The Discourse of the Sublime* argues creates the effect of self-consciousness: "The reflective surface which images the self . . . is internalized within the subject as that which is not self-identical: difference."[32] Like Smith's spectator, who aims to be both sane and insane, Wordsworth's speaker strives toward an equally paradoxical state—to be both solitary and social.

As a figure of thought the beggar is no longer utterly alien; he is vitally constitutive of the romantic subject. Given alms not because he is a member of an extended hierarchical family, the beggar is nonetheless related and familiar to his benefactors and relieved accordingly, for he occupies their intimate domain. Through this private, mental exchange, the poem restages the scene of benevolence that both produces and represents identity, but in place of deferential networks, mutual dependency, static and inheritable identities, "The Old Cumberland Beggar" constructs independent, developmental selves who have, through the course of the poem, internalized the patriarchal inheritance of status—"The Child is Father of the Man."[33]

"The Old Cumberland Beggar" therefore attempts to resolve the crisis in sympathetic recognition that characterizes the end of the eighteenth century by translating the scene of exchange to a "mental theatre," which is, I might add, pointedly untheatrical in some crucial ways, for it is neither public nor strictly visible, neither performed nor spoken. Despite Wordsworth's insistent use of visual imagery, his theater remains thoroughly textual and conceptual. Lacking interpretable visual cues, symbolic gestures, and lines to deliver in the social sphere, the old, nearly blind beggar has become an ambiguous metaphorical figure for a mental vision—"a silent monitor, which on their minds / Must needs impress a transitory thought." Clearly not a friend of the beggar, Wordsworth has instead become friendly with a concept, "truth," which he recognizes in the "Preface" as his "visible friend and hourly companion." In keeping such company, Wordsworth wholly transforms his indigenous community, even welcoming into his home at some future date the remote Sciences, which can conceivably (and only conceivably) become "a dear and genuine inmate of the household of man."[34] Because the sublime became mere spectacle over the course of the eighteenth century, transforming the ecstatic participant into passive observer, vision had to become visionary; this is Wordsworth's compensatory poetic economy for the blind inhabitant of the nineteenth century. And it is this displacement, not repression, of the theatrical and performative that has long dominated literary criticism and its literary narratives, thereby erasing the melodramatic mode from the historical record.

As an additional but not secondary result of these verbal maneuvers, Wordsworth's poem evacuates the public sphere and recreates an imaginative version of it that seems unmarked by its social and economic turmoil, as has recently been noted more generally by historicist literary critics of the romantic period. Marjorie Levinson's and Alan Liu's work in particular have charted Wordsworth's aggressive effacement of the material impact of market culture on the English countryside. As Liu argues, Wordsworth usually confronts history by choosing not to, but his solution was not universally adopted, despite the impression given by most modern literary criticism, which has accepted Wordsworth's naturalizing polemic and thus has accepted as true and natural his epistemological account of identity.

III

Although Charles Dickens, for instance, shared Wordsworth's hatred of workhouses, his response to their widespread use did not echo romantic poetry's interiority but sounded more like the melodramatic mode as it was implemented at various times and locations throughout the nineteenth century. While abhorring the changes occurring in society, the heterogeneous groups of people who enacted this mode continued to cleave to traditional forms of social exchange and their public constitution of identity. Directly addressing the incursion of the market into society, the rhetoric and behaviors of these groups represented a generally coherent attack on market culture's most salient effects, especially the various manifestations of the modern principle of classification, and offered an alternative, if deeply nostalgic, vision of society. In its various guises, the melodramatic mode restaged the theatricalized scene of exchange, not within a mental theater, but in the midst of the social sphere through public performances, protests, popular pamphlets, and literary texts.

Primarily operating within the realm of representation, but firmly engaged with historical events, the melodramatic mode, as I see it, took what were considered to be dehumanizing and materially influential rhetorics produced in market culture, such as bureaucratese and statistics, and translated them into narratives propelled by social feelings, not feelings for society. The disembodied agents of the bureaucratic state, whether the corporation investing in a theatrical venture, the distant London Commission of the New Poor Law, or the literally nonhuman legislation concerning marriage and divorce, were thus personified as villains in an inverted version of personification. Instead of universalizing a trait of the human individual, as Siskin would have it, this new sort of personification humanizes what were literally nonhuman institutions.

By means of socially saturated visual cues (physical features, conventional costumes, and standardized gestures) that did not demand a literate audience, the melodramatic mode created the conditions necessary for a dramaturgy of familiarity, an inclusive form of sympathetic exchange that strengthened patriarchal ties across the entire community. In these theatricalized exchanges, the customary props and plots of the melodramatic mode readily declared their meaning. Such a sense of "familiarity" was consolidated through sensational familial narratives in which estranged and alienated beings were always found to be related in time for the final familial tableau. Social feeling and patriarchal identity, quickly dissipating in a competitive, individualist culture, were once more produced and represented through language and gesture. Wholly recognizable and understandable, the melodramatic mode transformed spectators into actors again, thereby nullifying, if only momentarily, the distinction between private integrity and public persona.

Endorsing the social grounds of ethical behavior, the melodramatic mode continued to operate on the assumption that people are socially constituted and therefore recognizable to one another as long as they participate in sympathetic exchange. In this regard, the melodramatic mode directly addressed the bifurcated identity (difference in sameness) that was aggressively enforced by the modern principle of classification and incessantly figured in romantic poetry. As my next chapters will explore more fully, the changing structures of the English economy and the government's response to those changes were perceived to have caused the complete evacuation of a vibrant public sphere of deferential feeling. In its place was a bifurcated subject who performed empty roles in public, as Thomas Paine observed, while cultivating a private identity that was markedly disconnected from the larger community. One need only glance at the subjects of the high Victorian novel, Mr. Bulstrode in *Middlemarch* or, as we shall explore, Diana in latter portions of *Diana of the Crossways*, to see represented this combination of psychic complexity and social alienation. From the perspective of those who deployed the melodramatic mode, these private selves were always presumed to be engaging in secretive transactions, often represented as economic and sexual conspiracies designed to consolidate their self-interest. The publicizing representations of the melodramatic mode aimed to uncover these hidden selves and reintegrate them into a society where public exchange remained possible, where the beggar, as well as his benefactor, could both see and be seen. Obviating the necessity of becoming both a lunatic and rational man, the melodramatic mode traded instead in the clash of moral absolutes. In every melodrama, there is a villain and a hero. In every plot, the villain haunts the hero, but he haunts him noisily in the public sphere where the villain is represented on stage, not in the hero's psyche as a "silent monitor."

What might strike us now as highly exaggerated portrayals of villainy and heroism should not, in fact, be assessed in terms of their realism, for as we have seen the very concept of "realism" was largely a result of the crisis in sympathetic recognition that these performances sought to alleviate. The typical melodramatic tableau of a heroine's virtuous remorse, played on stage or in the home, not only aspired to convert spectators into actors, but sought to break down the newly erected boundaries between theater and reality. During these moments, the melodramatic mode reimagined a theatricalized deferential culture in the midst of a rapidly consolidating class society.

In these gestures, one can see some of the common concerns and aims between Wordsworth's poetry and melodramatic tactics. Just as Wordsworth hoped to embody, familiarize, and befriend the sciences in an effort to forestall their dehumanizing tendencies, so melodrama strived in strikingly similar ways to transform science's bureaucratic manifestations in the public sphere. However, it is the melodramatic mode's firm position within the public sphere that points to their irreconcilable differences.

Insofar as the romantic subject cultivated a private and exclusive identity, it did not share the melodramatic mode's agenda. In fact, the melodramatic mode provides a location, both historical and textual, to look at the romantic subject from a different perspective. A great deal of modern literary criticism on the romantic period has reified the romantic subject, accepting perhaps too unquestioningly Wordsworth's naturalizing polemic. Although Wordsworth was undeniably an opponent of market culture and many of its perceived alienating practices, his poetry does not transcend that culture any more than does the melodramatic mode. Because of its modest revisionary impact on the social terrain of early-nineteenth-century England, the melodramatic mode enables one, for instance, to see the subtle connections between the subject constituted by modern principles of classification and the romantic subject.

In contrast to the melodramatic mode's public constitution of identity, the romantic subject, as portrayed in "The Old Cumberland Beggar," is what one might be tempted to describe as a romanticized version of the private identity of class society. Characterized by its internalized psychic activity, the romantic subject merely displaces the sexual and economic transactions that, according to practitioners of the melodramatic mode, usually take place in this hidden mental space and replaces them with spiritualized and intellectualized transactions.[35] This substitution undoubtedly enables specific individuals to retreat from, or as Wordsworth and his admiring critics would have it, to transcend "the pent-up din" of capitalist England. It would also, later in the century, enable certain professions to distinguish themselves from trade, but it does little or nothing to prevent those less intellectually blessed or those with no time to spare from being classified within the public sphere in terms of their economic function, their class.[36] In spite of Wordsworth's poem, the old Cumberland beggar, if he had survived, would have become an inmate in the workhouse under the New Poor Law of 1834. In this regard, the romantic mode, contrary to the impression conveyed by modern formulations of its power, was no more successful than the melodramatic mode.

Regardless of the moralistic substitution offered in romantic poetry, the romantic subject's internalization of feeling and virtue still results in a form of identity that is seen to be private and essential, the exclusive possession of the individual. Furthermore, despite the presence of spiritual glimmers and social feelings, this consciousness of self has also internalized the more ominous results of classification, thereby revealing the romantic mode's close ties to the capitalist culture it so often reviled. According to Wordsworth's poem, the romantic subject's acquisition of moral and social feeling depends on the "monitor" of one's thoughts, a phrase that not coincidentally conjures up the more material setting of Jeremy Bentham's panopticon.[37] Lacking the disciplinary presence of an omnipotent deity, a god who enforces the Golden Rule, the romantic subject must internalize a policing agent—the "monitor" of one's thoughts—just as the inmate of the panopticon is expected to do. Rather than the mutual exchange of glances between actor and audience enforced by the melodramatic mode, the romantic subject (almost always presumed to be a man) knows he is seen within his own private space but cannot see in return; he therefore cannot see himself whole. This scene of surveillance is the melodramatic mode's version of poetic justice, for the romantic subject, like the felon in the panopticon, has committed a crime against society—he has withdrawn from it.[38]

IV

Despite appearances to the contrary, then, melodrama and "the poor" will not always be with us, nor have they always been. Literary genealogies have until now erased the history and historicity of melodrama and thus the melodramatic mode's influential participation in the rise of market culture. Its historical record indicates, at the very least, that "class society," "class consciousness," and romantic conceptions of subjectivity also have histories with a beginning and probably an end.[39] The explanatory power of these influential terms needs to be measured by this "other" history that has underwritten their appeal. The following chapters provide an inaugural account of that history.

The Old Price Wars

Melodramatizing the Public Sphere in Early-Nineteenth-Century England

Late in 1806, the Covent Garden Theatre in London premiered the lawyer William Dimond's latest melodrama, *Adrian and Orrila*. As was traditional at the completion of a performance, two of the leading actresses stepped forward on the stage to address an epilogue to the audience. The epilogue elaborated a timely conceit that likened the evening production to an unseasoned political candidate seeking office and the audience to a group of proud electors. In so doing, it made topical reference to the elections then taking place out of doors in the Westminster district where Covent Garden was located:

> *I* come to *canvass,* you, Box, Gallery, and Pit,
> For *you* return *our* Parliament of *Wit*:
> While here, in *Covent Garden* still, a *hustings* stands,
> And *Sheriff Mattocks* asks—a *shew of hands,*
> For a young Candidate (tho' not *untried*).[1]

Such supplications to the audience had long been considered standard etiquette in the theater, expected of acting companies whose traditional obligations to their spectators had been most famously described by Samuel Johnson in 1747:

> The Stage but echoes back the public voice,
> The drama's laws the drama's patrons give,
> For we that live to please, must please to live.[2]

The chiasmatic balance of Johnson's phrasing and the rhyming ease of the lines suggest that the deferential and causal exchange he describes between the stage and the public was easily achieved, an assumption which by 1806 seemed quaint if not blatantly misleading. As Porter's extended conceit confirms, pleasing to live had become a political issue.

Even if a reflexive relationship existed within the theater during Johnson's lifetime, by the time of *Adrian and Orrila*, alterations in both drama's laws and its patrons were transforming the nature of theatrical exchanges. The emergence of melodramas such as *Adrian and Orrila*, on a patent theater stage, often replacing the high canonical forms of tragedy and comedy, is perhaps the most obvious sign of this altered relationship between drama and its patrons. During Johnson's era, aristocrats and royalty dominated the audience and administration of the much smaller licensed theaters. Thus, the "public voice" presumably echoed in the drama belonged quite accurately to those who could be "drama's patrons" and who would, in another setting, write "drama's laws." In the last decades of the eighteenth century and the beginning of the nineteenth, however, successive enlargements of the patent theaters and an increased urban population, especially in and around Westminster, altered audience demographics.

Although the social composition of theatrical audiences during this transformational period is difficult to characterize with precision, it is certain that changes were occurring. The large and often crowded pit registered the shifts in London's population. Professional men—lawyers, doctors, merchants, men of letters, especially theatrical critics—spending a "stag" night at the theater, continued to prefer, as they did in the previous century, the proximity to the stage that the pit allowed. Yet, the pit also seemed to provide seats for tradesmen, master craftsmen, and some apprentices. It thus displayed, to a limited extent, the fluid demarcations among the various English ranks, especially as they then existed in Westminster.[3] The galleries were inhabited by a more notable addition to the local urban community—a quite numerous population of the lower ranks. In attendance were large numbers of servants, prostitutes, thieves, apprentices, and those working men and women, presumably single, frugal, or the marginally skilled, who had expendable income after payment for necessities (see Figure 1).[4]

The melodramas then being performed with increasing regularity before such new and unfamiliar audiences were not mere echoes of them. Indeed, in a city where the rural poor, the urban poor, and various others (the lum-

Figure 1. "The Boxes," by Thomas Rowlandson, 1809, comically renders the varied patrons at the Covent Garden Theatre during the Old Price Wars. In the pit are stationed the angry rioters, supported by the sign-wielding occupants of the lower boxes, all of whom are stationed at a distance from the "gallery gods," who share their environs with owls. Courtesy of the Print Collection, Lewis Walpole Library, Yale University.

penproletariat, petty bourgeoisie, and professional bourgeoisie) were transforming the social composition, "echoing back the public's voice" became a much more complicated procedure. "Theatre royals," for instance, rarely enjoyed the presence and backing of the royalty, as they had only a few years earlier, and now more fully depended on profits in a competitive market, profits that derived from the humble members of the pit and upper galleries as much if not more so than from the highborn in the boxes. Having paid their one or two shillings (somewhat more for the pit), these holders of cheap seats were, as purchasers, unarguably patrons in the new commercial sense but were hardly construed by the proprietors as patrons in the Johnsonian sense. Moreover, their admission into the "public" and their right to frame law, even dramatic law, were less certain and had become the subtext of many of the debates taking place in the elections out of doors.[5]

In the rapidly urbanizing London of the early 1800's, the parameters of and membership criteria for the "public" were deeply contested, and the theaters in Westminster registered the historically specific terms of this contest. Within the theater that opening night in 1806, seated in "box, gallery, and pit," there was a much more diverse gathering of London residents, if not of voters, than one would have encountered in Johnson's theater, and yet such diversity, though now occurring frequently in the patent theaters, had become rarer elsewhere in London. Covent Garden and the other patent house, the Drury Lane Theatre, were therefore two of the very few indoor places in an increasingly segregated London where a broad cross section of its populace, from a tailor's apprentice to the prince regent himself, might congregate to join in the same endeavor. Because theatrical customs were more tolerant than contemporary social restrictions, these theaters had become the primary public location where all kinds of people could be legally heard and where they could be "dramatized" as contentious voices in public debate. In a theater, if not in a parliamentary election, these people could "vote" their pleasure. Unlike the strict regulations against combination then in operation outside the theater, unlike the imposing censorship criteria applied to the drama itself, theatrical law had traditionally allowed the audience more freedom of speech than the players, at least insofar as the ticket holders were guaranteed the right "of Applauding, or Disliking the Performance of any particular Actor," as mentioned by Sir Richard Steele in 1720, who was then part proprietor of the Drury Lane Theatre.[6]

As these gatherings of heterogeneous ranks engaged in the common act of forming an audience, they were widely considered to be emblematic of larger versions of community and the "public" that were undergoing renegotiation during these volatile years. Moreover, their newly emerging and distinctive exchanges with the drama on the stage seemed of particular significance to these renegotiations. Once melodrama made its way to a patent theater in 1802, where it was performed under the close scrutiny of governmental censorship but before an array of voluble ticket holders, it could not merely "echo back the public voice" as comedy and tragedy were perhaps simplistically presumed to do for the more unitary audiences of the past; rather, it was both a contributing voice and an echo of these revolutionary exchanges between the stage and its new "patrons," exchanges that necessarily accompanied the contemporary increase in the urban population and the evolution of capitalist modes of production.

These newly emerging theatrical exchanges at the turn of the century were perhaps most spectacularly enacted and prodigiously recorded during a series of riots in the Covent Garden Theatre in 1809. In these "Old Price Wars" we not only see melodrama on the stage but also off of it—in the pit, the galleries, and the city streets. And it is these sites of theatricality off the stage that situate melodrama in its social setting so that we can see it as multiply determined and multiply determining—something other than an opiate for the tasteless masses, as many of its critics have long argued.[7] In the Old Price Wars, an inchoate manifestation of the melodramatic mode took center stage, acting out its political, economic, and social roles in early Victorian culture.

I

When the Covent Garden Theatre Royal opened for its new season on September 18, 1809, not quite three years after the 1806 elections and the successful run of *Adrian and Orrila*, the audience was greeted by several changes: a completely rebuilt theater, necessitated by the fire that had destroyed the old building the previous year; a new management headed by John Philip Kemble, formerly of Drury Lane, which was at this time closed due to its own devastating fire; and most notably, an increase in ticket prices, which until that day had remained fixed for many years. Formerly, boxes cost six shillings; seats in the pit, three shillings, six pence; and places in the lower and upper galleries, one to two shillings. On opening night, only the gallery paid the traditional price, while the audience in the boxes was now charged seven shillings; those in the pit, four shillings.

This rise in ticket prices occasioned what was soon known all over London as the Old Price Wars. Beginning that night, spectators seated in the pit, sporadically joined by those in the dress boxes and gallery, exercised what they considered their ancient right to express approbation and disapprobation in the theater. As soon as Kemble began to deliver his prologue, the audience interrupted him, drowning out his voice with its own voices, rattles, and cat-calls, a procedure that continued at the theater, with variations, for sixty-seven nights until an agreement was reached on December 14, 1809. The London newspapers of the day quickly took sides and committed large amounts of copy to the nightly events. Soon pamphlets, books, poems, and caricatures joined the print debate, and in time the evening riot at Covent Garden became a cultural ritual, engendering a dance, a medallion, and a hat.

I am concerned here with the distinctive exchanges between early English stage melodrama and its heterogeneous audience, which included the ranks of the O. P. faction and many others whose resistance to changes in the the-ater formed part of "a melodramatic mode." As will become apparent in the course of the riots and the performance of the plays, this melodramatic mode articulated an idealized version of a more traditional formulation of the pub-lic voice, an articulation audible within the theater and beyond.

Few modern historians have mentioned the O. P. Wars, and most of those who have are historians of the theater who are concerned almost exclusively with stage performances and therefore with the theaters only insofar as they facilitated those productions. When the rare discussion of the O. P. Wars' pol-itics arises, a residue of class bias usually emerges; for instance, one historian assessed the O. P. Wars as "the triumph of mob-rule in the English theatre."[8] Such implicit class bias is especially telling in analyses of the O. P. Wars be-cause it marks the triumph of an admixture of "class thinking" and aesthetic evaluation that was then taking shape and that formed one of the central subjects of contestation during the conflict. The opponents in these wars were much more diverse, their complaints much more complicated, their goals much more ambiguous and yet consequential than the phrase "mob-rule" suggests.

The Old Price Wars were never simply a protest against prices, even on that first night, since the increase was insignificant for most of the people who generally populated the pit and boxes.[9] Other controversial changes accompanied the new prices. On entering the theater, for example, the au-dience confronted architectural alterations that had affected the seating arrangements. The long and open upper gallery of the theater had been replaced by large arches beneath which the lowest-paying spectators, com-monly called the "gallery gods," were gathered closely together in "pigeon-hole" spaces quite distant from the stage. Most of these theatergoers, then, could neither see nor hear the performance. Along the sides of the theater, where open boxes had once lined the walls, private boxes and adjacent ante-rooms were built, all of which were intended for the exclusive use of those who bought season tickets. Such boxes now amounted to half of all seating in the theater. In addition, the new dress boxes, constructed above the private tier, were so close to the ceiling that the actors' voices were inaudible to the occupants.

Given the symbolism attached to the many-tiered audiences within the patent theaters, the restructured interior was almost immediately construed as a realignment of social relationships.[10] Combined with the price increase, the new seating amounted to, as one outraged commentator described it, "the absolute seclusion of a PRIVILEGED ORDER from all *vulgar contact*."[11] In addition to imposing segregation, the enlarged theater made it virtually impossible for those in the dress boxes and gallery to see the same performance as those in the private boxes, as if the new theater space were institutionalizing the social demarcations already associated with the various theatrical genres. One disgruntled theatergoer alludes to these generic distinctions when complaining of the new Covent Garden design: "Shakespeare may be played to the pit and side boxes, but he will be little better than dumb and blind shew to the people in the basket [top-tier dress boxes]."[12] As will become evident, the constitutive relation asserted here between the architectural renovations in the seating and the theatrical fare on the stage is not merely polemic, but a crucial insight into the dynamics of this cultural contest.

The proprietors of the theater seemed to be entirely restricting the entertainment of the poor, limiting the pleasures of the middle ranks, and selling large portions of the theater to the rich. But more crucially, they were emphasizing through seating arrangements the distinctions among ranks rather than the communal, though layered, identity of the audience, which was usually associated, in turn, with the hierarchical, yet interdependent, organization of English society. In a song sarcastically dedicated to John Philip Kemble, the most visible and thus most demonized of the proprietors, the lyricist quite explicitly links the new seating to a redefinition of not just the audience, but the nation: "He next in his National booth, you all know, / De-nationalized the very first row."[13] By privatizing a large portion of the theater and disregarding the old prices, the owners exercised their property rights rather than fulfilled their traditional obligation as patent holders—to amuse the nation with rational entertainment. A letter to the editor of the *Constitutional Review* stresses this age-old responsibility: "Theatres in a country under a monarchical form of government can never be considered as private property, but as a great national concern; as a powerful political engine."[14] Much of the succeeding debate therefore centered on whether the patent theater constituted private property (as the proprietors argued) or public domain (as the O.P. faction maintained) and, if private property, on the relation between private enterprise and the constitution of the nation.

The proprietors and their supporters—including the *Morning Post* and eventually, if inconsistently, the *Times*—found it useful to attach more hyperbolic associations to these contending parties by characterizing themselves as loyalist Englishmen and the O. P. faction as Levellers or Jacobins. It was the O. P. faction, then, who "originated a *civil* war, of which, community of property seemed to be the chief object."[15] Like the lyrics of the above song, this quotation demonstrates how this theatrical confrontation was almost immediately viewed, especially after the second night, as an implicitly political struggle about property and privilege.

On this second night, September 19, when the noise from the audience continued unabated, the proprietors called on the Bow Street magistrates to impose order. When their presence seemed to have little effect on the shouting, hissing, and scampering in the pit, the two chief officers, Read and Nare, went to stage center and proceeded to read the Riot Act to the audience, thereby communicating that the noise the audience considered a traditional right was deemed by these representatives of the law to be a violent breach of the public peace. One poet put this action into its political context:

> Who, therefore, damn'd a bad new play,
> Had *bred a riot* they might say;
> And those by whom 'twas not admir'd,
> Against the poet had *conspir'd*;[16]

In an apparent reversal of Johnson's law, Kemble and his associates had attempted to subdivide their increasingly diverse audience through architectural renovations and then, when that seemed inadequate to their ends, through legal prescriptions in order to regulate and manipulate the public whose voice they wished to echo. Rather than seeking to please drama's patrons, officers Read and Nare sought to convict and thus silence a specially designated portion of them so as to please drama's owners.

The *Times* confirms the proprietors' complaints that the composition of the pit had become noticeably and disturbingly diverse: "Jews, Turks, Hibernians, Bow-street Officers, pugilists, pickpockets, all jumbled together."[17] The O. P. faction, however, quickly countered that the Jews, the Irish, and the pugilists were paid by the management to taint the social composition of the protesters so as to provide a justification for their invasive actions. By giving disreputable people free tickets, the managers wished to strike a note of discord and, perhaps, to incite physical violence. A journalist sympathetic to the protesters outlined still another devious strategy: "Multiplied gratis admissions were issued to the lowest of the people . . . to create a false appearance of assimilation . . . to the views of the proprietors."[18] In this plan, boos and catcalls were to be drowned out by hurrahs and applause. With the disbursal of well-placed funds, the owners thus gave the impression that they were shaping "drama's laws" merely according to the pleasure of "drama's patrons" and thereby simply adhering to traditional theatrical custom. In fact, this opponent alleged, they were pleasing themselves, not their public. And they did so through secretive transactions with mercenaries. "The house is nightly filled with orders . . . in order to fill the house with persons *hired to applaud*, and to *resist the public voice*."[19] Although the proprietors long denied planting people in the pit, by the end of December they were grudgingly conceding their contractual relationship with Dutch Sam and Daniel Mendoza, certain Jewish pugilists who had frequently cheered the performances, fought in the pit, and regularly brought O.P. protesters before the magistrate.[20]

In addition to their effort to stage their own preferred version of the public voice, the proprietors also sought to discredit the voice that had erupted in protest. Rather than listening to the criticism of its audience, the theatrical company chose to hear the "halloo of drunkenness." J.K., perhaps John Kemble himself, wrote to the editor of the *Constitutional Review*: "We are impudently told, that the confused noise that takes place is the voice of the public; but let it be designated by its proper titles,—it is the halloo of drunkenness, assisted by ignorance, buoyed up by disaffection."[21] In effect, the proprietors reinterpreted the voice of their increasingly diverse clientele, translating their traditional right to express opinions into nonsense that the owners then felt justified in squelching. A *Times* account makes this strategy explicit when it describes a typical night in the pit: "It appeared a second Babel, as well from the variety of its occupants as from the regularity of its clamour. . . . [They] seemed to consider it their first and most imperious duty, never to cease from one universal and discordant bellowing."[22] The reporter immediately reduces the voice of protest into "Babel," "clamour," and "discordant bellowing."

Perceptions of the pit inhabitants had altered greatly over the course of one century. In the eighteenth century, the critics usually seated themselves in the pit; consequently, that region of the theater had been considered the site from which issued the rational voices of public taste, voices that regularly spoke to one another in the London press. In 1809, by contrast, the pit was charged with being the site from which bellowed the "discordant" mob. One commentator complained: "He [the protester] provides himself with a rattle or a dustman's bell, appropriate emblems of his function, to make that noise to which his unformed baby voice is inadequate: and then, *he* too is one of the PUBLIC!"[23]

At this juncture, it is important to stress that the crucial phrase "the public voice" embraces a wider definition than might be apparent to a modern observer. The meaning that the O.P. protesters attached to "the public voice" included both physical and verbal expression, action as well as voice. In this context, the new theater was accused of committing censorship by rendering large sections of the theater out of earshot, while simultaneously obstructing some of the spectators' views. Furthermore, when the proprietors refused to acknowledge the audience's "voice" of protest regarding these changes, its specific right to act out its opinions was being curtailed. And finally, when the Riot Act was read and protesters were taken before the magistrate, the owners were seen to be questioning not just the audience's right to express and act out theatrical opinions, but its right to have political opinions more generally.

The proprietors' policies of hiring Jewish and Irish pugilists to incite violence in the pit and of reserving the private boxes exclusively for the rich convinced many O.P. sympathizers that a conspiracy was afoot, one it is tempting to label a class conspiracy, where one class deviously conspires against another. Using the term *class*, however, is at least doubly misleading in this instance, since the two sides of the controversy neither split solely along what have come to be defined as "class" lines, nor articulated a fully elaborated consciousness of class affiliation.[24] Some of those supporting the O.P. faction, like solicitors, though certainly of a lower socioeconomic group than those who would generally occupy the exclusive private boxes, might be considered in the same rank as the opposing proprietors, while still others in favor of the old prices, apprentices, for instance, would not be considered in the same group as either the antagonistic proprietors or the sympathetic solicitors. This diversity of socioeconomic standing was apparent within the New Price faction as well. Mostly speculators, the proprietors were primarily not of the same economic group as the aristocrats in the box who were their nominal supporters.

Despite allegations of mob rule and Jacobinism, despite what might otherwise look to us like class warfare, the nightly protests against alterations within the theater were more comparable, though by no means identical, to conservative, ritualized uprisings, such as the food riots in the English countryside, which sought to return prices to customary levels and economic relationships to more traditional bonds. Another rough parallel might be the anti-Enclosure protests of the eighteenth century, which fought the transformation of common lands into private property.[25] Even more precisely, the O.P. protesters seemed to oppose the modern principle of classification itself, insofar as its imposition divided the theater audience and, within the private boxes, subdivided the elite into public and private roles. The protesters saw the changes in seating and prices as arising not from the natural or economic differences among theatergoers but rather from the self-interested coercion of the mercenary proprietors. In response to these disciplinary measures of classification, the O.P. supporters formed a version of what they considered to be a more natural social formation.

William Reddy and David C. Moore, among others, have begun to study the way various European peoples in the nineteenth century continued to coalesce around traditional codes of honor, the ideological remnants of the deferential behaviors that had cemented together the status hierarchies operative during the previous century.[26] According to this view, people from disparate economic categories who shared a belief in these codes might not only have behaved similarly, but also formed a coherent protest group to oppose a common enemy. While the O.P. faction fits this pattern, its adherence to deferential codes was also the content of its polemic. Confronting the classificatory alterations in the theater and their regulation of social exchange, this group insisted on the continued viability of older theatrical conventions and the apparently natural forms of social exchange they underwrote. The expression and enactment of this uniquely conservative and somewhat nostalgic view constitutes the melodramatic mode. For the O.P. protesters, a return to old prices presumably symbolized a renewed commitment to inclusive, instructive entertainment; a reduction in private boxes signaled a rejuvenation in communal ties among the ranks; and a resumption of audience commentary represented a renegotiation of the public voice.

In contrast to the communal and hierarchical bonds idealized by the O.P. faction, the proprietors' ties to the aristocracy were economic and contractual, the very terms of social exchange with which they hoped to legislate in the renovated theater. In purchasing the theater, the owners had secured exclusive patent privileges that the king had traditionally granted their many predecessors as a gift. The current proprietors had, in effect, bought the status conferred by the exclusionary patent rather than earned it through deferential behavior to a royal patron. Additionally, the social relationship between proprietors and aristocrats was becoming more obviously one of market exchange. Because the owners depended on the richest ranks' occasional presence at the theater to render theatrical attendance fashionable for the upper classes as well as for those humbler people who emulated them, John Kemble sought to solicit their business. Moreover, the proprietors were possibly affiliated with the aristocracy in more directly economic ways, since the owners relied on wealthy investors to support their purchase of the theater, though these investors were not exclusively aristocrats.

Because of this possible contractual relationship and especially because of their leasing of the new private boxes, the controversial alterations and subsequent disputes in the theater were blamed on the aristocracy, not just the proprietors. Instead of heading a deferential community, the patrician occupants of the private boxes, which one observer called "snug retreats," appeared to seek ever more refined distinctions among the orders, even seg-regating themselves from the middle ranks, who used to sit within sight.[27] As one observer complained: "There is something autocratical and super-cilious, to a degree of reasonable offence, in the idea of separate apartments, separate channels of communication, and separate entrances for the wealthy and the proud."[28] By absenting, perhaps even hiding, themselves from a tra-ditional scene of hierarchical unity, the rich enacted an alternative social for-mation, a prototypical class system in the modern sense. In so doing, they encouraged others to think in terms of horizontal rather than vertical alle-giance, to operate in "separate channels of communication." A letter to the editor of the *Morning Chronicle* explains the process: "When distinctions of accommodation are made at public places, the company which frequents them naturally divides itself into classes; and for any individual to be seen out of his respective class, mingling exclusively with those who form one of an inferior description is, at least, looked on as derogatory from his rank, and frequently disgraceful to his character."[29] Even as the new seating ar-rangements physically emphasized class distinctions and even as Dutch Sam's presence in the pit accentuated them, proponents of the new prices also verbally emphasized class distinctions by categorizing by income a broad array of occupations that in an earlier era were often seen as discrete social positions. For instance, one journalist supportive of the changes complained: "Clerks, apprentices, linendrapers' foremen, hairdressers, and knife-grinders, have been the dignified leaders of this most dignified mob; and upon *these* the name of the *Public* has been conferred."[30]

To the insulted members of the O. P. faction the private boxes particularly came to represent an "abdication on the part of the governors," to adopt a well-known phrase from Thomas Carlyle. One observer of the events rec-ognized "a dangerous precedent." Secreted in their anterooms, rather than spectacularly displayed in elegantly decorated open boxes, where they once presided over the lower orders like emblems of patronage, the rich appeared to abdicate any recognizable public role in, of all places, the "place where all orders of the community assemble for the purpose of forgetting their sepa-rations."[31] This architectural expression of the principle of classification therefore seemed to have concrete effects on the constitution of patrician and plebeian identities. Indeed, the new layout of the boxes could be interpreted as material evidence of the structural changes that had been taking place throughout English society in the previous century.

Jürgen Habermas has noted in *The Structural Transformation of the Public Sphere* that eighteenth-century society began to demarcate appropriate spheres for what came to be considered distinctive public and private behav-iors. In the increasingly bifurcated culture of the 1700's, educated elites led

45

private lives of family and business, then only occasionally gathered together in public forums to authorize state power through the operation of their influential opinion. This division between the public and private, Habermas claims, contrasted with the social structure of earlier feudal systems, where court life determined all forms of social existence.[32] In keeping with this account, the new boxes in the Covent Garden Theatre can be seen to manifest an even more pronounced bifurcation of patrician identity. The lingering theatricality of broad-based social interaction in the eighteenth century was now reduced to the size of a framed box and equipped with an escape route.

Although I accept Habermas's description of this gradual reorganization in eighteenth-century culture, the democratic thrust he attributes to the new public sphere conflicts with the experiences of those who were explicitly excluded from, or who refused to participate in, what he concedes were elite realignments of state power. For the O.P. faction, the unmistakable division into private and public realms evinced by the boxes' design extended the classificatory categories that defined identity according to economic exchange: the price one paid for a ticket. To those denied access to a private box, therefore, its recessed anteroom figured the contemporary patrician's retreat to a private life of exclusivity and secrecy. Furthermore, the box's rarely occupied balcony seating symbolized the aristocrat's seemingly empty performance of a public life that in fact narrowly represented the hidden interests of a secluded existence.

For the O.P. faction, this stratification of the theatrical audience and the disjunction between the public and private roles of the aristocrat were deeply related to the contracts that it assumed were signed by the proprietors and aristocrats. Kemble and his business colleagues were the main actors in this apparent economic conspiracy against the humbler orders that momentarily focused on issues of accounting during the last week of September. Covent Garden closed its doors that week while a committee investigated the theater's finances to determine whether the price rise was justified. Appointed by the proprietors, all the members were either aristocrats or recipients of aristocratic largess, and all were reputed to be sympathetic to the patent theater's cause.[33] Based on a review of the theater's financial books, their report supported the new prices by contending that the theater made only a meager profit from current ticket income.

The committee's bias aroused suspicion, but more important, its focus on the profitability of bulk ticket sales further attests to the structural shift from a patronage economy to a market economy. From the vantage point of the O.P. faction, this represented a shift from an old and familiar vertical system of status relations to a new and unfamiliar horizontal system in which transactions were commercial, private, and contractual. They intuited that implicit in this horizontal formation is contention, for, as one writer noted, "rival prejudices would arise in the rival classes of society upon those exclusive appropriations."[34]

When the royal boxes were filled with "drama's patrons," who paid a fixed single-night fee, and when the price of tickets for the general populace was determined by tradition, the source and amount of profit also seemed fixed and traditional and, to some extent, visible as a ritualistic bestowal of favor.[35] The nobility seated in the open boxes presided over these public acts of patronage. But once the proprietors raised prices in the name of an inflationary marketplace, once the rich paid a single fee to disappear from view for an entire season, the source and amount of profit became mysterious, dependent on unseen market forces instead of common consent, and hidden in private books never open to the public view. These private books, like the private boxes, concealed the economically determined social exchanges between the aristocrat and the proprietor that were replacing the public, deferential exchanges among all ranks.

Despite this canny reading of the events in the theater, the O. P. protesters certainly did not describe the conflict in terms of the alienating effects of market culture and its inherent class contention. Such a critique did not emerge in a fully coherent fashion in England until the late 1830's. Experiencing the early effects of a nascent class system, they responded to it with the assumptions of an earlier era. In their view, the upper ranks seemed no longer to exercise their power openly by dispensing punishment and generosity downward, but to transact private "business deals" with the criminal element. Although prostitutes, pimps, and bawds had been a regular component of theatrical audiences for generations, their illicit affiliations with the aristocracy were now presumed by O. P. sympathizers to occur in the comfort of anterooms rumored to include couches. From the perspective of the O. P. faction, such accommodations seemed to condone "the exotic association" between the highborn and the criminal and even, perhaps, to institutionalize their sexualized economic exchanges.[36] "These select retreats . . . will degenerate into receptacles of just concealment for the Darlings of degraded Dukes, the titled Concubines of impoverished Peers, and the frail Inamoratas of intriguing Valets."[37] This affiliation of market exchange with criminality and illicit sexuality was not new nor was it a rhetorical gesture soon to disappear. For those newly exposed to the operations of a full-scale market economy, market exchange seemed indistinguishable from theft and perversion.[38]

Because of this sexual-economic association between aristocrats and prostitutes, the O. P. faction found it convenient to remind John Philip Kemble and his business partners that Elizabethan law considered actors as well as prostitutes to be vagrants.[39] Through guilt by association, Kemble and his company became very much like prostitutes when they took the stage: "However great a person's talents in this way, yet the exercise of them *for the sake of gain*, is but *'a sort of public prostitution.'*"[40] Of course, the proprietors' decision to freeze the prices of the gallery seats and their subsequent hiring of pugilists seemed to be the most obvious indications of this three-tiered collusion among owners, prostitutes, and aristocracy. Soliciting prostitutes often frequented the lobbies of these upper galleries, and the Covent Garden district was a favorite location for houses of prostitution. One report notes what appears to be evidence of this collusion: "The lower and upper galleries remain at the old prices, evidently, *ad captandum vulgum*, that is to say, to conciliate the gods [those seated in the top balconies]."[41]

The formation of these two factions, the O.P. and the N.P., vividly depicts the unpredictable shape that contending groups could take in the early nineteenth century. On one side, the aristocracy paradoxically teamed up with myriad unsavory representatives of the cash nexus—speculators, pugilists, and prostitutes—all of whom shared a commercial interest. On the other, the humble and middle ranks, ordinarily considered the laboring and commercial populations, found their rallying point in an opposition to market relations, manifested in their nostalgia for older forms of community and their self-proclaimed strict adherence to ethical law.

Many historians and literary critics, some of whom otherwise conscientiously historicize their terms, nonetheless apply the term *class* as if it were a universal, essential, and unchanging component of all societies. Carrying connotations of theoretical precision, the term has nonetheless too often become a loose descriptive device for divvying up portions of society without recourse to analytical and/or historically relevant criteria, thereby creating the impression, for instance, that the same group of people called a "middle class" has existed for centuries, even though the middling group in the early Renaissance had significantly different relations to production than the middle class of Victorian England. Over the course of English history, there have, in fact, been many distinctive middle classes that demand more explicit definition and identification if we wish to avoid distorting the historical record.

In addition to contributing to historically specific definitions of early-nineteenth-century classes, I also hope to refine our current historical record of class consciousness during this period. The O.P. faction's own conception of its rhetoric and actions, which is vital to an understanding of the melodramatic mode, confirms that it did not mobilize as a self-conscious class. For example, the O.P. faction did not consider itself to be a proletarian consciousness demanding individualized representation in the franchise.[42] It did not represent any class; it opposed an emergent idea of class. This emergent idea was a heuristic device of political and disciplinary intent that gradually coalesced over several generations in the eighteenth and nineteenth centuries. It did so in relation to a complex interaction between increasingly specialized economic interests, such as the Covent Garden proprietors, and an increasingly heightened awareness among portions of the population of how those economic interests might affect public and private identities. It was this version of classification that largely formed the terms of debate among the participants in the O. P. Wars.

II

By November 1, 1809, when Henry Clifford was arrested for wearing the initials "O. P." on his hat while standing in the pit of the Covent Garden Theatre, he had become, in print at least, the symbolic voice of the O. P. faction. Consequently, many wished to associate the O. P. protesters with more explicitly political radicalism. Indeed, by this time, rumors about the Radical party's direct involvement in the riots, rumors largely spread by conservative newspapers, had become common. An active member of the Radical party, Clifford was a good friend of Colonel Bosville, who was reputed to be a friend of William Cobbett. In fact, Clifford was reported to have just left the colonel's home before his appearance at the theater the night of his detainment.[43] Some argued that Clifford had actually worked for Major Cartwright and other notable Radicals.[44] Moreover, when the Old and New Price factions met at the Crown and Anchor Tavern on December 14, 1809, to work out an agreement, the man who wrote up the O. P. resolutions was J. J. Stockdale, who had served as a treasurer for the Radical party during the Westminster elections of 1806 and later as the editor of the Covent Garden Journal, a weekly compilation of newspaper accounts of and letters about the O. P. Wars.[45] Whether the Radicals infiltrated an ordinarily apolitical audience in order to create a "corresponding society" within the theater when such societies were at that time illegal outside of it will probably never be known.[46] Marc Baer suggests that the mainly Radical members of the "O. P. Committee," which was founded several weeks into the disturbance, probably organized a handful of the evening protests, and certainly orchestrated the Crown and Anchor peace talks, but was never fully in control of the riots. After all, the heterogeneous crowds of O. P. supporters had to approve the results of the O. P. Committee's negotiations with Kemble.[47] Despite the uncertainty regarding Radical involvement, I am confident that the protesters' critique of theatrical power structures does seem deeply implicated in some of the same issues that had been raised by the Radicals during the 1806 Westminster election, the election invoked in the epilogue to the melodrama

Adrian and Orrila. In both instances the aristocrats seemed to be merely playing at their public roles, and in both instances the intended audience interpreted their performances as a sign of the aristocrats' disappearance from the public sphere.

The race for the Westminster seat occurred between the Whigs and the increasingly popular city Radicals, whose political agenda was noticeably at odds with the Whigs but far less revolutionary than many modern observers suppose. Although out of power for a number of years, the Whigs were favored by the infamous Prince of Wales, whose assumption of the throne seemed ever imminent as the reign of his aged father George III lingered on. (The prince would become prince regent in 1810.) Despite their absence from the ministry, the Whigs were a significant cultural and political force, the core of which was the London aristocracy centered at Holland House. Often accused of lacking a coherent oppositional philosophy, the Whigs only occasionally flirted with reform, particularly those measures that would further the separation of the church establishment from state authority. In contrast, the Radicals committed themselves more vociferously to parliamentary reform and thus, at times, the alteration of the franchise, but it would be a mistake to characterize the majority of them as advocates of rational individualism and its political manifestation, universal suffrage. Resistance to excessive taxation during these Napoleonic War years and the increasingly pervasive complaint of establishment corruption marked the Radical rhetoric far more often than a call for one man one vote.[48]

References to the theater and drama had of course been common during this election, since one of the Whig candidates running against the Radical James Paull had been Richard Brinsley Sheridan, a noted playwright and the owner of the other patent theater, the Drury Lane. In 1806, Sheridan had also been the employer of John Philip Kemble. In his *Political Register*, Cobbett set the terms for the Westminster debate when he disparaged an actor's life. This criticism was couched in terms of rank in order to highlight the contrast between James Paull, who embodied humble origins and the meager social status of an India merchant, and Sheridan, who as a friend of the Prince of Wales aspired to a position of rank and privilege. In focusing on his theatrical connections, Cobbett's criticism of Sheridan therefore symbolically lowered the proprietor's social rank: "If there be any calling lower than all other callings; there be any the most degrading."[49]

It was not simply to provide rhetorical color, however, that the Radicals deployed theatrical terms and concepts in their polemic against Sheridan and the Whigs; it was also to convey their growing conviction, seemingly corroborated by Sheridan's selection as a Whig candidate for Westminster, that state power was deeply theatrical and that its representatives were actors and playwrights creating an illusion. In articulating their criticism through theatrical language, the Radicals were adopting the perspective of another radical thinker, Thomas Paine, who saw only affectation and insincerity in the theatricalized and choreographed gestures of the English elite.[50] Rather than participating with aristocrats in an exchange of deference and paternalism, during which theatricality is a naturalized affect, the Radicals had become critical spectators, eyeing the actors with suspicion as they put on public performances.

During the election, for instance, Sheridan solicited the aid of his theatrical company and one day organized a procession down St. Giles's Street in the theater district, thereby eliciting Radical spectators' wary reactions. One of the marchers carried a banner with the emblem of a tailor, the profession of Paull's father, another was dressed as an ape with tailor's tools, while another was in French revolutionary costume labeled with Paull's name. The *Times* reports the event: "Parties of Mr. Sheridan's friends were preceded by a posse of Hibernians from the purlieus of St. Giles's, armed with cudgels, roaring *Sheridan for ever!*"[51]

This rhetorical conflation of Irish thieves threatening violence and Sheridan's players putting on a spectacle seems to confirm for Cobbett and Paull that the state's power to represent was political, theatrical, and fraudulent. Not unlike the three-tiered collaboration in the theater that the 1809 O. P. faction would be quick to discern, Paull understood this other sort of theatrical collaboration between what he called "stratagem, stage trick, Ministerial influence, or Treasury gold."[52] Patronized by Whigs and royalty, both as a candidate and as a patent theater proprietor, Sheridan had the material and official means to lampoon Paull. Three years before the O. P. Wars, then, actors and aristocrats, the "monied interest," as well as prostitutes, deployed theater against the humbler ranks. In 1809, it was to be police officers who, in stepping out of the trapdoor, took roles as actors. In 1806, it was actors who, in stepping down the street with cudgels, turned into police officers. Either way, both sought to enforce their version of the public voice by combining dramatic roles with state rules.

This perceived collaboration between political power and the theater implied for such spectators that the state's power to represent was, in fact, the secret of its authority and that, counter to tradition, the state depended on the theater, rather than the other way around. Such insights were soon given explicit articulation. Near the end of November 1806, Sheridan narrowly defeated Paull and celebrated the victory by putting on another show. Riding in a gilded "theatrical car," Sheridan and Hood, the other successful Whig candidate, were the central attraction in a procession that included a grand carriage containing nobility surrounded by a large accompaniment of police. Cobbett described the event:

> The car had been constructed by the people of Drury Lane, was surrounded by beadles, constables, police-officers, and police-magistrates, and as even their own venal prints informs by the numerous officers of the Thames police. "The People," of whom they talk as *huzzaers*, consisted of the play-actors, scene-shifters, candle-snuffers, and mutes of the Theatre, aided by a pretty numerous bevy of those unfortunate females who are some sort of inmates of that mansion.[53]

Confronted once more with a simultaneous show of physical force and theatricalized procession, Cobbett and Paull did not need to walk backstage to perceive the mechanisms generating this political show of power, for the illusion seemed to be exposing its own inner workings—state power as low-brow drama. As Cobbett observes: "Altogether the procession bore a very strong resemblance to that of *Blue-Beard*."[54] Or as James Paull commented: "Who introduced the low mummery and pantomimical tricks this day exhibited, to give *stage effect* to the proceedings of those performers? The public have been to-day amused by the first-act of *Robin Hood* and the farce of the *Forty Thieves*."[55]

The theatricality of eighteenth-century governance has been widely noted by modern critics, who have mainly emphasized its coercive force, a force that noticeably lingered long after many of its other dramatic symbols had come to be seen as "low mummery and pantomimical tricks" to observers like Cobbett and Paull. Throughout the eighteenth century, the power exerted over the common people by the "spectacle of terror" at the scaffolds, in courts of law, and at the processions preceding the quarter sessions probably far exceeded the actual physical force the state could, or was willing to, muster. "The assizes," Douglas Hay has written, "were a formidable spectacle in a country town, the most visible and elaborate manifestations of state power to be seen in the countryside." Philip Corrigan and Derek Sayer describe this "ritual of rule" as "spectacles of terror and patronage, punishment and benevolence . . . that allowed the surveillance of this social audience from those on stage."[56]

Such displays of "occasional dramatic intervention," as E. P. Thompson calls them, were still crucial to maintaining national order in the early years of the nineteenth century, even as, according to Habermas, more democratic, though still elitist, formulations of the public sphere were becoming concretely realized.[57] In fact, these two apparently contradictory forces were effective, if not always intentional, collaborators, especially when supported by the more tangible authority of an emerging police force. Theatrical spectacles of state power diverted attention from the activities of those fortunate few who had been invited into the enclaves of power. These men, like the proprietors of Covent Garden Theatre, were often the architects of the economic and bureaucratic restructuring of hierarchical England into a class society whose members, like the holders of the private boxes, were split personalities—public representatives of class interest as well as private individuals cloaked in secrecy.

The effects of their opponents' collaboration reveal why many Radicals did not lobby primarily for universal suffrage. In this context, representative government, premised on the interests of private individuals aggregated into classes, seemed to be a vacuum that sucked meaning from the more traditional sites of social exchange, such as London's patent theaters or England's country parishes, like those celebrated by Cobbett in *Rural Rides*. The struggle over the dimensions of the public and its voice was not, therefore, identical to the extension of the franchise that also took place over the course of the nineteenth century. In the Westminster district, a classic scot-and-lot borough in which any rate-paying resident could vote, there was already a comparatively large and inclusive electorate, such that issues of suffrage were not necessarily pertinent to local political debate.[58]

In the Westminster election of late 1806 issues other than the franchise were paramount. Given that governance had come to be seen as bawdy and bodily pantomime, Sheridan seems an ideal member of Parliament and the perfect representative of a state that depended on stagecraft for statecraft, on the theatrical display of physical dominance more than on the possession of it. Of course, Sheridan's selection was in some ways too perfect, inviting by its explicitness Cobbett and Paull's insight into these "rituals of rule." Once such "spectacles of terror and patronage," devised in private, were publicly demystified into pantomimes and farces in which the exercise of terror could be seen as a stage trick and the reputed recipients of patronage as "scene-shifters" dressed up to play the people, the awe-inspiring props could be easily distinguished from the "Hibernian pugilists," police officers, magistrates, and beadles.[59] The distinction between theater and some distinct "reality," between spectators and actors that had become evident in much commentary at the end of the eighteenth century became operative in this instance also. Theatrical exchanges of deferential benevolence and gratitude had mutated, so the rhetoric goes, into confrontations of coercion and resistance.

As a metaphor, pantomime clearly plays a complicated role in both the Westminster and O.P. War debates, and so its features need to be described at length. It was the most purely physical and gestural of theatrical genres at the time. Although contemporary pantomime included speech, "little in it was unexplainable by action," and its two major characters, Harlequin and Columbine, never spoke.[60] By the first decade of the nineteenth century, the traditional harlequinade, the second portion of the pantomimic performance—in which the hero, heroine, and villain transform into Harlequin, Columbine, and Pantaloon, respectively—was characterized by exaggerated physical antics, much more so than its eighteenth-century parent. The pursuit of Harlequin by Pantaloon, who in the first half of almost any panto was usually depicted as Harlequin's superior, and the often sexualized play of the Clown produced, in the words of a recent historian of the genre, "innumerable scenes of comic violence and destruction."[61] To contemporaries, then, pantomime almost always signified this broad humor of the harlequinade that was in turn associated with the violence of Pantaloon, the sexual licentiousness of his companion, the Clown, and the silent flight of the harried Harlequin. Consequently, pantomime easily represented both the farce of state power and its physical oppression of the silenced underdog. These more aggressively antic pantomimes experienced great popularity at Covent Garden in the early years of the nineteenth century due to Joseph Grimaldi's famous portrayal of the Clown.

Perhaps, then, Cobbett's comparison of the Westminster election to a performance of *Blue Beard* was more than a reference to the play's current popularity; perhaps he referred to its theme, best expressed by one of its comic songs where violent physical coercion threatens the voice of the downtrodden wife:

> How many there are, when a wife plays the fool,
> Will argue the point with her calmly and cool;
> The Bashaw, who don't relish debates of this sort,
> Cuts the woman, as well as the argument, short.[62]

When Paull claimed he had seen pantomime enacted during the Westminster election, it enabled him, as well as Cobbett, to draw a connection between the bodily force exercised by the state and the silencing of voices, in this case, the voices of Paull and his supporters. The main intent of Sheridan's procession, despite its grandeur and its claim to entertainment value, was to combine physical power and its censoring aggression; Sheridan intended to exert bodily force against the public voice in the same way that Bluebeard had done to many of his argumentative wives: "The play-actors of Westminster assum[e] a sort of corporate and political capacity; [stand] forward in a body to join the body of the nobility and that of the clergy; and with them co-operat[e] to stifle your voice."[63]

The centrality of the physical and visual in the pantomime could also resolve another representational dilemma for the Radicals. In Radical rhetoric the figures of pantomime transform all unfair economic transactions into corporeal and implicitly sexual interactions. In so doing, this rhetoric gave a body to exchanges that seemed in all other ways utterly disembodied, out of their sight. Cobbett emphasizes both the body and its sexualized mode of exchange when he writes that an actor "exhibits his person, displays his limbs and strains his voice for the *amusement* of the spectators."[64] This urge to incorporate and visualize the absentee activities of their opponents most explicitly links the Radical cause with the O.P. rioters. Not surprisingly, Cobbett in 1809 shared the O.P. rioters' hatred of the private boxes.[65]

On the first night of the disturbance at Covent Garden in 1809, three years after Sheridan's election campaign, many of the theatrical terms of the argument about the constitution of the public voice remained strikingly the same. When the magistrates were admitted through the trapdoors on stage in order to point fire hoses at the audience in the pit and then to read the Riot Act, it was evident to many that the state's "engines or instruments of torture" had become pantomime again—this time in a literally theatrical way.[66] Although not technically a stage play, the magistrates' performance was immediately considered a drama by contemporary observers and was even reviewed by the theatrical critics attending that night. "And even two or three respectable Magistrates turned actors, and came forward on the stage . . . as if it had been a dramatic piece got up for the occasion."[67] As in 1806, it seemed that once again playactors before the stage and nobility behind the scenes were cooperating "to stifle" the public voice through bodily coercion and indecency. The events of 1806 provide more than ample explanation for the O.P. faction's political interpretation of the proprietors' actions.

The audience in Covent Garden, however, did not merely observe the pantomimic gesticulation of Read and Nare, but helped to create it by silencing the magistrates' dramatic locution of the Riot Act with its own collective voice, as numerous commentators noted: "It might as well have been Pantomime, for the voice of the Actor was never heard."[68] The rioters' enforcement of pantomime on the stage constituted a particular social response to the N.P. faction's economic and "theatrical" exchanges with the audience. For this faction, pantomime had become, like the seats in the theater, a sign of class. Given the restrictions that made it illegal for nonpatent theaters to perform legitimate spoken drama, pantomime and its permutations had become associated with these theaters and with the lower ranks of spectators who frequented them. Elliston's Circus, one of these nonpatent theaters, was mentioned by a commentator two nights into the O.P. disturbance:

It is somewhat whimsical that the two plays which have hitherto been brought forward should so exactly tally with Mr. Elliston's exhibition. . . . He [Elliston] has performed Macbeth and Macheath, in a great degree, by show and gesticulation, in obedience to the mandate of the law, and nearly the same circumstances have occurred at Covent Garden Theatre, from the temporary will of an enraged audience. How long this race of pantomime is to run, time only can inform us.[69]

"Show and gesticulation" were more than a creative response to the law, however; they were to most Englishmen, including members of the New Price faction, the appropriate language of the lower classes. In affiliating this behavior with specified ticket holders, the N.P. faction supported the concept of what is called "class thinking" and ultimately implied that such audiences possessed limited means of expression inherently as well as legally; the law against illegitimate theater, the new ticket prices, and altered seating arrangements can be seen as simply legalizing "natural" behaviors. If Macbeth had become panto in a patent theater, the New Price faction argued, then it was because the recent audiences, indigenous to nonpatent theaters, had caused it to become so. Such people preferred physical gestures and visual displays. The audiences thus demonstrated their limitations by degrading high tragedy into low pantomime for their prurient enjoyment. After all, as one theatrical critic commented, "the boisterous rant of violent anger or perturbed indignation, the start of astonishment . . . by the million will ever be more applauded."[70]

Throughout the disturbance, the N.P. faction had insisted, contrary to tradition, that the protesting voice of the audience was, in fact, no voice at all. According to them, it was the "halloo of drunkenness," the sounds of an "unformed baby," or, as the famed actor William Macready recalled in his memoirs, a "'hubbub wild.'"[71] In sum, it was an inarticulate noise that originated in the aggressive physical body, not the expressive heart. In the poem "On the nightly Uproar at Covent Garden," the poet translates the O.P. voice into bodily violence by means of a reference to pantomime and thus demonstrates once more how genre was increasingly seen to be determined by its exchanges with its audience, in this case an audience identified by class: "The downfall of sense and ascendance of sound; / Where pantomime gains an accession of force, / And long sinking dialogue's finally drown'd."[72] For the N.P. faction, pantomime operated as a synecdoche for the mob violence frequently erupting throughout the eighteenth century, the violence that state spectacle sought to quell. One writer in the *Constitutional Review* directly equated the O.P. faction with this native violence: "The physical strength of a nation lies, not in the governors, but in the governed."[73] Indeed, several drama critics, as they looked into the pit on the night of a disrupted performance, could see only the traditional staging area for a pantomime; they saw "an admirable fac-simile of Bartholomew Fair,"[74] or, alternatively, "a Cockpit."[75] The fistfights, the dances down the rows of benches, the jostling of the crowd, whether instigated by hired ruffians or Henry Clifford's friends, were pantomimic scenes of the lower classes that had finally polluted the stage itself.

The members of the O. P. faction, however, saw the pantomimic *Macbeth* they caused not as a sign of class affiliation and therefore another justification for the suppression of the poor as a group but as an exemplary exchange between the audience and the stage. This new exchange initiated a process of inversion and hybridization that, rather than silencing the faction's voice, formulated an inclusive, collective presence in the public sphere of the theater. By hissing and hooting at Kemble and by reducing his company's performances to "show and gesticulation," the O. P. audience developed a hybrid drama wholly dependent on the interaction between the actors on stage and the audience in the seats, a form of drama increasingly difficult to produce in the three-thousand-seat Covent Garden Theatre. In this hybrid version of tragedy, a false king is exposed by the public, rather than a true one deposed by usurpers. Before the O. P. disturbance, many theatrical observers wondered whether "it is possible that imagination might, in her frolicksome flights, persuade an Acting Manager that he was in reality the King or Cardinal he was to personate."[76] After the first night of demystified theatricality, the audience seemed on its way toward convincing such an acting manager "that *Macbeth* is only the tinsel Sovereign, and that the Public is the real Dictator of a Theatre."[77] This *Macbeth*, played by actors and audience, then, exploded the traditional parameters of genre as well as the emergent class terms of the various genres. In effect, *Macbeth* was not pantomime, but a melodrama, for the O. P. rioters had found it necessary to transpose the bawdy and bodily satire of the pantomime into the familiar and familial sentiment of the melodrama.[78]

In this melodramatic formulation, the public was asserting its right to political participation as well as reasserting the traditional hierarchy of deference: "[The players] would learn that they are the servants of the public, and that the nature of their employment will not warrant them to place themselves on a footing with the Nobles of the realm."[79] At the end of the evening's performance, the actors on the stage were alone consigned to mummery—the pseudolanguage of the body, the lower echelon of theatrical entertainment, and perhaps most important, the mark of exclusion from participation in the public sphere. Kemble's decision to perform actual pantomimes on stage, especially around the Christmas holidays, only seemed an admission of his company's degradation.

Instead of converting everything to pantomime, the O. P. faction was actually looking for a more expressive theatrical vehicle. At first glimpse, the O.P. faction's critique, like Cobbett and Paull's, seems typical of the "countertheater" that the "mob" often staged in the eighteenth century as a reply to the "theater" of their rulers. E. P. Thompson argues that in these performances, the contending sides "moderated each other's political behavior."[80] Although the O.P. Wars were certainly a form of countertheater, with real political impact, the crucial difference between these protests and typical acts of countertheater, such as effigy burning and window breaking, was that the O.P. faction soon refused to communicate through such physically violent gestures, staunchly avoiding the taint of the harlequinade.

By drowning out *Macbeth* with their own voices, the O.P. supporters avoided the silent gestures and terroristic physical aggression characteristic of the harlequinade. They thus directly challenged the claims of the proprietors, who, as one observer defined their strategy: "Thought to make the gentry quiet" by proving "that *words* were *acts* of riot."[81] One J. Loraine, sympathetic to the O.P. faction, responded to this strategy in a letter to the *Times*: "I should be glad to be shewn . . . where clapping, hissing, hooting, or catcalling, at a theatrical representation, is declared to be an offence, or symptom of riot at all."[82] During the trial of Henry Clifford, the identical debate was repeated, a debate regarding whether riot was to be construed as physical, vocal, or a combination of the two. These court proceedings highlight once more the conditions under which the O.P. faction struggled to find an appropriate vehicle of public expression. At the trial, the proprietors claimed that Clifford's hat, decked with the letters "O.P.," and his alleged comments while seated in the pit were unlawful; to borrow the phrase, "they sought to prove that *words* were *acts* of riot." Judge Mansfield, perhaps less than impartial, encouraged the jury to interpret all hissing and hooting as "a deliberate and preconcerted scheme" and a "conspiracy."[83]

There is some evidence from contemporary sources, however, that the O.P. faction ultimately sought to limit its expressions of protest to terms of "legitimate criticism" by shouting words such as "shocking bad" or "horrid."[84] After John Kemble's basement windows were broken one night, the faction's sympathizers explicitly and publicly, through the *Morning Chronicle*, condemned the act, thereby verbalizing the stark ethical standards that would thereafter consistently characterize their rhetoric. Forged in the midst of legal proceedings, shaped by the laws of censorship and patent, this public presence, a constitutive feature of what I call the melodramatic mode, necessarily spoke its first words in a language of judgment and taste, claimed from a traditional right of theatrical criticism and presumed to be within the law. This response was no doubt meant to contrast with the empty theatricality of Kemble's company—their exotic spectacles, trick-filled extravaganzas, and acrobatic pantomimes of the stage, including the one when police with fire hoses emerged from the trapdoors. All of these performances too clearly seemed parables of an oriental despotism in decline, in which the bashaw cuts the woman as well as the argument short. As J. J. Stockdale complained: "Who called upon them to produce their Pizarros, their Blue-Beards, their Sleeping Beauties, and Cinderellas? Not the British public."[85]

Using the terminology of theatrical criticism and the strategies of the melodramatic mode, the O.P. faction expressed its political views. Just as Cobbett had preserved the reputation of the people from the collusion of the three-tiered conspiracy by distinguishing between the people's voice and the bodily (and sexual) exchange of the others, so the O.P. faction fashioned a verbal and physical presence of propriety, deference, and charity to intercede between the indecent bodily exchanges of the high and low, which were seen as sexual, economic, and deceptive.

Primarily because the exercise of state power outside of the theater was beginning to be seen as theatrical, the representation of a monarch's overthrow (King John Kemble) in the theater, or alternatively, the silencing of tragedy with pantomime and its simultaneous recreation of the audience's voice, resonated ominously beyond the walls of Covent Garden. As one concerned citizen wondered: "Is it advisable to suffer the Theatre to become a school for opposition, to teach practically the effect of the *voice* of the people. . . . May not the same voice which now makes the Theatre resound . . . aspire to shake the dome of more exalted structures?"[86] The "practical effect" of the people's voice in the pit, however, aimed to expose false kings, not to overthrow true kings or their "exalted structures." It wished to bring out onto the stage, before the audience, that which had been recently rendered private and mysterious and to make it public and explicable again. If the theater proprietors and their illicit supporters wished to interpret the public's opinion as violent, senseless gesture, then this new public would insist, in contrast, that all gesture must be sensible, indeed nearly as expressive as the voice itself. In effect, pantomimic antics become melodramatic convictions about the visible operations of the public sphere.

Despite the negative connotations attached to their bodily actions, most members of the O.P. faction did not wish to be limited to vocal expression any more than they wished to be limited to pantomime.[87] Avoiding the secret bodily exchanges of the aristocrats and proprietors, the O.P. faction insisted on the visibility of the body and its public significations. Thus, this public "voice" does not reject the body; rather it reconceives the violated, commodified, and secretive body as visible voice. In this way, people both on and off the stage are wholly recognizable and fully present in the social sphere; they are not like the private boxes that contain both a hidden space given over to economic exchange and a public space that masks empty shows of sociability.

Casting themselves as the respectable members of the middle and laboring ranks, the O.P. protesters hoped to reverse the gaze of state power so that the "surveillance" and classification of the audience by those on stage would become instead the consolidation of the audience and the demystification of the stage, along with its backstage strategies. One placard in the theater phrased it succinctly: "In an English Theatre all should see and be seen."[88] This shift in the direction of the gaze also signaled a reverse in its source of authority—from physical coercion into "classes" to moral suasion by the group.

Its emphasis on moral examination seems to align the O.P. faction with the broader ethical movements of Regency England, most notably represented by the efforts of William Wilberforce and Hannah More. Members of Wilberforce's Society for the Suppression of Vice, founded in 1804, like the commentators of the O.P. Wars, expended much energy gazing at the immorality of the aristocracy, a practice that is exemplified in More's book, *An Estimate of the Religion of the Fashionable World* (1791).[89] These common ethical concerns, however, should point only to the prevalence of moralism in Regency England and not suggest any coalition between two politically distinct groups. Wilberforce was a social reactionary whose associates regularly and energetically joined him in his condemnation of all theatrical entertainments, and Hannah More, once a respected playwright, found it necessary to abandon her career on conversion.[90] By contrast, the O.P. faction was not at all averse to a version of the theatrical exchange. It was through such mutual exchanges that morality existed in the public sphere. Rather than being engrossed in the moral surveillance championed by Christian evangelicals, which was a form of spectatorship only, the members of the O.P. faction were crucial enactors of the melodramatic mode. As eager as they were to see the activities on stage and to see the aristocrats in their public seats, they were equally eager to be seen.

III

The melodramatic mode provided an alternative representational model to the one newly presented by the Covent Garden Theatre's proprietors and actors. According to supporters of the old prices, the theater had once seemed a public place, an open community, but had become a divisive setting where spectacles camouflaged a private space of economic relations that avoided eye contact with the audience. A *Morning Chronicle* columnist recognized the power of this privacy and the specific power of representation it afforded:

This would, indeed, be a very convenient doctrine for those Authors who only require pen, ink, and paper, to make comedies (so called) . . . as they would then not have the fear of the public before their eyes, and might very successfully and profitably carry on their trade, in defiance of taste, propriety, and common sense.[91]

This interpretation, in keeping with the O.P. faction, follows a strict logic. Proprietors and their hired playwrights write plays conceived in private, devised to appeal to particular classes of playgoers. These plays are thus as tainted with economic motive as the liaisons in the private boxes. Both "trades" are exclusive transactions possessing despotic powers of representation because they evade the scrutiny of the community and its voice of "taste, propriety, and common sense."

In response, the O.P. faction clamored for open boxes, for open financial books, for open ticket sales (first come first served), and for a public realm defined both by its accessibility to all ranks and by its dedication to more traditional forms of social exchange premised on the visibility of the public sphere.[92] The O.P. faction acted out a resistance to what would become class alliances by renegotiating the terms of the economic, sexual, and theatrical exchanges between those in the highest- and lowest-priced seats. As a writer to the *Times* perceived the protest, a central issue was the monitoring of these exchanges: "In a theatre every one should be able to see what *is passing* in every part."[93] Ultimately, the O.P. faction won the battle if not the war: dining with his opponents at the Crown and Anchor on December 14, 1809, Kemble instantly agreed to five of their six resolutions, which included: pit admission returned to three shillings, six pence (box prices remained at the new level); private boxes reduced in number; and all prosecutions and legal proceedings abandoned. In this way, the O.P. faction interceded in the economic and sexual "trade," but perhaps most tellingly, it defined the language of "taste and propriety" in the theater by demanding of the Covent Garden managers a public apology, which fittingly took place on stage. In short, the O.P. faction forced Kemble to reveal his secrets.

The negotiations between the two sides aimed to resolve the deep and undoubtedly frightening social contradictions the O.P. faction perceived in the elite's exchanges with the criminal elements. The "exotic" association of aristocrats and prostitutes, as well as the contractual agreement between aristocrats and proprietors, was generative of the classes of seats within the theater and thus suggested a division within the community, both a patriarchal estrangement among the ranks and a dispersal within England itself. As for patriarchal estrangement, the liaisons in the boxes posed the threat of illegitimacy, a corruption of the aristocratic lineage that structured English society, a corruption that would necessarily affect all ranks. Not only did the immediate sexual-economic exchanges exclude the lower orders, but the result of the liaisons, whether an actual class of illegitimate aristocrats or simply the institutionalization of these relationships, also threatened to deprive other ranks of access to aristocratic protection and material wealth.

As for national stratification, the corruption of noble lineages unsettled the hierarchical communities that consolidated the nation by alienating the humbler English subjects from those regional landowners they formerly considered their protective superiors and whose participation in a newly atomized culture could only signal a retreat from a more social, more visible, and more recognizable public sphere. Undoubtedly, the O.P. activists were prone to idealizing this passing social order, especially since London culture had long ago abandoned many of these rural rituals, but perhaps some of the surging numbers of displaced rural workers living in London formed part of the O.P. faction. Moreover, one must hasten to add, deferential culture was far from a golden age; it, too, served best the needs of the ruling orders, and thus many patricians who were sympathetic to the O.P. faction's aims had more to preserve—both emotionally and materially—than did the plebeians with whom they protested.

The apparent dissolution of the deferential ordering of society also signaled to many the demolition of traits that were fast becoming considered distinctively English. This anxiety partially accounts for the additional criticism directed at the Covent Garden proprietors when they hired the Jewish-Italian soprano Madame Catalani for a particularly large fee. From the perspective of the O.P. faction, her hiring attested to the proprietors' disregard for a pure English bloodline, as if they were conspiring with their patrician friends to taint it with a foreign invasion, just as France threatened to do throughout the Napoleonic War years. "I never hear of any new *opera-singer* or *dancer* having arrived in this country, but I consider them as *spies*."[94] Her appearance on British stage also expressed a disregard for the much-honored English theatrical heritage, which had lately become a crucial component in nascent expressions of nationalistic pride. In the *Political Review*, Redhead Yorke, a radical turned ultrareactionary, complained: "This insolent imposture they endeavored to cram down the throats of the public, when they know that their engagement with the unfeeling Jewess, Angelica Catalani, is of itself calculated to banish the genius of our native poets from the stage." By banishing "native poets," Yorke argues, the owners estrange the audience from the highest of theatrical forms, tragedy and comedy, which were the genres of and about the aristocracy, and replace them with "detestable trash, of which, under the names of opera and melo-drame, the public are forced to be spectators."[95]

IV

It is at this place in the O. P. Wars that stage melodrama explicitly, if complicatedly, enters the theatrical debate about social representation and public expression. Melodrama's emergence on the stage elicited predictably polarized accounts of its origins. Even though Kemble and Sheridan had personally introduced versions of this genre into the patent theaters, they attributed its appearance to their regrettable financial dependence on the mob. Other detractors of melodrama, such as Yorke, emphasized its Parisian beginnings and its implicit connection to revolutionary politics.

By contrast, some theatrical critics, including some who sided with the O. P. faction, noted melodrama's spectacular effects and its profits for the proprietors. From their seats, melodrama could easily look like another instrument of power, and they therefore characterized it as a genre of oppression and estrangement, polluted with the marks of patriarchal and national atomism and contaminated by the deviant economic and theatrical exchanges between the higher orders and the criminal population. Frequently labeled "monster melodrama" because it was a form of "illegitimate drama," it was the result of mixed breeding, the contested bastard to "legitimate drama."[96] According to a drawing, "The Monster Melo-Drama," in the *Satirist*, 1807 (see Figure 2), melodrama is neither male nor female, human nor animal, but a monstrous combination, the offspring of "exotic associations" between Shakespeare and Harlequin and between English and French dramatists.

The aristocratic and nationalistic bloodlines of genre, were, in melodrama, "promiscuously jumbled together," and this was sometimes associated with the sexual exchanges in the private boxes, whose mixed occupants demanded mixed fare on the stage and whose reduction of human sentiment to economic transaction reflected melodrama's purely mercenary antecedents— the "melo-dramatic gentry writers" who will write anything "as long as they are paid for it." These "phalanx of melo-dramatists" join with the proprietors, "justices of the peace, Bow-Street officers, and understrippers" and, like Sheridan in 1806 and the bashaw in *Blue Beard*, seek to become "arbitrary tyrants" who "overawe their best benefactors."[97] Both the hybrid content and the relative youth of melodrama rendered the form susceptible to these varied readings.

The O. P. faction and its supporters rarely isolated melodrama from their

Figure 2. "The Monster Melo-drama," from the *Satirist*, 1807. A hybrid creature nourishes contemporary dramatists while treading on "Regular Dramas." Collection of the Harvard College Library.

jeremiad against contemporary theater and usually simply denounced this bastard form as yet another private and coercive spectacle of terror. Situated as they were in time and place, many members of the O.P. faction did not recognize that the distinctive presence they formulated over the course of the O.P. Wars constituted a melodramatic mode that they were enacting simultaneously on and off the stage.[98] When the O.P. faction insisted that the theater's proprietors return to traditional forms of deferential exchange and the social values represented through such exchanges, they exerted in a more vociferous and perhaps colorful manner what London audiences had been implicitly demanding for several years. They thus exerted material influence not only on the managerial procedures of the theater but on its productions as well. After all, they had already transformed *Macbeth* into pantomime. As proprietors became increasingly dependent on their mixed audience's approbation (even on the night when Nare and Read recited the Riot Act), they were obliged to finance the development of a genre that interacted with —and thus to some extent reproduced—the public, visible, and moral values of the audience. In this way, the proprietors of Covent Garden Theatre sought a profit through plays that staged in their interactions with the audience a coherent opposition to the market culture in which the owners and investors participated. It is in this paradoxical context, during a period when deferential and market cultures were fluidly intermingled, that the melodramatic mode and its stage version, melodrama, took shape. Resistant to market exchange, it nonetheless took shape at the site of that exchange. Indeed, it relied on its audience's new power as purchasers to wrest representational authority from the proprietors.

Not unlike the state's "engines and instruments of torture," early melodramas did aim to inspire momentary awe in their audiences through mechanical visual effects. Yet this comparison, by suggesting that melodrama was the deviously planned offspring of one specific interest, uses an overly simplistic notion of melodrama's mode of production. Although most theatrical historians consider the first English melodrama to be *A Tale of Mystery*, produced in November 1802 at Covent Garden, this play actually succeeded numerous productions that contained many of the ingredients usually attributed to the form: stirring incident, virginal heroines, evil villains, gallant heroes. Such productions—which combined French melodrama, English sentimental drama, and an infusion of the gothic—emphasize the motley nature of the genre, which is not sui generis but multi generis, a hybrid.[99] If the "ancient rule was that," as one contemporary phrased it, "tragedy displayed the overwhelming misfortunes of the great," while comedy displayed "their frailties and follies, as well as those of the lower orders of society," then melodrama combined the two, dramatizing the misfortunes of the high and low orders even as it uncovered both ranks' "frailties and follies."[100]

By including all social ranks and studying both their misfortune and frailty, melodrama not only suggested that all levels of people were subject to fate, but that all people were susceptible to the same sort of moral failure and were judged by a standardized set of ethical criteria. From this narrow, and ultimately misleading, vantage point, English melodrama seems a close sibling to the French melodrama of revolutionary Paris and provides the new, humbler portion of its audience a "representative" form of drama, "'a trades-man's tragedy.'"[101] Breaking the "ancient rule" that distinguished between tragedy and comedy, melodrama can be conceived as a lawbreaker, a revolutionary leveler of all hierarchies, whether based on class, theatrical genre, or taste.[102]

As will be seen, the melodramas of Covent Garden never attained this revolutionary spirit. English melodrama did first emerge as a literal law-breaker, however. Covent Garden and Drury Lane Theatres were the only places of entertainment in London that were licensed to perform the "spoken drama," according to the patents given to them by Charles II in 1660 and further regulated by the Licensing Act of 1737. The latter act amounted to a severe restriction of speech and was, it is often said, a response to the volatile political comment in theatrical productions mounted by Henry Fielding. Other theaters established in the city, whose mere right to exist the patent theaters continually challenged, were legally limited to pantomime and song. Over time, however, there evolved on these stages ingenious types of performance that mixed pantomime and song, musical doggerel and gesture, dialogue and music, until these productions hardly differed from the spoken drama. The proprietors avoided arrest by categorizing their works as burletta, "Comic, Pathetic, Historic, Anachronasmatic, Ethic, Epic Melange" or melo-drame.[103]

What we now term melodrama and some of the pieces that were performed at these early-nineteenth-century unpatented theaters may not share any attributes, since dramatic labels were intentionally deceptive rather than descriptively precise. *Burletta, comic opera, spectacle, pantomime,* and *melodrama* were inexact terms that embraced diverse and heterogeneous dramatic forms. Melodrama, despite its imprecision, was arguably the most hybrid of these heterogeneous forms and the one most imitative of high tragedy and comedy. It was originally associated with the illegal popular drama emerging from the unlicensed cheap theaters that catered to the less elite peoples of London. The patent theater's traditional, aristocratic patrons believed these nonelites to be lacking in taste and considered some of them, like

Cobbett's Radical associates, to be Jacobins.[104] Unfortunately, most of the plays associated with the cheap theaters are lost to the historical record.

The melodramas suitable for the patent theaters, reviewed by theatrical critics who would rarely deign to be seen in any other theaters, are the source material for the earliest definitions of the genre that we have inherited. These melodramas were, to a very large extent, nothing more or less than audience solicitations. Unlike Shakespeare's plays, which were, despite variations in script, production, and interpretation, textually somewhat stable, melodramas were rarely formally printed. They were, moreover, often pirated and were frequently broad translations from the French and German. Usually hired annually by proprietors, most melodramatists were not well paid or well respected, nor were they usually members of the upper ranks "free" to write from inspiration. They wrote and plagiarized for a commercial interest whose profits were determined by a socially diverse audience that often exercised its right not to attend. The playwright's "artistic intention" and translation skills combined with the proprietors' profit motive and the varied tastes of a motley audience, whose preferences, in turn, were shaped by other economic and social considerations. Even Sheridan, who possessed influence and independence, would not have been able to control the significations and the ultimate impact of *Pizarro*, one apparently melodramatic play he authored.

Most crucially, perhaps, melodramas were continually revised during performance as the performers gauged the response of the audience. Audience response, be it laughter, hisses, or tears, is perhaps the single constant criterion in the definition of stage melodrama, far more constant than the usual thematic and formal criteria cited in modern-day genre studies.[105] Villains, heroes, and heroines; "telling incident"; and exciting plot twists were all employed in an effort to elicit audience response. The traditional right of the audience to express their opinion was thus fast becoming a structural feature in melodramas, for the need for the audience's enthusiastic presence (and its admission money) had been interpolated into the dramatic dynamics of the performance.

Once melodrama made its way to a patent theater in 1802, it became subject to the conditions of these large establishments, and so, despite diverse early perceptions of the genre, its hybridized format, as played on a patent theater stage, can now be seen as a protest against classification in the context of the O. P. Wars. The insistence on a standardized moral code applied to all its characters is, therefore, not a sign of English melodrama's republican tendencies, but an instantiation of traditional deferential culture's ethics in which a "good character" is distinct from class affiliation.

Although early melodrama certainly inspired awe in its audience, as observers were quick to note, such awe was not intended to induce obedience, as it was in state spectacle, for melodramatic incidents were premised on the audience's awareness of, even participation in, the terror's theatricality. In this regard, the average audience at a melodrama shared the wary attitude toward spectacle of William Cobbett. The villain's threats to murder the hero and ravish the heroine, the armies sent to wrest power from a rightful heir—these are terrors that melodramas staged in order to expose, and in exposing them, to overcome.

As melodrama self-consciously mimicked and disarmed "instruments of terror," it elicited a collective moral response from a dispersed audience elsewhere threatened by atomization and the resultant disintegration of communal values. Undoubtedly, the often "exotic" villains of these dramas—oriental despots, Tartars, Magyars, and pirates—helped accentuate the growing perception of the categorical (and geographic) differences between the now alien and alienating aristocratic authorities and their subject audiences, just as the overthrow on the stage of these utterly foreign villains confirmed the reality of the audience's own collectivity. At a given moment, certain of these melodramas might interact with their audiences so as to elicit a sense of collectivity that could be accurately called "Britishness," as Linda Colley would argue, while other dramas performed on alternative nights might evoke an expression of "Englishness," as Colls and Dodd suggest in a collection of essays by that name. In these instances, such performances can be seen as early participants in the formation of a British imperial identity, but one can press this argument too hard, for still other melodramas of this type might provoke a less precise notion of solidarity, such as "fellow feeling" or "family feeling," that was much more provincial than metropolitan in its motivations.

Melodrama offered stark moral choices in discernible dramatic forms so that all levels within the audience—literate or illiterate, those in the cheap seats or in the stage boxes—could respond. At every turn—through stereotypically expressive costume, stock gesture, and standardized heroes and heroines—the genre publicized (made public) itself. Its emphasis on the visual, the emotive, and the audience aside were structural signs of the audience's importance, not merely as an observer of the action but, most significantly, as a participant in the plot. Michael Harvey guesses that as much as 60 to 80 percent of a script was spoken directly to the audience.[106] In contrast to an exclusive drama composed in secret, written with pen, ink, and paper in a private room, melodrama systematically and spectacularly unfolded its private subplots before the gaze of its inclusive audience. Even Shakespearean plays, when produced at Covent Garden, were staged in what might be called a melodramatic format. Actors would speak directly to the audience, emotional vignettes would be heightened, and action scenes prolonged. Such melodramatic productions contrasted with various contemporary attitudes toward Shakespearean drama that increasingly treated the plays as "closet dramas," poetry to be read in solitude rather than as dramas to be enacted in public.[107]

When critics condemned certain melodramas for unabashedly pandering to the audience, they attributed this exhibitionism to the contaminating influence of capitalism. In *Elbow Room*, "the great bursts of applause" that come from "the promiscuous audience of the Pit and Gallery" take on the association of sexual exhibitionism, once more conjuring up the riotous and licentious bodies of the harlequinade. These displays are distinguished from the upper ranks in the theater, "who almost consider it a breach of good-breeding to ruffle themselves by a violent agitation of the arms."[108] In a strict sense this reasoning seems valid, for it captures melodrama's desire to please, which in a market setting is inevitably a desire to sell. But one might argue that within the world of the market, even in the midst of a market exchange where shows are put on for the purchase of a ticket, these public exchanges between the drama on the stage and the audience seated in the theater reformulated market relations. Such choreographed exchanges were in fact markedly similar in detail to the exchanges staged by the O. P. faction. As a reformulation of patronage within a rapidly consolidating market economy, they avoided the proprietors' recourse to mysterious and invisible market forces whose secrets were hidden in private books. By inviting, indeed depending on, the audience's traditional right to express approbation and disapprobation, melodrama's transactions remained both visible and vocal, formative of as well as dependent on the heterogeneous public's gaze, voice, and judgment. Instead of oppressing the lower orders, early melodrama represented the responses it solicited and thus helped to unite audiences of diverse rank and to civilize the "hubbub" and "halloo" into a politicized and collective presence on the public scene, a scene devoid of private spaces. In the preface to his published melodrama, *Not at Home*, John Dallas defines this inclusive public:

In saying PUBLIC I am glad of this opportunity of stating what I mean by that word at a Theatre. I mean that cultivated Company who usually occupy the circle of dress boxes; I mean those judicious Critics who take their station in the Pit; I mean my worthy friend John Bull, who is found in either gallery.[109]

Melodrama's emphasis on the visual, what seems like its gaze of surveillance, may encourage comparisons between melodrama and contemporaneous panoptic procedures that were often part of the classificatory impulse melodrama resisted. Insofar as the two developments were responding to the same cultural phenomenon—the increased estrangement, both physical and experiential, among the ranks—they shared the desire to see what had become alien. Both melodrama and panoptic procedures are a testament to the heightened suspicion within English communities, where the motivations of others seemed increasingly hidden from view, notably absent from the performative public sphere. Like melodrama, the original design of the panopticon, as described by Jeremy Bentham, presumes that close inspection of the perceptible can lead to knowledge. In the panopticon, inspectors are situated so as to monitor the inmate, who is "confined in one of these cells" with "every motion of the limbs, every muscle of the face exposed to view."[110] Despite these similarities, however, the panopticon is more in keeping with the measures instituted by the Covent Garden proprietors. In segregating, classifying, and monitoring their clientele, the proprietors believed that they were accurately enforcing what seemed to them the essential nature of the audience and so, like inmates of the panopticon, the audience was to internalize these spatial regulations. As Bentham remarks, "Men become at length what they are forced to seem to be."[111] The enforcement of an initial stage of dissimulation—"what they . . . seem to be"—in the service of producing essential behaviors assumes a distinction between seeming and being that melodrama would not countenance.

From this perspective, then, such panoptic practices differ markedly from the melodramatic mode because they privilege private spaces, private subjectivity, and private exchanges. By contrast, melodrama derives its ethic of visibility from traditional codes of social display, such as those embodied in Renaissance sumptuary laws or, more contemporaneously, in the public scenes of relief under the embattled, but still operational, Poor Law.[112] Through these displays, English people witnessed the exchange of deference and beneficence that expressed the relationships among the various levels in a hierarchy, not the essentialized traits of class. Unlike the panopticon's invisible inspector, all actors in melodrama, on stage and off, must "see and be seen."

By the end of an early melodrama, the spectacular was no longer the instrument of terror and the protector of privacy; instead, it reified the visible, transferring relationships among private interests to a transparent public sphere devoid of class demarcations and the divisions between private and public identities. Thus, in *A Tale of Mystery*, the evil Romaldi, who silences his own brother by cutting off his tongue, eventually must realize, as should the aristocrats in their anterooms, that "No den, no cave, can hide me!"[113]

Melodrama's urge to publicize the private—or, in Christine Gledhill's words, its "aesthetics of the visible"[114]—is concomitant to the O.P. faction's call for a public sphere of visible morality, its insistence that "at the climax of an English melodrama, all should see and be seen." The social codes of honor, which had helped to identify the positions of individuals within a status hierarchy, were to be represented and reaffirmed in melodrama; consequently, reputations, the visible side of moral character, are essential to the genre. At the end of *Tekeli; or, The Siege of Montgatz*, the Hungarian hero turns to the audience to unmask himself as the deserving heir and to expose a pretender to his throne; at the end of *Adrian and Orrila*, Matilda reveals her son's parentage, and Rosenheim confesses his youthful indiscretion—just as Kemble was shown to be a false Macbeth. As Bonamo, a character in *A Tale of Mystery*, intones: "Good seldom accompanies mystery."[115]

If, as John Bender and D. A. Miller variously contend, the novel became that "cultural institution," to borrow Miller's words, that upheld privacy and the existence of an "autonomous 'secret' self," then early melodrama—as it was written, adapted and performed before English men and women—was the mode that, by exposing the secrets of the self and other private sites, insisted on the primacy of an older ethic.[116] This ethic operated through mutual dependency and socially determined and representable codes of honor. Attending a melodrama is a public, inclusive event, whereas reading a novel is a more private and personal experience. Since melodrama, unlike the novel, does not have an ethic that emanates from the individual psyche, its dramatis personae do not manifest distinctive or complex subjectivities. In a melodramatic scenario, characters are not split personalities, private selves with public appearances; they are entirely social beings, in most cases literally related to one another. Orphans find their parents, prodigal brothers meet their siblings, and estranged husbands claim their wives. They embody what appear to be universalized moral identities that are familiar and recognizable to everyone. Through the mutual recognition of these qualities, a potentially stratified audience is united rather than individuated into unique personalities.

Ultimately, then, melodrama situates law and morality in a public performative space inhabited by social and familial relationships rather than within the private spaces of individuals or in God. The public sphere itself, defined by social feeling and filial action, is both the site and origin of melodrama's powerful operation of providence so that sacred human communities, not an individuated God or fate or a despotic ruler, provide the instructive lesson. A typical passage in one of these melodramas teaches a lesson about community through the narrative of one of its reclaimed members: "And let us hope, that the example of this protected orphan may terrify the unjust man from the abuse of trust, and confirm the benevolent in the discharge of all the gentle duties of humanity."[117]

O.P. Wars: Melodramatizing the Public Sphere

As contemporary critics noted, early melodrama displays an obsessive concern with national and familial alienation, which is not unrelated to the genre's communal bias. *Tekeli*, for instance, begins with the noble Hungarian, Count Tekeli, deprived of his legitimate title by the emperor of Austria, while *Adrian and Orrila* opens with Matilda, Adrian's mother, estranged from her son's father, Rosenheim. These typical opening scenes of national and familial estrangement and political illegitimacy certainly bespeak ruptured bloodlines and, more important, a conspiracy of secrecy, a crucial private subplot that enables such dislocations to occur. Matilda, for example, declines to inform Adrian of his parentage, which stemmed from an illicit love between her, a common woman, and the nobleman Rosenheim, while Tekeli must hide in the woods to protect himself from the murder plot the emperor has privately devised to dispose of him. Private transactions between high and low breed secrecy, and this secrecy is always linked to illegitimacy and familial dispersal, as it was in the O.P. faction's speculations about the transactions in the private boxes of Covent Garden. Such secrets necessitate their own public revelation through the spectacle of melodrama, which unrelentingly strives to expose them in order to nullify the divisions they cause within the community.

In defining its version of a public sphere, an early melodrama mediates between the two collusive and much reviled genres frequently invoked in the O.P. Wars debate: spectacle, translated as coercion of the body, and pantomime, a synonym for oppression of the voice. State spectacle regulated the awed and submissive body of the mob by silencing the voice that was seen to be always already physically riotous, while plebeian pantomime acted out, as if to corroborate spectacle's edict, the speechless body's riotous gestures. Melodrama reworks these terms in the process of publicizing each plot's secrets. Consequently, it contains the traces of its mixed blood but also necessarily resolves those old lineages into a new lineage. Vestiges of pantomime inhere in the structure of these early melodramas in the form of characters who necessarily rely on gestures to communicate: a blind girl figures prominently in *The Dog of Montargis*, a deaf mute in Holcroft's *Deaf and Dumb*, the tongueless Francisco in *A Tale of Mystery*. In addition, extended segments of an early melodramatic performance, especially as it neared its climax, consisted of spectacular scenes of pursuit or rescue, as if refiguring the harlequinade. In *A Tale of Mystery*, Francisco pursues his evil sibling across a mountain range after the evil Romaldi has silently plotted his brother's murder.

In contrast to pantomime, however, the physical gestures of melodrama are granted the expressiveness and clear intention of voice and therefore are nearly as communicative and interpretable as vocal language.[118] Theodore, the mute count of Harancour, abandoned as a youth by his usurping uncle, is befriended and instructed by a teacher of sign language, the Abbé de L'Epée, so that "even in dumbness, [the count is] eloquently intelligible."[119] Through these broad gestures of sign language, Theodore will surely be understood and applauded by everyone in the theater, including the gallery gods, who were seated hundreds of yards away. The riotous bodies of the harlequinade are thus recast in this melodrama as something akin to the "public voice" that expresses approbation and disapprobation at the theater, the melodramatic mode of the O. P. faction, for they use both vocal and physical expression to assert their legal right to take part (or parts) in the community.

Melodrama attempts to turn all gesture into rational discourse but at the same time to retain within that discourse the passion and simplicity of gesture—hence the usually schematic, almost symbolic, dialogue: "Francisco is an angel, Selina is an angel, Stephano is an angel."[120] Because of these expressive criteria, early melodramas obsessively meditate on the relationship between body and voice. While the villains and their secret plans still dominate the early portions of a plot, the laws of state spectacle inhere: the voices of the dispossessed and marginal are silenced by awing their bodies, as if these voices were merely body parts and thus subject to physical torture. In *Tekeli*, the Austrian emperor's soldier is threatened with amputation of an ear if he mentions having seen Tekeli in the forest, just as Bluebeard's wife faces beheading if she argues with her husband. These are the terms of despotic spectacle and its political counterpart, feudalism, as Cobbett had understood in the 1806 Westminster elections. The politically powerless are figured as mute, aggressive bodies—the mob—while the authorities exert physical and verbal coercion. During the O. P. Wars, this type of terroristic threat when dramatized in a play was considered far more than a melodramatic technique. One O. P. placard explicitly expresses its contemporary political valence; the sign advertises a "Grand unfinished Tragic Ballet of Action, called JOHN OX; or The cruel Attempt to Despoil John Bull of his Noble Parts."[121]

These early forms of the melodrama also manifest a predilection for transformations and disguises. In this regard, early melodrama recalls the close of the first half of the pantomime when the individualized characters of each play transform into the stock figures of the harlequinade. Many an oppressed hero changes his role, almost always dressing down, in order to elude bodily torture, though this type of disguise is not allied with the hybridization and private deceit of the oppressor. Despite their apparent secrecy, these gestures are wholly public; often the decision to don a disguise is revealed to the audience during an aside. Indeed, even the deceptions perpetrated by the villain are not long concealed. In whatever manner the revelation is achieved, it is always communicated to the audience well before the other characters in the play discover the truth. There are never secrets between the actors and their audience.[122]

These powerfully plot-driven plays work toward the climactic moments when the formerly silenced, the alienated, and the marginalized—all these victims of secrecy—say, "He is before you—I am Tekeli."[123] At this point, melodrama asserts both its right to be spoken, legitimate drama and the right of the hero and the audience to be legitimized identities within an extended, patriarchal family. In thereby claiming its "privilege of place" in the generic hierarchy, not as bastard but as rightful heir to tragedy and comedy, melodrama also defies classification's corruption of the "bloodlines" of social hierarchy.[124]

Indeed, these final scenes of truth and justice expose privately conceived coercions as illegal appropriations of power and reunite family members who have been estranged. The orphans, foundlings, and bastards that abound in early melodrama, often dominating the plots as well as the titles of the plays, achieve a final recognition that affirms not only familial lineages, but the patriarchal lineages that bound the audience and, by extension, the English nation before market exchanges began to associate these relationships with class.[125] The count of Harancour returns to his home and title; Francisco reclaims his name from Romaldi's treachery; Tekeli returns to rule Hungary; and, in the most explicit terms, Adrian the bastard is legitimized as the son of Rosenheim.

In restaging rank and patronage, early melodrama aggressively domesticates, even as it absolutizes, the public sphere. Plays that seem to open as nationalistic allegory, promising myths about the overthrow of usurping tyrants by rightful heirs, resolve into tales of hearth and home. This should be seen, however, not as the domestic circle of mid-Victorian ideology, but as an idealized emblem of eighteenth-century status hierarchies purged of their oppressive theatricality and celebrated for their familial and thus familiar organization of society; they are nostalgic, not bourgeois, utopias. *Adrian and Orrila* does not conclude with an assertion of historical continuity and a triumphal celebration of Adrian's inclusion in the line of primogeniture, for such a closure would require the staging of a royal procession, like that of Sheridan on St. Giles's Street, which would involve exclusions and coercions. Nor does this melodrama celebrate the self-interested privacies of the nuclear family. Rather, the play ends with a woman's recognition of a domestic but also insistently social identity. Once abandoned but now recognized, Matilda speaks the final truth regarding the mutual dependence of consciousness and community. As a mother, she best represents the continuity of the familial lineage. As a lord's wife, her words resonate beyond the palace walls to the surrounding cottages. In her monologue, she explicitly resists the classification of society and the atomization of people into private and public selves. No doubt turning to the audience in a stock melodramatic pose, Matilda declares:

Wondering, trembling; touch'd with pious awe—I muse; am conscious; and adore. But now I stood upon creation's verge, a lonely hermit atom—living, yet unallay'd to kindred life—lo! even as moment; husband; offspring; friends; with all the heaven-born social charities, endear existence and invite me to a HOME.[126]

In this soliloquy, Matilda looks back to the extended "familial" groups characteristic of patriarchal hierarchies, which defined rank by kinship and transactions among these ranks as "social charities." Kings can remain kings and lords, lords, but they must live and govern their people like benevolent fathers, not despots.[127] These melodramas do not counsel revolution; rather, they mythologize the centrality of all moral beings within a hierarchical society.

Many of these melodramas include courtroom scenes—or at the least, as in *Deaf and Dumb*, scenes that mimic the courtroom setting—with characters fulfilling the roles of witnesses, examiners, and judges. Such scenes conclude the narrative's dramatic evolution from the despotic rule of bodily terror and secrecy to the hierarchical rule of visual and spoken justice. At the close of *Deaf and Dumb*, Franval cross-examines Harancour's villainous uncle, Darlemont, in his home, hoping that the uncle will abdicate his title in favor of his nephew so that public shame will not ruin his deserving son's prospects. Darlemont cannot bring himself to speak. By writing his confession instead of speaking it, Darlemont enacts yet another private transaction, as if to emphasize that certain aristocrats, with their "pen, ink and paper" were evasive private subjects, hidden from view. The letter, however, is read eventually aloud to the audience in the theater, which stands in as the judge as well as the jury. In this way, the "secret self" of Miller's formulation becomes a public reputation—visible, audible, and susceptible to communal judgment.

These "courtroom" scenes are also the dramatic analogues of the Henry Clifford trial, the culmination of the O. P. Wars. The voice of justice that the lawyer Franval uses to renegotiate the terms of patronage and rank in the final "exchange" with Darlemont in *Deaf and Dumb* is the same voice whose legal status was deeply contested at the quarter sessions on December 5, 1809. This is the "voice" of the melodramatic mode. During this trial, the melodramatic mode was thus performed on a stage usually reserved for state spectacle. The chairman of the sessions during the Clifford trial apparently heard the political content of this melodramatic mode when he warned the jury: "The audience of a public theatre cannot be considered as a court of justice recognized by the law of the country: it has no legal means of enforcing its decrees, or compelling obedience to its orders."[128] Despite the judge's attempt to privatize the jury box like the boxes in the theater, to counsel its members to think in terms of the proprietors' self-interests, the jury itself judged in favor of Clifford and the audience, opening the way for the resolution of the dispute at the Crown and Anchor—a local, and as the historical record shows, momentary victory for the melodramatic mode.[129] By the late 1830's, once "free trade" had effectively ended the monopoly of patent theaters, the classificatory impulse manifest in the Covent Garden architecture had resulted in class-denominated theaters, a more aggressive version of social segregation.

V

A tableau of a legitimate family grouping, with all members in their appropriate hierarchical positions, often closes an early melodrama and defines the only suitable type of privacy in the entire play. This home can eventually move out of the public gaze and beyond the narrative of the melodrama in some atemporal sphere precisely because it has been formed by the public; its privacy is always already publicized, since its premises are universalized and institutionalized in the social realm. There are no secrets. At last, the curtain can fall, separating but not alienating the audience from the players. In this moment and for only a moment, all the spectators—though dispersed throughout the pit, boxes, and galleries according to their economic worth— could nonetheless imagine their "familial" cohesiveness. When, in *A Tale of Mystery*, the conniving Romaldi dares to scorn as "mere ceremonies!" the patriarchal absolutes of landed culture, the traditional absolutes toward whose realization all melodramas strive, he is chastised by Bonamo, who invokes the rules of law, genre, and primogeniture: "Ceremonies! Bethink yourself; lest marriage become a farce, libertinism a thing to laugh at, and adultery itself a finable offense!"[130] In early melodrama one may laugh or cringe at the spectacular terrors of the usurping despot, but never at the ethical exchanges of a deferential culture; they are not farce.

Nor were the O.P. Wars, despite what critics often alleged. Rather, in confronting an early expression of the modern principle of classification, the O.P. faction itself also staged a melodrama, as one placard announced: "The Uproar!, or John Bull and the manager. A melo drame performed six nights, with unbounded applause, at the Theatre Royal, Covent-Garden."[131]

THREE

Storming the "Bastile"

Oliver Twist and Melodramatic Resistance to the New Poor Law of 1834

Within days after *Bentley's Miscellany* published in its pages the first number of *Oliver Twist*, the major London daily, the *Times*, reprinted on January 31, 1837, a portion of this Charles Dickens story. Under the headline "A Board of Guardians of the Poor," the newspaper excerpted the scene in which Oliver first meets the trustees who preside over the union and its affiliated workhouse. The *Times* borrowed the Boz text most obviously because it expressed antagonism toward the operations of the Poor Law Amendment Act of 1834 and therefore shared the widespread discontent that had fostered, since the law's inception, a national repeal movement. The *Times* and its owner, John Walters, strongly supported the protest and delegated many inches of copy to the cause.[1]

Dickens's story shared more than negative sentiment with many of the *Times*'s reported accounts of New Poor Law cruelty. Not only did such articles often prove to be just as fictional as Dickens's creation, but they sounded the same and looked the same.[2] For instance, the mixture of reportage and romance evident in the novel exemplifies the permeable boundaries between fact and fiction, news and novels that typified much of the anti–Poor Law literature and indeed much published journalism at this time. Walters and the other spokesmen of the movement differed significantly in their backgrounds, in their basic religious and political convictions, and even in their proffered solutions to this new relief legislation, but most of them employed a similar style of protest that, among other features, favored affect over fact. In this regard, they were speaking, writing, and sometimes even acting within the same rhetorical field as Charles Dickens: the melodramatic mode.

Anti–Poor Law speeches, editorials, reports, pamphlets, and sermons were almost all marked by the techniques that literary critics have consistently noticed in *Oliver Twist* and that have been described as "melodramatic" because of these techniques' similarity to those employed in stage melodrama.[3] That stage melodrama itself has been a widely disregarded field of study or, when considered, notably difficult to define renders this common comparison to the stage a rather empty analytical gesture. To say that *Oliver Twist* or a *Times's* editorial is melodramatic is to say in fact very little. If melodrama as a category or the melodramatic as a descriptive term are to wield any explanatory power in studies of nineteenth-century English literature or history, a more precise definition is required. In detecting "a melodramatic mode" in the anti–Poor Law literature, which includes *Oliver Twist*, I argue that melodrama has a social function and significance outside the theater that can perhaps lead to a more theoretically substantive and historically specific analysis of these theatrical terms.

The characteristic mode of anti–Poor Law literature does share with stage melodrama many structural features and, to that extent, justifies the comparison and the common term *melodramatic*. These features include graphic depictions of gruesome incidents, scenes of physical danger and inflicted torture, plots premised on criminal behavior, affected verbalizations of overwrought emotion, an aura of atmospheric menace, and narratives of familial and social crisis. The *Northern Star*, a working-class newspaper and mouthpiece for much anti–Poor Law protest, published a typical example of this prose in November of 1838. Like other examples of Poor Law protest, including *Oliver Twist*, the address adopts these melodramatic techniques particularly when describing union workhouses:

We have now reached a most portentous crisis, and every man ought well to weigh the question, how he would like to become the inmate of a union bastile; there to have his hair cut short, his manhood brutalized, his wretched body subject to a ruffian's stripes, branded as a felon, tethered like a beast, worked like a beast, and fed worse than a beast; no friendly eye to look upon him, no woman's tenderness to soothe his desolation, no little ones to gladden his dull soul, the partner of his bosom pushed back by menial hands, the mother's breast with all its wholesome nourishment dried up through very grief, and when death ensues, you may be handed over to the surgeon for dissection.[4]

In truth, workhouse inhabitants under the New Poor Law were not as a rule "fed worse than a beast," though they were fed sparingly and sometimes with adulterated foodstuffs; nor, presumably, were wives regularly "pushed back by menial hands" from their husbands, though husband and wife did live in separate parts of the workhouse. Also, dead paupers were not immediately handed over to a "surgeon for dissection," though the Anatomy Act of 1832 did allow workhouses to sell unclaimed bodies to medical schools. The *Northern Star* speech heightens the physical and psychological details for thrilling effect and plays loosely with facts, thereby jarring modern standards of serious journalism. Even so, it provides insight into the ideology of the 1834 Poor Law Amendment Act; its madness has method. The newspaper passage's reference to a union "bastile," a coined and consistently misspelled term within the movement that denotes a workhouse while evoking the famous French prison, cannily zeros in on a real confusion Poor Law reformers experienced when trying to differentiate paupers from criminals. Furthermore, the tableaux of bodily torture in this article that aim, as we shall see, to replace terms of psychological "reform" emerge from a more gestural, theatrical tradition of representation, one that seeks here to wrest rhetorical control from the managerial bureaucratese most often used by the new law's supporters. The effect achieved by such prose, therefore, was not simply a matter of exaggeration and hyperbole, but was trenchant, substantial, and complex.

This chapter concentrates on the ideological work of the New Poor Law of 1834 and the varied melodramatic responses to it, including that offered by Dickens in *Oliver Twist*. The New Poor Law revised the legal definition of a poor person and thereby significantly contributed to the massive reorganization of English society occurring in the 1830's. The melodramatic mode used by the anti–Poor Law movement, rather than signaling the movement's philosophical depletion and political ineptitude, furnished it with a powerful critique of this new law's transfiguring domestic policy and articulated a viable, if ultimately unsuccessful, alternative to the new society envisioned by Poor Law reformers.[5]

As evident in the *Northern Star* passage, the protest movement focused particular attention on the "bastiles," those reorganized workhouses of the new law that Edwin Chadwick supposedly modeled on the panopticon prison conceived by Jeremy Bentham, his mentor.[6] Although those workhouses that were built did not, in fact, look like Bentham's circular structure of surveillance, they sought identical results: the regulation, both physical and mental, of an unregulated population, in this case, paupers. Separate rooms for men, women, and children, along with rigid schedules and close supervision, all point to the new workhouses' affiliation with the philosopher's model prison. Both realized, in architectural shape, the principle of classification that, as a heuristic device, so dominated nineteenth-century libertarian reform. In order to address a wide range of social problems, this principle of classification took many forms. Its most powerful manifestation, the figure of economic class, is the primary regulative norm insistently pursued and imposed by the New Poor Law. Seen in these terms, economic classes, such as the classes of people in the workhouse, were prescriptive as well as descriptive devices. It was this general principle of classification and its reputed disciplinary effects, apparent in the workhouse but implicit throughout the new law's edicts, that attracted the anti–Poor Law movement's animosity and that determined the movement's melodramatic response.

Without the benefit of Foucault's famous argument regarding the internalization of the carceral framework and its engendering of modern subjectivity during the early nineteenth century, those who criticized the new law, including Charles Dickens, were nonetheless dissenting against these ominous and alien results of state regulation and privatization. Foucault's archaeological perspective, though valuable, leads to the impression that the power structures of "social control" preempted any significant attempt at resistance. Yet resistance did exist, and it took the form of melodrama because only melodrama could publicly stage this storming of the "bastile."

I

Unlike earlier legislation, including the Reform Bill of 1832, the New Poor Law of 1834 reached into the homes of even the poorest of the poor all across England and Wales.[7] It was a law empowered to alter daily habits. Earlier reform had been conceived neither on such an intimate scale nor on such a national scale. The New Poor Law redefined "the poor," who constituted the majority of English subjects, but no less significantly, its centralization and uniformity of procedure helped create a national identity where there had formerly existed myriad regional and urban identities. Its framers sought to reform relief procedures, but in so doing they assisted in the transformation of an older culture.

The Poor Laws in existence prior to 1834 formed a motley and piecemeal collection of local regulations and procedures that had revised, altered, even ignored, at times, the 1601 Act of Elizabeth that had stipulated that each parish was to maintain its own poor.[8] This emphasis on local jurisdiction expressed the Elizabethan state's just appreciation of the operational demands of the paternalistic status hierarchies that governed the English countryside and that enabled commentators to conceptualize the parish unit as a patriarchal family. Such comparisons at this time between the parish unit and the patriarchal family were not merely literary ornamentation. The parish unit was in many respects an extension of the family, the means by which a patriarchal structure was also a national and institutional one. Parallel if not always identical codes of rights and obligations served as ties between landlord and tenant, father and son. The aristocracy and gentry of each parish, those wellborn and propertied, determined, as a father would, how and to whom the levied poor rates would be dispensed, while the poor, the father's obedient children, generally respected his rules. Much changed in the intervening centuries, and sundry modifications to poor relief had been introduced, and yet in the early nineteenth century England was still a rural society mostly guided by these channels of deferential authority. This perception is demonstrated by David Davies who, in his *The Case of the Labourers in Husbandry stated and considered,* saw a supportive family when he looked at rural England in 1795: "It is manifest that our laws consider all the inhabitants of a parish as forming one large family, the higher and richer part of which is bound to provide employment and relief for the lower and labouring part."[9]

Despite Davies's confidence in this parochial family, signs of stress were becoming increasingly apparent in the latter half of the eighteenth century.[10] Although this mode of governance seemed to eighteenth-century observers providential, natural, and efficient, even within their complacent observations lurked the contradictions that would become most troubling in the next century. In 1759, for example, Adam Smith wrote confidently in his *The Theory of Moral Sentiments* about this social organization: "Nature has wisely judged that the distinction of ranks, the peace and order of society, would rest more securely upon the plain and palpable difference of birth and fortune, than upon the invisible and often uncertain difference of wisdom and virtue."[11] In this passage, Smith assumes that "birth and fortune" are the sole criteria that distinguish among ranks and that respect for them solidifies the ties among these "family" members. If Smith's analysis of the grounds for deferential hierarchy were accurate, an English nobleman would have been able to demand and receive obeisance even from unfamiliar agricultural laborers living in another region of the country, because differences of birth and fortune would be conspicuous, instantly recognized through manner and attire. This no doubt was a comforting belief for those who lived in the latter half of the eighteenth century. Significant population growth, increased mobility, economic crises, urbanization, and widespread enclosures of common land had put physical and emotional distance between the various ranks. In many parts of England, farm laborers ceased to live in the farmhouse near where they labored, and thus no longer formed a literal component of the parochial extended family. Especially in the north and midlands, laborers even ceased to work all year round for the same farmer because job shortages and seasonal variations encouraged laborers to move among employers. Meanwhile, landlord absenteeism had become proverbial. Given this dispersal, the importance of "plain and palpable" difference became crucial, but despite Smith's hopeful formulation, "birth and fortune" were no longer (if they had ever been) sufficiently palpable. There were other more palpable, if more impermanent, differences that stabilized society.

The stability of rank in the eighteenth century in fact relied on the operation of what David Moore has called "deference communities" that developed most strongly among people with both personal knowledge of one another and shared interests.[12] Parochial communities easily met such criteria. For instance, the lower ranks were usually quite able to see their local landowning family acting beneficently toward them. Just as essential, then, as "birth and fortune" was an aristocrat's publicly established reputation for honor and benevolence, otherwise denoted as a good character, and this could be best attained through visible acts witnessed by the local community.[13] Such acts of authority and privilege, sanctioned by but not identical to birth and fortune, were the truly "plain and palpable" differences that motivated and legitimized deferential behaviors and thus preserved status hierarchies.

The Old Poor Laws, which had for centuries provided an institutional framework through which public acts of beneficence could be staged, contributed much to the cohesion among ranks. Familiar people operated the machinery of the Poor Law. The overseers of the poor, those who actually dispensed the relief, were unpaid members of the parish, usually men of the middle ranks, while the highest appellant authorities were the local magistrates who were also the local landowners. To request relief, a poor person appeared before the overseer, whose presumed knowledge of this parochial neighbor dictated the amount and, perhaps, the kind of assistance (whether money or bread). If the relief recipient disagreed with the overseer's decision, he or she appeared in person before the magistrate, whose own knowledge of the complainant guided his final judgment on the case.[14] The frequency of these face-to-face meetings among the high, middle, and low ranks enabled each group to witness the public revelation of character that was so necessary to the maintenance of patriarchal ties. At least in theory, the poor had to reveal to their superiors their impoverished condition, while the rich publicly, and quite palpably, revealed their beneficent nature.

By the end of the Napoleonic Wars, inflation brought about economic crisis and with it a widespread conviction, which was partly true, that the poor rates were rising to unprecedented levels.[15] Thomas Malthus's dire predictions about population growth and food shortage seemed to be coming true and offered one explanation, among the many that were circulating, for the increasing poor rates. At the same time, social unrest brought urgency to the debate; there were labor uprisings in the country, rick burnings, and food protests. By the late 1820's, many among the upper ranks had become convinced that all these social evils could be traced to the wasteful administration of the Poor Laws. Precisely how this perception of the Poor Laws emerged from an earlier, eighteenth-century view that attributed to them England's incomparable domestic serenity is difficult to trace with precision. Undoubtedly, economic downturns, bad harvests, and genuine population increase were interrelated and substantively contributed to both the increased poor rates and the growing suspicion of the laws.[16] Most significantly, this increased antagonism toward the Poor Laws arose simultaneously with a more pervasive antagonism among the ranks, which was, for so many commentators, tantamount to communal, if not familial, dissolution. The 1834 Report on the Poor Laws, written by the framers of the New Poor Law to substantiate its planned reforms, especially noticed "that the very labourers among whom the farmer was to live, on whose merits as workmen, and on whose affection as friends, he ought to depend, are becoming not merely idle and ignorant and dishonest, but positively hostile; not merely unfit for his service and indifferent to his welfare, but actually desirous to injure him."[17]

While the Commission of Enquiry established in 1832 to review the operation of the Old Poor Laws and to recommend reforms was more inclined to blame the poor, each rank at one time or another accused the others of creating the antagonism. All ranks, however, appeared to experience this failure in intimacy in concrete ways. Wage labor turned formerly resident employees into strangers, while increased populations rendered personal contact more difficult. One commentator mused on the alienating ramifications of out-of-house farm labor: "Formerly, on reaching [the age of fourteen or fifteen], they passed into the houses of masters who kept them under effectual restraint until they married. The master in both town and country deemed it essential to have their conduct constantly under his eye in his dwelling. Now, to a large extent, they never enter the houses of masters. The farmer in various parts no longer boards and lodges his servants. . . . Under the old system they could not well grow into other than moral men and women; under the new one they can scarcely avoid becoming the contrary."[18] As Richard Sennett has argued, knowing the character of another person became nearly impossible in cities and industrial centers, where physical proximity had paradoxically fostered affective distance.[19]

Clothing, in particular, had traditionally affiliated a person with a specific region, rank, or profession, in part because of its reliance on local fabric and skills and its responsiveness to variations in climate and working conditions.

Clothing thus carried the signifying weight of "costume," for it provided visible signs of a person's identity. As I have argued in an earlier chapter, in a static, hierarchical culture these costumes were not allegorical signs in need of decoding, but were perceived as the tangible constituents of identity. In some sense, clothes did indeed make the man (and woman). By the early nineteenth century, urban dress had become far more uniform, at least within classes, while for those central mediators of class society, the servant population, clothing had, in some sense, become a disguise. Throughout the eighteenth century, the commercialization of fashion encouraged emulation so that servants were more likely to wear their mistresses' used garments or to purchase cheaper versions of them.[20] Amidst these cultural shifts, people and places became, rather than knowable entities, inscrutable sites of mystery.

England's market economy encouraged, if not caused, this alienation. The nature of market exchange, as Karl Polanyi succinctly observes, "aims at a gain that can be attained only by an attitude involving a distinctive antagonistic relationship between the partners."[21] Even as relationships became mediated by market transactions, by geographic distance, by the specialization of labor, and by other barriers to physical intimacy, a concomitant alienation arose that was figured as interior and, as the century progressed, psychological. The outer, visible person appeared to possess little relation to his inner, utterly invisible "character."[22] Not only one's costume, but the body itself was now seen as a disguise, an "outside" more often than not out of sync with an "inside." Of course, human beings had before this period imagined distinctions between body and soul; however, late-eighteenth-century England "rediscovered" a version of this difference as a deceptive disjunction precisely because of the culture's emergence from a theatricalized society that widely imagined identity in social terms, with comparatively little emphasis on inner-outer paradigms. Contemporary formulations of this disjunction were articulated in distinctively theatrical terms—costume, actor/actress, spectacle—that had now taken on pejorative connotations.

In this climate, partners in a transaction could accuse one another of unfair practices; the Commission of Enquiry, for example, could accuse workmen of ignorance and dishonesty. Not surprisingly, in this pervasive market culture, tableaux of patriarchal togetherness disintegrated into chaotic scenes of anarchy. In place of the idealized affection of the landlord and his fatherly bestowal of wages and poor relief, commentators spoke of "the producer and the capitalist" whose transactions with the worker were "no other than a barefaced though legalised robbery."[23]

The poor rather than the rich were the group most often accused of theft in the rapidly proliferating literature on the Poor Laws. The poverty discourse of the 1820's and 1830's is saturated with the conviction that poor relief recipients were in fact robbing the rich instead of seeking familial support. Not only was property "stolen" by the poor as their increased dependence on the poor rates depleted the ratepayers' capital, but even benevolent feelings themselves were presumed to be obtained through illegal means; the poor were robbing the rich of their sympathy through false entreaties. Henry Mayhew, in his journalistic investigations of the London poor in the late 1840's, classifies street children into two categories, the latter of which instantiates this thieving beggary as a type of profession: "Mixed with the children who really *sell* in the streets, are the class who assume to sell that they may have the better chance to steal, or the greater facility to beg."[24] This is a most explicit indication of the market's inversion of sentiment and sympathetic exchange. Market exchange had saturated the consciousness of English culture so thoroughly at this time that the socialized feelings necessary for the operation of deference communities—sympathy, benevolence, altruism—were in danger of becoming utterly subject to laws of political economy and its central motivating influence: self-interest. For instance, in her novella *The Parish*, which was written to explain and proselytize for the 1834 Poor Law, Harriet Martineau suggests that the incentive behind the exchange between begging poor children and their superiors is not deferential expenditure, but mercenary profit. They beg, "not to *pay* respect to travellers, but to ask pence of them."[25] In this newer economy, givers had become takers and the metaphoric coin of respect had been converted into literal pence. Belief in such widespread imposture and deceit inevitably strained the performative premise of the Old Poor Laws.

Industrialization and population increases, especially in urban areas, accentuated the defects seemingly present in the internal structures of the Old Poor Laws. Expanding parishes and mobile day labor, for instance, introduced large numbers of strangers into a system that relied on personal recognition to identify those worthy of deference or benevolence. Under these newer, more obfuscatory conditions, an overseer could more readily feel suspicion and impute the poor with deception. The Royal Commission of Enquiry, which was deputed to capture the essence of the Old Poor Laws, filled its enormous volumes with instances of "imposture"—the standard term used to describe various individuals' dishonest, if not precisely illegal, attempts to get relief when they did not need it.[26] "Imposture," a conceptual combination of imposition and deceit, was the dirty underside of theatrical performance, the term used by the audience when it no longer was willing to believe in or indulge the actor. The report of the commission claims that one-half to two-thirds of all able-bodied workers seeking relief "are cases of indolence or imposture." The report quotes a Mr. Walker, who argues that poor people "resort to every trick and artifice" in order to get aid, while a Mr. Whately speaks of the "ragged clothes" that "were kept by the poor for the express purpose of coming to the vestry in them."[27] In these instances, one can explicitly see the transformation of the actor into the liar, the costume of "ragged clothes" into disguise.

By many, the poor were no longer considered poor; they seemed simply to be acting poor. The vestry stage, where the poor traditionally came to reveal their need to the public, had become the scene of disguise and duplicity. The well-to-do imagined that the Old Poor Laws simply did not work anymore because lack of proximity between the high and the low and its attendant ambiguity corrupted the assumptions that underwrote the laws' procedures, encouraging manipulation of the scene of relief. In arguing for reform, Lord Russell developed this theme, noting that "the idle labourer . . . went to some distant magistrate and made out his false tale of distress."[28] The 1834 report, relating a similar instance of imposture, argues for a major alteration in the laws. There was, its authors recall, a pauper seeking relief who in actuality was "found to have saved large sums of money, without the fact having been known or suspected by the members of the same family living under the same roof."[29] This story demonstrated to the commission how even poor families themselves, let alone a patriarchal family unit, seemed to have become a collection of intimate strangers. Elsewhere, the commission report laments, "Now pauperism seems to be an engine for the purpose of disconnecting each member of a family from all the others."[30] Given these conditions, the report concludes, "how should a neighbour, much less a parish officer, be expected to have a better knowledge of the real means of the individual?"[31] In the 1601 Act of Elizabeth, traveling players formed a distinct and dangerous population under the vagrancy laws, but by the 1830's, all relief recipients had begun to be perceived as traveling players—strangers invading the community portraying mysterious and menacing roles. The New Poor Law was designed to manage these rootless and possibly riotous performers.[32]

II

The Royal Commission of Enquiry was formed in 1832, within one year after the Captain Swing Riots, whose perpetrators acted under cover of aliases and masks. With these antagonisms and impostures foremost in its members' minds, the Royal Commission of Enquiry considered social unrest one of its primary concerns.[33] One observer of its efforts agreed that the threat of violence shadowed the commission's endeavors: "In a matter so deeply involving the moral and physical condition of the mass of people, and, by consequence, the safety of society, the results of failure must be of a most awful character."[34] In launching their comprehensive investigation of the Old Poor Laws, the commission thus focused on the problematic and problem-causing poor. Convinced beforehand that the supposed exorbitant increase in the poor rates and in procedural fraud grew out of an expanding pauperized population, the commission sought, above all, to regulate this alien cohort. But first it had to acquire knowledge of these aliens.

By the early 1830's, statistics had become the method by which knowledge and, by extension, truth, was obtained even in regard to social issues.[35] Consequently, the commission set out to amass statistical information regarding the operation of the Old Poor Laws and the poor who were said to profit by them. It sent out lengthy surveys to thousands of parishes throughout England and Wales and dispatched twenty-six investigators to three thousand townships and parishes. The findings, gathered together in several large volumes, were summarized in the commission's final report and recommendations, published in 1834.[36] Although fewer than 10 percent of the surveys were returned, and only 20 percent of the population were represented in those returns, and that twenty not a cross section of the country, the statistical information derived from the surveys was considered almost irrefutable.[37] Before and after the passage of the new law, these materials were quoted repeatedly as convincing proof of the new law's superiority over the old. Michael J. Cullen has argued persuasively that these investigations sought not to deduce conclusions from the findings, but to confirm predetermined assumptions held by the investigators. Indeed, it was a question of considerable current debate whether the distinctions between statistical induction and deduction were even defensible. The surveys, for instance, only asked questions about how the relief procedures of the old laws affected the poor rates, without making, as Cullen observes, "any attempt to assess the effects of low wages or unemployment."[38] From the outset it was assumed that the old laws themselves, not the vicissitudes of the economy, increased the relief rolls.

The commission certainly shaped the survey to suit its own assumptions, though whether this was occasioned by fanaticism, statistical amateurism, or a little of both remains unclear. What is clear, however, is that the commission did believe that statistics would supply impartial knowledge to take the place of the local sentiment toward poor people that Chadwick provocatively called the "blind sympathy" of the Old Poor Laws, a phrase that recalls the disjointed exchanges between the Cumberland beggar and his humble benefactors. Nassau Senior, a member of the commission and an influential framer of the 1834 law, thought that "Man is seen to be an enigma only as an individual, in mass, he is a mathematical equation."[39] The methodology of local sentiment consisted of anecdotes, which are distinctive narratives about individual cases. Anecdotal evidence had until then been used as a reliable measure of variation in a culture where individuals, regardless of minor deviations in personality, were primarily seen to be a predetermined and given part (e.g., "the poor") of a larger, sanctioned society.[40] Local differences among the poor did indeed affect the distribution of relief, but those differences did not transform the poor into something else such that they threatened the basic premise of the law. Not until the 1820's, when the hierarchy of status was perceived to be in decline, did the plethora of cases among "the poor" appear to enfeeble this category's descriptive and functional efficacy. It was at this historical "moment" that statistics sought a quantitative profile of the poor, thus expressing the framers' need to define this now alien "mass" as "a mathematical equation."

Under the Old Poor Laws, the commission contended, anecdote had proven extremely susceptible to fraud and imposture; a poor person could easily tell, as Lord Russell describes it, his "false tale of distress." Statistics, by contrast, would generate an abstract and impartial knowledge about the nation's poor that local instances of imposture and the attendant "blind sympathy" could not overrule.[41] Anecdotes, the framers argued, focused on the singular and thus created poor laws premised on the existence of exceptional cases, a law full of variations.[42] By contrast, "statistics," as Theodore Porter observes, "tended to equalize subjects. It makes no sense to count people if their common personhood is not seen as somehow more significant than their differences."[43] Do not be misled, however, into thinking that the commission was inspired by a spirit of democratic egalitarianism. Although they were committed to the equalization of subjects within a statistical cohort, the commission was not committed to a philosophy grounded in universal resemblance.

By accentuating the "common personhood" of the poor, the commission created a national population of theoretically equal subjects, but it did so by separating them from their local relationships and therefore from their place within a deference community. In practice, of course, these statistics emphasized the similarities of the poor throughout England and Wales in order to emphasize even more their differences from the rich. Statistics applied in this way were just as much a cause as a symptom of the alienation among the ranks. By relying on this methodology, the commission committed itself to an enormously radical and comparatively new procedure for organizing and seeing people within society.

Historians like to claim that the Commission of Enquiry and the subsequent 1834 Poor Law substituted the political economy of Smith, Ricardo, and the Utilitarians for the moral economy of an older patriarchal society.[44]

This interpretation can be enormously misleading because it suggests that the New Poor Law was without moral assumptions. In fact, the political economy of the 1834 Poor Law was also a moral economy, but it was a new one that redistributed good and evil among the population.

In status hierarchies, people possess a ranking in relation to other people in their community. Unlike classes, ranks are differential and relative and each possesses no intrinsic identity that is associated with moral meanings. Eighteenth-century social philosophy did not generally attribute good and evil to groups but to what was usually called "character," a universal and natural property possessed by all people. "Character" was not an exclusive property of any one rank, though its moral value did vary from person to person.[45]

Unlike anecdote and the relativity of deference, statistics and classification conceptually segregated the poor from the rich and thereby provided the rationale for the eradication of what was then deemed the inaccuracy of local sentiment and the treachery of "blind sympathy" in the administration of the Poor Laws.[46] In the New Poor Law of 1834, which almost entirely adopted the recommendations of the Commission of Enquiry, parishes were amalgamated into unions governed by Boards of Guardians that adhered to nationally uniform procedures. Because these guardians represented several different parishes, they usually did not know the individuals requesting assistance. The men who physically dispensed the relief, relieving officers, were unelected officials who lacked any vested interest in the impoverished. Ultimate authority no longer rested with the local magistrates but with three men in London, who were appointed as Poor Law commissioners. Because of these reforms, discretionary judgment and individualized public acts of patronage were replaced with mandatory classes of relief for specific classes of the poor, all of which were defined by this distant and unelected committee.

As is evident in the above account of the new law, in place of status rankings for people, the commission divided people into what it called "classes." This process of classification differs most markedly from status rankings in not deriving its distinctions from relationships among the various vertical groups. Instead, class demarcation abstracts the presumably intrinsic, essential features of horizontal groups. This "common personhood" was defined by the commission in terms of ethically saturated labor functions. In a classificatory society dominated by the laws of political economy, poor people were designated as workers or paupers not primarily because of their differential relationships with other people or even with one another, but because laborers, as a group, were supposed to be industrious, frugal, proud, and "well-regulated" internally as well as externally, while paupers were theoretically idle, spendthrift, shameless, and unregulated through and through because they did not work. The imposition of this moral and economic difference between the pauper and laborer presumably reflects their distinctive, essential qualities, not their relationships with one another. Individuals within these classes do not possess an identity constituted in terms of an external entity, such as another person or group, but rather in terms of their own essence. Political and moral economy combine here to define the parameters of subjectivity in the class culture of nineteenth-century England. Classes are therefore aggregates of individuals, individuals identified according to their economic function in the market and whose interactions with individuals from other classes are dictated by contractual exchanges and ultimately explained in terms of self-interest.[47]

Classification, then, not only segregated the poor from the rich, but crucially differentiated among the poor. It problematized the term "the poor" as well as its subjects; indeed, they were one and the same issue. The institutionalization of this differentiation seemed to the commission to be the first and most crucial step toward reforming the Poor Laws, since imprecise definitions, Chadwick claimed, had contributed to the increase in those considered qualified for relief and, consequently, had caused the rates to rise—"We believe that modern history scarcely furnishes an example of verbal ambiguity by which greater mischief has been done, than by the ambiguity of the word 'poor.'"[48] According to his logic, language as well as costume and distance blurred one rank's perception of another.

For Chadwick, the term *poor* rendered too many individuals eligible for relief, since most Englishmen were poor, in the sense of living at a subsistence level. He and his colleagues preferred to "draw a distinction between the poor and the indigent. By the poor they understand that large section of the human race whose lot is to earn their subsistence by their labour."[49] These people, labeled "independent labourers," were not eligible for relief because their subsistence-level wages were presumed to be naturally sufficient for them.

The Speenhamland system, an eighteenth-century addition to the Old Poor Laws, especially committed this linguistic error and was therefore the commission's main object of criticism, even though the system was not universally used. Speenhamland, the commission members contended, conflated wages and relief and confused workers with paupers, because it furnished allowances in aid of wages. Under this system, all poor people, working and nonworking, could receive relief if, according to complicated equations based on the price of bread, a man's wages fell below the amount computed as necessary for the maintenance of his family.[50] The Speenhamland system thus gave what amounted to bonuses to those families who had many children and therefore it seemed to subsidize large families instead of discouraging them. This older system was also thought to "encourage" early marriage and large families by interfering with hiring practices. A farmer usually hired family men instead of unmarried men, since he could pay the same wage to them as to single men and yet receive the labor of the married man's family at no extra cost because he knew that the poor rates would provide any necessary supplements that the employee would need to feed his family. According to the commission, this outmoded practice wrongly considered the laborer's need, or rather his family's need, as the "natural" level for income, whereas the commission, in obedience to the laws of market supply and demand, considered the market wage as the "natural" income, regardless of whether it could feed a family or not. Giving these workers aid in addition to wages, like an "attempt to control the tides," was thought to disrupt the natural order because its subsidies presumably threatened to sponsor the workers' admission to the middle ranks, a corruption of the seemingly preordained distinctions among the orders.[51]

The so-called free worker, ideally, the single male laborer, was the fundamental labor unit around which the New Poor Law was organized. As a laborer, a man's identity suddenly became knowable again according to the terms of his class designation. This sort of knowledge, however, was not readily displayed in performance, embodied before the spectator, but needed to be interpreted—"discerned." When looking at a laborer, "there is a sense of moral feeling and moral dignity easily discerned," claimed one active supporter of the commission's work.[52] These laborers were in some senses independent, as the commission labeled them. They were independent of relief, and they were independent of familial and regional obligations; however, they were wholly dependent on the market. Their labor had become a commodity to sell, and like other commodities, they could be alienated from their homes. Not surprisingly, the New Poor Law had provisions for migration; it would pay the costs of transportation for an independent laborer who sought work outside his parish.[53]

By differentiating the independent laborer from the rest of the poor, the commission swiftly reduced the number of applicants eligible for relief, but it had yet to isolate the population that was presumed the most greedy and thus disruptive to the system—the able-bodied unemployed. Just how many able-bodied unemployed existed in the early 1830's is unknown, but the commission seemed convinced that this population was large and rapidly growing.[54] More than their employed counterparts, these able-bodied unemployed were the fraudulent impostors who had corrupted the Old Poor Laws and who could in the future disrupt the principles of the new. The able-bodied unemployed threatened the law of supply and demand because they were not constituted by it. Unlike independent laborers, whose wage labor under the New Poor Law submitted them to market forces, unlike the elderly, sick, and impotent (children and the insane), whose incapacity clearly disqualified them from participation in the market and whose residence in the workhouse physically marked their irrelevance to it, the able-bodied unemployed confounded a classification system based on labor functions. As able-bodied poor people they were by nature supposed to labor for a living. Instead of working, however, they lived like independent laborers, often in their own homes, while at the same time living like paupers by receiving relief.

Committed to just two classes of the poor, those who work and those who cannot work, the commission as well as many of their contemporaries could only theorize that the able-bodied unemployed were those who could work but pretended to be disabled.[55] These were the men thought to be "travelling players" who moved from parish to parish looking for the most generous— and thus remunerative—relief and thereby speculating on poor relief as if it were their capital and the Poor Laws a free market. These were the women capitalists whose wombs were imagined as factories for the production of their excess profit, such as the woman who "is now in the receipt of 18s. per week, the produce of successful bastardy adventures."[56] These were the impostors who seemed to blur the boundaries that differentiated the employed from the pauper and, perhaps most frighteningly, the rich from the poor. And therefore, these were the people the commission most needed to classify and regulate.

For those administering the Old Poor Laws, these pretenders had played paupers too convincingly, but the New Poor Law was determined not to succumb to "blind sympathy." Through the operation of the workhouse test, New Poor Law administrators intended to obtain what Chadwick calls "clear perceptions."[57] The workhouse test was conceived as a self-acting mechanism through which a poor person would reveal his true class—not, significantly, his true character. The workhouse test was based on the principle of "less eligibility," whereby the life-style of a pauper was presumed to be "less eligible," or less desirable, than that of an independent laborer. When a person requested relief, he or she was to be given a choice: either come live in the workhouse and live the life of a pauper divorced from the market, or live without relief under the terms of the marketplace. In theory, if a person entered the workhouse, he or she acknowledged destitution and accepted the identity of a true pauper. If one did not accept this definition, one proved to be an independent laborer only disguised as a pauper, a person who could in fact work, as demonstrated by the decision to go home.

The workhouse test preserved classification's explanatory power because it preserved the integrity of the law's two classes of the poor. At the same time, this test replaced the discretionary judgment exercised by local officials with an illusion of the calculus of self-interest, and in doing so it rejected outright both the possibility of one person knowing the character of another and the relevance of that knowledge. Chadwick noted that he had

found that most attempts to administer public relief according to character . . . have created great dissatisfaction. Character being made up of habits, and habits being made up of a series of simple acts, (which we sometimes find it difficult to determine on in our courts of law . . .) it is not surprising that persons in wealthy or superior stations . . . usually fail of estimating them, so as to adjudicate justly.[58]

In this passage, Chadwick rejects the explanatory power of everyday, habitual acts and champions in their place a test that "discerns" the attributes of class by cutting through the distractions of behavior and appearances. Chadwick's rejection of character, however, does not mean that he planned to subtract moral value from the law's calculation of an applicant's worthiness for relief; on the contrary, moral value was considered crucial, though it inhered in classes of people, not in individual characters. The minute an independent laborer requested assistance, he lost his worthiness, no matter his former diligence or his good reputation in the community. A supporter of the new law describes the process wherein a man loses not just his character but his class: "He has become a pensioner on parish bounty. . . . *He has lost his character as an independent man*, and has begun a downward course, which leads, *if he pursue it to the end*, to dependence, degradation and discontent."[59] According to this moral logic, certain "good" classes will receive relief, while "bad" classes will not.

Poor women complicated but did not forestall this process of moral classification. As women, they should have been theoretically presumed more virtuous than men; as poor women corrupted by the operations of the Old Poor Laws, however, they were deceitful calculators who became pregnant either to force their partner into marriage or to live idly on the relief that the parish would provide in lieu of the father's support. The Bastardy Clause of the New Poor Law attempted, among other goals, to prevent this deception by making the woman herself support the child. Although most of the New Poor Law received a warm welcome from the majority of Englishmen, this clause encountered resistance even among reform-minded Whigs. Its reconstitution of the poor female into an entirely usurious and self-interested speculator and of the poor male into a passive victim contradicted too explicitly the gender stereotypes of the day that, though qualified by issues of economic classification, were not erased.[60]

The significance in this shift from the Old Poor Laws' presumption of character to the New Poor Law's theorem of class cannot be overemphasized.

During the 1838 Select Committee of the House of Lords, which was a series of hearings evaluating the early operations of the New Poor Law, a Mr. Bowen, supporter of the Old Poor Laws, compared the new workhouse test to a version he had used under the old laws. His conversation with the 1838 committee, a group that was heavily in favor of the law, contrasts the two contending philosophies. Bowen recalls, "We did not apply [the workhouse test] in the same Way as at Present; it was always applied by us not as a Test of Destitution, but of Imposition."[61] Bowen seems to be quibbling merely about terms, but he points to a genuine difference. According to the new law's logic of classification, the workhouse test was designed to uncover the social position and thus the moral nature of the applicant. By examining for destitution, the new test supposedly identified paupers, who were truly poor, and the able-bodied unemployed, who were truly impostors. Destitution and imposture constituted, therefore, two alternative labels for these two distinct classes: the poor and the able-bodied unemployed, respectively. In contrast, the older workhouse test did not test for destitution; neither did it seek to reveal a class of destitutes because, under the terms of the old laws, destitution was both readily attributed to the applicant (for why else apply for relief?) and utterly irrelevant to a determination of his or her moral intentions. Only a test for imposture could disclose moral character if, for some reason, knowledge of moral character were required.[62] Despite the framers' stated intention, Mr. Bowen stumbles on the actual result of the amendment: the new workhouse test assigned the classificatory place of a poor person, while the regional and rarely used older test revealed the character of a poor person.

These two versions of the workhouse test also help to elaborate the two philosophies of dispensing relief. Under the old laws, a poor person generally received some sort of relief regardless of his or her moral character because destitution was not generally considered a moral quality per se. It should be noted here that even in the eighteenth century this conceptual separation between moral character and economic condition was not universally accepted. Some evangelicals, for instance, considered poverty to be God's punishment for immorality, and others believed that a pauper might, in fact, be destitute because of improvidence and thus willful moral failure. Most people, however, attributed destitution to fate. Prior to the amendment, legal handbooks described three forms of destitution: "poore by impotency and defect," "thriftless poore," and "poore by casualty."[63] In this formulation, one may be thriftless, but one is still legally destitute and therefore eligible for aid. Under the new law, at least under ideal conditions, a poor person received relief only when he or she was a true "pauper," that is, a member of a moral and morally sanctioned class of nonworkers.[64]

Despite this theory, the commission warned that the newer workhouse test would not operate under such ideal conditions in the years just after its inception. The able-bodied unemployed, enervated by habitual dependency, might prefer the workhouse, thereby flouting the principle of "less eligibility." Consequently, the newly restructured workhouses were intended to enforce, and thus clarify, the difference between a pauper and a laborer by making a pauper's life significantly less appealing than a laborer's life.[65] After the passage of the law, the sick and elderly could still receive outdoor relief if they desired, but theoretically, able-bodied recipients had to move into the workhouse, even if this meant that the father had to quit his low-paying job and the family had to sell all its belongings. In order to preserve the distinction between pauper and laborer, and the consistency of economic law, the commission was even willing to quarantine the semi-independent but impoverished worker to prevent him from infecting the self-sufficient market with his superfluous needs. In the workhouse, paupers were housed according to subclass designations rather than in familial groups. The four groups were: the aged and impotent, children, able-bodied females, and able-bodied males. According to the assumptions of the classificatory system, the pauper family required segregation because it formed an inefficient unit of labor, unlike the independent laboring family, which was alienable, mobile, and divisible. Once divided according to labor function, paupers were supposed to be strictly regimented, closely supervised, and scantily fed a uniform diet devised by the Poor Law Commission in London. As a result, they were to live less independently than the independent laborer.

As pauper pretenders, able-bodied unemployed were accused of increasing the poor rates because they bred too much, spent too much, and, crucially, desired too much.[66] The workhouse ingeniously responded to all these excesses. By separating family members, the law easily inhibited population growth. By providing relief in the form of room and board, the law withheld discretionary income. By instituting Benthamite principles under the rubric of "the well-regulated workhouse," the law ultimately hoped to produce, like Bentham, self-regulating individuals, or in other words, independent laborers.[67] This result seemed particularly challenging to achieve since the able-bodied unemployed especially resisted this categorization. While the independent laborer possessed an economic independence that manifested its independent character only within the confines of his class, the able-bodied unemployed exercised an unclassifiable and thus dangerous temperamental independence. The model "independent laborer" desired only to subsist, but the able-bodied unemployed desired to capitalize on the Poor Law, perhaps even to imagine themselves capitalists. As the 1834 report notes: "It is abundantly shown in the course of this inquiry, that where the terms used by the public authorities are vague, they are always filled up by the desires of the claimants, and the desires always wait on the imagination, which is the worst regulated, and the most vivid in the most ignorant of the people."[68]

In order to regulate the imagination, the framers decided that the workhouse would have to reach the inaccessible mind through the body. The commission, after all, repeatedly asserted that the workhouse sought not to hurt paupers but to humble them. As Richard Hall, an assistant commissioner of the New Poor Law, asserted: "I attach Disgrace to the Term Pauper."[69] This decision to regulate the inner space of a pauper also clarifies the new marginalized status of the needy body under the 1834 law, for it is primarily figured as a dependent, if collusive, agent of the mind, an agent whose own reform is insufficient as long as the mind remains unregulated. Special clothing, repetitive labor, and supervised family visits did not physically harm workhouse residents, the reformers insisted, but did deprive their senses and constrict their desires. And ultimately, as Foucault noted about prisoners in the panopticon, the external restrictions on the physical body of the pauper were ideally interiorized into a carceral subjectivity that took over the workhouse's policing function. A reformed pauper is decidedly not a traveling player performing before receptive audiences.[70] Not surprisingly, the 1834 report speaks of the able-bodied pauper's "conversion" into an independent laborer.[71] Like a religious document, the report envisions moral conversion, but like a tract on political economy, it calculates the economic conversion of paupers into independent laborers, and thereby typically mixes moralism and money.

III

On February 23, 1837, one month after publishing its excerpt from *Oliver Twist*, the *Times* printed a letter by the Reverend George S. Bull that protests against the Poor Law Amendment Act of 1834. The minister intones:

Deceit and oppression are mentioned in many places of holy writ as inseparable companions. And thus in this act the word "amendment" really means the retention of some of the worst parts of the old system with sundry hateful additions out of the commissioners' own store. The word "guardian" really means a mere delegate of three despots; the word "relief" means grief and deprivation: the term "relieving officer" is applied to men who are appointed to screw down the poor to the last point of endurance: whilst the officials under this act are boasting of making "independent labourers."[72]

In this passage, one of the most vociferous mouthpieces for the resistance to the New Poor Law, the appropriately named Bull, translates the law's terminology of bureaucracy into the emotionally charged language of melodrama. Most of the prominent figures in the anti–Poor Law movement were, like Parson Bull, translators engaged in a representational conflict with the framers of the new law.

Some historians might take issue with this apparently poststructuralist claim, which seems more concerned with words than with material conditions.[73] The example of the Poor Law Amendment Act largely disputes, I think, the usefulness of this binary opposition, for the law significantly altered the material conditions of the poor, their social interactions, and the constitution of their identities precisely by restaging the poor man's "representation" before two audiences: the new law's Board of Guardians and the general public. Institutionally, the new law replaced the poor man's "tale of wo" told before a familiar relieving officer with abstract classes judged by strangers and supervised by the invisible forces of the Poor Law commission in London.[74] In the discursive sphere, the new law replaced familial metaphor and a syntax of deferential sentiment with statistical cohorts and a hedonist calculus.[75]

The old law's syntax of deferential sentiment—sympathy, benevolence, kindness, and respect—referred to relationships existing in deference communities, but it would be anachronistic to regard these words as signifiers of personal, spontaneous feeling, which belong instead to a romanticist idiom. Rather than an expression of private emotion, such words described modes of public and universal behavior, "social feeling," that had regulated welfare exchange and other forms of cultural interaction prior to the reforms of the nineteenth century.[76] In fact, the internalized gestures of the romantic mind, by privatizing these sentimental behaviors and articulating the narrow parameters of the individual conscience, demonstrate one of the ways by which the social utility of sentiment was problematized and rendered inefficient in the eyes of the new law's framers.[77]

The battle between the two sides to influence public opinion, which continued with varying intensity from 1834 to about 1842, was more than just a debate; the public's acceptance of the new laws' discursive representations of the poor were to be interpreted as a sanction of that law's institutional treatment of the poor. The framers of the new law had, of course, a decided advantage in the public forum because they possessed government authorization and officially funded means of dissemination. Chadwick and the Commission of Enquiry were fully aware of the need to win public approval for their representational system. While amassing their information between 1832 and 1834, the commission rushed to publish several thousand copies of an interim report in an effort to introduce early their representative classes of the poor. Chadwick noted, "What a mass of evidence is requisite to convince a whole nation!"[78] The government, at least, was very convinced by the report. The consequent law, when put up for a vote, passed both houses by a landslide.

By contrast, the voice of opposition to the new law articulated the sentiments of a dispersed and relatively marginal group of radicals, Tories, clergy, working men, and landed proprietors. Anti–Poor Law agitators included John Fielden, a Cobbettite M.P. and industrialist; Joseph Stephens, an ultra-Tory anti-Anglican; Richard Oastler, a church-and-king Tory; John Walters, a landed gentleman and owner of the *Times*; and Reverend Bull as well as hundreds of less famous men and women. The North of England offered the most extensive and best-organized resistance, perhaps because of its already well-developed network of political activist groups, but overall the opposition suffered from this group's premises. Its preference for community determination and local experience provided it with neither a national identity nor a nationwide plan of attack, and consequently the movement lacked focus and momentum, in direct contrast to the campaign of the framers of the new law. Indeed, the term *movement* is not even an accurate word to describe this protest effort. Despite the *Times*'s adherence to the cause, the opposition relied primarily on the unstamped press, open-air speeches, and both organized and spontaneous protests to disseminate its response to the official pronouncements of the new law's influential supporters.

The framers' dominant voice in print, combined with the material effects of the new law's misrepresentations, created a climate in which the authors' diction of bureaucratic engineering, devoid of human agents and expressions of social obligation, could be complexly experienced by its detractors as both emotionally and physically oppressive. Although writing of relief measures, Chadwick and his associates seemed oblivious to those measures' human exactions, especially their infliction of bodily harm. Consequently, the New Poor Law opponents continually depicted scenes of physical violence and suffering in order to give a feeling body to, for instance, the workhouse test, as Parson Bull did when he translated "relief" into the melodramatized emotion of "grief and deprivation" and "guardian" into the melodrama's favorite orientalized villains, "despots." Such translation was an especially crucial strategy, given that the intended penalty resulting from confinement in a workhouse was largely a psychological one and thus not readily visible to an average spectator. The opponents thus relied on a gestural and a theatrical component in the print debate, as if to force the issue into a more traditionally public arena, to render it in a more generally accessible iconography.

In short, the anti–Poor Law resistance responded to the statistical depictions and material oppression of the poor through the expression and enactment of the melodramatic mode. By the 1830's, melodrama had become a recognizable, if still somewhat irregularly defined, theatrical genre, but had nonetheless become the undisputed rhetorical narrative of the dispossessed—orphans, paupers, estranged spouses, prodigal sons.[79] These dramas of familial dissolution and reunion were structured to involve their audience in a scene of recognition and reconciliation that would reify, through the use of visual and verbal cues, the patriarchal bonds of family within a fragmenting society. Perhaps some people in the movement to resist the New Poor Law, who shared melodrama's vision and its distinctive language, knowingly adopted its style, though certainly they lacked a theorized consciousness of its myriad effects. I have argued in the previous chapter that the structures of theatrical melodrama, rather than providing a model for replication, participated in and reflected the more extensive structures of this melodramatic mode. This melodramatic mode articulated and enacted the resistance's effort to dramatize the culture of deference communities in a country increasingly marked by alienation, classification, and privatization.

Partly because of food riots and rick burnings, the poor, who were now defined as paupers, were commonly perceived as an unruly, unregulated mass. As Raymond Williams has observed: "The aggregate of distress and sorrow has only to move, collectively, to be converted into its opposite, and be seen as a howling mob."[80] Indeed, some of the early opponents of the law in the mid 1830's stormed actual "bastiles," for instance in Heckingham in Norfolk, where a crowd attempted to "rescue" the incarcerated and burn down a workhouse.[81] Such gestures, no matter how their details might be symbolically interpreted by generous observers, could be easily construed by the proponents of the new law as riot. As was true in the melodramatic rhetoric of the Old Price faction, the melodramatic rhetoric articulated by the antagonists of the new law thus downplayed the aggression of the protesters, accentuating instead the familial and moral bonds among themselves and with those inside the workhouse.

The melodramatic resistance thus gave a rational voice and a suffering body to the poor, a voice and body that they needed in order to transform their predicament into a recognizable moral force that could participate in public debate. "Moral force" became a frequently used term in the anti–Poor Law movement. Initially used by the Whig government, the resistance adopted it to represent its effort to humanize the intentions of the rowdy body of the mob. As a Mr. Hill noted in the *Northern Star*, "The people had now a moral force, in the control of which they could exercise over the vote of the electors."[82] This moral force, however, was not always exactly equivalent to the voices and bodies of the paupers themselves—for most vocal members of the opposition were gentlemen and most bodily representations were through verbal imagery and illustrations; rather, it was a communal resistance against the social implications of these procedures of classification that often presumed, in a consistent paternalist attitude, to include the paupers' voice in its collective response. As a group championing a hierarchical social order, the opposition to the New Poor Law could not be expected to have a democratic organization intent on the radical empowerment of the marginalized individual. Rather, the opposition dramatized, in often sentimental word and histrionic gesture, a traditional society that was seemingly under direct attack by the new law.

IV

The Poor Law Amendment Act of 1834 aimed to substitute a national classification system for the deference communities that had until then mostly governed England and Wales. As a result, it helped to institutionalize the growing divisions among the ranks and redefined the terms of their social interaction. Its success, however, is still a subject of debate among historians and should, at this point in my argument, be discussed. A significant number of parishes, especially in the North and in rugged, rural regions, managed to avoid the reforms entirely; another group of parishes returned to their old ways after initially yielding to the law. And no one can ever be certain about the number of parishes that appeared to adhere to the law while behaving otherwise. Nevertheless, the assumptions of the law percolated into English culture, and not until after the First World War did a Poor Law Amendment outline a radical alternative to this 1834 relief philosophy.

Whether or not they were thoroughly successful in achieving all their wide-ranging reforms, the framers did manage to write a law without the old law's syntax of sentiment or philosophy of social feeling; as Chadwick wrote to a friend, "We should keep to the windward of the humanity mongers."[83] Instead, the new law presumed that individuals acted according to their self-interest in the so-called free market. The new law's restaging of the scene of relief dramatized this pervasive restructuring of social exchange. This new scene of relief insistently refused to stage what were now conceived to be deceptive performances by the poor designed to manipulate the audience. One writer to the *Times*, sympathetic toward the old laws, sorrowfully describes this new scene: "A claimant for relief is brought to a general board of guardians, only a small number of whom know anything of the case; yet the whole board sits in judgment upon it, only the smaller number . . . having . . . sympathy for the claimant as applies to the knowledge of his sufferings."[84] From the perspective of this opponent, the framers legislated against traditional forms of social feeling. As one opponent regretted: "The whole measure, in my conception, is pregnant with cruelty and injustice—makes war upon the most helpless class of society—and tends to tear asunder all those important and tender sympathies between the middling and lower ranks of life, which are so necessary towards maintaining the real happiness and strength of a state."[85] The new law's scene of relief, repeatedly represented in the framers' propaganda, trained its bureaucratic and national audiences to be unmoved by public performance. Rather than eliciting fellow feeling and paternalistic intervention, this scene instilled distancing objectivity and forbearance, even suspicion. In one contemporary stage melodrama, *The Factory Lad*, one of the characters explicitly complains about what was perceived to be disingenuous suspicion and studied forbearance among people who should certainly know their poor:

Aye, or a pauper, to go with your hat in your hand, and, after begging and telling them what they know to be the truth—that you have a wife and five, six, or eight children, one, perhaps just born, another mayhap just dying—they'll give you eighteen pence to support them all for the week; and if you dare to complain, not a farthing, but place you in the stocks, or scourge you through the town as a vagabond![86]

One protester elaborated further on the effects induced by the new law when he described its "threefold object" as "tranquilizing, soothing, and lulling the consciences of the rich" so that they would not be "disturbed, even in the midst of their enjoyments" by "the hideous and revolting spectacle of the wretchedness existing around them."[87] Unlike the theatrical spectacle of melodrama, this spectacle avoided direct appeals to the sentiments of its audience, appeals that would presumably lead to "blind sympathy" and unregulated benevolence as practiced under the old laws. Disdaining the traditional exchange of feeling between the scene and its audience, this performance taught its audience to be passive spectators.

In order to warm cooling public sentiment, to alter the new law, and ultimately to restore the dynamics of paternalist social exchange, the resistance to the Poor Law Amendment deployed the melodramatic mode. Like the language of sentimentality, melodrama attempts to elicit compassionate feeling, but it confronts an audience, unlike sentimental literature's unitary readership of the literate middle class, that is disunited and suspicious. Through its recuperation of specific theatrical techniques, melodrama regenerates paternalist attitudes among estranged "family" members and was therefore the ideal mode for the New Poor Law resistance, whose members experienced the new law as an attack on the patriarchal order of agrarian Britain.

Since deference communities were presumed to operate like extended versions of patriarchal immediate families, the amendment's abolition of outdoor relief and, especially, relief in aid of wages seemed to its opponents to be an act of disinheritance because it denied to the poor the assistance that had been formerly considered a birthright, an inheritance from their parochial fathers theoretically like the land a gentleman's son inherited from his father. The 1834 report mentions an employed shoemaker, who, on being rejected for assistance, responded that his relief *"was like a freehold"* to him.[88] S. W. Nicolls, who had implemented in his parish some of the new law's procedures prior to 1834, argued against this conception of relief as a form of common property: "The great body of the Poor, Have no more distinct claim on the property of the country at large, than any single pauper has on a private fortune."[89]

Relief had been one of the few proprietary rights the poor still retained in 1834, and its withdrawal symbolized their abandonment. The aging William Cobbett, one of the early opponents of the law, insisted: "What was the New Poor Law but an abdication of responsibility both by those who held the land and by the government?"[90] The poor no longer had access to common land on which they could graze an animal, and very few had a garden plot by their cottage in which they could grow vegetables. They could not even hunt, since wild animals were regarded as the property of the proprietor on whose lands the animals were found. After 1834, the poor were, in law, wholly supported and constituted by their wage labor. Instead of extended family members, they were legally commodities, and as commodities "the long line of glorious ancestry is a thing unthought of; equally so is the line of posterity."[91] The impoverished classes of the New Poor Law were, by definition, creatures of subsistence—without legacies, without lineal connections to their superiors, without histories, without homes. The law intended "to persuade the rich that the poor have no claim on them for protection; that all their old associations may be safely broken up, and their feelings trampled upon; and to reduce the poor to that degraded condition in which they are assumed to be already—a burden to their country—citizens not of England, but of a workhouse."[92] The only lingering inheritance remaining to the poor were the idle and dissolute habits of their pauperized parents: "When once a family has received relief, it is to be expected that their descendants, for some generations, will receive it also."[93] Even this legacy, however, was withheld from them when they entered the workhouse. Once there, mothers, fathers, sons, and daughters no longer lived, died, and bequeathed as members of a family; instead, they became male paupers, female paupers, and children. As the resistance continually emphasized: "The new poor law provides that the poor shall be . . . separated the husband from the wife . . . the wife from the husband, the parents from the children!"[94]

From the perspective of the Poor Law resistance, the new law, especially as it was institutionalized in the workhouse, determined that familial and lineal identity were now the exclusive possessions of the upper ranks. Family roles, like commons land, had become enclosed, privatized, cut off from the public realm where patriarchal ties had formerly flourished. Many recent scholars have discussed the unique qualities and lasting influence of this Victorian version of the private sphere.[95] The idealized Victorian family existed in a domestic haven theoretically protected from, but supportive of, the public world of the market, a private sphere where the upper ranks largely reserved familial feeling and moral virtue for their own use. According to the laws of classification, unlike the idle and dissolute paupers, unlike the industrious and regulated independent laborers, the upper ranks, as a property-owning class, embodied wisdom and virtue and possessed them as essential, individualized traits within the context of the private sphere.[96] While the "working" class was defined entirely in accordance with labor function and productivity, the emergent middle class was able to avoid a purely economic determination by seeking refuge in the market-free zone of domesticity.

By reconstituting the poor in terms of their market function, the Victorians abandoned them to a wholly economic sphere. The independent laborer, as an alienable commodity, could not, by definition, inhabit a domestic realm of familial values. Instead, a good laborer behaved according to the golden rule of the market and the institutional structure that upheld it. During the years leading up to the new law, the pauper seemingly did not obey this rule, did not participate in the market, and was therefore perceived in a new light by those who were now embracing, indeed living, the rigid dichotomy between private and public spheres. To these people the poor lived a private life, but this sort of privacy was utterly unlike the regulated and supervised home life of Victorian domesticity. It was private insofar as it was inaccessible to their surveillance. And one should note that "surveillance" becomes a meaningful concept for the ruling classes at this juncture precisely because they had conceded the demise of an inclusive social sphere unscarified by divisions between private and public. Under the new law, the workhouse's segregation, its close supervision, and its other panoptic features were aiming to eradicate this sinister, private life and make the pauper, like the laborer, a creature of a newly reconstituted public sphere where older, familial versions of socialized sentiment and virtue had no place.[97]

"Relief" had become "welfare" in a public sphere regulated by punitive bureaucratic institutions whose perceptual dissonance with a still largely agrarian, provincial populace was continually reproduced in hybridized prose and pictures. Such dissonance was cannily articulated by a *Punch* author when he combined the familial images of deferential culture with the perceptions of utilitarian reform, a collision of idioms typical of the melodramatic protest. Instead of mother's love, the writer wryly notes, pauper children were raised by an "automaton Poor-Law mother . . . dandling, kissing, fondling its pauper multitudes."[98] For the reformer, it is implied, the only relationship imaginable between the rich and the poor was mediated by a mechanized bureaucracy, "automaton Poor-Law mother," and the only feelings possible among the poor were mercenary, hence the numerous accounts of poor mothers who sent their children to beg and of poor parents who bred for profit. And yet, both author and illustrator (see Figure 3) persist in conforming to the familial rhetoric of the opposition and thus staging a melodramatic scene in which moral polarities are embodied by good mother / bad mother and superintended by the providential fates of a devil and an angel.

In Robert Blakey's *Cottage Politics* (1837), a book that addresses poor law legislation, there is a woodcut that also struggles to illustrate the radical transformations that were only partially comprehended. The woodcut portrays the decline and perversion of deferential exchange under the New Poor Law, but also seems to represent the resulting bifurcation of identity that was also addressed during the Old Price Wars. Through the actions of its relieving officer, the New Poor Law creates a mediating barrier, both physical and psychological, between rich and poor (see Figure 4). In one half of the woodcut, the officer wields a whip in the presence of a poor man seeking relief, an iconized tableau of torture typical of melodramatic staging; in the other, divided from the adjacent action by what appears to be a solid wall, he bows obsequiously to his superior, another standard scene in melodrama. Because the officer cannot, of course, inhabit two spaces at the same time, the two sections of the woodcut might at first encourage a sequential reading, as one might read a comic strip, but the three-dimensional space suggests simultaneous action, as if the artist were attempting to depict in architectural form and theatrical space the relieving officer's duplicity, as if straining to give a body and a place to what twentieth-century critics might wish to figure alternatively and anachronistically as psychic strife. Between this dramatized illustration in *Cottage Politics* and our contemporary notion of subjectivity lies the panopticon.

By forcing paupers to internalize their class definition, the amendment denied to the poor the right to be good men and impoverished men at the same time.[99] Although the new law could distinguish the pauper from the independent laborer, and both from the upper ranks, it would not, perhaps could not, distinguish the imposing, posturing, entrepreneurial pauper from the criminal, since both lived off of the upper ranks without joining the legal labor force. In line with this reasoning, the new law did not provide graduated relief based on moral distinctions among individual paupers—all paupers were to reside in the punitive workhouse. As one of the speakers at a

THE "MILK" OF POOR-LAW "KINDNESS."

Figure 3. "The 'Milk' of Poor-Law 'Kindness,'" from *Punch*, 1843. A villainous matron, representing the New Poor Law, wrests an infant from a beseeching mother in a stock scene borrowed from stage melodrama. The devil and angel in the background accentuate melodrama's stark moral polarities. Collection of the Sterling Library, Yale University.

Figure 4. The poor-law overseer's two faces, untitled illustration from *Cottage Politics*, 1837. In the first portion of the diptych, the overseer administers the harsh justice of the New Poor Law, while in the second portion, he obsequiously defers to his aristocratic superior. Collection of the Library of Congress, Washington, D.C.

Bradford anti–Poor Law meeting asked rhetorically: "But did the new law draw a line of demarcation between the good and evil? No, in the bastile they found the most virtuous people crowded with the most vicious people on earth."[100] The new law considered all able-bodied paupers criminals and poverty a crime punishable by a sentence in the workhouse, or, as the resistance knowingly labeled it, the "bastile."

The Poor Law resistance therefore sought to free the poor from this literal bastille and its imprisoning representations; it sought to release them from this panoptic public sphere while at the same time republicizing the sentiment and virtues that seemed to have become exclusively managed by the rich under the new law. On stage, melodramas had enacted for decades just such sensational scenes of escape and rescue, and the melodramatic mode pursued similar effects in this discursive realm. If the new law's workhouse test revealed the class of an applicant for relief, melodrama, like the imposture test of the Old Poor Laws, revealed the applicant's character by reasserting the significance of an individual's reputation in a public realm constituted by patriarchal ties, not institutional regulations.

Resisting the carceral framework of statistically sanctioned classification, its imprisoning connotations and internalized effects, the anti–Poor Law movement publicized one melodramatic anecdote after another about the courageous endurance and familial devotion of paupers with incorruptible good characters. Usually, these stories tell of a father or a mother, sometimes with a name, sometimes without, who starved to death, gave birth in the street, or murdered a baby rather than seeking relief in a workhouse where the child would be taken from the parent. These scenes of physical suffering were often factually inaccurate, but they achieved their purpose. They embodied and publicized the intended mental terrors experienced in the workhouse, which were as private, because internalized, as the panoptic regimen was public.[101] In the melodramatic mode, as in the censored early versions of stage melodrama, the body spoke through these anecdotes for those individuals without a sanctioned public voice. But, most crucially, the embodiment of torture rejuvenates a more traditional method of constituting the individual—not as a body disguising inaccessible thoughts and motivations, but as a recognizable being whose pain is visible for all to see. One of the resistance's more prolific letter writers, George Baxter, compiled *The Book of the Bastiles*, which contains hundreds of pages of such anecdotes.[102] (See Figure 5.)

Neither case studies of individual psyches nor prescriptions for a statistical cohort, these anecdotes, a form of evidence culled from more classical methods of rhetorical contestation, became instead a catalogue of moral types. The catalogue's subjects were individuated mainly insofar as they were family for the doctor to attend her until it was too late, and the consequence was, that she died from neglect."—*Rev. Edmund Dewdney (of Portsea), at the Freemasons' Tavern Anti-New Poor-Law Meeting*, Feb. 19, 1838.

"Under the present law, he knew that in Suffolk many cases had taken place, in which a delay of ten days had occurred between the application for, and the administration of, relief."—*Earl Stanhope, House of Lords*, March 22, 1838.

"An investigation of considerable importance was made last week at Cambridge, touching the death of an infant, which, with its mother, had been removed from Tuplow to Cambridge by a brute of an overseer. The child died in consequence of the removal, and to carry his hardheartedness still further, the overseer refused to give a single farthing towards the funeral ! Upon being remonstrated with for not giving relief, and in ordering the unfortunate mother and babe to be removed, he said, ' *he believed the child would die soon, and so the matter would be dropped.*' The coroner summed up the case in a most able manner, and quoted several cases to show that if a party be guilty of negligence, and death is the result, the party guilty of such negligence is also guilty of manslaughter. The jury immediately returned a verdict of *manslaughter*, and the overseer was committed to gaol forthwith."—*Halifax Guardian*, Jan. 26, 1839.

"An investigation was held on Thursday, at St. Mary's Cray, Kent, on the body of a pauper named Burgess, who died in the workhouse of the Bromley Union. It appeared that the deceased having applied for relief to Mr. Palmer, Relieving Officer of the Lewisham Union, that gentleman (?) had him sent forward in an open cart to Coodham, his alleged legal settlement. Burgess was exceedingly ill at the time, and died shortly after his arrival at Coodham. Mr. Palmer, in his defence, said he did not know that the man was in a dangerous state at the time of his removal. After a long investigation the coroner summed up, and, in doing so, observed, that the jury were to determine if any party was to be made responsible for the death of the deceased. The jury retired for about an hour-and-a-half:—*Mr. Snelling* (the foreman) ' We find Mr. Palmer guilty of neglect of duty, not knowing the state the deceased was in at the time.' *Coroner*—' But what is your verdict in reference to the deceased?'

Foreman—' We find there has been neglect of duty; we can't soften it.' *Coroner*—' Do you intend a verdict of manslaughter, or not?' *Foreman*—' We leave that to you, Sir.' The jury-room was now again cleared, and after above two hours had elapsed the public were admitted, and the jury delivered a verdict of ' Manslaughter against George Harding Palmer, accompanied with a recommendation to mercy' (?). The coroner then made out Palmer's commitment to Maidstone gaol."—*Examiner*, March 31, 1839.

"An inquest was lately held on the body of Mary Hancox, at Ampney Crucis. The deceased was a poor woman, aged 55, the wife of James Hancox, a poor old cripple. Being destitute, the deceased applied to the Cirencester Union Board on the Monday (distant from Ampney about three miles). The day was piercingly cold, and after waiting at the Board a long time without getting relief, she returned home in a very weak and shivering state, and went to bed ill. On the Tuesday, application was made for medical assistance, and medicine was sent on the Wednesday. On Friday she was attended again, and had more medicine; and on Saturday morning she died. After a long and patient investigation, the jury returned a verdict—' That the deceased died by the visitation of God, and that her death was accelerated by the intensity of the cold to which she was exposed in attending the Board of Guardians on the preceding Monday.' "—*Gloucestershire Chronicle*, March 31, 1838.

"Perhaps the worst and most decidedly *un*-English part of the new system is, the separation of mothers from their children, husbands from their wives, in the New Bastiles, and the driving *men* from the marriage bed to sleep with *boys*."—*Weekly Dispatch*, Feb. 21, 1836.

"In this day's paper, we give some particulars of scenes at Rolvenden, in Kent, connected with the removal of aged and bedridden paupers in the depth of winter. It will be seen that some of the victims died under the operation, and that others were subjected to sufferings that made them pray to the Almighty to release them by death."—*Ibid.*

"Jacob Pike, a poor man, weak in intellect, who had, for many years previously to the introduction of the New Poor-Law, been an inmate of the Soberton Poor-house (he was then a stout, robust man, he is now dwindled away and exhi-

Figure 5. Pages 136 and 137 from Baxter's *The Book of the Bastiles,* 1841, which represent only two of the many pages that catalogue the cruelties

bits a pale-faced, half-starved appearance) ; for the last twenty years this poor innocent creature had been supplied with tobacco by private charity, but even this is now denied him by the rules and regulations of the House."—*Rev. Stephen Butler's (of Soberton), "Letter to the Ratepayers of the Droxford Union,"* 1838.

" I found in one room (of the Droxford House) 14 children confined with the itch ; one little girl had been shut up in this apartment eight weeks and was not then recovered ; another was in such a state of salivation as to be laid on a bed, spitting up blood, which I was informed she had done for a week."—*Ibid.*

" A man with a large family went into the —— Union workhouse. As soon as they were washed and got the workhouse dress on, the Governor said to another woman, ' take that child from that woman's (the man's wife) arms and carry it to the nursery.' The poor mother thought she should drop. The woman took it with tears in her eyes and said she would take care of it. The mother could only say, ' Pray do.' This was on a Friday, and on the following Sunday, one of the women stole away the child from the nursery and brought it to the mother in the chapel, and she suckled it during the service, and two or three days after she did the same again......This woman was locked up with others in a close gaol of a washhouse, containing the linens of the dead, diseased, those having the venereal complaint, &c., &c., and, day after day, though in a very weak state, could only have the door open a little time by chance, as that was contrary to the ' Rule.' The matron of the workhouse said to this poor woman, ' I know you and the rest all want and desire some extra or better living. I dare not give it you !!!' This family *cost too much in the Bastile,* and were sent for out again ; a farmer promising the man work because his family cost 30s. or 40s. per week in the House : but he had not worked for him many weeks before he was jeering him with how well they lived in the workhouse, &c., &c. The poor man said, ' Yes, indeed ! look how they have treated my son.' (This son had married a widow with a family, and, to oblige the Union officers, went to Lancashire and got a good contract there. But his master died, and his son refused to abide by the contract, which the magistrates could not enforce, but sent the whole family back by orders, which this poor family could not

help. But on their return, they were treated worse than beasts. Indeed it is enough to break any one's heart to read their story—I have written it from their own mouths.) The master of the poor man in question, still continued his jeers and sneers, till the poor man said—' Damn the House ! I wish it was blown up,' &c., &c. The master discharged him that night, and said he would every man that made use of such language, and gave him notice to keep off his premises. The poor man replied, that he had committed no crime, or done anything to be so cruelly treated ; and if he did not come to ask him for work, he might be sent to prison, or refused all relief, because he had not done all he could to obtain work, and keep his family from becoming chargeable. After this, the best work he could get, was picking stones off the land to mend the roads. Himself and four children, 16, 14, 12, and 8 years of age, were five weeks earning 40s., which, reckoning the children at 2d. per day, (including Sundays) each, left him not 6d. per day for himself. In fact such work is only fit for women and children, who can pick up more than men very often."—*Extracted from a Letter of a Southern County Correspondent to the Author,* dated Oct. 2, 1840.

" A poor man, with a wife and child at the breast, was last winter obliged to go into the Union workhouse. The woman's child, which was only a year-and-a-half old, was taken from her, *as usual,* and they were treated so badly that they came out again at the end of one week, when she suckled the child again. But the man could get only four days' work, and after that was again forced into the 'House,' with his wife and child. The poor woman, on this their second admittance, begged and prayed her child might not be taken from her, as she had suckled it again since she had been out ; but all in vain. The jolly babe was crammed into a ward were the scarlet fever was raging, and the mother had great difficulty to be allowed to nurse her own child ; but it recovered from that ; and as soon as given up again to the matron, the father, by stealth, found it in bed with a child that had got the measles ; and, before he could get the mother to it, the child had lain 48 hours in the most filthy, horrid state ; from which, in spite of all the mother could do, it died from neglect of their keeping the mother from it ; and she has since declared, that she would live upon half-a-bellyful of potatoes per

and injustices of the workhouses under the New Poor Law. Collection of the Sterling Library, Yale University.

members; they were sons, daughters, and especially mothers. Rank and family relation identified the person; good and bad public acts, those habitual behaviors so derided by Chadwick, identified that person's character—whether it be heroic or villainous. According to the logic of melodrama, good and evil are public property, not the private possession of any one class, and thus they are both visible and available to the entire community. In this way, the anecdotes displayed the public reputation that was typical among the poor, though not definitive of them.

In these melodramatic scenarios, public reputations expressed through visual cues or prescriptive social behaviors become crucial. Accessible and easily interpretable to the entire community, they expose to a dispersed audience the good or bad character of every actor in the story. These polarities of good and evil, so characteristic of melodrama's ethical universe, are perhaps simple but by no means simplistic moral binaries. Although modern critics universally condemn stage melodrama's moral binaries as evasive tactics, a fool's refuge from real-life complexities, they do so usually without considering the real-life complexities of early-nineteenth-century England. The opponents of the new law derived their definitions of good and evil from a more unitary and consensual society, and though they perhaps underestimated the divisions in contemporary England that were fast problematizing these definitions, they continued to believe in the self-evident justification and social utility of these definitions.

In the enormous theaters of the early nineteenth century, the people at the back or in the second balcony needed broad, moral types to render visible information that they might not otherwise be able to see or hear. In English society at large, broad public gestures, expressive of an individual's reputation, also conveyed information between participants and spectators, ultimately breaking down the distance between them. Both stage melodrama and the melodramatic mode kept no secrets from their audiences. Like other spokesmen within the movement, an editorialist for the *Northern Star* wrote melodramatically in what would now be labeled simplistic polar oppositions but which should be seen instead as historical artifacts from a society of relative moral and social consensus: "The character of the people is unchanged—they are the same simple, peaceful, and confiding people that they ever were; and the character of the Whigs is unchanged—they are the same selfish, grasping subtle, cowardly political gourmands that they always were."[103]

Melodramatic scenarios dispense virtue and vice across class lines; good and evil know no rank, no class, and they are generically social attributes: "Let there be no distinction made between the unvirtuous lapses of the

daughters of the rich and titled, and those of the poor and helpless."[104] Melodrama's moral absolutes were considered communal possessions that enabled
the Poor Law resistance to efface class differences by creating an ethical consensus among the members of its audience.[105] What we might analytically
label a "class society" may not describe a culture or segment of that culture's
recognition and/or acceptance of it. Patricia Hollis notes that from the perspective of many people of the lower ranks, "working class" was still a term
of degradation that defined a group that was without the vote and without
control over the products of its labor.[106] The resistance's melodramatic mode
thus overcame the crisis of estrangement by publicly revealing to the rich
man an alternative to the undesirable classification of the poor man. These
anecdotes were self-consciously rhetorical, scenic, and performative, as if
they were spectacles staged before audiences. A *Times* editorial directs, "Let
[any unprejudiced person] look at the miserable objects, complete pictures of
perishing destitution"; the *Northern Star* instructs, "witness the breaking up
of their once happy and social communities, and see a squalid race of living
skeletons marching in sad procession. . . . Behold then the misery."[107] These
vivid scenes of families and communities in physical torment, unlike the
scene of relief under the new law, brought the pain "home" to the audience, for they rendered the suffering in familial and thus familiar terms and
reenacted the more traditional operation of sympathy. Only by reestablish-
ing patriarchal, familial ties, such partisans reasoned, would the audience be
able to sympathize and benevolently intervene, so as to protect as a patron
should.[108]

The melodramatic mode's conservative adherence to patriarchy differentiates it from other contemporary responses (socialism, utilitarianism) to the
social and economic crises of the 1830's and 1840's. Perhaps the melodramatic
mode's politics, if such a term can even be applied to such a dynamic and
evasive cultural force, are most different from English socialist thinking in
their implicit estimation of the potential value of an aristocratic culture. The
distinctive phrases and gestures of the melodramatic mode seemed assertively to distinguish between an intact ideal of patriarchy and a more brutal
reality of capitalism. The social feelings and community obligations, the patriarchal lineages and deferential codes that form the conceptual basis of a
melodramatic lament were by no means seen to be analogues of the capitalist
system of exchange. Clearly embattled by this relatively new social order and
continually subject to its co-optation, these melodramatized tenets of a patriarchal society nonetheless represented to many a pure market-free zone.
By contrast, Robert Owen, the New Lanark socialist, and many, if not all, of
his followers, denounced the entire social structure that produced an aris-

tocracy, not least because of the aristocracy's perceived collusion with capitalism. For instance, Owen rejected the central patriarchal tie of marriage, whose contractual origin signified to him its market origins.

Although both Reverend Bull and Robert Owen might condemn emblematic capitalist behaviors and the apotheosis of *Homo Economicus* by telling the story of an aristocratic rake seducing a poor laborer's daughter, their narratives were informed by fundamentally contrary methodologies that led to dissimilar conclusions and calls to action. For Owen, William Thompson, and Anna Wheeler, to name some of the more prominent socialists, this rake's progress allegorized, as Barbara Taylor phrases it, "the rape of class by class."[109] For men like Richard Oastler, an anti–Poor Law leader still dedicated to older social forms, such scenes of seduction spoke instead of family breakdown, not class antagonism. Working within a sociology of patriarchy, Oastler sought solutions that would reunite the family and resocialize the alienated aristocrat so that he might grant the girl bread rather than steal her virginity.

These carefully delineated theoretical differences were nonetheless unevenly embraced and deployed by many contemporary human agents, who were uneasily straddling this transition between two social orders. The *Northern Star*, especially in the early 1840's, could juxtapose melodramatic scenarios of patriarchal benevolence with bitter tirades against aristocratic capitalists. Always a hybrid, the melodramatic mode rarely existed in any text or setting in an ideologically pure form; for this very reason, it can only be seen as a rhetorical and performative mode, not a fully realized and internally consistent ideology. The melodramatic mode can best be seen as a form of strategic dissent, sometimes offering only a momentary rhetorical solution or emotional response in a print debate and at other times a genuine material effect in a world where basic structures of social interaction were in conflict.

The melodramatic mode always resolves this conflict in the same way: all interactions are figured as familial; all people are family. Even as the workhouse reconstituted its inmates as able-bodied men and women, the men who criticized it staged typical melodramatic tableaux in which family identity and feeling are frozen into symbol: "A *massacred father—a famished mother—a debauched sister—a wife—a brother—a child that died in bastile agony!*"[110] As shown earlier, the magazine *Punch*, for instance, sketched in detail a child being torn from his mother. Unlike the drama of estrangement enacted every day in the workhouse, melodrama created a world in which everyone is related, where in the final scene strangers are revealed to be husband and wife, father and son. One resistance speaker intoned before his audience, "I care not whether you be Whigs, Tories, or Radicals, I claim your attention, demand your sympathy, and lay claim to your support. As Fathers, as Husbands, as Brothers, as Sons, as Friends, as Men, I address you."[111] At this moment in the drama, bodily oppression, physical separation, and class identity are overcome through a sympathetic exchange that is grounded in familial relation; ultimately, the suppressed voice is heard to say—"My father."[112] Both participants and spectators become members of a patriarchal family (fathers, husbands, brothers, sons), a now fully operational sympathetic unit. Near the end of one of his speeches, Reverend Bull looked into his audience and said: "I hear the suppressed but powerful and Heaven rending moan of the widow, of the fatherless, and of the friendless, saying 'Lord! how long?' and I hear the responsive sympathy of thousands who echo back the cry 'Lord! how long?'"[113] As Charles Dickens apparently understood as well, under the New Poor Law, poor people were always orphans and bastards, while under the law of melodrama, all people were family. Oastler entitled his periodical *The Home, the Altar, the Throne, and the Cottage.* The string of appositives here emphasizes their synonymous nature.

Even the Poor Law commissioners were considered family, but as in stage melodrama, they embodied the villainous sons or brothers who disrupt the family lineage and must be purged just as surely as the hero must be welcomed home. The resistance cast doubt on these men who were now considered to be their brothers by labeling them "those mean wretches" who "thus openly outrage every solemn and sacred tie of brotherhood among mankind."[114] Or alternatively, they cast them as the pimps, the sexual speculators on the market, who authorize "the first designing villain, (say a nephew or younger brother) . . . to undertake the ruin" of a daughter pauper.[115] Even here, however, one should note that family roles are still named. In this way, the commissioners were held intimately responsible for the disruption of the hierarchical lineages that were the traditional basis for connection between the peoples within England and Wales.

Melodrama identifies a family member as the source of evil in order to hold him or her responsible according to the rules and regulations of patriarchy. Furthermore, by transforming the villain into a family member, the melodramatic mode can render familiar institutional oppression, holding some recognizable body accountable for what otherwise seems to be disembodied aggression delivered in a bureaucratic prose devoid of a subject or agent. The three unknown, unelected commissioners in distant London, who were free from parliamentary oversight, seemed to many of the new law's opponents comparable to "the invisible hand" of the market that was supposed to regulate henceforward the lives of the poor. Chadwick had especially approved of this administrative independence precisely because it protected the overseers and the Boards of Guardians from "blind sympathy" or electoral bribery. From the perspective of the opposition, however, the commission epitomized the private realm from which the poor (and their supporters) were excluded. These three men formed "a banded conspiracy" that secretly plotted to disinherit the pauper.[116] As in a stage melodrama, the melodramatic mode exposed secret plots and plotters and appealed to the unifying moral absolutes of the audience.

In place of the conniving, secretive administrators, the resistance fashioned a sympathetic chorus of judges: "We appeal to the great tribunal of Public Opinion for its verdict; and we already hear the *united* and mighty sound of twenty millions of voices pronounce—GUILTY!"[117] In this way, the audience could cast out the offending relation, purify the lineage, reform the ranks, and ultimately recognize the pauper as the true heir to his parochial father's beneficence. By constructing a sympathetic audience, by translating class identity into family relation, and by insisting that moral character have public potency, melodrama storms the "bastile" and restores to the social sphere the sentimental relationships and egalitarian moral absolutes that rendered deference communities viable. As a consequence, the melodramatic mode restaged—through speeches, pamphlets, letters to the editor, and in *Oliver Twist*—the Old Poor Laws' representation of personhood.

V

Despite the *Times*'s embrace of the serial *Oliver Twist*, the potency of Dickens's critique of the Poor Laws in the novel, like much of his social commentary, was from the beginning discredited by his readers, usually because they focused on the narrative's apparent inaccuracies. For instance, one critic in the *Spectator* complained that even in those "earlier workhouse scenes," which were intended "to chime in with the popular clamour against the New Poor-Law . . . Boz has combined the severity of the new system with the individual tyranny of the old."[118] To a certain degree, this discrepancy is present in the novel. Dickens's characterization of Bumble the Beadle, who appears to be the object of this complaint, is anachronistic, since the beadle was a parochial appointment who was relieved of his Poor Law duties when the new law reorganized individual parishes into unions.[119]

Dickens's historical imprecisions have also generated confusion and impatience among twentieth-century critics. F. M. L. Thompson, perhaps likewise confused by Bumble's presence, suggests that *Oliver Twist* took place "in a pre-1834 setting," while Peter Fairclough in his appendix to the novel's Penguin edition contends that by the time Oliver was nine and returned to the workhouse from Mrs. Mann's care the new law had been put into operation.[120] Such ambiguities of chronology, which remain unexplained in the book, seem to many critics to underscore Dickens's general indifference to the Poor Law debate. James Brown, for example, complains that Dickens's scenes in the workhouse are merely tokenism: "Social criticism is embodied in self-contained passages . . . almost arbitrarily dropped into the casually unified mix of melodrama, sentimentality, and comedy."[121] Thomas Leitch airs a similar condemnation of Dickens's intent when he argues that Oliver's gentlemanly lineage uncovered at the end of the novel blunts the force of Dickens's message: "Oliver's sociohistorical or journalistic status as figure for the helpless poor ill accords with his status as the naturally good, because naturally well-born, half-brother of Monks."[122]

Despite these critics' complaints, which are usually supported by the observation that *Oliver Twist*'s plot abruptly leaves the workhouse behind, the novel shares much with the contemporary debate about the Poor Law Amendment Act of 1834. Most probably, Dickens was no more fuzzy about the details of the new law's bureaucratic features than were most people during its earliest years of operation, when the new law was at best inconsistently implemented and imperfectly understood. Dickens had at least heard of the new workhouses and their regimentation, and the law's premises provide the foundation for the novel's trenchant criticism of the new law, not the old. During the scene in which Oliver faces the board for the first time, Dickens refers to the board's "decision" made "that very day" to institute what appears to be the workhouse test (p. 54). This reference suggests that Oliver appears before the board soon after the act was passed in 1834, as Fairclough has argued. Bumble's cruelty, perhaps, does not so much represent Dickens's confused use of the "individual tyranny" of the old law, but rather enacts a melodramatic technique, which should by now be familiar, that personifies the institutional repressions of the New Poor Law. Although Bumble's anachronistic role as beadle certainly signifies a Dickensian gesture to the past, it is one of numerous gestures in the narrative toward an ideological past, a past most often invoked for its patriarchal connections and most often symbolized by the rural parish and its occupants. Moreover, Oliver's brotherhood with the proprietary gentleman Monks does not bluntly reveal, as Leitch and others have contended, Dickens's hypocritical yearning for a bourgeois identity, a class standing, but rather, in the iconography of melodrama, an almost visceral resistance to the breakup of the patriarchal family brought on by the new law's edicts. More often than not, *Oliver Twist*, like the Old Price Wars preceding it, protests against the concept and implementation of class.[123]

Oliver Twist, then, can be seen as a full participant in the contemporary melodramatic response to the new law, for throughout the narrative, this novel confronts, via the techniques of the melodramatic mode, the issues of personal identity, social status, and public relationship that the New Poor Law had altered throughout the country but had most graphically reorganized in its "bastiles." Like the Poor Law debate itself, the novel oscillates between the two conflicting definitions of identity offered by status hierarchies and classificatory categories. These two contrasting types of subjectivity are represented as two cultural spaces between which Oliver is continually and helplessly shuttled.[124]

When placing *Oliver Twist* amid the contemporary discussion regarding pauperism, I do not intend thereby to grant it a privileged status in the historical debate, claiming for it some preeminent aesthetic resolution of ideological conflicts that other texts and speeches of the Poor Law resistance failed to achieve. In truth, the novel never seems fully to resolve the particular conflicts that shape it, conflicts that, more than any cosmetic similarities, place it firmly within its time and place. First produced in serial form, then published later as a complete text, *Oliver Twist* muddied the already murky waters of the publishing market. A social diatribe and a story, a narrative with discursive adaptations of theatrical techniques, the text not only encompasses the contemporary debate between the old law and the new, but additionally evokes what might be called the debate between melodrama and the novel. Indeed, *Oliver Twist* indicates that these two seemingly dissimilar debates were, in fact, part of the same cultural argument.

The gradual erection of the generic boundaries between the novel and melodrama at this time seems to constitute another contemporary instance of the principle of classification and its radically transformative demarcations between the public and private spheres. Unlike stage melodrama, the novel was deriving its cultural distinctiveness through its association with procedures of privatization. In the realm of reception, the practice of novel reading was quickly becoming seen as an alternative to public attendance at theaters, while in the realm of production the battle for literary copyright, which was often centered on novels and novelists, resulted in an extension of the reach of private property and proprietary subjectivity. Furthermore, as D. A. Miller has contended, the Victorian novel's form and content, its containment of ideology and plot, implicitly contributed to the constitution of this private, proprietary and decidedly bourgeois subject. The Victorian novel, as modern critics have frequently argued, is both an instrument and a product as well as, less regularly, a critic of class society, and some writers, including Dickens, seem to have stumbled on this insight. The novel form at this time could thus be seen to share some crucial effects with the New Poor Law, for both law and genre attested to the spread of a classificatory paradigm that reified privacy, property, and class.

In fact, in *Oliver Twist*, novels are often depicted as agents of the same malign forces that are in operation at the workhouse and are therefore explicitly countered by the melodramatic content of the narrative. As a representative of class thinking, the novel as genre becomes a villainous figure in the melodramatic mode's reactionary symbolism. In the middle of *Oliver Twist*, Dickens directly, if only momentarily, addresses this contemporary debate about the respective cultural functions of the novel and the melodrama during a self-conscious discussion of his own authorial method.

Soon after Oliver has been recaptured by Fagin's gang, Dickens explicitly invokes melodrama. He pauses in his story long enough to discuss "the custom on the stage, in all good murderous melodramas." Although ostensibly a jocular defense of his narrative's abrupt transition from Oliver's capture in London to Bumble's clownish duties in the parish of Oliver's birth, this invocation of melodrama articulates Dickens's anxious awareness not just of the physical distance between once closely related people in the plot, but of a parallel critical distance that might arise between himself and his reading public. Speaking directly to them in this passage, Dickens reveals to his audience both his hopes and fears for this project. After describing the shifting scenes of a generic melodrama, Dickens writes:

Such changes appear absurd; but they are not so unnatural as they would seem at first sight. The transitions in real life from well-spread boards to death-beds, and from mourning weeds to holiday garments, are not a whit less startling; only, there, we are busy actors, instead of passive lookers-on, which makes a vast difference. (P. 169)

This "vast difference" between participation and spectatorship, Dickens suggests, can result in the kind of distance that causes "passive lookers-on" to condemn a performance "as outrageous and preposterous." According to this logic, then, the actors in *Oliver Twist* could be accused of absurdity, if not worse, because they perform before even more disparate and passive audiences than are encountered in a theater—audience members who read in private, often alone in their own homes. In evoking such criticism, Dickens thus confronts the possibility that his own novel might invite an accusation of empty theatricality, an accusation, as we have seen, that was pervasive in the 1830's and 1840's. In other words, his novel might well encourage and thus further the sort of distancing criticisms that arise in a society structured by privatization, social dispersal, and emotional alienation as he felt England in the 1830's promised to be. In writing his novel, he could become, in effect, Oliver's jailer rather than his rescuer. Just as the principle of classification instituted under the New Poor Law disrupted traditional modes of social exchange, divided the public, and reconstituted personhood, so might writing fiction for perusal in the private home facilitate the dispersal of community and inhibit the public exchanges of "social feeling" that Dickens so valued in the melodramatic performance.

The strategies of the melodramatic mode at work in *Oliver Twist*, as Dickens argues above and as I will elaborate below, do strive to break down the barriers between the readers and the characters in the novel, symbolically forestalling, as opponents of the new law had done, the critical distance and emotional forbearance of spectatorship. Lord Melbourne, the Whig prime minister who oversaw the passage of the New Poor Law, confided to Queen Victoria his low opinion of *Oliver Twist*, an opinion that attests to the novel's relative mastery over this crucial reader: "I don't *like* those things; I wish to avoid them in *reality*, and therefore I don't wish them represented."[125] Under the New Poor Law, as Melbourne no doubt knew, the rich could avoid looking at and having feelings about poverty, crime, and prostitution, but Dickens restaged this law's representation of the public poor before the private rich, forcing Melbourne to confront their reality.

Sitting as it does in the midst of a novel, however, this invocation of melodrama cannot wholly overcome the imputed incarcerating effects of its vehicle, as Dickens himself at times seems to realize. Once transmitted into print and then transported to the novel reader, the melodramatic mode in *Oliver Twist* operates at a disadvantage, deploying its performative strategies in an insistently untheatrical setting. Melodrama is thus seen by Dickens as the best available means to overcome social division and yet potentially susceptible to the aesthetic evaluations that are the product of the reading public's critical distance; the cure may turn out to be just another symptom. It is a tension that permeates Dickens's project to the very end.[126] It is also a succinct articulation of the melodramatic mode's continual susceptibility to co-optation by the features of market culture it most seeks to compromise.

Dickens's adoption of this popular theatrical style for the defense of sympathetic community and a passing theatricalized public sphere cannot entirely resolve another tension, a biographical one, that becomes apparent when one remembers the author's activist role in the copyright movement and his eager desire to define and be identified with the serious novel.[127] At the very moment when the publication of *Oliver Twist* expressed the novelist's deep, perhaps subconscious, reservations about the social and psychological impact of the novel form, Dickens was yearning to acquire the legal and cultural status of a middle-class professional. In this regard, Dickens was not unique. Just as passages adopting the melodramatic mode's syntax of deference and obligation sit alongside paragraphs articulating class contention in the *Northern Star*, so Dickens found in melodrama an emotionally coherent and incisive language through which to express his longing for a passing era even while jockeying for position in a new one. Similarly, melodrama and the melodramatic mode were often adopted later in the century by liberals otherwise intent on furthering the principles of class society. The melodramatic mode can be seen to be a stinging critique, developed through its dissonant relation to market culture, but its practitioners, living in and through the passage of time, subjects of and to uneven development, were often drawn to its expressiveness without wholly adhering to all of its implications.

In the chapters surrounding his brief discussion of melodrama, Dickens seems preoccupied with the drastic and substantive difference between melodramatic performance and novel reading. When he returns to Oliver after his interpolated reflection on melodrama and brief detour with Bumble, he stages a contrasting scenario of private reading in which he appears to map out the interrelations between the modern principle of classification and the effects of novel reading, both of which seem to reconstitute individual identity and to exacerbate social consensus in his text. Having been consigned once more to Fagin's world, the site of class identity in this novel, Oliver is put to bed in a locked room. Fagin provides the little boy with a book in which the "history of the lives and trials of great criminals" are classified, a narrative genre that mimics the novel form at this time. Only after snuffing the candle does he begin to read these narratives of "secret murders," hidden "bodies," and lonely men whose isolation leads them to crime (p. 196). Dickens never comes closer to depicting the inner consciousness of Oliver than he does during this scene of imprisoned reading in the dark. Furthermore, throughout the rest of the story, the closest approximations to representations of individual consciousness—Sikes's escape from the murder scene and Fagin's last hours—will look most like the accounts of secrecy and haunted conscience outlined in this anatomy of criminals. In this passage, Dickens explicitly contrasts the solitary reader Oliver, a "poor outcast boy who had never known the love of friends or kindred," to those who possess a relational identity within a community and family (p. 197). Unlike such people, Oliver is shown to be susceptible to criminal temptations precisely because of the isolated and enclosed subjectivity that private reading engenders.[128] Left to itself, such a subject is subject to everything.

As a collection of narratives, the catalogue of criminals epitomizes both the promise and peril of the private reading site in mid-nineteenth-century England; it figures the irresolvable conflict between melodrama and the novel that shapes Dickens's own larger narrative in *Oliver Twist*. At first glance, the catalogue seems to take on the traditional regulative function of a state spectacle, such as hanging, which was considered at the time to act as an agent of discipline. By viewing the brutal end of the villain, the public was to be shown the disincentives for crime. Indeed, criminal catalogues like *The Newgate Calendar* were structured to climax at the scene of hanging for this very purpose. The authors of a nineteenth-century edition of *The Newgate Calendar* emphasize the moral importance of the final hanging scene by paraphrasing "an able commentator on our criminal laws": "Punishment should succeed the crime as immediately as possible, if we intend that, in the rude minds of the multitude, the picture of the crime shall instantly awaken the attendant idea of punishment."[129]

Although the motivating force of such spectacles of punishment was coercion, the moral and material impact of these public punishments can be aligned with what I have described as the effects of melodrama. Both activities presumed the communicative power of the performance, its capacity to both generate and transfer moral value through a theatricalized exchange with its audience. In this regard, both are remnants of an eighteenth-century culture grounded in participatory theatricality. Initially, Oliver's reading material does sound like the standard plots of contemporary stage melodrama. Perpetrators of hidden evil are eventually exposed; bodies once buried in pools of water bob to the surface in passages that look like classic melodramatic scenes of exposure:

Here, he read of dreadful crimes that made the blood run cold; of secret murders that had been committed by the lonely wayside; of bodies hidden from the eye of man in deep pits and wells: which would not keep them down, deep as they were, but had yielded them up at last, after many years, and so maddened the murderers with the sight, that in their horror they had confessed their guilt, and yelled for the gibbet to end their agony. (P. 196)

Seemingly, the evil is made public and the villain is found out.

And yet a modern audience is more tempted to read psychoanalytic figures in these sentences, almost justifiably so, for they uncannily prefigure the emergent content of nineteenth-century personhood that later becomes the raw materials for psychoanalysis. The bobbing bodies in this passage are more closely equivalent to the silent monitor of thought that the old Cumberland beggar becomes in Wordsworth's poem, for they haunt the conscience of the criminal rather than reveal to the public at large the providential social order; these bodies are props in a mental theater. As the preface to *The Newgate Calendar* indicates, "*The picture* of the crime shall instantly awaken the attendant *idea* of punishment" (italics added). Rather than the standard vocabulary of melodramatic motivation, such as evil and villainy, Dickens uses what might be called the more psychic language of guilt and shame, the internal feelings of private subjectivity. And in place of the social tribunal of exposure and swift condemnation advocated in *The Newgate Calendar*, these criminals themselves encounter the surfacing bodies and call out for their own hanging—a classic trope for the return of the repressed and yet another sign of the internalization of morality. These narratives are not melodrama, nor, most important, are they the moral equivalent of a public hanging.

In fact, as Dickens is careful to imply, the narratives that Oliver reads are not seen to promise deterrence, like a public hanging, but enticement. Dickens depicts Fagin locking Oliver in the room with the book, notes the book's well-thumbed pages, and has the young boy fling it from his side as he prays for protection from its temptations. Although Oliver responds to the text as a warning, he is clearly seen to be unique in this regard, for one can presume that the pages were well thumbed by Fagin's gang and that Fagin himself hoped the book would have a similar impact on his newest charge.

According to the figurative logic in this scene, reading is depicted as constitutive of the private subject, here seen as intrinsically imprisoned and unenlightened; both, in turn, are linked to murder, the deepest expression of antagonized social relationship: "The terrible descriptions were so real and vivid, that the sallow pages seemed to turn red with gore; and the words upon them, to be sounded in his ears, as if they were whispered, in hollowed murmurs, by the spirits of the dead" (pp. 196–97). In this scenario, Dickens imagines the private subject as an internalized form of crime and punishment. Conscience is experienced as incarceration, a harrowing rendition of the psyche Bentham's panopticon sought to create.[130]

Oliver's sojourn with the catalogue of criminals seems to encapsulate the transitional moment that Foucault writes of in *Discipline and Punish*, when the mission of criminal narratives oscillates uneasily between warning and welcome. This "moment" marks a crisis in visual transmission in general and in the impact of criminal spectacle on its audience in particular, especially, of course, when the spectacle has become textual.[131] Ultimately, then, the catalogue's impact addresses the anxieties attendant on sympathetic exchange in a market culture of private interests and private transactions, including reading. The mediated relationship between the text and the individuated reader, a process dissociated from the moral consensus of an audience, was seen to encourage self-reflexive identification and, in the social sphere, egomaniacal self-aggrandizement. The sympathetic tear of sentimental fiction had become the murderous intent of the Newgate tales.

Taken out of the narrative context, the relations that Dickens draws among novel reading, private subjectivity, and insidious procedures of control and classification seem to anticipate D. A. Miller's argument in *The Novel and the Police.*[132] Dickens, however, does not invoke melodrama in chapter 17 in order to facilitate the project of novel reading and thus to imprison Oliver in the darkened domain of private subjectivity. Rather, with melodramatic techniques, Dickens hopes to continue the long defense of his popular subject matter and style that he had launched in his preface; in so doing, he also stages Oliver's escape from Fagin's "bastile," the site of private reading. Unlike its previous perusers, Oliver resists the temptations of the catalogue of criminals by enacting a classic melodramatic pose: he prays to heaven for aid, "to spare him from such deeds" (p. 197). In stage melodrama, such prayers are customarily viewed by the audience as a coded plea for its sympathy. In this scene, Oliver thus emotionally projects a deferential relationship in the vacuum of the bedroom. He solicits the "familial" benevolence and protection he lacks.

As a frequent visitor to the popular theaters in London, Dickens well knew that melodramas had the capacity to overcome "the vast difference" between "mere spectators" and "busy actors" that novels threatened to exacerbate. Through their narratives of patriarchal dissolution and reunion, melodramas involved audiences in their scenes of revelation, recognition, and reconciliation. Actors not only spoke directly to the audience, but encouraged its response and thus broke down the fourth wall that was becoming crucial to the design of Victorian "high" drama. Because Dickens could not enact *Oliver Twist* in the theater, he did the next, if distantly best, thing; he invoked both melodrama and its principles in the midst of his narrative.

Like a melodramatic actor, he spoke directly to his reading audience, thereby encouraging its participation even as he described to them a model for such participation. As a "good murderous melodrama," *Oliver Twist* was, ideally, to transform the members of Dickens's audience into "busy actors" undivided by critical distance, who then experienced patriarchal bonds and social feeling within a formerly fragmenting audience of private subjects. By means of its melodramatic techniques, *Oliver Twist* creates a hitch within the powerful advance of the modern principle of classification, including the classification of the Victorian novel as an ideologically totalitarian form.[133] The early workhouse scenes in *Oliver Twist* evoke the most timely instance of classification and therefore inaugurate Dickens's book-length melodramatic response to this relatively new social force and its radical reconstitution of the self.

Having been born an orphan with unknown parentage, Oliver could conceivably have been "the child of a nobleman or a beggar," if identified according to the ranks within a status hierarchy, but because he is born into the workhouse, his familial origins matter little; instead, he is "badged and ticketed, and [falls] into his place at once—a parish child—the orphan of a workhouse—the humble half-starved drudge" (p. 47). In these first scenes, Dickens demonstrates how the new law replaces patriarchal identity with class identity and neighbors within a community with disembodied abstractions. To Oliver the pauper, who is incapable of bureaucratic thought, the beadle is a hat, while the Board of Guardians is a table (p. 52).

Despite Oliver's hasty departure from the workhouse, he does not escape from the "bastile" of classification once he becomes apprenticed to Mr. Sowerberry, the coffin maker. Instead, Oliver witnesses the effects of Poor Law legislation when he goes to a tenement house to collect the body of a mother. This tableau of a separated and disoriented family echoes Oliver's own early experience of separation. After this incident, Oliver soon makes a daring escape from Sowerberry, but it merely lands him in the company of Fagin's gang—yet another cell within the prison of modern classification. The New Poor Law is thereby shown to be only one manifestation of a pervasive classificatory impulse at this time.

Dickens's most infamous recasting in *Oliver Twist* is his transformation of the kindly Bob Fagin of Warren's Blacking Factory into Fagin the receiver of stolen goods. Bob Fagin was a co-worker of Dickens during his childhood tenure as a manual laborer at his cousin's business. Rather than being an authorial act of vengeance against the boy who, Dickens later recalled, almost exposed Dickens's poverty by walking him home to his boarding room one night, this transformation enables Dickens to portray all market relations as criminal ones.[134] In place of the generous camaraderie of Bob, which had emphasized Dickens's class affiliation, Fagin, as archetypal Jew, epitomizes the criminal antagonism inherent in the market's class relations. In *Oliver Twist*, in fact, all "working-class" people are members of a criminal class, not primarily because Dickens thought poor people were all thieves and swindlers, but because once people are classed according to their market functions, as the poorer classes were by the utilitarian reformers, the connections among them are perceived as mercenary, confrontational, radically anticommunal, and, inevitably, criminal. The premises of classification were believed to perpetrate the new criminalized category, the working class, and therefore, as was seen during the Old Price Wars, classification was itself deemed a crime. Fagin's much-quoted discussion with Noah Claypole exposes the fallacy of a class collectivity built out of economic function: "The more you value your number one, the more careful you must be of mine; so we come at last to what I told you at first—that a regard for number one holds us all together" (p. 388).[135]

Whereas Oliver ultimately goes home to a family structured according to patriarchal tenets, Fagin, Sikes, and their Poor Law counterpart Bumble go "home" to the "bastiles"—the prison, the gibbet, and the workhouse, respectively. Although Sikes's public hanging may at first appear to be Dickens's desperate bid for the benefits of a traditional social spectacle, it is, like the criminals in the catalogue who call out for their punishment, a self-inflicted death, as much a result of Sikes's flight from his own tortured conscience as from the crowd that pursues him. Sikes, Bumble, and Fagin have internalized the hedonistic calculus, which for Dickens was tantamount to a private subjectivity that is always criminal and inevitably organized along lines of panoptic surveillance.[136] They, therefore, become for Dickens the only appropriate subjects in his story for what modern critics label "psychological realism." In some sense, a private psyche becomes Sikes's punishment for his crime against patriarchal, familial relationships—his brutal murder of his common-law wife. Like the narratives of hidden bodies that resurface to torment the murderer in Oliver's book, like the hidden supervisor in a panopticon, Nancy's eyes haunt Sikes's journey through the English countryside. Significantly, the only explicit relief to this solitary confinement of the psyche occurs when Sikes is in a public setting, cooperating with others to put out a fire, as if he were a member of their community. It is a brief moment from which Sikes ultimately flees. During Sikes's otherwise harrowing journey, Dickens's third-person narration momentarily impersonates his character's interior voice, as if to emphasize the murderer's psychic isolation.[137] Similarly, Dickens dramatizes Fagin's final hours by representing his private thoughts, which, like all such displays of consciousness in this novel, are simply an internalization of the prison: Fagin "continued to mutter, without appearing conscious of their presence otherwise than as a part of his vision" (p. 472). *Oliver Twist* displaces the public hangings of a more theatrical past and puts in their place scenes of incarcerated dementia. The incorporation of the gaol warden as internal vision—the silent monitor of one's thoughts—fulfills the outcome promised by Bentham's panopticon.

Fagin's gang therefore embodies the constitutive features of market culture—its adversarial social exchange, its classification and specialization of labor, its perversion of the patriarchal family, and, most crucially, its creation of a subjectivity that is, for Dickens, always self-torturing, like the self-regulating subjectivities produced in the workhouse. From the perspective of Dickens as well as members of the anti–Poor Law movement, the panoptic procedures of the modern principle of classification did not eradicate, as promised, the mystery surrounding alien beings such as the poor. Rather, by enforcing the internalization of surveillance, such procedures created the mysterious and criminal privacy of the self-conscious, alienated subject.

Fagin's lair, a microcosm of capitalist society, serves in the novel as the scene of familial estrangement and private conspiracy from which melodrama's plot traditionally begins. It is at this point in the story that many critics of the novel direct their complaints concerning Dickens's social commentary. Because they do not theorize the function of melodrama or adhere to a historically specific class analysis, critics have faulted what they perceive as Dickens's cowardly decision to "domesticate" and thus privatize social ills. Once Monks appears, one observer characteristically argues, "Oliver has become a different kind of victim—not a social victim of the workhouse, nor of the poverty which can lead to a life of crime, but the object of a specific malevolence [Monks's] very different from society's general indifference and scorn."[138]

Certainly the entrance of Monks alters the representation of Oliver's victimization, but it does not subtract social significance from the equation. Rather, Monks plays a major part in the melodramatic mode's complication of the smooth operation of the principle of classification and its alienating consequences in *Oliver Twist*. Through his characterization of Monks, Dickens gives a familial body and therefore integral place in the patriarchal lineage to what had been an alien and disembodied idea of social oppression. Monks, in effect, replaces the beadle's hat and the guardian's board and becomes the archetypal and highly visible villain of melodrama. The role of Monks does not in fact erase Dickens's criticism of the Poor Law, but translates the law's bureaucratic discourse—its statistical analysis, its calculation of quantitative need, and its evasive agency—into the syntax of patriarchal bonds and responsibilities, a rhetoric through which Dickens can condemn Monks according to a value system he both understands and generally embraces; at the very least, it provides an emotionally compelling solution to contemporary instances of disinterestedness and objectivity. In place of the distant Poor Law commission in London, the "invisible hand" of the market, or even fate, the melodramatic mode insists that social relationships must be described and judged in terms of the public yet familial relationships and codes of behavior characteristic of patriarchal status hierarchies.

In *Oliver Twist*, public reputations and their visible information thus become crucial to the reestablishment of patriarchal ties in the social sphere. The hideous disease that disfigures Monks's face—"an index even to [his] mind"—and the confession he gives are the tangible signs that reveal to the audience his evil character and his ethical brotherhood with Fagin's gang (p. 439). This recognition justifies his ejection from Oliver's family. In melodrama, the final recognition of patriarchal relation and the recognition of ethical relation are one and the same, for only through the channels of patriarchal, performative exchange can character be identified. Not until Monks publicly identifies himself as Edward Leeford and Oliver as his brother can he be condemned. Similarly, Oliver's and Rose's sweet countenances reveal their familial as well as ethical relationship to one another;

these relationships thus replace Oliver's class relationships with Fagin and Sikes. As with that of the villainous Monks, the initial description of Rose translates into prose the performative codes of melodramatic character embodiment. Unlike Fagin's first appearance in the novel, where his body, half cast in shadow, suggests concealment and duplicity, Rose is pure light, formal expressiveness, and tangible virtue: "Cast in so slight and exquisite a mould; . . . The very intelligence that shone in her deep blue eyes, and was stamped upon her noble head, seemed scarcely of her age, or of the world" (p. 264).

According to this melodramatic symbolism of family relation, Monks's hatred of Oliver should not be seen as personal or psychological—as a private matter—but as a corruption of the patriarchal bond that ensues when the market intercedes. Hence the language of inheritance, not personal animosity, must govern Monks's words when he finally speaks, even though these words ultimately reveal his capitalist soul. Instead of inheriting his father's heart, Monks inherits from his father a market relationship, a "prior claim upon his purse" (p. 458). And instead of an honorable public reputation, visible to all through acts of social obligation, his mother "bequeathed these secrets" to him (p. 459). From this tainted lineage, Monks gains a legacy of hatred for familial ties and an affection for private contractual relationships such as the one he devises with Fagin. As punishment for his lack of filial feeling, Monks undergoes at the end of the novel "a long confinement for some fresh act of fraud and knavery . . . and die[s] in prison" (p. 476). Having served his melodramatic purpose as the villain brother, Monks is finally banished from the realm of melodrama and consigned, along with Fagin and Sikes, to the "state" of private subjectivity.

As "the principle of Good surviving through every adverse circumstance," Oliver, in contrast to Monks, resists what most modern critics identify as the "realistic" portrayal of private subjectivity that becomes the fate of Sikes and Fagin (p. 33). With Oliver locked in Fagin's workhouselike hideout, Dickens could have depicted the torture of the boy's private consciousness, but instead he shows Oliver groping for the relational identity that physical proximity to others makes possible: Oliver "would crouch in the corner of the passage by the street-door, to be as near living people as he could" (p. 179). And later in the novel, rather than suggesting that Oliver, like Monks, conceal his true nature through plots of deception and disguise, Dickens depicts Oliver turning to Rose and Mrs. Maylie after recovering from his gunshot wound. Here, like a true melodramatic performer playing to the balcony, he offers to "show his gratitude" (p. 285). He expresses his desire to perform those "habitual acts" of errand running, those public displays of deferential feeling that

Chadwick abhorred; he thereby renders his character visible to those who would otherwise be uncertain.

Oliver embodies melodrama's insistence that virtue knows no class or, for that matter, blood. The classification of virtue under the New Poor Law granted to the upper classes the privilege of defining virtue's characteristics. In this way, the new law participated in a more widespread trend to doubly privatize morality—to remove it from the public sphere and, further, to attribute its origins to individual conscience, and thus to construct a distinctive, historically specific type of private subjectivity.[139] Rather than inherently possessing virtue, the lower classes thus needed to be instructed in it by their "betters." By contrast, because status was not psychologized, Oliver simply is good, even without any early form of virtuous instruction, be it in the workhouse school or the school of hard knocks.[140]

Not a pauper, not even primarily a proprietary gentleman, Oliver becomes a brother and a son. This traditional romance element in melodrama, in which the "pauper" becomes a "prince," should not be read in terms of class betrayal, since in this final portion of the novel, in the geographic space of rural England, identity is not primarily constituted in terms of class. In melodrama's symbolic economy, insofar as Oliver inherits a patriarchal identity and retains his good character, he demonstrates the continued viability of a culture organized in terms of idealized status hierarchies, not economic classes. In this culture, the poor will be recognized and welcomed home; in this culture, the scene of relief under the Old Poor Laws will continue to dramatize the exchange of social feelings. Paupers become princes only if they always have been.

Although the melodramatic mode plots the return of a society organized around a patriarchal family and its extended version in status hierarchies, it should always be remembered that it idealizes and thus revises to some extent that culture by purifying its lineages. The melodramatic mode of Dickens, of Bull, and other opponents to the New Poor Law eschews both utilitarian classification and the Whiggish "Old Corruption" of mere blood ties in which aristocrats bestowed favors and offices on other aristocrats. More often than not, these two forces seemed one and the same.[141] Estranged families reunite instead along primarily ethical lines that nonetheless seem dependent on the ideological coherence of the principle of blood lineage. In keeping with this logic, Monks must go to America, while Oliver's bigamist father and unmarried mother are just as well dead. Rose Maylie's fate best exemplifies this melodramatic narrative. Rose's connection with her sister's adultery could have tainted her public reputation, but melodrama privileges an ethical lineage while still superimposing it on an existing bloodline so that

Rose is not so much Alice's sister as she is Oliver's "sister." Similarly, Oliver is not so much his father's son as the recipient of Mr. Brownlow's patronage. Oliver's inheritance affirms his patriarchal/ethical identity, which is a melodramatic conflation that contrasts with both a revisionist class affiliation and an unreconstructed blood tie. Its conditions guarantee that the son, like any son within a status hierarchy, must be widely known to be good. He will inherit the money "only on the stipulation that in his minority he should never have stained his name with any public act of dishonour, meanness, cowardice, or wrong" (p. 458).[142] Stage melodrama and the melodramatic mode in Dickens's novel align ethical absolutes with the absolutes of patriarchal relationships in order to establish a familiar-because-customary form of exchange that can compel the recognition of moral ties among their dispersed audiences.

In keeping with a critical tradition that reads melodrama as a quintessential expression of the evolving civilization of the bourgeoisie, Northrop Frye has described these bonding effects of melodrama as "the advance propaganda for the police state, in so far as that represents the regularizing of mob violence."[143] In this formulation, Frye connects melodrama with mob violence and mob violence with the police. Unlike D. A. Miller, who associates the police with a wide range of "social controls" exerted against "the mob," Frye imagines the police to be a more civilized version of that mob, a step in the cultural progression of the middle class. Frye's rendition of melodrama, despite his dissimilar definition of the police, tends to keep Miller's critique of the Victorian novel intact. In this reading, melodrama becomes yet another punitive structure within the totalizing architecture of the novel.

Frye's characterization of melodrama, however, is essentially ahistorical and, when applied to the 1830's, anachronistic. The bourgeoisification of Victorian England is an unarguable fact in the historical record, but its ultimate dominance, seen in retrospect, should not result in the erasure of alternative formulations of social order. Indeed, the historical record documents the existence of a melodramatic mode that was affiliated neither with the police nor with mob violence. The increased interest in building regional police forces during the 1830's was a direct retaliation against the mob violence of agrarian unrest. Many of those who resisted the new law considered these police forces intimately "related to" the patriarchal estrangement and corruption imposed by the New Poor Law. They considered it just another sign of aristocratic benefactors reneging on their responsibilities and forging instead "unnatural" familial alliances that excluded their humbler relations. One commentator, expressing the melodramatic rhetoric of family relation, refers to "two such pests as the New Poor-Law and the Rural Police-Law (the latter is only the *bastard* of the former)."[144] Such connotations are applied to the urban police as well. Indeed, in Dickens's plot, the Bow-Street detectives, Blathers and Duff, are represented as a momentary threat to Oliver's admission into the Maylie family; they could, in effect, imprison him once more in a society dominated by class antagonism.

For a crucial moment in *Oliver Twist*, the crowd that pursues Bill Sikes to Jacob's Island is neither a barbaric version of the police, affiliated with Blathers and Duff, nor the stereotypical demoralized mob who stormed the original Bastille in Paris, but a mob whose members, through melodrama, had become ethically related: "It seemed as though the whole city had poured its population out to curse him" (p. 450). And yet Dickens cannot maintain this vision for long. Soon into his narrative of the mob's pursuit, Dickens loses sight of his characters. He writes vaguely of an "old gentleman" standing on the bridge, whom the reader can only surmise is Mr. Brownlow (p. 451). By offering a reward for the capture of a living Sikes, this gentleman attempts to civilize the mob, but at that very moment this deafening and deaf mob becomes "dreadful" as it nearly suffocates individuals who have failed to "extricate themselves from the mass" (p. 451).[145] At the close of this scene, the reader is left with a thoroughly "modern" urban landscape, one inhabited by anarchic mobs and suicidal criminals. Moreover, Dickens is left with a scene in which he, as narrator, becomes the accusatory "passive looker-on" whose distance from his own characters places him that much nearer a class society. If melodrama promises a grand scene of escape from panoptic structures, in this novel it nonetheless seems incapable of preventing those escapees from merging with the lawless mob. The story of the melodramatic mode often ends in this way; although an internally logical and powerful expression of rhetorical and behavioral resistance to market culture, its resistant energy rarely succeeds in substantively transforming the processes of classification, privatization, and competitive exchange that were altering the social terrain of England.

Within a theater, where the crowds were immense and yet entirely visible both to the actors and among themselves, melodrama could stage the familial reunion of its audience. However, within London of the 1830's, a city of unimaginable vastness to its inhabitants, even *Oliver Twist*'s melodrama seems overwhelmed by its innumerable and dispersed audiences.[146] Perhaps Dickens's apparently unintentional concession to melodrama's limitations accounts for the Bow Street detectives' curious story of Conkey Chickweed, a story that seems at first nothing more than comic relief (pp. 278–80). In urban London, melodrama cannot guarantee to its audience members unobstructed knowledge of their neighbors, and consequently, the anxieties haunting the operation of the Old Poor Laws reappear in the margins of the narrative. Pretending to be a victim of theft, Conkey is in fact the thief, just like those paupers of the Old Poor Laws who robbed the rich of their sympathy (and charity) through dramas of insincerity. It is strange urban neighbors like Conkey or even Dodger who created the need for detectives such as Blathers and Duff and, by extension, fictions of detection like those soon to be written by Dickens himself.[147] One might argue that the courtroom scene in *Oliver Twist*, during which the Dodger comes to justice, is a prototype of Dickens's later fictions of detection (pp. 394–96). Dodger, like Conkey, is an urban impostor who pretends in court to be a gentleman. His detection, like that of a pauper capitalist, requires the most sophisticated machinery of the modern legal bureaucracy—a prosecutor, a cross-examination, a witness and a jury. By contrast, the exposure of Monks follows a melodramatic format. Monks knows his prosecutor, Brownlow, and Monks's deceptions are revealed by visible signs and a confession staged in front of his family.

At the end of the novel, brutalized by urban secrecy and imposture, Oliver's family goes back to the English countryside. It is here that people can still recognize one another in the crowd. And, it was here that the New Poor Law's representation of the poor, conceived by London Utilitarians, seemed so inappropriate. Not surprisingly, Harry Maylie gives up "rank and station" in Whiggish London to become the head of a parish where, instead of the divisive effects of classification, "fancied barriers are leveled" between Rose and himself and no doubt between deferential paupers of the parish and his benevolent ministry (pp. 464, 465). It is significant that Harry Maylie affiliates himself with the parish structure, for his choice emphasizes the particular sort of "nature" idealized in these closing scenes. Unlike the old Cumberland beggar, lost in his own thoughts on a lonely road, Oliver becomes part of a community; this convergence of the Maylies and Mr. Brownlow "thus linked together a little society" (p. 476). In this society, haunted consciousness is replaced by demonstrations of filial loyalty; labor function is replaced by inheritable nature. Brownlow delights in Oliver as "his nature developed itself" (p. 479), revealing itself to be more and more like that of his biological father. To retain the social valence of melodrama in this novel, its rural location must be historicized and linked to the existing parish cultures of the 1830's. By creating unions out of these parishes, the New Poor Law threatened to introduce an urban class culture into a still rural hierarchical country. The melodramatic mode of *Oliver Twist*, like the protests of Parson Bull, the *Times*, and other expressions of anti–Poor Law resistance, responded to this specific danger.

This final familial tableau in *Oliver Twist* has understandably been seen by critics as the unproblematized bourgeois domestic circle of Victorian mythology, a mythology infused with various romantic assumptions regarding a socially evacuated nature.[148] The differences between that myth and the one

I outline above are muted and fragile, and in the novel, the operative distinction between these two ideals is even more arduously maintained. The rural locale of the novel's conclusion can certainly look like a retreat from the public sphere if seen from one perspective, and after all, in later novels Dickens returns continually to the warmth of a domestic hearth. If Harry Maylie and Oliver still seem viable actors in the drama of deferential exchange, Rose's role as melodramatic heroine seems by the end of the novel in dire jeopardy. Described as "shedding on her secluded path in life soft and gentle light, that fell on all who trod it with her, and shone into their hearts," Rose is now confined to "the fireside circle" (p. 479) that delineates the sharp demarcations between the public and private spheres of market culture. Contrary to the figural language of imprintment earlier in the novel that rendered Rose so susceptible to melodramatic representation and public exchanges of sympathy, she now seems an aggressively privatized locus of personal virtues. The classificatory impulse of market culture that melodrama merely forestalls in portions of *Oliver Twist* can be seen manifesting another of its prominent forms at the very end of the novel. Just as the poor had become the object of a classificatory logic premised on labor function, so women were soon to be subsumed into a class of their own, as the next chapter will explore more fully.

The melodramatic mode did storm the "bastile" of Poor Law reform and therefore ushered in a brief era of confusion, if not revolution. Melodrama's version of a status hierarchy, imagined as family, relies on a conception of moral nature divorced from class and only provisionally linked to blood and is thus extremely vulnerable. Insofar as blood ties are deemphasized, insofar as patriarchal terms lose their material antecedents, the melodramatic mode shows signs of its ideological depletion, veering toward pure nostalgia. If moral character is not precisely a function of blood, then what marks the difference within a status hierarchy? Without the physiological ties of blood, without the economic ties of feudal social organization, human beings can seem perilously equal to one another and potentially different from themselves. As one writer of the 1830's mused, "In respect to character, man has the capacity to be anything, and by turns, everything, as circumstances shall determine."[149] In fact, by late 1838, as we see by this quotation, segments of the Poor Law resistance, as manifested in the *Northern Star*, for instance, turned to the discourse of Chartism and the political polemic of universal suffrage. Not surprisingly, church-and-king Tories found themselves estranged once more from their brother radicals, many of whom lived in London or worked in a northern factory, not on a parish farm. These radicals usually dispensed with the language of the melodramatic mode and spoke in the language of class and of the New Poor Law: "The hand of every man is more or less raised against every other man—the interest of every class is opposed to the interest of every other class—and all other interests are in opposition and hostility to the interest of the working man."[150]

After the reforms of the 1830's, battered and weakened, the melodramatic mode was still available to various people in their attempts to resist classification and its private places, but mid-Victorian melodrama found it even more difficult than did Dickens in *Oliver Twist* to fashion a public sphere within an increasingly antagonistic market culture.

FOUR

The Queen's English

Melodramatic Rhetoric in Victoria's England

In the early decades of the nineteenth century, English stage melodramas, such as those written in quantities by Thomas Holcroft or Theodore Hook, had often borrowed their settings from historical or mythic events and exoticized, foreign locations, not least to avoid the suspicion of contemporary political provocation that would inevitably have invited the censor's hand. At this time, the melodramatic heroine shared star billing with a hero and a villain and was often supported by a comic subplot that by the drama's end helped to fill the stage with players. By the mid–nineteenth century, however, melodrama on and off the stage seemed to narrow its range, becoming less politically partisan and more domestic and gendered. In these plays, the curtain often fell on the solitary woman in a flood of light. Melodrama became the ideal genre for the narration of a woman's personal story and therefore the perfect vehicle for a popular actress. On stage, "domestic melodrama," a subgenre that focused on the trials and tribulations of women both good and bad, dominated the English theatrical venue.[1] Theatrical entrepreneurs were always eager for scripts devoted to the moral plight of women. Consequently, one of the most popular novels of the period, Mrs. Henry

Wood's *East Lynne*, first serialized in print in 1860, was quickly dramatized for the theater, where numerous adaptations played night after night, decade after decade, for American and British audiences that heartily applauded its themes of marriage, betrayal, and murder. The story of Lady Isabel, who, having abandoned her family and committed adultery, returns home to her unsuspecting children disguised as a governess, became one of the standards of stage melodrama.[2] True to melodramatic fare, these various dramatic versions of *East Lynne* contain dozens of climactic revelatory soliloquies, but perhaps none exceeds the pathos and mythic significance for Victorian audiences of the following speech delivered by the tormented Isabel, here reprinted from one of the dramatized versions:

Alas! what is to be the end of my sufferings? How much longer can I bear this torture of mind, this never-dying anguish of soul? From what a dream have I awakened! Oh, lady, wife, mother! whatever trial may be the lot of your married life, though they may magnify themselves to your crushed spirit as beyond the nature, the endurance of woman to bear them. Fall down on your knees and pray for patience; pray for strength to resist that demon who would tempt you to flee them. Bear them unto death, rather than forget your good conscience. Oh! I have sacrificed husband, home, children, friends, and all that make life of value to woman—and for what? To be forever an outcast from society, to never again know a moment's peace. Oh! that I could die, and end my suffering and my misery.[3]

By the final decades of the nineteenth century, stage melodrama rarely strayed from this obsessive spotlighting of the emotional revelations of the fallen wife, mother, or daughter. The Melville brothers, famed producers of sensationalistic melodrama of the 1890's, made a veritable career out of a variation on this theme, as we see in the iconic titles of some of their productions: *The Girl Who Lost Her Character*, *The Bad Girl of the Family*, *That Wretch of a Woman*, and *The Worst Woman in London*. The countless narratives of a woman who "sacrificed husband, home, children, friends" almost entirely financed theatrical melodrama during the late decades of the century when drawing-room realism and naturalism slowly eroded its market share.

The emergence of this domestic melodrama on stage parallels the melodramatic mode's offstage emergence as a rhetorical form of specifically domestic resistance during the middle decades of Victoria's reign. While *East Lynne* played to sell-out audiences, real families acted variations on its melodramatic narrative of fallen women and predatory men. And at least one wife expressed in public and in print its melodramatic sentiments of alienation and remorse. Not long after the success of the novel and the premiers of several dramatizations of *East Lynne*, Mrs. Caroline Norton, a novelist, poet, and celebrity of the previous generation, apparently accused Mrs. Wood of stealing the novel's plot from a sketch Norton had contributed years earlier to the *English Annual*.[4] Given the ubiquitousness of the fallen woman thematic at this time, it would have been nearly impossible to prove Norton's claim that Wood's story line was taken from her less famous fiction. Besides, Wood's plot seems even more derivative of some of Caroline Norton's nonfictional texts, arguably her most famous contributions to the printed word: *English Laws for Women in the Nineteenth Century* (1854), "A Letter to the Queen on Lord Chancellor Cranworth's Marriage and Divorce Bill" (1855), and various letters she published through the years in the daily newspapers. Through these documents, Norton recounted the copious and complex details of her marriage to, separation from, and litigation with George Norton—what amounted to her autobiographical melodrama of familial and marital discord.

Such prolific and, in many respects, repetitious publication was the printed manifestation of a social necessity; Mrs. Norton was burdened with, to use her words, "the sorrowful embarrassment of a 'story' to explain."[5] Norton's story demanded the deployment of a dizzying array of rhetorical strategies, for it combined what were then considered contradictory elements. The story paired a woman's voice with legal and parliamentary discourse; a gentlewoman's sensibility with physical violence, illicit sexuality, and public exposure; and a woman's domestic domain with politics and economics. Generated from these contradictions, Mrs. Norton's several completed polemical narratives look and sound very much like that hybrid of genres—melodrama, as Mary Poovey has elsewhere perceived.[6] That Mrs. Caroline Norton, like Mrs. Henry Wood, wrote melodramatically, with elevated diction and overwrought emotion, and even cast herself as melodramatic heroine on the grand scale of Lady Isabel, can be easily demonstrated. Simply compare Isabel's plaint of "never-dying anguish of soul" and her depiction as an eternal "outcast from society" to Norton's theatrically stagey description of society's attitude toward her as a harassed wife: "She, who if she has not a home has nothing—should be left stranded and wrecked on the barren sands, at the foot of the world's impassive and impassible rocks."[7]

By midcentury, then, both stage melodrama and Caroline Norton's offstage enactment of the melodramatic mode centered on the domestic narrative of the outcast wife. This paradigmatic narrative has seemed to most critics of melodrama to be a straightforward admonitory tale that promotes the dominant bourgeois ideology of Victorian England. By offering to women only one promising role—the wife/mother—such plays naturalize, these critics argue, the bourgeois distribution of social and economic power. As moral center in a middle-class home, so the story goes, the wife and mother navigates her family to a safe harbor, far from the storm-tossed waters of a masculine, capitalist society that continues its contentious activity out of doors and unabated.[8]

Such interpretations, revelatory as they have been for early feminist literary criticism, now inadvertently further the totalizing ambition that is essential to any ideology, for they portray the Victorian bourgeois social order as a spatial and temporal monolith, the all-powerful presence that dictates the conditions of existence for every human subject. These standard readings of melodrama thus presuppose a determinism most often associated in literary criticism with containment theory, which depicts the dominant ideology as always already absorbing competing cultural forces. Accounts that adhere to containment theory, therefore, cannot explain "bourgeois ideology's" embattled formation, a battle that was engaged quite frequently in Victorian England in surprising places, for instance, in what is often regarded as the archetypal and therefore least conflicted melodrama, Mrs. Wood's *East Lynne*. Nor can these literary accounts acknowledge the existence of other visions of social order that joined this battle. One of these visions, expressed through the melodramatic mode, struggled constitutively with the bourgeois version of social order even during its hegemony.

Jonathan Dollimore, in a canny response to containment theory, contends that any dominant ideology is a "containment . . . always susceptible (in principle, not a priori) to subversion by the selfsame challenge it has either incorporated, imagined, or actually produced."[9] By the midcentury, I will argue, certain trademark symbols of the melodramatic mode (the virtuous wife and mother especially) were indeed either produced by or quickly becoming incorporated into a market culture structured by bourgeois ideology. One might even argue that a fully realized capitalist culture determined the gendered valence of the melodramatic mode at this time, and yet the melodramatic mode could still retain its subversive potential as a challenge to the quickly consolidating truisms of bourgeois ideology. In arguing for this subversive residue, I am not thereby making the rash claim that all domestic melodramas, as we have come to define them in histories of the drama, exemplify a potential challenge to Victorian bourgeois ideology. Indeed, even among those domestic melodramas that contain traces of the melodramatic mode's resistant material, there is considerable variation in the degree to which melodramatic tactics dominate and shape the narrative message. In the original novel *East Lynne*, for instance, the strain of melodramatic techniques that invade the story line does not exactly result in a traditional melodramatic tableau of familial hierarchy, but these techniques do detract from the "happy ending" to such a degree that the triumphal assertion of domesticity rings in as a disappointing compensation for a failed community of deference.

Though it is tempting to read melodrama's concern with domesticity as domestication of the genre, this thematic obsession in much stage melodrama and in the melodramatic mode should instead be understood as a rumination on and response to the costs and sacrifices of this process of domestication that was becoming widely institutionalized in law and at home. Melodrama's spotlight on the woman within the family continued throughout the decades of Victoria's reign to often represent an alternative social model and to expose, if not at times to subvert, the principles of classification and market culture that had come to organize the middle-class home and regulate its intimate exchanges. Caroline Norton's polemical texts enact this melodramatic mode. Ejected into the public sphere during these middle decades of the century because of her estrangement from her husband, Caroline Norton could either have championed a radical, republican ideal and demanded "natural" rights for herself, as did a very few women of her generation, or plead for her return to the protectionist culture of the aristocratic family. Norton's melodramatic protest, through which she lobbied for the passage of the Infants and Child Custody Bill in 1839 and the Matrimonial Causes Act of 1857 and yet ignored the failed Married Women's Property Amendment of that same year, bespeaks her conservative, yet politically astute, decision. From the perspective of those, like the young Norton, who lived their lives in the deferential culture of the aristocracy, a joint public-private venture, the melodramatic thematic of the outcast wife and mother, was not a romance that ballasted a false consciousness, a state of mind usually attributed to the mystified wives and mothers of Victorian England. Nor was it a bourgeois sentimentalizing of the more systemic economic and sexual injustices of capitalism, but a cutting, comprehensive, and sometimes explicitly self-conscious reaction against this market system's classificatory effects on the patriarchal family and the more traditional ideology of deference.[10]

As a vehicle of protest in the middle decades of the nineteenth century, the melodramatic mode could empower its practitioners with rhetorical and behavioral strategies responsive to invasions of market culture, but the power so derived was nostalgic and regressive in its impact, a form of resistance especially difficult to see as resistance from a modern vantage point. This subversive potential has perhaps been especially difficult to see for liberal and feminist historians and critics with an understandable predilection for Whiggish history, albeit a revisionist version of it, that yet contains built-in apologias for the premise of liberal reform.[11] As Alan Liu has suggested when speaking of his academic colleagues, "In our own political climate (i.e., the academy), we do not expect—and cannot really understand—the possibility of a subversion expressed as total conservatism."[12] Furthermore, local instances of subversion become nearly impossible to accept as such when their position looks much like that held by members of the dominant caste, who, by the late 1860's, could also adopt the melodramatic mode for their own conservative, if dissimilar, aims.

By these middle decades of the century, many influential people, some of whom had once heralded the theoretically self-regulating mechanisms of the market, were witnessing periodic enactments of the market's inherent instability and found themselves, like the audiences at a production of *East Lynne*, attracted to melodrama's rhetoric of deference and scenes of hierarchical social order in which women both played the crucial role and formed part of the receptive audience. Often deployed in the past in opposition to governmental procedures, the melodramatic mode's protest against a classificatory society could be imagined in the 1860's and 1870's as the government's own method of defense against the market trends of speculation and class mobility. Such trends seemed by this time as uncontrollable as the desires of able-bodied paupers, which the market principles of supply and demand had once set out to regulate. In these instances, the melodramatic mode comes closest to collusion with the very forces its resists, facilitating the dominant caste's monopolization of market exchange, but even here, it should be remembered, melodramatic tactics work as a conservative force to delimit the extension of market behaviors. Its resistant strategies were ultimately available to a broad spectrum of political interests.

Beginning in the 1870's, Queen Victoria, sponsored by her government's cabinet, starred in what has been called "royal melodramas."[13] Although these theatrical events did not take place on a stage, in the theater, or even in the home, they employed many of the dramatic strategies, visual effects, and thematic motifs of the genre melodrama, with the goal of managing the energies of social change. Here, especially, the deferential ethic and the figure of the wife/mother, so central to this domestic melodrama, easily coalesced. In Walter Bagehot's influential account of the Parliament between the first two reform bills, *The English Constitution* (1867), he seems to corroborate, from a contemporary vantage point, melodrama's merger with the figure of the queen, for he describes the function of the monarchy as if it were a melodramatic drama and, almost echoing Caroline Norton in her "Letter to the Queen," depicts the queen as a melodramatic heroine.

Through an analysis of midcentury domestic melodrama on stage and in Wood's *East Lynne*, the melodramatic rhetoric Caroline Norton deployed in her polemical texts, and the stagings of royal melodrama during the 1870's and 1880's, I will discuss the varied use of the melodramatic mode as a mixed method of conservation and of subversion during the midcentury by a diverse range of practitioners. As I delineate these sundry uses, I will need to account for the melodramatic mode's representational fixation on the wife/

mother in a domestic setting. As a portable rhetoric in the middle decades, to a large extent detached in time and place from the material conditions that had grounded its original ideals, the melodramatic mode was beginning to serve multiple interest groups, all of whom were dedicated, if for different purposes, to the regulation of social energies devoted to free trade. This symbolic side of regulation increasingly relied on the wife and mother, or, more accurately, the theatricalized embodiment of the wife and mother's virtue. The continued representation of deferential virtue in the body of the wife seemed to many to promise the continued survival of the constitutional monarchy and its oligarchical governance in a market culture whose sudden booms and busts and whose periodic extensions of the franchise threatened central English institutions.[14]

I

The railway boom and bust of the 1840's and 1850's serves as an illustrative instance of the uncertainty of a free-market economy that ultimately rendered melodramatic tactics so desirable for both Norton and, later, liberal reformers. Although the development of the railway in England and Scotland experienced its first period of growth in the 1830's, its most dramatic expansion occurred after 1845, when Parliament approved the construction of double the number of existing lines. During this era of railway expansion and optimism, the historian S. G. Checkland has remarked, "Railway sponsorships passed from the cautious hands of provincial men of business to a new generation of projectors, for whom plausibility was more important than proof."[15] Rather than local businessmen from the region in which the trains would run, rather than the engineers who would actually build the line, city financiers now became the principal backers of these projects. Most manifest in the figure of "Railway King" George Hudson, such men devised investment schemes, many of them swindles, that encouraged widespread speculation.[16] The rise and fall of Hudson and others in the late 1840's and early 1850's, as well as the specious existence of many of these projects, reminded numerous proponents of the laws of classical political economy that what had once been considered the naturally self-regulating tendencies of the market were actually, in practice, its propensities for unpredictable behavior and that what was once believed to be its rational administration of finance was in truth its flights of fancy.[17]

These railway schemes did not generate income out of land or labor, nor did they obey the laws of supply and demand; instead they responded to their investors' desire for sudden profit. Instead of instilling in its participants frugality and consistency, the market now seemed to encourage what was then termed "speculative mania." During the rise and fall of the market in railway speculation, the culture of the landed gentry seemed seriously challenged by this alternative formulation of aristocracy and monarchy epitomized by the singularly unregal figure of the Railway King. Even the image of the mobile train cutting tracks across estates symbolized the liquidation of real property by commercial property. During this period, not just the Railway King, but "men and women of all sorts of station, trade or profession, high or low degree of means, age and persuasion saw themselves growing suddenly much better off *if they were quick enough.*"[18] Social status reliant on the possession of real property no longer seemed guaranteed by a fluctuating market that enabled all kinds of men, and even women, to grow rich in spite of the controlling mechanisms of labor.

The speculative symptoms of "railway mania" indicated a decreased reliance on real property as the source of wealth and influence in the country.[19] The specific principles and practices of landed culture—primogeniture, the consolidation of land through marital alliance, and the ideology of deference—seemed directly contested by a now-incompatible market, which was generating its own contentious, classificatory culture of monetary exchange. As this conflict developed, marriage, which was both the basis of familial reproduction in the aristocracy and the most intimate and crucial symbol of the deferential form of social exchange, not surprisingly became a site of contestation.[20]

By the mid–nineteenth century, the conflict between a deferential model of social exchange and a contractual model was most commonly enacted in the domestic sphere, partly because this sphere was a site where the ethic of deferential relationship could still be imagined and thus staged. Changes within the public sphere rendered the exercise of deference increasingly anachronistic in civic, business, and social spaces. As the public sphere became stratified according to class affiliation, few theaters, for instance, catered to the heterogeneous populations that had once favored the melodramatic mode's depiction of patriarchal social exchange. Strikingly unlike the program of the Covent Garden Theatre of 1809, mid-Victorian theatrical fare as well as its theaters had become associated with particular classes. Even the large patent theaters had by this time built separate entrances for their various clientele.[21] As the physical design of theaters reflected society's stratification, the stage within these theaters often became the site of representation for a deferential domestic sphere no longer manifest in the larger public sphere of the audience. Despite the battle won in 1809 by the Old Price faction, its heterogeneous members had indeed lost the war.

By contrast to the contentious relationships in the market world, the home, represented either on stage or in a house, seemed the last outpost of deferential community and social sentiment. Here the husband could still be expected to play the role of patron; his wife and children and servants, the various deferential ranks who sought and received his protection. The husband would provide food, clothing, shelter, status, and respect, while the wife represented the familial lineage by both producing and training the children. As Susan Staves has observed, "Many wished to preserve natural law in the family long after they had made the transition to natural right in the state."[22] In fact, the years between the two reform bills form a distinctive historical period during which many men of stature and influence appeared to regulate intercourse among each other in terms of natural right, while at least claiming to regulate their relationships with the poor and women in terms of natural law.

These contradictory methods of governance could coexist only as long as the two domains could be seen as distinct, functional, and mutually supportive. As long as the market reserved its contractual ethic for business and civic activity, the paternalistic ideology of reciprocity and the landed culture it underwrote could continue to organize familial relationships. By engaging in a criminal conversation suit against his wife in 1836, George Norton seemed to reject this deferential model of exchange and insisted instead that his family interact according to the laws of the market. In effect, he asserted his proprietary, speculative claims within the deferential home and, literally as well as theoretically, cast his wife out of the kinship society in which she had derived her identity. Just as the lower ranks had sensed the removal of aristocratic protection after the institution of the New Poor Law of 1834, so families like the Nortons were experiencing a crisis in patriarchal codes of behavior, a crisis that found expression through the melodramatic mode.

II

When George Norton filed a criminal conversation suit against Lord Melbourne, he revealed to Caroline the extent to which speculative culture had infiltrated their home. The details of Norton's twenty-five-year-long confrontation with her husband have been narrated by Norton herself as well as several others, and so I will provide information only as my study dictates.[23] Married in 1827, the Nortons were unhappy almost immediately. After a few brief, aborted separations, in 1836 George Norton prohibited Caroline access to her three children and soon thereafter legally proceeded against his Whig patron, Melbourne. Melbourne had been a frequent and acknowledged visitor to Caroline at the Norton home ever since George's appointment to a mid-level post in Melbourne's government.

Although criminal conversation cases had been in existence for generations, their economic assumptions were now becoming visible to people like Caroline because of the heightened contemporary concerns about speculation's potential erosion of the kind of virtue that had once been associated with the possession of land and the maintenance of the manor.[24] Under English common law, criminal conversation suits enabled a husband to seek damages from the man with whom he suspected his wife of committing adultery. Having convicted the accused man of adultery, the judge and jury would then determine the amount of damages to be rewarded on the basis of the husband's social standing—in a sense, the loss he incurred from having his property stolen. By seeking damages from the current prime minister, George Norton showed Caroline that he, supported by English law, considered wives to be the private, personal property of their husbands rather than inalienable guardians of the family name. In a sense, they had been a form of real property but were now managed as commercial property.[25]

As a woman of the upper ranks, Norton underwent a significant and exemplary transformation of identity through this marriage and estrangement: she not only witnessed, like the poor, her exclusion from the public theater of patriarchal relation, but became, as a result of the market's classificatory process of social organization, the site of antitheatrical privatization. Before the criminal conversation trial, Norton's tastes and heritage inclined toward what would now be considered most typical for an early-eighteenth-century woman of talent and lineage. Although from an impoverished nuclear family, she was well connected, mostly thanks to the political activities of her grandfather, Richard Brinsley Sheridan. Aristocratic by patronage if not in fact, Norton therefore made her debut with other beauties of the day at Almack's, the most fashionable gathering place in London society. The unmarried Norton was as much a promising public figure as many women of this older society had been, for that era condoned women who maintained public roles, particularly as a sign of family prestige or as a conduit for refined and sometimes politically influential conversation that cemented the dynastic connections among aristocratic families.[26] Subjected to published gossip and frequently quoted for her wit, Norton became one of a group of well-known authoresses often labeled the "blues."[27]

These ladies and their public personas were still products and by-products of the eighteenth-century aristocracy and were depicted as such in the early 1830's by the society artist Daniel Maclise, who painted them prettily seated around a tea table, engaged in lively conversation, and duly attended by a slave boy, a symbol of wealth and cosmopolitanism (see Figure 6). In keeping

Figure 6. "Regina's Maids of Honour," from *Fraser's Magazine*, January 1836. Caroline Norton (first seated figure from the right) joins a bevy of notable literary ladies at tea, which is served by a lavishly dressed African servant. Collection of the Sterling Library, Yale University.

with this persona, Norton wrote poems in Byronic verse and composed romances not entirely unlike those of the "silver-spoon" novelists of fashionable, aristocratic London then known as "the Ton."[28] Before her bitter split with her husband at age twenty-eight, Norton even attempted to become a politically influential woman, as other aristocratic, intelligent women continued to do through the middle of the nineteenth century. In 1835, she served as a go-between for Melbourne when he was working to build a coalition cabinet after Peel's resignation.[29] Anthony Trollope satirically depicted such contemporary political hostesses, who were primarily of Whiggish persuasion, in the figure of Glencora Palliser. George Norton's marginal influence and wealth, however, effectively prevented Caroline from participating in this elite culture, and as a result, she fell subject to an alternative set of bourgeois assumptions regarding the woman's role. The passage of time that commenced with Norton's young womanhood and climaxed in her separation from her husband, a passage of time that changed a woman who engaged in "conversazione" into a woman accused of "criminal conversation," charts in miniature a larger transitional period in English society. In fact, the conditions that transformed this woman from an influential and highly patronized family into a middle-class Victorian wife had been taking shape throughout the eighteenth century.[30]

Through legal and bureaucratic reform, such as the New Poor Law, and through other procedures of social organization that took place in the eighteenth and early nineteenth centuries, the "familial" members of the traditional patriarchal status hierarchies of feudal England were being divided up according to what contemporaries began to identify as economic class. In place of these parochial extended families, the nuclear family of husband, wife, and children came to constitute in law, in the economy, and in perception the standard social unit. This nuclear family was classified according to separate, but complementary, spheres of domestic exchange, on the one hand, and economic and civic exchange, on the other, that were associated with essentialized concepts of gender. Virtues and values that were once considered exchangeable among the members of the patriarchal family, the market, and the civic setting had thus been divvied up and had become affiliated exclusively with a single gendered sphere of this bifurcated culture.[31] The immediate family came to be seen as the germ of all private existence and, crucially, as the microcosm of the state, now represented as an aggregation of private family interests. As one journalist insisted, the family was "the first element and very foundation of the state,—the state in miniature,—and the state itself nothing more than a system of co-ordinated families."[32]

In this emergent society, "normal" women were supposed to represent the newly constituted "private" virtues that had once been valued as public duties and behaviors independent of gender and class. Such privatization and feminization of benevolence, to name just one of these virtues, necessarily altered the stipulated responsibilities of the husband of this nuclear family. Where the landowning lord had formerly been expected to protect an injured tenant's family, he now felt responsible only toward his immediate family members. Unlike public, ritualistic scenes of relief common during the seventeenth and into the eighteenth centuries, where magistrates and landowners bestowed their beneficence, philanthropic activities by the mid–nineteenth century were usually initiated by private women. These activities were characterized as a transfer of domestic virtue from one private home to another and were denominated as acts of isolated, personal charity, gestures of the individual conscience. As in "The Old Cumberland Beggar," the emphasis was placed more on the personal virtue such actions epitomized in the benefactor than on the benefit offered by the actions themselves. An article in *Household Words*, in describing this form of giving, emphasizes the superiority of its private origins: "There are the poor and the sick round her home; she will visit them, and nurse them, and teach their children, and fulfill her duty better thus than by walking the hospitals, or preaching on Sundays!"[33]

As many analysts of the eighteenth century have discussed and as the above quotation implies, this emphasis on a female's private virtues marked a significant change for wives of the upper ranks.[34] During the Renaissance, high-ranking wives publicized the relative status and generalized virtue of their families through the sumptuary splendor of their costumes. As late as the eighteenth century, aristocratic women continued to stage, through costume, social conversation, and public gestures of munificence, a standard of family prowess and civic virtue. In effect, they embodied the value of the family in the theatricalized public sphere. Many eighteenth-century women, however, were not embodying dynastic value through public displays of their clothed bodies as did their ancestors. Instead, in a market culture increasingly constituted by proprietary individuals and organized by economic classification, they represented the value of their husband's private property and did so through possession of spiritualized essences—private disembodiments rather than public bodies.[35] Just as members of the working class were seen to possess a standard moral profile, so females were seen by the dominant middle and upper ranks to be constructed by this specific set of virtues. Conduct books of the eighteenth and nineteenth centuries bluntly recommended such private, nontheatrical behavior for women, while implicitly negating the possibility of any activity with demonstrable public impact. In discussing marriage, Sarah Stickney Ellis, a prominent writer of conduct manuals, advises, "If you were never humble and insignificant before, you will have to be so now. . . . Be uninteresting as long as you live, to all except the companion of your home."[36]

Norton experienced this reconstitution of the female identity in her literary career when critical reception of her work, seemingly influenced by her controversial life, attempted to make her into a "poetess." In his review of "Modern English Poetesses," Hartley Coleridge traces this transformation in a single sentence. Referring to the modern type of poetess, and implicitly contrasting it with a more performative persona, Coleridge argues: "Affectation has disappeared with the uneasy singularity of position which provoked it; and the woman of genius or learning, who knows that men are conversing with her on a ground of respect and equality, learns to be humble and sincere."[37] Norton's heroic verse and idealized romance reminded Coleridge of Byronic verse—at one point he calls Norton "a lady Byron"—and such poetic emulation of Byron no doubt led to an unacknowledged assumption of Norton's marital emulation of that infamous man, an emulation that Coleridge, writing in 1840, obliquely characterizes as Norton's "uneasy singularity of position."[38] The critic therefore encourages the poetess to resist imitating that genre and that man, and to be, instead, "humble and sincere"—a phrase not too distant from Ellis's admonition to the wives of England to become "humble and insignificant." The Byronic verse troubled Coleridge in Norton's poem because she wrote, he claimed, too much "'*about* the heart,'" and not enough "'*from* the heart.'"[39] According to Coleridge, Norton had the audacity to universalize—to publish abroad—the heart's feelings, and in doing so she seemed hubristic.

From a twentieth-century vantage point, Coleridge's distinction is hard to grasp, but it expresses the changing criteria for literary taste and feminine behavior that were so evident in the middle decades of the nineteenth century. Norton's efforts to universalize the contents of her heart sounded like Byronic grandiloquence, but they also owed something to the personifying impulse in eighteenth-century poetry, an impulse that assumed the existence of, in Clifford Siskin's words, "a uniform human community." In the context of this uniform community, the poet "constitutes himself as the center of the community—the abiding presence who is its Spokesperson."[40] Coleridge, no longer believing in this unitary community, cannot imagine the existence of such a "Spokesperson" versifying in generalities "about the heart," especially a female spokesperson recently estranged from her husband, but can only imagine and revere a privatized and private female writing "from the heart." Norton's universalizing poetic effects are thus construed as "affectation" and her publicizing role of "Spokesperson" is represented as "an uneasy singularity of position." Once relegated to the privacies of the home, a woman's dramatic gestures in the public sphere can only be seen as "acting."

In Victorian England, Coleridge implies, the "poetess" should aspire to "humble and sincere" writing because this kind of writing was considered to be a dual product of a sanctioned privacy and a determinate gender. In this review, indeed in Victorian society at large, the married or not-yet-of-age woman writer could be turned into an entirely private entity, concealed from an audience just as commons land had become enclosed, because at home and in the law she was defined as the property of her husband or father.[41] Once married, under the law of coverture, any property a woman owned prior to the wedding or acquired during the union also became the sole property of her husband. Once married, a woman found it exceedingly difficult as well as economically and socially suicidal to divorce, since she possessed no legal or cultural identity within the public sphere.[42] Women were therefore expected to write conduct books or, alternatively, poems or novels that read like conduct books. Such homely writing fulfilled the requirements both of marital privacy and property by, to borrow Coleridge's words, "living in the hearts of men," not by publicly and promiscuously "commanding the favour of the town."[43]

Instead of locating herself within the context of an extended hierarchy of kinship where, as a Sheridan, she would have been constituted in relation to other members of that patriarchal unit, Norton was now primarily identified according to abstract virtues strictly associated with a lifestyle of domestic privacy. In this formulation, motherhood and marriage within a nuclear family comprise the sum of her relationships, thereby isolating her from other people—most pointedly, other men. In this context, just as her public writing about social feelings that were recently privatized took on connotations of promiscuity, so too did Norton's widely publicized, if privately held, meetings with Melbourne.

Prior to his allegations of adultery, George apparently defined these exchanges between Melbourne and his wife in terms of the rituals of patronage. As a second son, George had had little hope of obtaining status through the inheritance of land or other property or even through his poor wife's settlement. Chronically short of money, without significant land or capital, the Tory Norton relied on his wife to obtain for him a magistracy from Melbourne, then the leader of the Whigs and a family friend of the Whiggish Sheridans. At the beginning of the marriage, Norton had thus initially displayed his willingness to live according to the rules of patronage and to show deference to Lord Melbourne, but within a few years, George substituted the litigation of the criminal conversation suit for the deference of patronage. In this trial, the law did not perceive Caroline Norton as a link in the deferential network of patronage, nor was she seen as part of the inalienable real property of a familial dynasty; rather, it appeared to Norton that George, backed by legal precedent, considered her to be commercial property—a potentially profitable personal possession—and, perhaps most ominously, a proper object of his "speculative mania." Norton later described George's intention: "MONEY was his avowed motive."[44] Although the marriage and divorce laws had not in fact changed in the previous decades, the protectionist ethos that had surrounded them seemed to be dissipating, revealing the more proprietary assumptions that remained.

In her nonfiction prose, Norton arrives at this revelation through what comes to be her habitual gesture of solidarity with the poor. Because the divorce laws were so complicated, the poor were frequently ignorant of their regulations. To document this ignorance, Norton often cites instances in which poor men believed that they might sell their wives. Such instances, of course, merely recapitulate in more literal terms the underlying anxiety Norton felt in regard to her own position. In this scenario of the proprietary gentleman and his privately possessed wife, any "conversation" that might have taken place between a wife and another man could now be construed only as "criminal conversation"—property theft.[45]

From the perspective of George and a sizable segment of society, however, Norton initiated her own alienation because she chose to be a public woman, as Hartley Coleridge perceived. She composed Byronic verse that hubristically claimed a universal perspective; she had maintained a highly visible intercourse with the prime minister, and she had penned vociferous defenses of her behavior in the letters section of the newspaper. She had even continued after her separation her appearances at social functions. In a market culture where women were constituted by private virtues that were privately owned, Norton's public gestures presented a frightening prospect of social upheaval. Her attempts to incorporate herself in the public sphere were inevitably perceived as acts of imposture, while Norton herself was branded an actress who "played a role" rather than existed as a wife. In Victorian society, women in the public sphere could not be seen as public figures, but only as impersonators of private feeling. Fanny Kemble, herself a professional thespian, recalled that Mrs. Norton was "comically dramatic in her manner of narrating things."[46] Lady Eastlake complained of Norton in a letter to a friend: "No, she is a perpetual actress, consummately studying and playing her part."[47] And as late as the 1850's, when George once more engaged in litigation, he described his estranged wife's behavior in these terms: "All must remember it as the most splendid piece of acting ever exhibited, however much the sober mind of England must revolt against the disgrace of a court of justice being turned into the stage of Drury-Lane."[48] Although public agents in Victorian England were still occasionally likened to actors, these comparisons of Norton to an actress, unlike the traditional theatrical metaphors used in relation to public men, carried pejorative connotations that were deeply rooted in mid-nineteenth-century anxieties about the relation between the domestic sphere and the public stage of civic and commercial life, a relation whose frictions were otherwise suppressed in everyday practice. In a culture where the drama was seen to be in an aesthetic free-fall and whose artistic productions were most often celebrated for their studious realism and eschewal of theatrical tricks, tropes of theatricality were nonetheless ubiquitous, for they adeptly expressed the tensions between surface and interior that so characterized capitalist society, especially the identity of women in such societies. Actresses in particular embodied these tensions.

In midcentury England, actresses were perhaps the only female public figures living amid the upper and middle ranks of society.[49] Although the history of female actors on the English stage had by then spanned 170 years and they were to some extent tolerated by their culture, mid-nineteenth-century actresses were nonetheless commonly presumed to be prostitutes.[50] This assumption arose largely because actresses were in some ways like prostitutes—both displayed their bodies and sold them in the public sphere in order to earn a living. But perhaps this conflation also occurred because it was assumed that actresses were to some extent emotional impostors. They, too, feigned emotion in the execution of their trade. They, too, had become objects of suspicion in a culture for whom theatricality, especially in women, was a synonym for affectation, where bodies had become masks. While they expressed the feelings of a mother, wife, or daughter in the demure roles they played in the domestic drama of the Victorian stage, as working women they were patently not mothers, wives, and daughters, as commonly conceived. Hence, a disjunction between role and being was presumed. In one of Caroline Norton's early romances, *Woman's Reward* (1835), written before her initial separation from George, she depicts this contemporary conception of the actress. Lionel Dupree, the selfish but beloved brother of the heroine, expresses this by-now familiar condemnation of female actors, who are, like paupers under the Old Poor Law, nothing but speculators on the market, traders (and traitors) in feelings: "I must, however, beg leave to doubt the fact of any modest and feeling woman being *able* to carry on this trade in the passions, this export and import of different sensations—this exchange of loud mock heroics for private confessions of admiration, uncorrupted."[51]

As participants in market exchange, Victorian actresses and prostitutes were considered to have sacrificed their private identities within the home or, worse, to have bartered them in the public byways of the market. This sacrifice of their domestic identities, however, could not erase the private space in relation to which their public position was necessarily defined in a culture that was rigorously partitioned by the boundary between the public and the private. As a result, the private space remained, but it was shifted to a more interior, mysterious location.[52] In place of the geographic space of the domestic sphere they had rejected, a private, physical space was assumed that seemed always associated with the interior regions of an actress's and/or prostitute's body (those parts not visible on stage), as well as the impalpable feelings lodged there. Many nineteenth-century medical men believed that women were incapable of sexual arousal, but many also expressed the corresponding anxiety that fallen women, such as prostitutes or actresses, were motivated by the desire for sexual pleasure.[53] If true, fallen women necessarily experienced this pleasure out of view of men, who assumed women's erotic indifference. If fallen women felt sexual pleasure, men worried, they did so in private, both within the body and the mind. This physically grounded but psychological domain remained troublingly outside the panoptical and etherealized privacy wistfully attributed to the domestic sphere of virtuous womanhood and was considered inaccessible to surveillance, appropriation, or regulation, just as the paupers' motivations in the 1830's had seemed menacingly resistant to intervention.

According to the logic of the market, possession of any private realm entitled one to alienate it for profit, even if that private realm was an actress's imagined interiority. When embodying on the stage a paragon of virtue, an actress's body, like the private boxes in the Covent Garden Theatre, was often assumed to conceal, even to symbolize in itself, private, self-interested economic and sexual motives, a special form of private capital ever ready for exchange. One commentator alluded to this "property" of subjectivity: "The life of an Actress is to the world at large a curious *terra incognita*, peopled by forbidding phantoms of evil, or seductive visions of pleasure and success."[54] During the midcentury crisis in the market, many critics of the theater thus imagined a "speculative mania" breeding in this terra incognita. Such women, like able-bodied unemployed paupers, might harbor not only a secretive sexual desire, but an insatiable economic drive fueled by "visions of pleasure and success." Their proprietary behavior—their acting in and for the public and in exchange for money—symbolized the speculative desires that many contemporaries worried were becoming typical of all women during the 1830's and 1840's, those years when women invested in railways and star actresses could amass wealth of their own.[55] Without a home or family, an actress, a prostitute, or an estranged Caroline Norton ceased being the real property of a husband and became, it was imagined, the alienable property of her own proprietary self.[56]

From this perspective, surely the perspective adopted by George Norton, Caroline Norton's alleged adulterous liaison with Melbourne could be interpreted as the most explicit, but not the only, manifestation of her market behavior. Her other public activities as author and political hostess had already alienated her from her husband's ownership, exposing her to the market culture of the public sphere. Declining to live in her husband's heart, she was automatically presumed to prefer "the favor of the town." Public women in Victoria's England thus shared the fate of paupers, whose displays of social and familial emotion seemed to their former benefactors to be acts of imposture that concealed their self-interested motives. Norton, like other vagrants without a home, was doomed to be a traveling player, an actress.

III

In domestic melodramas of the day, actresses played out the ideological contradictions that hedged in Caroline Norton and upper- to middle-class women like her. Amid the multiplying speculations of the midcentury, of which "railway mania" is only one, it is not surprising that commercial drama capitalized on the interlocking associations among actresses, prostitutes, unmarried girls, outcast wives, and property. Alienated by profession, actresses were the ideal vehicles for the portrayal of marriageable women in what was anxiously deemed the marriage market and, through them, the depiction of families that were endangered by this commodity exchange. In J. B. Buckstone's adaptation of the French melodrama *Isabelle*, the narrative charts the life of the heroine in three acts entitled "The Girl," "The Wife," and "The Mother." Throughout the drama, Isabelle is the victim of the speculative appetites of the men around her. Her husband, Eugene, an officer in Napoleon's army, gambles away his regiment's pay and is bribed by his friend Scipio, who threatens to reveal this youthful mistake. Through acts of gambling and bribery, both men thus enact an exaggerated perversion of the contentious and contractual relationship typical of the speculative market. Closely associated with their speculative temperament are their insatiable desires—be they professional ambition, greed, literal hunger, or sexual appetite.

All such desires are depicted insofar as they exert effects on Eugene's marriage. Eugene ignores his wife and dallies with an aristocratic beauty, while Scipio "indulge[s] in a plurality of wives" for profit.[57] For Scipio, in particular, marriage becomes another form of speculation. By the second act, Scipio exposes Eugene, who then deserts his wife to wander shamefully abroad. Not until after the fall of Napoleon's despotic rule, with the resumption of the Bourbon monarchy, does Isabelle's family re-form, thanks to the bravery of her son, Vincent, a soldier in the Bourbon army, who slays Scipio on the mountainside. The son thereby eradicates this villainous, despotic, and predictably Parisian influence from the family and from the monarchical culture with which that family was affiliated. Explicit throughout this translation from a French melodrama are the contrasts between two political cultures—the Napoleonic and the Bourbon.

Napoleon's rise to power in France was not unlike a speculation that culminated in his assumption of quasi-monarchical powers in 1802, a year that inaugurated a new era of economic growth and expanded trade for France. However, Napoleon's attempt to replace the Bourbon dynasty with his own was complicated by his wife Josephine's childlessness, so in 1809 Napoleon divorced her and married the archduchess of Austria, who bore him the child on whom he later bestowed the title King of Rome. Despite his evident desire to originate an alternative patriarchal monarchy in France, Napoleon did not obey the patriarch's code of protection for dependents; rather, he, like Scipio, traded on and with his wives.[58]

Buckstone's English adaptation of *Isabelle* and other domestic melodramas address comparable concerns of midcentury England. During the railway mania of 1845 to 1847, George Hudson had been dubbed the "Railway Napoleon." Like the French emperor's success, Hudson's rise to power had opened up the prospect of an alternative aristocracy, in this case, one empowered by its commercial wealth rather than, as in Napoleon's, its military and bureaucratic might. This shift in the source of political and economic influence from inalienable to alienable property had great impact in England on the ideological significance of marriage. Formerly, in the late seventeenth and eighteenth centuries, political power had become less dependent on royal patronage and more dependent on the ownership of land. Without the influence of the monarchical lineage, to borrow J. G. A. Pocock's words, "inheritance . . . appeared more than ever before the mode of economic transmission proper to a society's existence in time."[59] As a result, the laws of primogeniture were of supreme importance and were strengthened by the laws of strict settlement; both insured the continuing influence of the patriarchal, landowning family through the generations. In this context, the purity of the familial lineage seemed increasingly crucial, and therefore a wife's chastity—her virtuous containment of physical desire—determined to a great extent the family value.[60]

By the mid–nineteenth century, land and those who owned it still exerted the most power in England, but well-publicized periods of speculative inflation threatened landed culture's oligarchic monopoly and, in turn, its conceptualization of the marriage bond. If marriage in the eighteenth century had "become more exclusively economic than it had been in the century before," the deferential codes that still lingered from feudal relationships had nevertheless managed to mitigate the mercenary motives in what was usually depicted among the upper ranks as a familial alliance among patriarchal dynasties.[61] By the mid–nineteenth century, however, the gradual shift in influence from the patriarchal dynasty to the private, proprietary self was registered in the representation of the wife, who embodied and then acted out this transition and the anxieties that attended it.

As long as extended patriarchal families controlled social exchange through spectacle, as long as the wife incorporated (in both senses of the verb) the family value, and as long as wives contributed to the prolongation of dynasties through reproduction and/or political conversation, a woman occupied a public role. Caroline Sheridan Norton, in keeping with her birth family's Whiggish loyalties, might mediate the formation of a coalition government in the company of Melbourne without arousing accusations of adultery. Just as the Old Poor Laws had operated on mutual recognition and knowledge between the benefactor and the recipient, so marriage could proceed on a similar set of assumptions, with George recognizing his wife's exchanges with Melbourne as the rituals of deferential exchange. However, once the laws of the market as well as the laws of the land began to give priority to the private, proprietary male self and once the existing laws seemed no longer capable of regulating that self, the contractual rights of marriage superseded the deferential code's system of reciprocity as it was expressed through the theatricalized exchange and display of women.

If, by the nineteenth century, intrinsic virtue or honor was widely considered constitutive of the woman's value and her social role, then its very abstraction perhaps rendered it peculiarly vulnerable to speculation. Rather than representing the stature of her family through her clothed body, she initially represented her own commodity value in the marriage market and, once wed, her husband's private wealth, measured in part by a quantitative and qualitative assessment of her personal virtue.

In another of Buckstone's midcentury domestic melodramas, anxieties about women's new status within a speculative culture receives even more direct expression.[62] In *Victorine*, a woman dreams that instead of doing "as all good wives do who love their husbands—save money, work hard, and take care of the children"—she becomes the mistress of a wealthier man. By rejecting the well-regulated home of her fiancé, she becomes, as one of her speculating (and thieving) friends describes her, "an excellent circulating medium."[63] Rather than embodying the inalienable property of landed culture, Victorine embodies currency. The heroine of this play represents the new woman of an unregulated market culture—she is an actress playing a wife turned prostitute, precisely the accusation lodged against Caroline Norton.

As Victorine's dream progresses, the drama charts her alienation in the market economy. From a frugal wife-to-be, she becomes, in turn, the familiar image of an insatiable female consumer, a "circulating medium," and a gambling house owner whose establishment, not surprisingly, is filled with the secret compartments typically associated in melodrama with economic and sexual transactions. This admonitory dream, which takes place the night before her marriage, thus explicitly emphasizes that the marriageable Victorine is a medium of exchange, the medium by which wealth is transferred from one man to another. Like money, she signifies value; like money, she is intrinsically alienable. Unlike Isabelle, however, Victorine shifts the terms of commodity exchange, moving into the entrepreneurial sector of the economy, becoming the proprietor of a gambling house. She, like prostitutes, actresses, and Caroline Norton, is presumed to be a "closet" speculator motivated by the private spaces that house her self-interest.

As *Isabelle* and *Victorine* thus suggest, such midcentury domestic melodramas could either address the market's impact on marriage through the depiction of the wife as a passive victim or an active agent. Isabelle, while remaining virtuous throughout, experiences familial alienation as the result of her husband's evil deeds. By contrast, Victorine, in a dream, or Lady Isabel, in the "reality" of *East Lynne*, become the agents of their own dispossession. Both, in fact, become laborers in the market, with Victorine, most ominously, assuming the position of an entrepreneur. Similarly, as their printed documents make clear, both Caroline and George Norton accused each other of harboring private interests within the marriage. Unlike the public displays of protection and deference that ensured the cohesion of the extended patriarchies of an earlier era, these private motives—sexual and economic—were seen to be intrinsically fatal to the cohesion of marriage because they undermined its ideological justifications. Mr. Dill, a secondary character in Wood's *East Lynne*, isolates the crucial connection between the patriarchal hierarchy of landed culture and marriage that was so threatened by the prospect of wandering wives. He identifies the importance of deferential recognition: "When I have a good master I know how to stick to him, though some wives don't know how to stick to good husbands."[64] Many midcentury domestic melodramas thus registered and, as I will show, tried to manage the growing apprehension that marriage had lost its power to represent and sustain the virtue of the patriarchal family unit, to unify dispersed people symbolized by these units, and therefore to preserve what were perceived to be the more solid values of landed culture.

True to their generic requirements, these domestic melodramas always conclude with a tableau of reunited patriarchies, thereby asserting their ability to fend off incursions from the market. As with other forms of melodrama, these plays usually recast the alienating influences of a contractual and proprietary culture into a moral drama about a patriarchal family's banishment of a fallen relative or mercenary friend. This villain's ultimate ejection from the family circle leads to the final tableau of reunion during which the wife, even if she herself has played the villain, is often given the concluding speech. In this climactic scene, she spectacularly displays her virtue or confesses her vice and baldly insists on the identity between honor and family.[65] Even the guilty Lady Isabel of *East Lynne* repentantly realizes in a passage already cited: "Oh! I have sacrificed husband, home, children, friends, and all that make life of value to woman—and for what? To be forever an outcast from society, to never again know a moment's peace." The self-interest that formerly motivated her is ultimately recast as the yearning for a familial connection within the serene boundaries of society.

In a culture where a woman's virtue was threatening to become either someone else's disposable property, or worse, the disposable property of the woman, these climactic scenes attempted to reassert virtue's function as the visible, familiar, and inalienable foundation of familial cohesiveness, and thus to reprivilege a much truncated version of the patriarchal family and its associated values over the proprietary individual. Whether the plot presented the frightening specter of a villainous husband or wife, its climax relied on the wife alone to symbolically display, through costume and body language and in the presence of an audience, the iconic virtue of the patriarchal family, not the hidden, sexualized desire of the proprietary self. The typical tableau of repentant womanhood—the actress on her knees, hands clasped before her as she faced a family tribunal—ultimately functioned as a reembodiment of a familial and social virtue, especially because it staged virtue in a relatively public space, before the eyes of husband, children, servants, and audience.[66]

This logic informs a crucial portion of the plot line in the novel *East Lynne*. Having reentered her home disguised as a governess—the market's most distorted and mediated version of maternity—the adulteress Isabel eventually casts off her green-tinted spectacles and gray gown to reveal herself as an unmediated wife and mother, a reincarnation of family virtue, thereby certifying, before she is banished from the family, the justice and benevolence of her former husband and the family he heads. To compel audience compliance with this message, but also to recover the communal valence of this virtue, such virtue needed to be as visible and interpretable in its own way as the signs of hereditary status, such as costume and accent, had always been.[67] This sequence in the plot therefore purposefully turns inside out the contemporary attitude regarding theatricality that the melodramatic mode so consistently resists in all its manifestations. Instead of a lavish costume simulating a false virtue or feigned modesty and thereby disguising the truer mercenary motive hidden inside the fallen wife, the muted uniform of the governess visibly embodies in true melodramatic style the literal incursion of the market into the family that the occupation of governess represented. When such clothes are shed, we do not see the prostitute lurking behind the virtuous-seeming actress (at least not at this late moment in the narrative), but the wife/mother liberated from the governess.

Often, and with only modest success, Caroline Norton's rhetoric and much midcentury melodrama struggle to resolve the crisis of representation addressed in *East Lynne*: the moment when virtue becomes doubly privatized—a wholly individuated trait as well as a possession of an individual. In the alchemy of the melodramatic mode that these plays conduct, virtue is not a private, domestic possession, but instead, to use the words of Lady Isabel in one of the dramatized versions of *East Lynne*, "a woman's priceless jewel."[68] Such a phrase reveals the mixed status of female social signification during the Victorian period and the degree to which remnants of deferential value inhered uneasily in market culture. It is a phrase that attempts to give a body to disappearing virtue—virtue no longer seen very often or very easily. The "jewel" represents virtue through its sparkling visibility, but it also evokes in its materiality a more performative era of sumptuary costume and real property; it is like an heirloom that exemplifies a family's wealth and status over time. Within the procedures of the melodramatic mode, "priceless" is meant to express virtue's freedom from the market; like an heirloom, it was not meant to be sold and thus had no price. Isabel's comparison here between real property and female virtue is therefore an anxious expression of melodramatic polemic that is intended as an argument against her fateful abandonment of family. Inevitably, of course, the phrase "a woman's priceless jewel" also evokes the tensions associated with the increasing dominance of commercial property that melodramatic performance can only partially overcome; after all, the woman, not the entire family, claims the jewel in this phrase.

Unlike heirloom jewelry and real property, both of which were legally inalienable, such "priceless" virtue was becoming increasingly easy to price, as Isabel's ultimate desertion attests. Through her hasty act of adultery, she barters the priceless jewel as if it were her own. In this unregulated market culture, marriage, instead of a pledge of familial alliance, could be considered more explicitly, by the fallen Isabel and by men like the penniless Sir Francis Levison, as an economic transaction, with the wife as commodity. Throughout their history, women had often represented value, but now, as with so much else, value lodged in the commodity form. Under contemporary law, married women were in fact more like commodities than they were like the proprietary selves of men. They could neither become a party to a binding contract nor hold others accountable for contractual agreements, but they could be circulated as tokens of value, as the procedures of the criminal conversation law indicate.

Melodramatic acting, as it developed through the early part of the nineteenth century, possessed a style and philosophy designed to accommodate the demands of these polemical dramas. Unlike, for instance, the drama of the early eighteenth century, with its fascination for layers of allegory and double entendre, melodrama was characterized by a hyperrealism that acquired its urgency from its need to compel belief from an audience habituated to what was now considered empty theatricality.[69] Melodramatic acting was therefore a style premised on the principles of revelation and disclosure, and it demanded of its actors and actresses a full measure of physical expressiveness, the use of body perhaps even more than the use of voice. In melodrama, the body is communicative of social virtue, not the container of secret sexual desires and pleasures or the private scene of self-interested economic exchange.

The features of this type of acting became, not surprisingly, the crux of many arguments defending virtuous women's participation in the acting profession. Acting in a domestic melodrama became a sort of training ground where women learned to become less restrained and artificial and thus more genuine. A woman's expressive body and voice rendered her more legible to the observing audience.[70] As one female defender wrote, "An actress's imagination and affections are constantly exercised, both mind and body are brought into service, she has the free use of all her faculties and limbs."[71] Standard acting manuals of the period outlined a "natural" method, which instructed novices to coordinate their physical gestures with their vocal expression.[72] More important, these manuals encouraged their students to feel in actuality the emotions they wished to portray, for "these are nature's own symbols of the passion she has inspired."[73] In this way, "mind and body" worked in synchrony to produce an authentic characterization of a mother, rather than working at cross purposes to yield an affected impersonation of one by an insincere actress.[74] Continually accused of affectation by her husband, Caroline Norton countered his criticism by adopting a similar melodramatic style that could express her wifely and maternal authenticity in the context of the deferential ethic of patriarchal culture.

IV

During the 1836 criminal conversation trial *Norton v. Melbourne*, Caroline Norton remained at home while her relationship with the prime minister was discussed before judge, jury, and courtroom observers. As the private property of her husband, she had no legal right to appear in court to defend herself. Her absence from the court perhaps gave the counsels for both husband and accused lover a broader freedom to represent the alleged iniquity. Based on a review of eighteenth-century criminal conversation cases, Susan Staves reports that "there was often a very specific contest of interpretation, the plaintiff's counsel trying to assimilate the facts to a tragic narrative and the defendant's trying to force them into a comic one."[75] Apparently, like classical forms of drama, these trials were considered to be highly theatrical.

The *Norton v. Melbourne* trial, however, seems more like a detective narrative in the tradition of the Conkey Chickweed tale in *Oliver Twist* than a classical comedy or tragedy. Without the wife physically in the courtroom, George's barristers proceeded to interrogate her indirectly and through this oblique questioning to construct the sort of culprit that only a market culture can imagine: a public stranger necessarily subject to police surveillance and uniform regulation lest he or she attempt to defraud anyone. In the most explicit of examples, a charwoman was brought to the stand to report signs of observed illicit behavior as indicated by the Norton bedroom's state of disarray and as registered on her lady's linen and bedclothes. No longer a clothed public figure of familial virtue, the fallen wife has here been literally stripped of her costume (and thus her right to public appearance in the courtroom). The linen itself becomes dirty linen—the perfect trope for an unregulated housewife. Like actresses and prostitutes, Norton had, the prosecution contended, feigned her marital and maternal feelings while harboring in the private compartments of her home and body adulterous ambitions. Underwriting this interrogation is the ideal of the well-run household of a proper bourgeois woman, whose home, free of dirty linen, is an internalization of this sort of surveillance. Esther Summerson's ring of keys to the varied housekeeping compartments in Bleak House is clearly only one of a number of Victorian images that trace the subtle conceptual dependencies among female subjectivity, domestic economy, the private compartments of political economy, and the panopticon.

When Norton determined to write her own version of the trial and twenty-five-year separation in *English Laws* and "A Letter to the Queen," she found it necessary to adopt what seems like a pronounced melodramatic narrative and to depict herself as a beleaguered heroine precisely because she wanted to employ the style of theatricality that privileged visibility, disclosure, and public authenticity instead of hidden meanings and allegorical disguises. Norton recognized that George's behavior in the criminal conversation trial prevented her from writing in the romance style typical of her earlier works: "Had there been no such proceedings,—then, instead of this pamphlet, the work I was occupied upon, would have appeared; harmlessly to amuse those who had leisure to read it. I give them, in lieu of such a work, this 'Story of Real Life;'taking place among the English aristocracy."[76]

Instead of writing romances, which amuse young women with idealized pictures of the aristocracy, of gallant heroes and virtuous heroines, Norton needed to write in a generic tradition that could reveal what had become of the aristocracy and the virtues of its culture. In place of romantic maidens and their happy unions with deserving lords, Norton portrayed herself as a victimized heroine of melodrama, for in this genre she could both embody her virtue and her husband's economic self-interest hidden behind his empty mask of the patriarch. She describes her belated 1853 courtroom appearance in these terms: "In that little court where I stood apparently helpless, mortified, and degraded—that bitterest of many bitter hours of my life,—I judged and sentenced him. . . . I sentenced Mr. Norton to be *known*."[77]

Melodramatic rhetorical strategies thus substituted for the courtroom sentencing of George that Norton was denied in 1836. In the 1853 courtroom scene, nearly twenty years after the couple's initial estrangement, Norton's debtors took George Norton to court for nonpayment of various bills. Under the law of coverture, wives were not responsible for the debts they incurred, and so the husband could be required to pay. As a material witness, Norton was this time present in the courtroom. In *English Laws*, she restages this 1853 confrontation as a melodramatic contest between good and evil. "I felt," Norton wrote, "that I no longer stood in that Court to struggle for an income—but to struggle against infamy."[78] In this phrase, Norton translates the legalese of contractual obligation into a syntax of honor typical of a melodramatic rhetoric and thereby attempts to translate what she experienced as the isolating and disembodied language of market culture back into the language of visible reputation that characterized representations of patriarchal culture.[79] Insofar as George had sought financial reparations in the initial litigation and thus emphasized his individual self-interest, he no longer represented his wife or family. Instead, he affiliated himself with laws that effectively broke up the traditional bonds of the family by means of their putative impersonality, objectivity, and forbearance. In this regard, the laws of marriage and divorce resembled the New Poor Law of 1834.

In Norton's texts, the law becomes the focus of attention precisely because it enabled George to free himself from the burdens of being a patriarch and, therefore, to absent himself from scenes of deferential exchange. Norton writes: "I am not now discussing this, with any reference to him [George] individually. Gone,—past—buried in unutterable scorn,—are the days in which I appealed, either *to* him or *from* him. I complain,—not of the existent husband, but of the existent law."[80] In order to recreate the conditions necessary for a scene of deference, Norton needed, in effect, to personify the impersonal law in the form of her villainous husband and thus to judge the law in terms of George's failed familial obligation. In "A Letter to the Queen," Norton stages the classic melodramatic scenario of virtuous heroine and mercenary villain, quoting Sir John Bayley, George's former counsel: "She treated her pecuniary affairs as a matter of perfect indifference. . . . I found her husband, on the contrary, anxious ONLY about the pecuniary arrangement, and so obviously making the love of the mother for her offspring a means of barter and bargain."[81] George is here portrayed as the evil family relation, riven by economic desire, who attempts to sell the woman's familial virtues as if they were his own property. By contrast, Norton, like Isabelle, Victorine, and the repentant Lady Isabel, enunciates the familial content of her thoughts: "I thought of nothing, day or night; but my children."[82] Rejecting the behavioral model of the melodramatic hero, George eschews patriarchal obligations; he is represented as self-interested and greedy, not protective and fatherly. As in the climax of a domestic melodrama, Norton reveals the content of the villain's thoughts: "If the husband be really high-minded, honorable, and injured,—it is a mockery to *pay* him for such injury; if he be *not* honorable, but base and grasping, it is a strong temptation to him to threaten such an action, or even to speculate on bringing one."[83] Through these scenarios Norton exposes the speculations of her husband who, unlike the local magistrate, landed gentleman, and paternalist he pretended to be, cared nothing for the patriarchal virtues of "high-mindedness" and "honor." Instead, as a fallen aristocrat and husband, George had alienated the hierarchical community which he had formerly represented in the public sphere, and like Isabelle's Eugene, had abandoned his wife, dispersed his family, and neglected the poor.

Having exposed George as the villain, Norton then attempts to persuade the legislators to appoint a reformed law as surrogate patriarch: "It becomes perfectly absurd that the law which appoints the husband legal protector of the woman, should not (failing him who has ceased to be a protector, and has become a very powerful foe) itself undertake her protection."[84] Although it is somewhat submerged in the broader polemic of the texts, the main aim of Norton's documents becomes quite explicit in the above commentary: to advocate reform of the laws regarding marriage and divorce so that the law and not the husband would be the ultimate source of benevolence and obligation in the family. In order to argue for this conservative-minded reform, Norton needed to extend the range of her domestic melodrama. Just as she exposed the self-interested motives hidden behind George's disguise as aristocratic gentleman, so she directed a similar criticism toward the Tory members of Parliament, whom she ironically described as "that 'nation of gallant gentlemen.'"[85] Throughout her conflict with her husband, Norton assumed that the Tory party had funded George's criminal conversation suit as a means of toppling Melbourne's Whig cabinet and, furthermore, that it had resisted various marriage bills in Parliament in opposition to the Whiggish interest that Caroline Norton shared. In response, Norton charged that these "gallant gentlemen" were speculative sectarians, whom she portrayed as a "circle of protected whist-players" who preferred to wager on cards and, implicitly, to hatch secret plots rather than to legislate and who resented card sharks and the loss of their gambling profits more than they resented brutal husbands or women's loss of virtue.[86] Mirroring the speculative pursuits of Eugene and Scipio in *Isabelle*, the members of Parliament had relinquished their patriarchal roles. Norton's complaint thus moved to a political plane; she laments the changing nature of all representation in a society where traditional constituencies have given way to modern interest groups—class politics.

This plea for legal protection in lieu of marital protection connects Norton's localized melodramatic rhetoric to a contemporary discourse that influenced one particular philosophy of legislative reform. Throughout the 1830's and 1840's, Parliament repealed many laws that were seen to interfere with free trade, while it opposed any new protectionist legislation. During the railway mania, for instance, when the market suddenly seemed incapable of self-regulation, many resisted government intervention. At the same time, members of Parliament who opposed free trade espoused a paternalist theory of protectionist legislation. Such legislation empowered the law to become the patriarchal presence in the social arena, in many parishes replacing the lord of the manor or the church as the public dispenser of beneficence, a type of statist patriarchy that prefigures the contemporary welfare state.

By tapping into this larger reservoir of paternalist sentiment, Norton could cannily avoid certain dangers in her argument. In calling for reform of the divorce laws, Norton also found herself demanding personal copyright so that she might live off the profits of her pen, contract privileges so that she might pay her own debts, individual maternal rights so that she might raise her sons, and, of course, the legal right to free herself from her husband's ownership, as if she were aiming to become as much a proprietary self as George. Because many legislators believed that the marital relationship was the prototype for social relations, they resisted reform of the divorce laws. Norton shared these opinions and yet wished to be free of a husband who seemingly did not. As a result, she portrayed the law as her surrogate "protector" and described her personal claims as requests for beneficence phrased in a syntax of social feeling, not as demands for natural rights.[87] Norton was no revolutionary, but a woman in search of "wholesome authority," as she explained to the queen in characteristic melodramatic tropes of despotism and enslavement: "Madam—in families, as in nations, Rebellion is a disease that springs from the *malaria* of bad government. WRONGS make REBELS. Those who would dwell submissive in the wholesome atmosphere of authority, revolt in the jail fever of tyranny."[88] Norton wanted to defer to a man, not because of his physical dominance, but because, like all decent lords of the manor, he theoretically filled his position in the status hierarchy and respected its code of reciprocity.

Fears that Norton wished to become a proprietary self always lurked in contemporary critiques of Norton's behavior, as they often did in portrayals of heroines in midcentury domestic melodrama. What melodrama stages as a female's theatricalized authenticity in the public sphere was often received as insincerity, less a transcendence of the dissonance between the public and private personas of the individual than a costume to disguise an inner ego-ism. Harriet Martineau, for instance, criticizes Norton's lust for celebrity and her "selfishness": "When I see an eloquent writer insinuating to everybody who comes across her that she is the victim of her husband's carelessness and cruelty . . . when I see her violating all good taste by her obtrusiveness in society, and oppressing every body about her by her epicurean selfishness every day, while raising in print an eloquent cry on behalf of the oppressed; I feel, to the bottom of my heart, that she is the worst enemy of the cause she professes to plead."[89] As a student of utilitarian philosophy dedicated to the principles of market culture and thus to analyzing the subject in accordance with these tenets, Martineau cannot conceive of any social behavior instigated by an individual that does not conceal some hidden self-interest, whatever that individual professes in public.

Norton's combination of her own familial narrative with an appeal on behalf of the poor, however, is part of her melodramatic rhetorical stance intended to counter this accusation of selfishness. By affiliating her own story of domestic cruelty with the suffering of the poor, by pleading for a protector for them both, Norton universalizes (in a pose she had adopted in her earlier poetry) her particular narrative into an emblematic melodrama of nationwide familial estrangement that appealed to a heterogeneous audience, whether its members were dispossessed by their husbands or their landlords. In so doing, she recreates the extended family of a deference hierarchy. Norton's maneuver also provides an insight into one probable form of alliance between wealthy women and the poor in Victorian England that does not express a socialist or progressive agenda but is nevertheless antagonistic toward bourgeois ideology. Moreover, Norton's position suggests that there were other ways of imagining womanly identity in Victorian England than the stark choice between selfishness and selflessness.

Through this linkage with the poor, Norton's melodramatic rhetoric thus rejected the most marked manifestation of market culture—class. Throughout her critique of the marriage laws, she points to the inequities that rendered it nearly impossible for a poor couple to divorce, and she argues for a more uniform law that enables the poor as well as the rich to end marriages. Such an argument, like her request for women's rights, could easily sound like egalitarian propaganda, but she was always careful to delineate the nature of the deferential relationship between the upper and lower ranks. In her 1845 poem, *Child of the Islands,* for instance, Norton ostensibly speaks to the young Prince of Wales, the son of Queen Victoria. In dedicating her poem to the prince, Norton recalls the patronage system even as the poem itself stages a resuscitation of the society that fostered it, a society that seemed particularly embattled by the 1840's. Written at the height of Chartist unrest, Norton's poem responds to Chartism's discourse of class conflict with a melodramatic rhetoric. Initially, she measures the emotional and physical distance between the little prince and various pauper families as the seasons progress. In autumn, the prince lives a pastoral romance, while nearby a man, weakened by labor, dies in a field. Although she thus concedes that these once-connected populations have become estranged, Norton attempts to recreate social cohesion by means of a melodramatic revelation that espies a community of feeling that she claims is easily visible in their countenances. She writes in her preface, "It is . . . a gleam of that union and kindliness of feeling between the Higher and Lower Classes, which it is the main object of the writer of these pages . . . to inculcate."[90] Although yet a child, in this poem the Prince of Wales is coaxed out of his enclosed garden to become the patriarch of the commons land. He, like Norton, must come close to the suffering poor, for only in the face-to-face exchange can he feel and see that "gleam of union."

In "A Letter to the Queen," Norton again stages a scene of patronage in which her request for rights becomes a direct plea for protection to the Queen of England. In a long preamble, Norton describes the celebrations attendant on the opening of the new hall of Lincoln's Inn in 1845 over which Victoria presided. Norton insists, with a devotion to cultural symbolism typical of melodrama, "Now this was not a great mockery; but a great ceremony."[91] In this ceremony, according to Norton, Victoria was honored as the patroness of justice and was therefore endowed with the power to exert appropriate influence on the successful passage of legislation concerning marriage and divorce. Victoria's dual role as patron and matron, as a protector and as a wife and mother, enables Norton to place her own argument in the context of patriarchy at the same time as she aims to annul her ties to her husband. Furthermore, Victoria's ownership of private property, her singular ability to contract even as a woman, her public position, and her simultaneous devotion to family provide, Norton claims, a model for women like Norton, who, by choice or otherwise, find themselves in the public spotlight yet divested of value. By insisting that the monarch take a public stand, Norton hoped to cast the queen in the traditional role of a woman whose public displays of virtue and sincerity were not misconstrued as imposture. Much more successfully than Victorine, Victoria could give voice to the central themes of domestic melodrama. As a matronly monarch, she could best represent the continued importance of the virtuous woman in the familial lineage. In "A Letter to the Queen," Norton encourages Victoria to imagine herself in these terms. Norton narrates other stories of royal women whose patience resulted in the ultimate preservation of the patriarchal line. Recalling a favorite of midcentury domestic melodramas, Norton speaks of Empress Josephine, whose "profligate" husband sent her home to her birthplace in the Caribbean but whose grandson nonetheless became Napoleon the Third after the 1848 revolution.[92]

By championing in public the familial virtues of the woman, Victoria was to support Norton's attempt to acquire rights—that is, rights of protection as a wife and a mother in a patriarchal order—that were not contingent on her husband's personal proprietorship. Although not precisely a fantasy of matriarchy, this representation is an act of substitution in a system of substitution that is, as we have seen in *Oliver Twist*, typical of melodramatic logic. Female virtue replaces male blood as the crucial bond in patriarchal lineages, a substitution that implies that female virtue is an unproblematic equivalent. In addition, Norton's melodramatic banishment of George and Tory party officials makes room for a distinctively matriarchal (and Whiggish) family reunion at the close of her narrative in which even Prince Albert is absent. In a culture dominated by men, Norton seems to run the risk of sexual and political isolation, if not outright contradiction, when she ejects their representatives from her patriarchal home.

Norton's polemical texts and midcentury domestic drama demonstrate that the market's complex impact on the family and the deferential ideology that lingered from landed culture were frequently expressed and managed by the melodramatic mode. However, these texts also suggest, especially through Norton's wish for a quasi-matriarchy, that melodramatic content, performance, and consumption had become almost exclusively associated with the female sex and the poor—a sure indication of the governors' abdication from patriarchal responsibility. Indeed, the discourse of paternalist reform that was so deeply linked to the melodramatic mode elicited a similar response from liberal-minded opponents, who allied its tendencies with stereotypically feminine characteristics. Here is how James Fitzjames Stephen, a Benthamite utilitarian, described Charles Dickens's legal critiques in *Bleak House*, which were often seen as representative of a paternalist plea for the downtrodden:

Freedom, law, established rule, have their difficulties. They are possible only to men who will be patient, quiet, moderate, and tolerant of difference in opinion; and therefore their results are intolerable to a feminine, irritable, noisy mind, which is always clamouring and shrieking for protection and guidance.[93]

Stephen's effeminized version of Dickens is succinctly distinguished in this passage from the explicitly male ideals of liberalism—moderation, patience, and tolerance. Melodramatic rhetoric is biologically antithetical to classical rhetoric. Rather than melodramatic expressions that compel sympathy and community, men possess differentiated opinions that demarcate the boundaries of the private self and its interests.[94] As early as the novella *Woman's Reward*, Norton had located this physical and discursive distance between the sexes at the most powerful, most institutionalized site of men's differences in opinion—the floor of Parliament. While the women sat in what Norton appropriately labels a "Strangers' Gallery" and peeked out, like the gallery gods in the Covent Garden Theatre, through small apertures high above the parliamentary floor, William Clavering, M.P., "prepared to exert his power of persuading and convincing, not over her weak heart or inferior understanding, but on the minds of men."[95]

As I have argued throughout this study, the melodramatic mode could be a useful rhetorical strategy for those who were, like women, paupers, vagrants, and actors, increasingly confined to society's "Strangers' Gallery," people who were no longer recognizable but instead were objects of suspicion. Not unlike Bulwer-Lytton's wife, who, from this gallery, once loudly proclaimed her husband's shortcomings to the assembled members of Parliament, Norton made use of the melodramatic mode—in particular its empowerment of the marginalized audience—to reveal the private transactions of Westminster's "gallant gentlemen." As long as there remained a receptive audience for an idealized vision of patriarchal social exchange, such melodrama would thrive; in Norton's case, her ties with landed aristocrats undoubtedly helped her campaign.[96] But once the cast of characters as well as the receptive audience seemed largely empty of those contemporary men who wielded genuine and direct political power—in effect, largely empty of patriarchs—the melodramatic mode necessarily entered a more symbolic, but by no means entirely depleted, phase of its existence.

In her prose, Norton had to resort to vaguely delineated representations of a matriarchal society headed by a queen with very little real authority. As Norton somewhat disingenuously admits in the first pages of "A Letter to the Queen": "The vague romance of 'carrying my wrongs to the foot of the throne,' formed no part of my intention: for I know that the throne is powerless to redress them."[97] Although Queen Victoria in "A Letter to the Queen" and the Prince of Wales in *Child of the Islands* are meant to embody a resuscitated ethic of patronage and patriarchy, they were, by the 1850's, largely supernumerary figures, as were many of the rhetorical figures on which melodrama relies.[98] The husband heading a nuclear family seems a poor substitute for the lord of the manor; likewise, the monarch, as embodied by the dependent Victoria, may suggest to us a weak substitute for the local aristocrat, especially because of Victoria's reclusive existence after the 1861 death of the prince consort. In the years following his death, Victoria sought refuge from the public eye, abandoning her frequent visits to the theater, for instance, to mourn in the privacy of her home—a withdrawal into the privatized, domestic sphere from theatricalized public spaces that both fuels and confounds the melodramatic mode's ethic of visibility.

The melodramatic mode's detachment from concrete referents in Norton's texts anticipates melodrama's discursive portability in the three decades surrounding the second and third reform bills (1860 to 1890). Moreover, the progressive diminishment of public spaces epitomized by Victoria's own withdrawal from the theaters and the prevailing suspicion of theatricality expressed by those like Harriet Martineau inevitably exerted pressure on and thus altered traditional melodrama's message and its reception. During these thirty years, the extension of the franchise and the growth of the popular press, combined with the liberal ideal espoused by men like Fitzjames Stephen, imposed complex demands on public forms of spoken, social exchange, including the melodramatic mode.

V

Consistent with the deferential political thrust of melodramatic rhetoric in the early decades of the nineteenth century, Norton's polemic outlined a plan for conservative reform that challenged the organization of capitalist culture into rigid private and public realms. These reforms aimed to manage the alienating effects of market culture by insistently recasting its proprietary selves as deferential family members and thereby redirecting their insatiable exchange of private property for profit. In the late 1850's, when the extension of the franchise was receiving renewed consideration, the threat of an enormous increase in these speculative selves and their impact on English culture became one of the major themes stoking the opposition to electoral reform. It is hardly surprising, then, that the melodramatic mode put in an appearance in the various debates concerning the connection between the franchise and the capitalist market, though the political outlook of its newest practitioners is indeed surprising.

For the social conservative Thomas Carlyle, one of three results of this upcoming electoral reform would be the emergence of the "hundred-and-fifty millions free . . . to follow each his own nose, by way of guide-post in this intricate world." Even though the vote would not automatically endow poorer men with the means to speculate, its constitution of them as independent political voices appeared to confirm their right of private self-ownership, and thus, like actresses and prostitutes, they would presumably join the melee of the marketplace. Such newly proprietary selves, Carlyle continued, would lead the nation to "unlimited Free Trade,—which some take to mean 'Free racing ere long with unlimited speed, in the career of Cheap and Nasty.'"[99] This passage presents a classic nightmare image of a libertarian market society of unprincipled competition, immoral profit, and inferior value.

As with reaction to the railway crisis of the 1840's, the extension of the franchise was presumed by men like Carlyle to encourage market behavior within relationships that had until then remained mostly deferential, at least in theory. Most modern historians and critics have come to assume that class culture and class conflict uniformly describe the exchanges among the ranks in Victorian society and that only delusive reactionaries could imagine themselves engaged in deferential exchange. This description may not accurately depict the practice or, at least, the expectations of some of those engaged in these exchanges; furthermore, to diagnose such aristocratic expectations and deferential practices as "false consciousness" discounts the very real material effects that these so-called illusions could have, for they could surely determine whom one might engage in transactions. Even in the middle decades of the nineteenth century, there were people, people of quite opposite political perspectives, who believed that some working version of the patriarchal model of deferential exchange provided a moral code for behaviors, both social and economic. Aristocrats turned capitalists could conceivably continue to manage their labor pool according to the rituals of deferential exchange, as Patrick Joyce contends in *Work, Society and Politics*. Although we might argue that deferential exchange was then more pervasive in British colonial societies and their bureaucracies than in England, we must concede that these old customs lingered, shaping conservative reaction to an extended suffrage and the social mobility it seemed to stimulate.

Despite these fond attachments to a deferential ethic, however, by the middle of the nineteenth century, the traditional social code of deference had become in practice irretrievably mingled with the newer values of a consolidated capitalist economy. In direct opposition to these old customs of deference, certain segments of society communicated that they no longer believed that their social superiors adequately represented their interests; they thus demanded the vote. They did not necessarily include in their demands a plan for radical redistribution of wealth and power, but it often seemed so, as Carlyle's concerns attest. When women expressed their desire to leave a marriage, they, like the working classes, could be seen to be critiquing the entire social hierarchy, implicitly demanding self-ownership and the means to barter that self in the public sphere.

To appease these suspicions, Norton found it useful to deploy the melodramatic mode when narrating her story, and it was the use of this rhetorical strategy, more than the adoption of a plot line, that marked the similarity between Mrs. Henry Wood's *East Lynne* and Norton's stories. In Wood's *East Lynne*, the election contest between another Carlyle—Archibald—and Lady Isabel's lover, Sir Francis Levison, seems at first only a backdrop to Isabel's decision to leave home, but it is, in fact, a broader societal version of the very same problem. The novel thus articulates the constitutive relation between domestic and parliamentary politics that Norton also noticed. As Mr. Dill suggests, Isabel's failure to know a good master when she sees one is just like an elector of East Lynne not recognizing a good candidate. In the novel, melodrama's revelatory effects expose not only Isabel's error of recognition—the pivotal error of melodrama—but also Levison's murderous and speculating past that disqualifies him from the borough race. In so doing, the disclosures affirm Carlyle's role as patriarchal representative within the family and also within his regional district.[100]

Mrs. Wood thus appears to use melodrama for the same purposes as Caroline Norton. Like Caroline, Isabel travels the lonely path from aristocratic theatricality to bourgeois domestication. And, like Caroline's story, there are brief moments in Isabel's story that struggle to reassert patriarchal order and its ethos of visibility. *East Lynne*, however, is scarcely a plagiarism. Less firmly attached to aristocratic culture than was Norton, Wood registers in her seemingly inconsistent characterizations of heroes and heroines an especially complicated entanglement of old and new value systems that we have already seen partly articulated in the image of the "priceless jewel."

It is generally agreed that the novel's main trajectory exhibits an obvious class bias. The gouty Lord Mt. Severn represents the decadent and literally decayed body of the aristocracy, while the commoner Barbara Hare confidently introduces domestic economy and domesticated femininity into East Lynne. Moreover, Archibald Carlyle's purchase of the indebted estate not only exemplifies the canny business sense of a middle-class investor, but also provides an explicit symbol of the middle-class's buy out of the upper classes.

This inescapable class parable, which is sometimes explicitly articulated by characters and narrative voice alike, is nonetheless undercut by the discontinuities created by the melodramatic mode. Through its techniques of display and performance, centered mainly in the person of Lady Isabel, it dominates considerable portions of the plot. In a manner far more pronounced than Norton's texts or its own stage versions, *East Lynne* celebrates market behaviors, but it does so by superimposing them onto an attenuated yet still recognizable image of a deferential social order that lingers to the very end of the novel. This entanglement between new and old in the novel parallels the historical record and undoubtedly exceeds the conscious intentions of the author. The result is a particularly hybridized form of the already hybridized melodramatic mode that projects its vision of a traditional social order and adheres to its ethos of visibility even as the novel celebrates what we now recognize as the bourgeois virtues of modesty and prudence. Despite the narrative interpolations that directly admonish Isabel, the biased comparisons between Isabel's household management and Barbara Hare's, the torture that the plot imposes on Isabel—despite all these obvious signs of bourgeois cheerleading—many contemporary and modern readers note the ambivalence with which Isabel is finally dispatched, the niggardly praise directed at Barbara, and the hollow bonding between Carlyle and his new wife that closes the novel. Wood, like many men of her day, harbored an uncloseted if complicated nostalgia for a deferential culture in which aristocrats played their roles well. It is the recent "abdication of the governors" that haunts Isabel's suffering and modulates Wood's triumphal tones.

The formal disjunctions in *East Lynne* that mark the presence of the melodramatic mode are most easily detected in the author's treatment of the wife/mother's body, which, as we have already seen in the social reaction to Caroline Norton, serves as a barometer of family and social change. The presence of a revised melodramatic perspective is most revealingly evidenced early in the novel when Wood struggles to interpret the visible display of Isabel's aristocratic body. Before attending her music teacher Mr. Kane's recital, Isabel dons diamonds and a fancy lace dress. On seeing her costume, Lord Mt. Severn and, later, Wood's narrative voice chide Isabel for vanity; Severn transforms melodrama's ethic of visibility into a seedy burlesque when he warns Isabel, "'You will have the whole room gaping at you.'"[101] Like Harriet Martineau's criticism of Norton, the narrator's assessment of Isabel's behavior (voiced, oddly, by the most dissolute of aristocrats) is motivated by bourgeois standards of subjectivity—private, internal, egoistic— that assume Isabel is seeking personal admiration.

By contrast, Isabel defends herself by articulating the principles of theatricality explicit in melodrama's set scene of deferential exchange. Her costumed body represents and confers value; her open display of patronage, like aristocrats in open boxes in a theater, encourages other beneficent acts: "'I thought I would show those West Lynne people that *I* think the poor man's concert worth going to, and worth dressing for.'"[102] In spite of the narrator's voiced opinion, the plot seems to justify Isabel's reading of social behavior, for her presence results in a large audience that comes to watch her performance as much as it comes to hear the recital.

Mrs. Wood's discomfort with the very melodrama she uses points to melodrama's often compromised status in England's quickly consolidating class culture. This conflict is also apparent in the figure of Archibald Carlyle. Archibald's "middle-class" virtues of duty and frugality could be seen to threaten a standard melodramatic message upholding the principles inherent in deferential display. Archibald, however, also evinces a generous paternalism that extends to townspeople and family alike. This uneasy mixture of middle-class individualism and rural paternalism could indicate Mrs. Wood's failed characterization of her hero if one adheres to static and ahistorical notions of class, but Carlyle embodies instead an uneven historical development that often typifies midcentury examples of literary melodrama as they grapple with a changing society. Carlyle's "middle-class" virtues are, for Mrs. Wood and for many of her contemporary readers, universal virtues; the emphasis critics of the novel place on class obscures Wood's own emphasis on Carlyle's substitution for, not replacement of, the profligate Lord Mt. Severn. Carlyle, after all, moves into East Lynne; he does not resell it for a profit. It is at least useful to recall that what we might wish to see as contradictory class positions are presented by Wood as viable, if ultimately historically delimited, composites: an aristocratic rural culture of face-to-face deference and acts of benevolence is simply peopled here by professional men and their wives and daughters (Barbara Hare), who still display virtue, but a virtue that is increasingly difficult to display.

Throughout this novel, the admixture of deferential ideology and the bourgeois ideology of market exchange produces a modernized version of the melodramatic mode that is undeniably a dilute solution in comparison to the corrosive effect manifest in the melodramatic behavior and rhetoric of the Old Price rioters. Not just female novelists like Mrs. Wood, but liberal-minded commentators of the midcentury were producing startling texts with similarly hybrid combinations of the melodramatic mode. Such people, despite their more open allegiance to the principles of capitalism than Wood's narrative expresses, shared Thomas Carlyle's concern that the extension of the franchise represented an unwelcome extension of market behavior, both in the home and in the halls of Westminster.[103] Like Caroline Norton, like

Mrs. Wood, they thus turned to the melodramatic mode for familiar images of social and cultural stability. If still a disruptive figure in the computations of capitalist speculation, the melodramatic mode was nonetheless part of its equation. Its critique of market behavior and social organization could be deployed by its practitioners and received by its audience as a regulative mechanism rather than as a fundamental challenge to the new order. Lady Isabel functions throughout *East Lynne* as a voice of deferential order, an expression of cultural stability, only to be permanently replaced by Barbara Hare.

One liberal-minded commentator was Walter Bagehot. His famous rendition of government operations between the first two reform bills, *The English Constitution*, was written on the eve of the 1866 bill, when change was inevitable and imminent. Although a stout liberal, Bagehot echoed Carlyle's worries. Soon, poor men would be able to vote; even a few women were expressing their desire for electoral representation. On this eve of transition, Bagehot noted that the public's fascination with political life had already diminished campaigns for parliamentary seats into a form of social competition, a trend that a broader electorate would only exacerbate.[104] The upcoming reform bill haunts Bagehot's pages, for it threatens to commodify members of Parliament as George Norton commodified his wife. This specter of political speculation was no doubt fueled by the anticipated changes in the property requirement for enfranchisement. In the 1866 Reform Bill, even more markedly than in the 1832 bill, liquid capital was construed as an adequate fulfillment of the property requirement and was thus considered nearly on par with the traditional requirement of real property. As a result, men with modest, alienable wealth were now, in effect, to be represented in Parliament. With this further extension of the franchise, successful but common men never before seen in Westminster could realistically imagine themselves winning a borough election. Bagehot's submerged subtext grew into a major concern on passage of the Second Reform Bill, and this concern is addressed directly in subsequent parliamentary legislation. Although the financial chicanery of parliamentary elections had been tacitly accepted and therefore never seriously monitored, after the Second Reform Bill there was renewed interest in regulating campaign expenditures. Rather than emanating from an idealistic desire to protect new voters from bribery, these regulations, it might be argued, were an attempt to restrict the speculation on parliamentary seats and votes that might arise.[105]

As Bagehot looked back on the years between the first two reforms, he believed that despite this troubling trend toward electoral speculation, the English constitution as it then operated mostly controlled the "free racing ere long with unlimited speed" that Thomas Carlyle deplored. This "race of expenditure" was confined to a very few people precisely because the monarchy as the apex of society superimposed a hierarchy of blood on this competition, reminding the contestants that no one of them could ever expect to attain first place.[106] As one commentator on Bagehot has characterized this notion: "Reverence for rank mitigated the idolization of wealth."[107]

According to Bagehot's text, the constitutional monarchy that governed England between the first two reform bills consisted of two influential parts—the "dignified" and the "efficient"—that were distinctive and yet mutually supportive in their efforts (p. 61). The monarchy, and to a lesser extent, the House of Lords, constituted the dignified part, and the Parliament with its Cabinet constituted the efficient. The monarchy—more successfully than the larger House of Lords—served the vital function of exciting in the populace deferential and, crucially, inheritable feeling for government. Bagehot notes that "semi-filial feelings in Government are inherited just as true filial feelings in common life" (p. 60). The royal lineage not only secures the throne through time, but as an extended patriarchal family, guarantees obedience from its people generation after generation. It induces this allegiance by exerting theatrical influence over its audience:

The elements which excite the most easy reverence will be the *theatrical* elements—those which appeal to the senses, which claim to be embodiments of the greatest human ideas, which boast in some cases of far more than human origin. That which is mystic in its claims; that which is occult in its mode of action; that which is brilliant to the eye; that which is seen vividly for a moment, and then is seen no more; that which is hidden and unhidden.

Such a theatrical display is that "which yet comes *home* to the mass of men" (emphasis added), who rely on the monarchy to symbolize in its royal lineage the English extended family to which they imagine themselves to belong.[108]

This "mass of men," mass being a common term for those without the vote, is "unable to comprehend the idea of a constitution—unable to feel the least attachment to impersonal laws," but its members are greatly attached to the familial affairs of the royal family. Bagehot takes as an example the marriage of the Prince of Wales, which excited considerable response, especially from English women, who "care fifty times more for a marriage than a ministry." In relating this example, Bagehot is quick to point out that women form "one half of the human race at least" (p. 85). Bagehot therefore believed it to be an especially happy coincidence that the current monarch was a queen, for she, more than a king, could "be a visible symbol of unity" for a largely female disenfranchised population (p. 90).

Bagehot's somewhat cynical description of the monarchy portrays with an almost uncanny precision what I have presented as the theatrical and social procedures of midcentury manifestations of the melodramatic mode—its "mystic claims" of outrageous coincidence, its often "occult modes of action," its scenes of disclosure and revelation, its insistence on the embodiment of patriarchal relations rather than the disembodied "impersonality" of laws, and, most especially, the centrality of the "visible symbol" of the virtuous and aristocratic wife and mother. As in Norton's polemical texts, the queen plays the dual role of patron and matron, and like the heroines of midcentury domestic melodramas, such as the dying Isabel, Victoria's theatricality is a "visible symbol of unity" for an otherwise dispersed population. Like other species of melodrama, this royal melodrama seems to manage the market's incursions into English culture. Just as *East Lynne*'s reification of marriage implicitly justifies patriarchal and thus regional representation in Parliament rather than democratic and numerical representation, so the marriage of the Prince of Wales seems to support the limited franchise, because, like Mr. Dill, most people still "know how to stick" to a "good master." Just as Norton's melodrama banished the mercenary George, so royal melodrama banished the frightening prospect of that "race of expenditure."

All these species of melodrama aim to preserve hierarchical society and its code of deferential exchange, but with varying degrees of thoroughness, sincerity, and intent. In Bagehot's description of royal melodrama, the "vague romance" of monarchy that troubled the practicality of Norton's vision of reform becomes a full-blown mythology for the masses. Rather than a visible embodiment of a genuine social structure, the monarchy "acts as a *disguise*. It enables our real rulers to change without heedless people knowing it" (p. 97). In Bagehot's text, the costumes have become disguises, the roles have become impostors, and the melodramatic mode has become, under these circumstances, a ruse. At this point in the nineteenth century, as Caroline Norton discovered, the theatricality inherent in the melodramatic mode could be seen to be pretense, but a pretense that could be useful. Bagehot notes that when the queen wrote a letter to Mrs. Lincoln after the president's assassination, "it was," for the masses, "a spontaneous act of intelligible feeling in the midst of confused and tiresome business" (p. 86). Indeed, behind the disguise of royal melodrama, with its familial narratives, its scenes of face-to-face exchanges expressive of "intelligible feeling," the Cabinet proceeded with, to use Bagehot's significant choice of phrase, its "business." As described by Bagehot, this royal melodrama seems specifically designed to obscure rather than reveal the secret transactions going on in private boxes and, to this extent, is opportunistic.

Instead of wielding her influence in the name of the dispossessed, the queen was apparently using melodramatic tactics to hide the secret transactions taking place in Parliament's own version of a private box—the "secret" Cabinet (p. 69). Within these meetings, political deals were made that had far greater economic consequences on the populace than did the debates in Parliament. During the decades after the First Reform Bill, when party politics in England came to dominate political culture, the Cabinet did in fact consolidate its power and became the true executive branch of the English government. Despite its national significance, it was also the "effectual secret of the English constitution" because there was no official precedent for its existence—it was a mid-nineteenth-century creation (p. 69). All of its meetings were confidential, and no minutes were recorded, let alone disseminated to other branches of the government or to the general public, unless members decided to leak information. Unlike the floor of Parliament, the secret Cabinet was explicitly untheatrical; it had no Strangers' Gallery from which the audience could participate and keep on eye on its exchanges.

Despite Bagehot's assured tone and comprehensive analysis, his depiction of midcentury government is, as David Cannadine notes, more prescriptively hopeful than descriptively accurate.[109] The mourning Victoria's decision to avoid the public eye at the same time that the Cabinet perfected its secretive procedures of governance threatened to evacuate the public sphere just as effectively as had the private boxes in the Covent Garden Theatre or the privatized commons in the English countryside—even in spite of the apparently wider participation of the populace in government after 1866. Not surprisingly, by the late 1860's and early 1870's, the ramifications of this withdrawal from public view manifested themselves in allegations of a by-now familiar form of conspiracy. Charles Dilke and other Republicans, who were enjoying an increase in their numbers at this time, charged that the savings accrued from the royal household's civil list had been transferred to the queen's private account.[110] Rather than the beneficent lady of the manor, even the queen had begun to seem like the selfish governor who had abdicated the paternal role. Needless to say, the gambling, whoring, and merrymaking of the Prince of Wales encouraged this representation. Painfully aware of Victoria's seclusion and Bertie's idleness, Bagehot wistfully imagined a form of "royal melodrama" that had to wait until history supplied the outrageous coincidence, menacing fate, and spectacular familial reunion that such a genre requires. Bagehot did not need to wait long.

In 1871, ten years almost to the very day when Albert succumbed to typhoid fever, the Prince of Wales fell gravely ill with the same malady. Although he was near death for several days, the prince defeated the infection as his mother stood watch by his bedside. Soon thereafter, London experienced its first large-scale royal celebration since the marriage of Victoria.

Late in February, large crowds assembled to witness the royal progress to St. Paul's Cathedral on a day of official thanksgiving for the recovery of the prince. In an open carriage, the queen, her pale son, and his wife acted a fitting climax to the previous days of illness, forming a familial tableau that would do justice to a final scene in any stage melodrama and, apparently, exacting the proper emotional response from the audience. A reporter for the *Times* describes the street scene in this royal melodrama called the "Day of Thanksgiving":

The sight of the Mother and Son had, of course, an immediate effect upon all. A throb of sympathy passed through the spectators when it was seen how much the Queen was moved by the glad homage of her people on the recovery of her Son from well-nigh mortal sickness, and with what fond tremulousness she directed to him the salutations that hailed their approach.[111]

In spite of the pomp and scale of the celebration, depictions of the event nonetheless strove to capture this standard melodramatic scene of face-to-face exchanges of sympathy among the members of the royal family and, more important, between the royal family and the spectators. Such a large-scale ceremony certainly marked a new era for the staging of the melodramatic mode. It would be a mistake, however, to claim that melodrama had by this time become simply another version of state spectacle, as Bagehot seems to imply.

By the late 1870's many changes had occurred in the more stylish London theaters that further impeded stage melodrama's affective impact on its audience. The advent of the proscenium arch, permanent seating, and the star system all in their separate ways contributed to the illusion of realism on the stage and thus discouraged the actors' direct interplay with the audience that had created the conditions for an exchange of sympathy. Managers even included clauses in their contracts with artists that forbade direct address to the audience.[112] These changes in the more exclusive theaters reflected the continuing aestheticized process of class stratification in England; they did not, however, accurately reflect the style or effect, at least as it was described in contemporary accounts, of the thanksgiving day progression or even of the later Golden Jubilee. The queen was not "Olympian, aloof, and detached."[113] Riding in an open carriage, wearing a bonnet rather than a crown, surrounded by her family, Victoria presented the impression, if not the reality, of accessibility and familiarity; she was, to borrow Bagehot's phrase, "a visible symbol of unity." The melodramatic mode became increasingly detached from its concrete and historical context, but this loss rendered its symbolism proportionately more poignant, its interchange of sympathy more crucial.[114]

On arriving at the cathedral, the archbishop of Canterbury narrated the harrowing scenes leading up to this climax of mutual sympathy:

In those dark December days and nights of undefined dread, never to be forgotten, when, hour after hour, sounding in our anxious ears in this city the striking of a church clock or the tolling of any passing bell startled us with apprehension lest our worst fears were realised, all the people of this United Kingdom—the whole British race everywhere, all of every blood who own allegiance to our Queen—joined in prayer as one family, a family wide as the world, yet moved by one impulse, watching over one sick bed, yearning with one heart for one precious life.[115]

In this introductory passage from the archbishop's sermon, most of the terms of the melodramatic mode can be seen—the atmospheric menace, the familial yet pointedly patriarchal motif, the overcharged emotion. Here as elsewhere these terms continue to resist class affiliation and market incursion even as they managed new anxieties in a changing English nation. On the one hand, the threat of class conflict, for decades a haunting influence on the mechanism of melodrama, remains central to the rhetoric. The rich and the poor, themselves regardless of class, continue to recognize their mutual likeness, not difference, through the operations of sympathy staged by the melodramatic familial setting; the minister continues, "Thus we were all drawn close together through those family affections which are the birthright and blessing alike of rich and poor." The new members of the English electorate do not engage in class politics through the consolidation of their private interests, but are seen to be staunchly attached to their extended, patriarchal family interests in spite of their political power. "The love of law, the love of liberty . . . are inseparable from those intense feelings which make us reverence, not abstractions merely, or multitudinous bodies corporate, but individual living souls." Such people, elsewhere labeled by Carlyle as the "hundred-and-fifty millions free . . . to follow each his own nose," do not in fact become mercenary speculators in a corporate culture, but, when witnessing the royal family's progression, themselves embody family members and express, in the words of the *Saturday Review*, "genuine, unbought loyalty."[116]

On the other hand, the ever-expanding empire, whose colonial inhabitants threatened an even more essential alienation, are also included in the tableau, invited to the intimate domestic (but not domesticated) event of a sickbed vigil. The process of forging a national consciousness during the latter half of the nineteenth century out of a historically provincial country has been widely analyzed and discussed.[117] Although it is not within the scope of this study to address such a broad issue, melodramatic narratives such as this supplied the process of nationalization with useful representations of unity and continuity. These representations articulate one particular strain of nationalist identity formation among many extant. The increase in bureaucratic technologies that led, for instance, to the institution of the New Poor

Law in 1834 standardized procedures of social exchange on a national level and in so doing constructed another version of national and imperial identity premised on the proprietary self in a free market. Images of international tradesmen circulating their wealth or narratives of English bureaucrats rationalizing the natives are related to this ideology.

Melodrama, by contrast, imagines a national identity premised on the familiar and patriarchal, an intrinsically social and therefore inclusive ethic—"a family wide as the world."[118] In this formulation, Victoria was not so much the monarch of England, but the queen mother of the English people. The intimate and local was superimposed onto a national consciousness of "Englishness," with complex results. For example, the melodramatic mode's insistence on familiarity could also breed racism, jingoism, and xenophobia.[119] Both of these seemingly contradictory tendencies—inclusion and exclusion—were as apparent in the stage melodramas of the 1880's and 1890's as they had been in the melodrama of the early nineteenth century.[120]

As Bagehot obliquely sensed, the extension of the franchise and the growth of "the whole British race everywhere" rendered the effects of royal melodrama all the more valuable. Even though the thanksgiving day celebration certainly mobilized these effects, it remains an open question as to the extent to which the Cabinet and Gladstone, the current prime minister, specifically masterminded the thanksgiving spectacular and thus compelled the widespread expressions of loyalty that ensued.[121] Those preferring a "great men" style of political history or who accept Bagehot's analysis without question assume that such displays performed solely propagandistic functions for the state by appealing to the poor and women, who were presumed to prefer melodramatic fare.[122] It is then tempting to represent Gladstone in this instance as the master of spectacle and the large London crowds as his gullible audience. Even within these terms of operation, such a conclusion seems questionable. Gladstone himself harbored profound feelings about the symbolism of monarchy.[123]

Furthermore, the long-standing pervasiveness of melodramatic rhetoric among both the rich and poor, as this study has attempted to show, suggests that a public outpouring of face-to-face deferential sympathy hardly required Machiavellian machinations by the powers of the state; contemporary culture was suffused with the conditions favorable to its existence. Even if Gladstone, like Bagehot, had hoped to quell the "free-racing" of social and economic speculation with the "disguise" of melodrama, he also honored melodrama's values, sharing this affection with many of those he wished to moderate. He might stress duty and frugality when others emphasized protection and beneficence, but he treasured these theatricalized scenes of a familial reunion in which strict patriarchal hierarchy remained intact.[124] Most

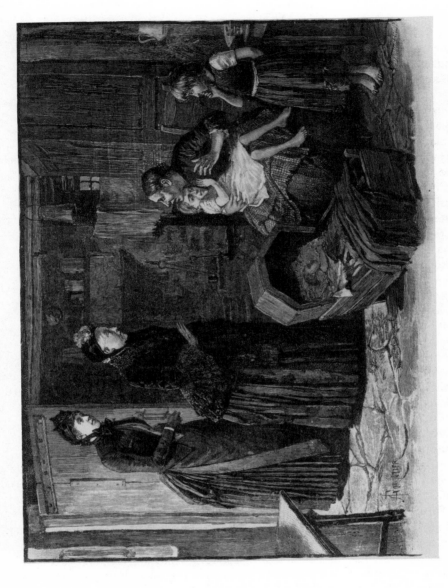

Figure 7. "The Queen Visiting a Poor Cottager at Balmoral," from *The Illustrated London News,* Diamond Jubilee Number, 1897. Victoria surprises one of her impoverished tenants in an illustration that combines the private philanthropy of womanhood and the public benevolence of the

of the spectators on the Day of Thanksgiving probably preferred to think of themselves as loyal subjects of the queen rather than as proprietary selves, just as Norton preferred to represent herself as passive victim and heroic wife. Like Gladstone, they too yearned for social stability in a familiar and recognizable shape.

Many of the ceremonial details and theatrical representations of the Day of Thanksgiving found amplification many years later in the queen's jubilees of 1887 and 1897, especially the former, when the progression to Westminster Abbey consisted of a display of Victoria's extended blood family.[125] Comprising a large portion of the European heads of state, this reunion provided a concrete display of the hierarchical, familial deference on which England's supremacy was presumed to exist. The fact that these triumphal displays might have been a response to the early signs of imperial decline only argues further that the melodramatic mode—its surcharged emotion, obsessive familial tableaux, and insistence on "intelligible feeling"—was the appropriate representational vehicle in an era of imperial breakdown, national dispersal (Irish Home Rule), and rising trade unionism.

By the 1870's, the lord may have appeared to abandon his manor and the people on it, but the queen had not.[126] Years earlier, Caroline Norton had hoped that Victoria could combine the domestic virtues of the wife with the social virtues of the traditional aristocratic gentlewoman; in the public progressions through London typical of the later decades of her reign, Victoria, clad always in mourning, finally embodied that role—enacting, albeit on a grand, metropolitan scale, the face-to-face and public interplay of benevolence and respect so crucial, in melodrama's terms, to a moral society. In the special Diamond Jubilee edition of the *Illustrated London News*, a half page was thus fittingly devoted to an engraving of Victoria entitled "Queen Visiting a Poor Cottager at Balmoral" (see Figure 7). Although the newspaper picture shows Victoria visiting the home of an impoverished laborer, its dissemination throughout the nation transforms this private act of charity into a deferential performance of patronage.

FIVE

Blows into Whispers

The Melodramatic Mode and Intellectual Culture in the 1870's and 1880's

> Women, and the mob! the canaille, the profane vulgar, the
> swinish multitude!   William Thompson

In his study *The English Constitution* (1867), Walter Bagehot describes in detail the processes of parliamentary governance in mid-Victorian England. At one point in his analysis, he charts a normal sequence of events during which "opinion out of doors" precedes debate on the parliamentary floor, which in turn precedes what he calls the "melodrama" of Parliament. Like the abrupt reversals in fortune typical of a standard stage melodrama, parliamentary melodrama climaxed in the hasty collapse of one government and its sudden replacement by another. Bagehot laments the chain of cause and effect that is mistakenly implied by this progression of political occurrences. These spectacular reversals in Parliamentary melodrama "impress men even too much," Bagehot complains, because they misleadingly convince men that changeable public opinion outside the walls of Westminster determines not only the content of parliamentary debate, but even selects the ruling party and its Cabinet. In making these remarks, indeed, in arguing throughout *The English Constitution* that the Cabinet, not the public, was the "efficient secret" of Victorian government, Bagehot aimed to diminish the importance of another characteristic similarity between stage melodrama and parliamentary melodrama—their obliging and unsecretive relationship with their audiences. Although he does not elaborate on his chastening remark about parliamentary melodrama, Bagehot seems to use the complaint as a means of regulating in his text the potential power of public opinion outside of Parliament in order to enhance instead the impact the debate inside exerts on those closed Cabinet meetings. He asserts a chronological and qualitative distinction between a relatively exclusive procedure of official debate and the inclusive, unpredictable, and undeniably "inefficient" unfolding of public opinion. For climactic scenes in the play of government, Bagehot prefers walls and cabinets, not open-air theaters.

In Bagehot's regulatory formulation, the parliamentary floor becomes the scene of popular instruction, not a staging of the popular will. The debates are, to borrow Bagehot's terminology, a "prologue" before "the play," a typically untheatrical moment when the audience receives interpretive guidance and frequently a narrative preview concerning the impending performance.[1] Only after the instructive and revealing debate on the floor of Parliament can the now anticlimactic melodrama that overthrows governments take place. The prologue's the thing. Through this theatrical conceit, Bagehot detaches the audience from its obliging melodrama and thus dissociates a probable cause from its effect; he steals thunder from the troubling prospect of a potent and yet uninformed popular voice, a prospect framed no doubt by the imminence of the Second Reform Bill, which promised to enfranchise large numbers of men traditionally associated with the ill-informed mob.[2]

In parliamentary debate, Bagehot finds an ancient origin and historical justification for a style of social exchange that had become a central premise of mid-nineteenth-century liberal ideology and its constitution of the liberal subject. Perhaps best seen as an evolved version of eighteenth-century Enlightenment ideals that were formerly associated with the rational conversation of the coffeehouses, the orderly exchange of reasonable opinion had not only become a favored method of social interaction, but the source of social identity for noted liberal men of the day, many of whom extolled its virtues in print. For men like the journalist Walter Bagehot, the writer and Liberal politician John Morley, and the novelist and poet George Meredith, all of whom aspired to positions of influence in English society, rational exchange was the premier feature of an ideal social order, a society perhaps first fully envisioned in the work of John Stuart Mill. Mill represents an originary figure of sorts for this population of intellectual elites who would champion throughout the second half of the century his model of civic, political, and social exchange. In Mill's libertarian philosophy, as espoused in *On Liberty* (1859), the exchange of views among reasonable men comprised the ground for a free society and, most crucially, the necessary environment for the nourishment of an individualism premised on reasoning ability. Men like Bagehot, Morley, and Meredith discerned in these principles of exchange a rationale for a new and exclusive social class of professional intellectuals, of particular men conversing in a particular room, sheltered from and oblivious to the tempestuous passions that consumed the masses. As dictated in Bagehot's version of the instructive debates on the floor of Parliament, the exchange of views among informed men would even help to civilize the populist tastes of these newly enfranchised masses by providing the prologue before the play that would moderate their taste for melodramatic spectacles of toppled governments and therefore their predilection for the more insidious revolutionary views such turns of political fortune implied. In effect, rational exchange produces through its powerful performance a society where mob rule on an open-air stage seems no longer thinkable, where, instead, reasonable gentlemen in a room sit down and talk to one another and, in so doing, chart the course of a nation.

Bagehot's celebration of the exclusivity of party debate and cabinet politics seems to confirm the existence of those "protected whist-players" of Parliament that Caroline Norton melodramatically excoriates in her approximately contemporaneous polemic in *English Laws for Women in the Nineteenth Century*. Despite their diametrically opposed assessments of this style of governance, both texts stage a contentious but vital relation between parliamentary debate and the effects of melodrama, a textual relationship that rhetorically dramatizes a very real confrontation that grew increasingly contentious and explicit as the century progressed. Mill and Bagehot's prescriptive images of a society organized around the reasonable exchange of opinion did not then merely aim to minimize the potential impact of those melodramatic scenes of parliamentary crisis and the popular disputes that seemed to cause it, but as a hegemonic form of social organization, such images of rational exchange also sought to counter all other disputatious developments of popular sentiment and the resultant scenes of melodrama that might otherwise noisily interrupt calm discussions among men. By and large, these prescriptive images succeeded, but not without frequent and costly encounters with the alternative representations produced through the melodramatic mode.

During the later decades of the nineteenth century, especially in the 1870's and 1880's, melodramatic situations—toppled governments, fallen women, despotic rulers—proved to be quite pervasive representational figures of opinion "out of doors," most noticeably on the stages of theaters and music halls and in the pages of the popular press, perhaps culminating in W. T. Stead's sensationalistic reportage in the *Pall Mall Gazette*.[3] The patriarchal ethos of melodrama and the deferential society it envisioned found an especially congenial outlet in nationalist expansion and colonial relations and thus accounts for stage melodrama's immersion in imperialist themes and settings during this era. But, as J. M. MacKenzie notes, melodrama had once more moved beyond the stages of the East End. One need not have attended a theater to see an imperialist melodrama, for "empire had become its own melodrama."[4] The merger of melodrama and empire is perhaps best exemplified in Victoria's assumption of the title Empress of India in 1876. As a mother and monarch, hereditary heir and imperial hero, Empress Victoria's rhetorical and pictorial representations symbolized through her aristocratic female body a familiar and familial unity in an acutely dispersed culture. During the 1870's and 1880's, England was experiencing some of its most severe class antagonisms at the same time as it attempted to assimilate under the rubric of empire what were anxiously perceived to be even more alien classes than England's own poor.[5]

Continuing the trend of earlier decades, then, the melodramatic mode was clearly being deployed in otherwise nontheatrical, nonliterary controversies. Still a dramatic vehicle for the dispossessed, still expressing reservations about market culture, still declaring allegiance to a by-now highly attenuated and nostalgic rendering of deferential exchange, the melodramatic mode could still be seen and heard in numerous venues on and off the stage. During the national movement to repeal the controversial Contagious Diseases Acts, Josephine Butler, the movement's spiritual leader, made ample use of the melodramatic mode's polemical tools of resistance in responding to what she perceived as market culture's structural reorganization of the traditional terms of social exchange among the classes and between English men and women. At times, Butler's polemic can sound very much like an echo of Caroline Norton's own rhetoric.

Rather than losing their efficacy with the passage of time, various features of the melodramatic mode—its familial narratives, criminal situations, overcharged emotionalism, and uncanny responsiveness to its audience—came to typify a style of public opinion formation in late Victorian England's emerging mass culture that was categorically unlike the discussion on the floor of Parliament. It was this popular discussion "out of doors" that was presumed capable by many of reversing fortunes and even toppling governments. Often produced by and through an emergent mass culture industry, the melodramatic mode that surfaced in popular culture during the last third of the nineteenth century still evoked the features of melodrama but displayed a somewhat revised style of deferential exchange that often emphasized an inclusivity more populist than paternalist and a sentiment more shrill than stately. Moreover, in clear contrast to the typically masculinized renderings of rational exchange, late Victorian scenes of melodrama were most often associated, especially by its critics, with women.[6] Such associations were not entirely unfounded. As in midcentury, women were among those most likely to be victims of the bureaucratic and economic streamlining of England and thus were logical benefactors of the melodramatic mode in many of its myriad manifestations.

Combined with its power to alter the course of fate, the melodramatic mode's inclusive and deferential model of social organization threatened both the values of the liberal elite and their own social value in Victorian culture, despite—or perhaps because of—melodrama's affiliation with women and the poor. In effect, the confrontation between the melodramatic mode and the culture of liberal debate, and therefore between the distinct forms of social exchange they epitomized, was a battle over cultural capital that greatly influenced the ways and means by which public opinion and social status were formulated, packaged, and disseminated in late Victorian England. This confrontation was also, inevitably, mutually constitutive, with liberal culture and its club of reasonable men engaged in conversation taking shape in relation to a late-nineteenth-century version of the melodramatic mode and its often female cast of clamoring open-air crowds.

This chapter will therefore document the melodramatic mode's contribution to the formation of public opinion in late Victorian mass culture as well as its unforeseen contribution to the institutionalization of a class of professional intellectuals who abhorred, feared, and then assertively responded to the melodramatic spectacle of public sentiment by taking possession of it for their own ends. In order to unearth these remnants of the melodramatic mode that once exerted such a strong influence on late Victorian culture, it is necessary to start with the liberal culture's confrontation with it. Only through this interaction can one tease out the lineaments of this melodramatic mode from a historical record that has long eradicated most of its traces.

I

Although political and intellectual histories might now paint a calmer landscape when discussing the history of liberalism, Mill's ideal of enlightened debate among rational individuals was, from the beginning, under siege; indeed, his book was composed as a response to nineteenth-century political reforms that threatened to usher in an era of majoritarian rule by public opinion. Later changes in the political climate further endangered the environment for rational debate. The 1870's saw Gladstone take his ministerial program to mass gatherings in the North, while in 1884 to 1885, the Third

Reform Bill enfranchised agricultural laborers, for the first time making the working classes the majority of the electorate.[7] It was during these same decades that party journalism, a form of print debate, declined in the wake of an emergent "new journalism" that sought and produced broad cultural constituencies rather than elite, political ones.[8] On the eve of the Third Reform Bill, one contributor to *Macmillan's Magazine* explicitly mourned the anticipated demise of that most revered form of rational exchange, parliamentary debate: "The House of Commons is already tending to become an assembly for transacting the routine business of the nation, and carrying out the decision which by means of discussion outside its walls (already, alas, gaining steadily in worth upon debates within them) the nation has arrived at."[9] Instead of forging a party program solely out of parliamentary political conflict, instead of educating the populace about these programs through the exchanges in party newspapers and journals, both parties, the writer concedes, found it necessary to confer with the expanded public on matters of national policy. In so doing, politicians revealed their increased recognition of the powers of public opinion and, following Bagehot's terminology, its articulation through the tropes, techniques, and plots of popular melodrama.

As is evident in Bagehot's trope of parliamentary melodrama, the version of melodrama most often envisioned by its critics was not by any means an accurate, measured, or comprehensive rendition of the melodramatic mode on its own terms, but it does focus on those features that presented the greatest threat to a liberal ideal of social organization. The melodramatic format of populist disputation was invariably seen by both Tories and Liberals as dangerously different from the rules of debate. What we recognize as a melodramatic mode apparent in the "new journalism" was a particular danger, for it was perceived to be both violent and explicitly oppositional to the liberal ideal of individualism. John Morley sensed both of these dangers lurking in the new world of publishing: "The multiplication of journals 'delivering brawling judgments unashamed on all things all day long,' has done much to deaden the small stock of individuality in public verdicts."[10]

In addition to its fascination with violence and its antagonism toward individualism, the melodramatic mode's overt emotional expressiveness and its preservation of the patriarchal ethic through the clothed body of the woman represented a further threat to the masculine preserve of individuated and rational debate in all its manifestations, whether in Parliament or in Morley's *Fortnightly Review*, a journal dedicated to the publication of opposing opinion and thus engaged in the rigorous enactment of debate. Josephine Butler's often strident polemics and fearless physical activism, which occasionally resulted in brawls among her audience and physical danger to herself, seems a specific incarnation of Morley's worst fears. As she lobbied against mandatory examinations of unclothed prostitutes and for the veneration of womanly authority, Butler was often considered a demagogue who valued populist sentiment more highly than reason. Henry James, a younger contemporary of Morley's, in documenting this perceived change in public opinion formation explicitly affiliates it with gendered stereotypes, perhaps recalling activist women like Butler: "The masculine tone is passing out of the world. . . . It is a feminine, nervous, hysterical, chattering, canting age."[11] On reading this Jamesian complaint, one should recollect the quotation in the previous chapter from the Victorian James Fitzjames Stephen, who stipulated a gendered distinction between "men who will be patient, quiet, moderate, and tolerant of difference in opinion" and the "feminine, irritable, noisy mind, which is always clamouring and shrieking for protection."[12] In a quickly consolidating mass culture where information technology was becoming increasingly sophisticated, the formation of public opinion was inevitably swayed by majorities, but at least in the views of these men, such undifferentiated majorities were, oddly enough, distinguished by hysterical women with unregulated mouths.

The populist version of the melodramatic mode in the 1880's was clearly perceived to be something other than a frail, feminine plea for protection in the tradition of melodramatic stage heroines. As demonstrated in Victoria's assumption of the crown of empire, the feminine voice of the melodramatic mode could be seen to be militantly masculine in its own right. A drawing of this period, for instance, departs from the maternal representation of the mother/queen and sketches instead a manly Victoria in battle dress (see Figure 8). Even the queen is auditioning for and winning traditionally male roles. As depicted through the perceptions of its detractors, most often the liberal intellectual elite, performances of the melodramatic mode in the 1880's suffer from very nearly the same flaws as earlier manifestations of it in 1809 and 1834. Rather than signifying for these critics a coherent resistance to market culture, the melodramatic mode incarnated that male-oriented culture, embodying its competitiveness, its insatiable desires, its manias.

This particular criticism arises from a perhaps inevitable misapprehension of the melodramatic mode's always complicated relation to market exchange. Although resistant in principle to market culture, it operated within an increasingly urban, stratified, and commodified society; Thomas Richards comments that by the 1880's "the question of whether anything was once *not* a commodity becomes moot."[13] As a populist vehicle of expression, it was necessarily transmitted through the urban mass market's material organization of popular exchange and consumption—newspapers, music halls, and, later, movie houses. Through this transmission, the melodramatic mode was

Figure 8. "A Modern Melodrama," by Tom Merry, from *St. Stephen's Review*, 1887. Victoria dons battle armor and a manly likeness to adjudicate between two warring European factions in another stock scene from stage melodrama. Collection of the Harvard College Library.

shaped, and it inevitably acquired traits associated with the urban market. Equally important, however, its traditional themes and symbols were then reinterpreted through the filter of a dominant consumer culture. For example, the melodramatic mode's special appeal to the populace was read, not without justice, as pandering to its audience.[14] Critics of market culture, especially those inspired by Arnoldian aesthetics, thus condemned melodrama as a form of entrepreneurship in their attempts to rhetorically and, ultimately, materially distinguish between their own model of consumption and exchange and the market's version of consumption and exchange.

In enforcing these distinctions, opponents exploited a familiar heuristic device: the principle of classification. Stage melodrama, and thus any form of public performance linked to melodrama, was associated, rather inaccurately, with particular classes of people, usually women and the poor, and was evaluated within this conceptual framework. In a theater staging a melodrama, for instance, members of the audience as well as the management itself were constructed and perceived as participants in an economic exchange, not a cultural one, and were therefore identified solely in terms of their economic function in the market—as producers, laborers, and consumers. Such a perspective informs the description of them provided by Henry Arthur Jones, an influential playwright and theatrical critic of the 1880's: "They [the audience] come jaded from the impure air of shops, factories, offices, from the hard stress of business, professional, or domestic duties." Once at the theater, Jones continues, they take in a melodrama, staged by "cheesemongers" and "managerial shopkeepers" who perform the function of theater managers.[15] As economic entities, not social or familial members, these audiences' appreciation of such theatrical fare can only be figured by Jones as a business transaction, the purchase and consumption of a commodity by a sundry crowd of laborers and lumpenproletariat. Women, coming from the "hard stress" of "domestic duties," are lumped with this crowd of laborers through the transforming magic of consumption, even though elsewhere they were more frequently figured as standing outside the market. In their consumption of melodrama, women are like laboring men and so Jones must deny them the moral and aesthetic powers of discrimination.

In part because of these material and rhetorical representations partially governed by principles of economic classification, the expanded public of the 1880's was seen by many contemporary commentators to intensify a familiar concern about unchecked social and economic appetites, a concern formerly voiced with less vehemence by men like Walter Bagehot. Bagehot, though worried for the future of English society, was far more sanguine than the writer in *Macmillan's Magazine* about the business in Parliament. For Bagehot, the real business of government was mainly limited to the oligarchic and private transactions within the Cabinet. By the 1880's, however, the market ethic seemed to have permeated the entire House of Commons. Such perceptions were not entirely whimsical. The Parliament of 1880 was the last to consist of a landowning majority; subsequent Parliaments contained significant numbers of men representing or embodying commercial interests. Whereas Bagehot had worried that parliamentary seats might become commodities in electoral districts, by the 1880's, the floor of Parliament itself was in danger of becoming a marketplace, a site for transactions among contending commercial interests. Indeed, candidates for election were increasingly considered to be akin to commodities. At this time, Alan Lee has commented, a "new morality" emerged that condoned the candidate's adoption of policy positions for the express purpose of getting elected. Although this is, of course, standard electioneering procedure in the twentieth century, it came into acceptance only late in the nineteenth. During its period of emergence, Lee remarks, critics did not perceive the public forums during which these policies were offered to the electorate as a scene of debate, but, like other scenes of populist expression, these forums were perceived as markets in which the candidates sold political policies and bought votes.[16] If candidates were businessmen and elections were marketplaces, it was only a matter of time before the floor of Parliament started to look like the stock exchange.

Invaded by the melodramatic mode of public discussion, tainted by that mode's presumed participation in economic exchange, parliamentary debate was losing its esteemed reputation, but the principles of debate and the civilized society it engendered continued to engage the intellectual heirs of J. S. Mill. Most of these men were sons of the educated middle class, and most of them sought prestige and status in English society, despite their lack of hereditary rank and the absence of patronage that the aristocracy had once offered educated men like them. Although not all of these men were members of the Liberal party, they espoused the liberal ideals of rational exchange and tolerance. John Morley, editor of the *Fortnightly Review* until 1882, Liberal member of Parliament, and later the secretary for Ireland and then India, wrote the now little-read *On Compromise* (1874), a book that celebrates these liberal ideals. Owing much to Mill's *On Liberty*, Morley's book discusses the moral means and ways of "wise suspense in forming opinion," "wise reserve in expressing them," and "wise tardiness in trying to realise them."[17] In effect an etiquette of rational exchange in a civilized society, *On Compromise* worried about the threat political expediency posed to the convictions of the individual in a largely enfranchised population.

Like Morley, such men of the educated middle class were eager to advance in society but nevertheless increasingly eschewed free market ideology and its practices—industry, trade, and market speculation. The reasons for this oppositional attitude toward market culture remain obscure, not the least because such attitudes remain prevalent today in England. Martin J. Wiener suggests that the English aristocracy traditionally disdained industry and thus disseminated this attitude downward through the ranks, while Harold Perkin rightly questions this hypothesis because it disregards the fact that "the aristocracy before and during the Industrial Revolution were the most economically progressive and profit-oriented ruling class in Europe."[18] Perhaps some of the causes of this antimarket stance lay in larger structural factors in the economy. Unlike real property, commercial property was volatile and unstable, subject to market upheavals, bank failures, and speculative surges. Furthermore, commercial property may have lacked the cultural, if not monetary, status of real property, since it was often believed that anyone might amass a large commercial fortune. Whereas real property traditionally conferred lifelong and exclusive privileges to its possessors, commercial property potentially offered unpredictable privileges to nearly everyone.[19]

From this perspective, neither real nor commercial property could provide a sufficient degree of stability and exclusivity required to ground the liberal ideal of the individual. Periodic economic crises, such as the railway mania of the 1840's and the bank failures of the 1860's, seriously undermined the image of a self-regulating market, not to mention the havoc such "mania" wreaked on the image of a self-regulating, self-possessed individual. In many respects, the market culture that had constituted possessive individualism had failed to sustain it, but another sort of property was rapidly becoming, for men like these, a fully theorized substitute for real and commercial property—namely, what I will call "mental property."[20] Mental property is equivalent to Harold Perkin's conception of "human capital." Like human capital, mental property is a form of property "created by education and enhanced by strategies of closure" that emphasize "skilled and differentiated labour" and "selection by merit."[21] Like owners of human capital, possessors of mental property participated in the professionalization of English society, as I will briefly discuss later in this chapter.[22] I use the term "mental property" rather than "human capital" in order to separate the exclusive category of intellectual services from the more inclusive category of human services, a distinction that emerged from this period. Mental property consists of the unique possessions of the individuated intellect and provided a revised version of subjectivity that was insistently differentiated from both the free-trading, amoral, and possessive individual of market culture and the "shrieking," "brawling," and "hysterical" voice of populist melodrama. I will call this revised subject, for lack of a better term, the "intellectual individual."

Like Henry Arthur Jones with his theatrical criticism, men who represented and enacted intellectual individuality actively distinguished between intellectual culture and other forms of cultural organization. Unlike real property, mental property did not rely on antiquated modes of deferential exchange in which a lingering reliance on blood, status, and community effectively excluded or underemphasized most intellectuals and their idealized conceptions about the free play of thought. Moreover, unlike commercial property, mental property was scrupulously disassociated from market culture and its contentious tendencies. Such men were proprietary individuals, but their possessions were perceived to consist of ideas and convictions, not stocks and bonds, and their self-possession, what Morley describes as "coherency of character," consisted of "a commanding grasp of principles," not, at least overtly, their grasping command of money amassed through free agency in the market.[23] As will be demonstrated below, this feature of intellectual culture is both its most crucial myth and deepest contradiction, for in order to transcend the vagaries of the market, one needed to control one's destiny within it, to create, for instance, a labor monopoly, as Morley and his intimate friend George Meredith sought to do in the field of authorship.[24]

This intellectual individual, along with its variant conceptualizations of rational exchange, imagined a new economy in which power and prestige were distributed according to intellectual ability and professional expertise. Although it would be inaccurate to claim that late Victorian England represented a realization of this society, as Perkin is perilously close to arguing, an intellectual elite did acquire cultural capital as the century came to a close. The increasing value attached to mental property is documentable in the apotheosis of the man of letters as a representative gentleman of late Victorian society. The possessive individual of market culture, endowed with commercial wealth, found himself in social competition with intellectuals, endowed with brains. By the 1890's, the novelist and poet George Meredith could embody for English people a lionized sage, in effect replacing the exalted industrialists of midcentury, such as the entrepreneurial engineer George Stephenson, whom the British elite had honored with a funeral cortege to Westminster Abbey in 1859.[25]

The lionized Meredith's highly regarded novels of "philosophy in fiction," to adopt Meredith's own term, contributed to the theorization of mental property and the intellectual individual who owned such capital. Literary historians have assigned to Meredith a supporting role in the refinement of realist fiction, but they have not examined the ways in which Meredith's distinctive brand of novel—his "psychological realism"—helped to articulate and promote the ideals of intellectual culture, especially its cherished ideal of rational exchange. Through strategies of plot and characterization, Meredith frequently represented individuated intelligence through a revamped depiction of the exchange of ideas.

Because of this emphasis on the exchange of ideas, the intellectual individual and his mental property can be seen as the direct conceptual heirs of the liberal individualism Bagehot had celebrated. Similarly, because of her emphasis on patriarchal ethics, Josephine Butler's melodramatic ploys to formulate public opinion can be seen as the heir of Caroline Norton's melodramatic rhetoric of the 1850's. These parallels between the histories of liberalism and the melodramatic mode are not coincidental. The remaining sections of this chapter will therefore analyze the mutually constitutive interplay between the melodramatic mode and the professional aspirations of the intellectual liberal elite through an examination of representative instances—Josephine Butler's melodramatic polemic against the Contagious Diseases Acts and Meredith's later career, especially as it is obliquely represented in one of his most celebrated philosophical fictions, *Diana of the Crossways* (1885). In so doing, I will also make an exploratory contribution to the long overdue study of the historical constitution of psychological realism and the political content of its version of subjectivity.[26] Literary critics and historians have been far too hesitant about historicizing these two concepts or narrating the story of their genesis, no doubt because so many of the assumptions involved have become naturalized in literary history and the history of ideas. Instead of pursuing explications of the internal coherence and logic of psychological realism as a literary genre, I will document its confrontation with and ultimate translation of the popular rhetoric of melodrama, thereby placing those naturalized assumptions back into the fray of cultural formation. Finally, through this comparative study of Butler's texts and Meredith's career, I will continue the attempt begun in the last chapter to add precision to our definition(s) of "feminism" in nineteenth-century England, which a knowledge of the melodramatic mode facilitates.

II

During the height of George Meredith's career in the 1870's and 1880's, one of the most persistent topics of public discussion concerned the Contagious Diseases Acts of 1864, 1866, and 1869. Billed by their supporters as military reforms, these three acts sought to control the spread of venereal disease among enlisted men. The laws focused their attention not on the infected soldiers and sailors, but on the prostitutes who plied their trade in garrison and port towns throughout England. Under these acts, plainclothes policemen were empowered to identify women as prostitutes. These women were then submitted to a pelvic examination conducted by a physician. They could either volunteer for the examination or be constrained to submit to it by a magistrate's order. If found to be diseased, women were confined up to three months in what were called "lock hospitals."

Passed quietly in Parliament, these acts became the center of public outrage and of a nationwide movement that sought their repeal. The movement did not win the repeal of the acts until 1886, after a protracted and often brutal fight. This repeal movement embraced many kinds of supporters with diverse concerns and goals, and by the 1880's there were dissensions in its ranks, but what unified opponents to the legislation was the fact that the acts appeared to legalize prostitution in England, to place the onus of the venereal disease "epidemic" on women alone, and to discriminate against poorer women, the ones most likely to be suspected by policemen. It is not within the scope of this chapter to provide a more detailed narrative of this movement, which was led in large part by Josephine Butler.[27] I want instead to concentrate on a sampling of Butler's published speeches and pamphlets because, as Judith Walkowitz has observed, they adopt melodramatic scenarios and a melodramatic rhetoric to communicate to their audiences.[28]

These texts not only attest to the continued vitality into the 1880's of the melodramatic mode, but provide a contemporary instance of the populist behaviors that proved so threatening to and formative of intellectual culture in the 1880's. I have chosen these texts for another reason as well. Although the melodramatic mode was deployed in other public discussions during the 1870's and 1880's, particularly in the populist press, its operation in Butler's polemic accentuates the parallels between her efforts and Caroline Norton's in the 1850's and thus provides a point of connection with Meredith's *Diana of the Crossways*, my exemplary text of psychological realism and central artifact of intellectual culture. The novel is loosely based on Norton's life. Furthermore, Butler's engagement with issues concerning women—their social rights and personal desires—furnishes further points of thematic congruence between contemporary melodramatic rhetoric, which was continually perceived to be a feminine expressive vehicle, and Meredith's novel, which became the fiction of choice for "emancipated women" in the late 1880's.[29]

Because Butler supported equal property rights for women under the law and female suffrage, she cannot be called the immediate heir of Caroline Norton, who, being more than a generation older than Butler, held more conservative views. Nonetheless, both women sought to initiate public discussion about issues concerning women that were considered taboo during their day, and both women initiated such discussion in order to bring about changes in laws that directly affected people who had no hand in their construction. Butler commented, "Let it not be supposed that it has cost us little to break through the rule of silence imposed by society upon women."[30]

In this regard, Norton and Butler continue the tradition of the melodramatic mode—its use as a vehicle of expression for censored or repressed voices. In fact, these and many more parallels between the campaigns of Butler and Norton are also analogous to the protests of the O.P. faction and the 1834 Poor Law opponents, despite the years that separate them. Such parallels underscore the extent to which the melodramatic mode was a coherent and viable response to very particular social and economic changes that became characteristic of English governance throughout the nineteenth century.

The Contagious Diseases Acts, like the New Poor Law of 1834 or the 1809 renovations in the Covent Garden Theatre, instituted a system of bureaucratic classification that aimed, in this particular instance, to professionalize and nationalize England's armed forces. The acts constituted the soldiers and prostitutes under their jurisdiction in terms of an essentializing economic function, not as a priori social entities defined according to community and family connections. Rather than daughters and sons within a patriarchal family unit, both prostitutes and soldiers were now represented by the acts as independent—and alienable—wage laborers in a national economy.[31] As proletarians, the prostitutes shared the fate of able-bodied paupers under the New Poor Law and estranged wives under the marriage law, for they were conceptually and, if diseased, physically separated from their communities and families. The new acts therefore privileged economic-sexual exchange among these two groups of independent workers rather than the more traditional deferential exchange among the ranks and the sexes. Paradoxically, through this economic reclassification that resulted in the literal and figurative isolation of prostitutes, the laws also firmly fixed these women in a moral economy, for they now represented beings who had repudiated, rather than were repudiated by, the domestic ideology of Victorian society.

Through these statutes, then, the acts recall the procedures of seating and ticketing at Covent Garden Theatre, the operations of the New Poor Law, and, especially, the results of midcentury constructions of the marriage and divorce law in which male-female exchanges are of central importance. Also like these older laws, the new acts brought into being measures that sought to name, to place, and to control populations that were assumed to be unrecognizable, deceptive, and unmanageable. Just as the workhouse test empowered wardens to "discover" impostors among the paupers, so the Contagious Diseases Acts empowered plainclothes policemen to detect prostitutes among the women in the streets and, then, authorized physicians to conduct what amounted to moral as well as physical examinations on the unclothed bodies of women. The physical exam, a particular point of contention with repeal proponents, echoes the judicial examination of Caroline Norton's charwoman conducted by George Norton's legal counsel, for both acts engaged in a disrobing that discredited the symbolic function of the clothed female body.

Given these important parallels, it should not be surprising that the melodramatic mode emerges as Josephine Butler's preferred behavioral model or her rhetoric of choice in texts such as "Letter to my Countrywomen, Dwelling in the Farmsteads and Cottages of England." In this piece, Butler deploys nearly all of the features of the melodramatic mode. For instance, in this title, she emphasizes familial, local, and rural associations; at the end, she signs her "letter," an intimate vehicle of communication, with a universalizing, moralized identity tinged with a hint of aristocratic privilege—"An English Lady."[32] Throughout the campaign to repeal the acts, Butler consciously used this hybrid form of hierarchical yet populist rhetoric to engage people of all classes. Like the actors and actresses of melodrama on the stage of the Covent Garden Theatre, Butler directly addressed her audiences. She appealed to their familial, regional, and national affiliations—in that order—gradually enlarging on their most immediate feelings of connection and sympathy until audiences in the North of England could be convinced that prostitutes in Dover were "daughters" and "sisters" deserving of pity and protection. Rather than a bourgeois nuclear family, she reconstructed a deference hierarchy, replete with reciprocal rights and obligations, by exploiting the traditional forms of respect due women and the traditional forms of authority due powerful men. Although it is certainly true that neither Butler nor many of the politicians she hoped to influence were authentic aristocrats, many of them were familiar with and susceptible to the remnants of this deferential culture.

Like the opponents of the New Poor Law, Butler tells the typical melodramatic narrative of estranged patriarchal families, wrenched apart by the mercenary evil doing of a villainous family member who has succumbed to the dissolute pleasures associated with secretive market transactions. Prostitutes "fall" because "no tender mother ever spoke to *them* of God or Christ; no kind father ever shielded *them* from temptation . . . rather, they have been sold—yes, sold—into their life of bondage by those who ought to have died to save them from such misery."[33] For Butler, then, the fall into prostitution is not a story of willful abandon, but a story of victimization and coercion, a theory only confirmed by W. T. Stead's later reports of white slavery in London.

In some instances in Butler's rhetoric, this classic narrative of the victimized heroine seems an allegory of class oppression, symbolizing the aristocracy's rape of the laboring classes. Although Butler was surely aware of class conflict, she was not engaged with proletarian labor struggles or bourgeois ideological battles, but with patriarchal ones. Her language should be glossed accordingly. Simply labeling someone an "aristocrat" did not always constitute a class appellation, as the history of class language shows. The term *aristocrat* could be alternatively applied as a status identification, even in the last decades of the century. As status identification, the term does not carry with it the economic, social, and competitive connotations of class.[34] When rakish aristocrats ravage a virginal peasant or working girl in Butler's anecdotes, a linguistic emphasis on what appears to be class affiliation is instead a rhetorical expression of dismay regarding the subject's perceived abdication from his position in the patriarchal family unit, the greatest sin within the deferential ideology of melodrama. This drama, more than dramas of class struggle, dominated Butler's imagination. As in other instances of the melodramatic mode, the behavioral traits negatively associated with class identity—deception, greed, and lust—and even the symptoms of "class thinking" itself constitute the punishment for one's repudiation of deferential graces.

Class affiliation and class conflict are symptoms of, or alternatively, punishments for one's rejection of the hierarchical extended family. Butler writes disdainfully of "worldly and impure men" who think "they can separate women . . . into two classes,—the protected and refined ladies . . . and those poor outcast daughters of the people whom they purchase with money, and with whom they think they may consort in evil whenever it pleases them to do so, before returning to their own separated and protected homes."[35] In the patriarchal world of melodrama, virtuous aristocrats are synecdoches for virtuous husbands and fathers, while rakish aristocrats are incarnations of the villainous principles of economic classification. Only these latter men are capable of making specious distinctions between their wives and their purchased inamorata, whom Butler, in defiance, continues to perceive as "daughters." In response to these "worldly and impure men," Butler collapses their system of class affiliation into a universe of ethical identity: "'We will have no more class legislation; England shall be governed *by* the people *for* the people'—this had been long their watchword, and they could not therefore stand coldly by and permit laws for the advantage of the vicious few to be forced upon the virtuous many."[36] Butler highlights the segregationist thinking typical of class, but she refuses to adopt its competitive logic, preferring instead the logic of inheritance, as did Charles Dickens in *Oliver Twist*. Calling a gentleman procurer "worldly and impure" rather than a man of the "upper class," Butler then reasserts the villain's unavoidable—and ethical—connection to family, which culminates in a melodramatic scene of recognition: "The poison is in his soul. His children inherit the mixed tendencies of their parents—good and bad; and what security has this prosperous man of the world that the one who is to inherit foul blood and warped brain may not be his *daughter*!"[37] Through the inheritance plot of blood ties, Butler eschews class boundaries, even downplays bourgeois relations, and reinvigorates the patriarchal, familial connections among the people of a stratified society. Indeed, in the above passage, circuitous prose nearly manages to identify the fallen prostitute with the client's own daughter, superimposing an almost incestuous network of relations on an otherwise rigidly stratified scenario of procurement.

Butler's melodramatic rhetoric clearly relies on the traditional tenets of a deferential ideology, even if, by the 1870's, this ideology had become highly attenuated, characterized by nostalgia and conservative idealism, and, at times, complicit with some bourgeois ethical virtues. Despite these revisions, the values of deferential exchange within the hierarchical family continued to influence people like Butler, whose protests were more often reactionary and patriarchal than radical and democratic, as commentators have noted.[38] Like melodramatists of the early 1800's, Butler resolves her narratives of familial and national estrangement with elaborate restagings of deferential exchange, as when she describes her visits to poor prostitutes. By redramatizing these visits in large open-air speeches or in published letters and by deriving from them a social model of exchange, she casts herself as traditional lord of the manor rather than as the philanthropic lady of the private home. Such scenes usually culminate in the poor girl thanking her new protector, thereby rendering into tableaux the code of reciprocity inherent in the beneficent exchange typical of melodramatic denouement.[39] By the end of these scenarios, then, the "fallen girl"—"by pure and kindly contact" is taken out of "the concubinage market" and placed in one of the many "homes" that were springing up as alternatives to "lock hospitals" and gaols.[40] Through this compact symbolism of melodrama, the face-to-face benefits of deferential exchange extricate the prostitute from the market and place her in a family, thereby achieving the magical transformation from prostitute to wife, daughter, or mother. This scenario in particular reveals the extent to which members of the bourgeoisie, antagonized by market exchange, found justification for their interventionist philanthropy in a nostalgic reversion to some, if not all, tenets of deferential culture, even at times resuscitating the royal prerogative.

Like Norton in "A Letter to the Queen," Butler also invokes in "An Appeal to the People" the female monarch when, for instance, describing the mandatory medical examinations—"Such treatment of women will never be allowed in England while the Queen lives" (p. 140). In this passage, as in Norton's text, the monarchy represents deferential ideology in its national form, but throughout Butler's polemic the queen as wife can also uphold the deferential ethic within the nuclear family. Butler thus goes public with the privatized family, attempting, from yet another angle, to connect disparate peoples through highly stylized and compelling scenes of regal protection. Through a process of syllogistic logic, the mother, wife, or daughter becomes constituted as the queen in the family. Rather than the alienable property of her husband, rather than a self-proprietor, she has "absolute sovereignty over her own person" (p. 126). Butler, like Norton, thus clearly rejects the proprietary model in this instance and in so doing marks the limits of her liberalism. Although supportive of working women and committed to a woman's right to her own property, Butler did not want women to become possessive individualists—subject to and thus subjects of the laws of the market. Neither as property nor proprietor did a woman retain the familial and virtuous identity that for Butler most empowered women in Victorian society. Butler opts instead for a model of "absolute sovereignty" that conjures up a queen's court and the deferential ideal practiced there. She calls for a revival of "chivalry and generosity towards women" (p. 127).

By introducing the queen into texts that also contain the various men of government who instituted the Contagious Diseases Acts, Butler brings to her argument the tensions between monarchy and Parliament that characterized Bagehot's *The English Constitution*. Butler, however, sees through the spectacle of monarchy that Bagehot deemed so effective a shield for the Cabinet. For instance, Butler discusses the situation of "harlots," who, on being examined and declared "clean" by the doctor, assume that "they have the sanction of the *Queen* for the continuance of their profession—for Government to them means the Queen—and that so long as they are clean and orderly in their profession they have satisfied the Queen and thus they satisfy what remains to them of conscience" (p. 135). Although the poor prostitutes are duped by this sleight of hand, Butler's melodramatic "public appeal," like those previously discussed, reembodied disembodied bureaucratic procedures; such a public appeal, she claims, "compelled the enemy to show himself."[41] In detecting the governors who really sanctioned these laws, Butler reenacts the crucial melodramatic gesture of Norton's polemic. She reveals the "selfish and unrestrained" "animal appetites" of men, desires that ultimately lead to prostitution.[42] Butler thus differentiates between the "absolute sovereignty" of women and the government of men, whose "passions" are their "rulers."[43] Virtuous (and fully clothed) heroines are thus pitted against rapacious despots and their slaves in true melodramatic fashion. This binary in Butler's polemic, between a matriarchal monarchy of morality and a male despotism of desire, is descriptive of both social and personal governance and expresses the political content in the melodramatic mode. Resisting the insatiable and tyrannical appetites of men as they were constituted in market culture, Butler imagines a sense of identity that is neither proprietary nor alienable, but, like a sovereign, absolute and eternal; the body is inseparable from the costume and the role. In this regal scenario, women cannot be bought and sold but instead embody and display a corporate virtue, that of the family, the nation, the empire.

Because the first Contagious Diseases Act passed quietly through Parliament with little debate, let alone public discussion preceding it, the acts were perceived to be the result of conspiracy; they were also considered to be products of calculation and coercion, a melodramatic portrayal of parliamentary exchange. Butler argues: "It is a law worked out in secrecy, mystified by indefiniteness, upheld by violence."[44] In melodrama, as we have seen, these three characteristics are usually interconnected; secrecy almost always veils economic speculation and physical/sexual exploitation. Recalling the secrets of the "protected whist-players" in Norton's "Letter to the Queen," such Cabinet secrets become the moral antecedent and legal precedent for prostitution in Butler's polemic. They offer a model of business transaction for the more crucial transaction in the Contagious Diseases Acts debate—the business transaction known as procurement. According to Butler, these secret transactions within the government inexorably lead to the legalization of prostitution. Having transformed the halls of Westminster into a market of their passions, these men then proceed to trade their passions in the streets.

Butler, like Norton before her, battled laws that reconstituted wives, daughters, and mothers as either laborers or commodities in the market. In effect, the Contagious Diseases Acts considered prostitution to be an ahistorical given and prostitutes to be intrinsic features of a naturalized market economy. In response to this representation, Butler used religiously tinged language that superimposed on prostitutes a moral history. In so doing, she suggested that such women possessed a past and projected a future. Instead of the class appellation of prostitute, they were "fallen women," women "betrayed into it by deceit, or driven into it by despair."[45] Such narratives, above all, resist imputations of female sexual or economic desire. Even prostitutes will not be subjected to or become subjects of market culture.

It should be obvious by now that Butler's defense of women who become prostitutes is also a defense of women in general. It should also be obvious that her attack on the Contagious Diseases Acts is also an attack on the male preserve of market culture, whose values seem to have fathered the acts. For instance, her moralized language of good and evil, so typical of melodramatic rhetoric, pointedly countered the calculus of political economy voiced by supporters of the Contagious Diseases Acts, who were clearly capable of fitting all women into their system, prostitutes and wives alike. In the following passage, one of the most notable medical proponents of the law, Dr. William Acton, explains the natural causes of prostitution. As he does so, he easily interpolates these women into a supply curve, transforming them into "artificial" consumer goods:

Supply, as we all know, is regulated by demand, and demand is the practical expression of an ascertained want . . . the desire for sexual intercourse is strongly felt by the male . . . this desire of the male is the want that produces the demand, of which prostitution is a result, and which is, in fact, the artificial supply of a natural demand.[46]

In this sentence, Acton also naturalizes male sexual desire through an economic model, thereby equating sexual and economic appetites. The congruence, if not identity, between these two drives was a crucial assumption in midcentury thought. Within utilitarian philosophy, free-market ideology, and liberal ethics, men in general, not just soldiers or able-bodied paupers, were often described in terms derived from this economic model of supply and demand. Acton's prose especially manifests this assumption, for it regularly conflates the sexual physiology of man and the circulation of the market: "Nothing costs the economy so much as the production of semen, and its forced ejaculation."[47] For this economic model of sexual order to operate smoothly, it too relies on the self-regulating mechanisms of the market. Moral women, wives and mothers, were frequently represented as the perfect emblem of regulated supply for men's sexual demand because they were believed to be naturally devoid of their own sexual and economic desires. Moreover, unlike factory production's ceaseless and geometric increase, a woman's reproductive capacity was periodic and limited. Acton himself demonstrates the intersection of these concepts: "Many of the best mothers, wives, and managers of households, know little of or are careless about sexual indulgences. Love of home, of children, and of domestic duties are the only passions they feel."[48] Note how, in an eerie echo of the *Norton v. Melbourne* proceedings, a fine "manager" of a household—an expert in domestic economy—is explicitly disassociated from indulgent sexual desire and implicitly associated with the market's self-regulation, despite her location in a putatively market-free zone. In Acton's account, both prostitutes and wives become part of a calculus that Butler abhors.

Despite her vehement antimarket sentiments, however, Josephine Butler necessarily operated in a market culture that figured women as commodities and entrepreneurs. Through her use of the melodramatic mode and its inevitable transmission through the newspapers and magazines that characterized the market's organization of popular exchange, Butler was therefore frequently regarded as a component of the populist menace in antagonism to which men like Morley and Meredith outlined intellectual culture and its version of subjectivity. Indeed, Butler's melodramatic tactics aimed to bring about genuine alterations in national law and policy in a manner that to some observers might have seemed evasive of conventional legislative procedure, such as parliamentary debate. Her direct appeals to the larger public that sought to arouse populist sentiment did not comply with the gentlemanly standards of debate; to use Morley's criteria from *On Compromise*, they were neither formed with "wise suspense" during an intimate exchange of ideas nor expressed with "wise reserve." Indeed, Butler's polemic unflinchingly investigated the sexual desires and habits of her opponents—the rapacious aristocrats and lascivious doctors who were the villains of her melodrama. In this particular regard, she whetted the appetite for scandalous speculation and gossip that Meredith and Morley detected and condemned in contemporary novels. Butler's speeches themselves, often filled with thinly veiled sexual accusations and personal anecdotes about innocent women wrenched off the streets (a traditional tactic of the melodramatic mode), could be experienced as the very archetype of gossip. Rather than a rhetoric of the self-sovereign woman in a deferential society, the melodramatic mode in its various manifestations could be and often was construed by the liberal intelligentsia as an expressive vehicle of unregulated female desire, the medium of womanly speculation.

Even though some women had always traded sex for economic support, the regulation or, alternatively, reformation of prostitution emerged once more as a central concern in the 1870's and 1880's, particularly because prostitutes' behavior stimulated broader concerns about female desire at this time. Although the passage of the Married Women's Property Acts in 1870 and 1882 seems on the surface irrelevant to contemporary discussions about prostitution, it was not. These acts were reforms that extended the reach of proprietary definitions of identity because they secured a married woman's right to the ownership of property. Just as prostitutes owned and alienated their bodies, so married women now owned and could alienate their possessions; they could become proprietors and entrepreneurs. Not surprisingly, conservative resistance to these bills articulated itself in these terms. Members of Parliament worried that there would be "two powers" in the family; that the woman would become a domestic contradiction—"a partner . . . with separate interests."[49] As Caroline Norton had predicted, the conflict of market exchange had disrupted deferential exchange within the home; by the 1880's, husbands and wives could be described, albeit hyperbolically, as contracting partners merely. As indicated in the plot of Trollope's *The Eustace*

Diamonds (1873), men even imagined wives selling family heirlooms and thereby trading away the symbols of family status that had once been worn by those wives.[50]

By the 1880's, traditional constraints seemed to many unable to stave off the proprietary behaviors of women, especially women of independent property, who were regulated neither by subsistence wage nor, increasingly, by childbirth. Although birth control was still largely unavailable, it was discussed, with trepidation, among certain circles and it marginally contributed to the growing impression that bourgeois women were independent operators. This was the specter that so haunted men like George Meredith and determined their reception of melodramatic outbreaks.

III

In 1885, George Meredith published what proved to be a widely read and discussed book, *Diana of the Crossways*. As Meredith himself admitted privately to Robert Louis Stevenson, the novel's heroine, Diana Warwick, was "partly modelled upon Mrs. [Caroline] Norton," who had died in 1877.[51] The narrative, although telescoping several decades into several years, faithfully follows the major events in Norton's life, except the birth of her three children. Nevertheless, *Diana of the Crossways* is not a historical biography, but a novel deeply involved in the contemporary issues of the 1880's—the rights of women and the Irish question, to name two.

The novel faithfully documents Norton's marriage, her estrangement, her friendship with the Conservative M.P. Sidney Herbert, her husband's death, and her eventual remarriage. A lengthy segment of this quasi-biographical novel, however, focuses not on a verifiable event in Norton's life, but on a rumor. According to this widely known and frequently accepted rumor, Norton leaked information to the press that ultimately defeated the government of the Tory prime minister Robert Peel. Norton, having learned from Herbert, a Cabinet member, of the prime minister's intention to repeal the protectionist Corn Laws, was believed to have sold this secret to John Delane, the editor of the London *Times*. His premature publication of the news resulted in a fatal crisis of confidence in Peel's ministry in 1846.[52]

Meredith's decision to concentrate on a possibly spurious rumor seems especially odd given the opening chapter of *Diana of the Crossways*, in which his narrator disdainfully relates the idle gossip, both spoken and written, that his heroine has elicited from the public. The narrator declares: "It is a test of the civilized to see and hear, and add no yapping to the spectacle" (p. 7). As Meredith explicitly confirms, this rumor, indeed the entire rumor-ridden life of Diana Warwick that he proceeds to narrate, performs a crucial role in his story, for it will function as a "test of the civilized" when administered to his readers; it serves as a means of distinguishing between his reading audience and those who would yap at a spectacle. In effect, Meredith places a narrator's prologue before a standard melodramatic plot of familial and national estrangement and of secrecy exposed in order to transform that drama. He does so by separating the audiences who employ and enjoy the melodramatic mode from those who would savor his own retooled fictions. Here, as in Bagehot's disquisition on Parliament, the prologue's the thing.

Although it is true that at this point in the novel Meredith does not specifically identify such public gossip with melodramatic rhetoric and behavior, there is already ample evidence of this equation. The mention of observers "yapping" their response at a public spectacle recalls any number of contemporary descriptions of theatrical audiences attending a melodrama. Moreover, Meredith lines up a chain of associations that repeatedly labels as gossip both the content of public discussion in newspapers and at social gatherings and links the purveyors of such gossip with speakers and writers of melodramatic romance. Perhaps most persuasively, *Diana of the Crossways* follows a familiar melodramatic plot, strikingly like Bagehot's parliamentary melodrama. In response to "opinion out of doors," the novel enacts the toppling of a government. When the heroine facilitates the publication of the Cabinet secret, she transforms exclusive knowledge into public gossip and places a national government in jeopardy. Diana's transaction also initiates her own estrangement from her lover, the Cabinet minister Percy Dacier, and thus continues the theme of familial estrangement so crucial to the melodramatic plot. The spectacular revelation of secrets forged in private spaces, be they boxes, cells, or parliamentary cabinets, had always been a staple of melodrama and the melodramatic mode.

Even if Meredith did not read Bagehot's *English Constitution* or attend the Covent Garden Theatre or witness Butler on the stump, his novel associates Diana's indiscreet act—her public exposure of a Cabinet secret and its potential to topple a government—with her submission to the popular taste of melodrama. Like Caroline Norton and Meredith himself, Diana Warwick is a novelist, and just prior to her midnight journey to the editor's office, she attempts to work on her latest story. Her inspiration seems fueled by what must be described as the melodramatic mode: "And strange to think, she could have flowed away at once on the stuff that Danvers [her maid] delighted to read!—wicked princes, rogue noblemen, titled wantons, daisy and lily innocents, traitorous marriages, murders, a gallows dangling a corpse dotted by a moon, and a woman bowed beneath" (p. 302). Bagehot had worried that such melodramatic scenarios might perhaps overly impress those out of doors because they overemphasize the impact of ever-broadening public opinion. In the rest of this passage, Meredith merely shifts this general observation about public opinion to the arena of fictional taste, but he still links melodrama and the public, a public divided by class but joined together by an insatiable appetite for melodrama. Diana recognizes that

she could have written, with the certainty that in the upper and the middle as well as in the lower classes of the country, there would be a multitude to read that stuff, so cordially, despite the gaps between them are they one in literary tastes. And why should they not read it? Her present mood was a craving for excitement; for incident, wild action . . . any amount of theatrical heroics, pathos, and clown-gabble. (P. 302)

Through this narrative, Meredith links melodrama with gossip and both with gender. In addition to the reference to the female maid Danvers's taste in fiction, Meredith accentuates Diana's own sudden preference for "clown-gabble," a rhetorical mode whose description recalls not only Henry James's account of the public tone—"feminine, nervous, hysterical, chattering, canting"—but also Fitzjames Stephen's "feminine, irritable, noisy mind, which is always clamouring and shrieking for protection and guidance." Perhaps most compelling, however, is the example of *Diana of the Crossways* itself— a novel that explicitly tells the story of a melodramatic and female romancer.

According to Meredith, therefore, all forms of populist and thus public opinion formation, including popular fiction, were unhappily seen to be versions of a feminine, if not precisely female, "yapping at a spectacle," a rhetorical form that one might less judgmentally call the popular media version of the melodramatic mode. Like many stage melodramas, like the speeches of Josephine Butler, the new journalism and melodramatic romances were public vehicles that transformed private individuals into public spectacles in order to render them interpretively visible in society and through this accomplishment to assert the social grounds for identity. As Morley rightly noted, such rhetoric certainly did "much to deaden the small stock of individuality in public verdicts," for it sought instead a communal verdict that would emanate from a more unitary, cohesive society. Furthermore, the "brawling" opinions that Morley so thoroughly condemned were probably the highly publicized, often aggressively verbalized assertions of popular conviction that users, like Butler, strategically deployed in order to expose what they considered to be the antisocial behavior of their opponents. Observing woman dragged from the streets into a lock hospital, Butler "yapped at the spectacle" by denouncing publicly the police and Parliament, describing their own less-than-virtuous desires and publishing those speeches in frequently reprinted and widely distributed pamphlets.

For men like Meredith and Morley, however, this "yapping at a spectacle" is notably devoid of the "wise suspense," "wise reserve," and "wise tardiness" that Morley had identified as characteristic features of rational exchange. Indeed, it was through contention with these melodramatic traits of public exchange and consumption, especially regarding political issues like that concerning the Contagious Diseases Acts, that Morley's *On Compromise* was formulated. Likewise, the presence of melodramatic gossip and rumor in *Diana of the Crossways* demands "the test of the civilized" that formulates through opposition Meredith's "philosophy in fiction" and his personal share of the literary market.

By Meredith's own definition, melodramatic romances were populist commodities designed for popular consumption by a wide range of men and women. Consequently, like other forms of commercial property, these novels had promised, throughout most of the nineteenth century, unpredictable and potentially fleeting income for nearly anyone, including women. Although female novelists were often able to carve out a living in spite of the vagaries of the market, male novelists, more often heads of households, found it difficult to build a stable career. Indeed, Morley and Meredith's early years as writers were characterized by extreme financial hardship and, in Meredith's case especially, social anonymity. Careers, unlike livings, required a regular income to maintain a household as well as social prestige to sustain a gentlemanly standing. Women flooding the mass market with fiction, snagging the attention of the public press, simply reduced the market share (of monetary and cultural capital) for men like Meredith. Given his disappointing entry into a mass market of public opinion often dominated by women, an experience undoubtedly shared by many literary and political men of his generation, Meredith understandably mistrusted feminine gossip and the romances it engendered, for they led, as Walter Bagehot had noticed in Parliament, to melodramatic climaxes and sudden changes in national and personal fortune. As I have mentioned in the previous chapter, women entering the marketplace as both producers and consumers during the middle decades of the nineteenth century induced considerable anxiety among many observers who predicted domestic dysfunction, social chaos, and anarchy. The prospect of a fiction market dominated by women writers and women readers elicited, it seems, a comparable anxiety.

In response to the threat posed by melodrama's economic, political, and vocal empowerment of women, Meredith proceeds to regulate the content and broad-based appeal of the melodramatic mode through his "philosophical fiction," a variety of fiction that produces and represents the intellectual individual. Meredith's strategies become most apparent in the climactic scene when Diana sells the Cabinet secret. More than any other single (and documentable) event in Caroline Norton's life, this publication of a Cabinet se-

cret and its impact on government epitomizes Norton's melodramatic reputation as a social and political actor. As depicted by Meredith, however, the
scene occludes the political effects of Norton's midcentury efforts and presents her instead as a sordid speculator. Rather than including in his novel a
reference to Norton's texts and their influence on legal reform, Meredith
chose to ignore this aspect of Norton's life. Instead, he represents at length
the rumor of a melodramatic act and depicts it as a fit of speculative mania.
Meredith suggests that Diana sells the secret not simply out of need, but in
expectation of her increased value in the eyes of the formerly scornful editor
Tonans. There is a certain symmetry in this reading, since Diana sells the
news (the repeal of the protectionist Corn Laws) that heralds the arrival in
England of a free-market society in which, many both hoped and feared,
everything can be for sale and everyone can experience a sudden change in
their personal fortunes. Through this maneuver, Meredith implicitly misrepresents the intent of Norton's original melodramatic polemic against Parliament and the law, thereby diminishing its value and replacing it with the
appetite for "clown-gabble," the rumor of a sold secret, and the chaos of a
market society. The trade in rumor or, alternatively, the speculation in gossip
thus become conflated with speculation in the market, and both sorts of speculation illustrate the uncontrollable melodramatic tastes of a broader public,
embodied by a voluble woman who simply cannot keep her mouth shut.

By means of this interpretation, Meredith achieves two ends that are complicatedly related to one another. His interpretation enabled him to condemn
the economic and social appetites that elite commentators, like Henry Arthur
Jones, associated with melodrama. It was these consuming appetites that encouraged writers to pen such journalism and fiction and thus to fight over
market share with the unwilling and yet needy Meredith, whose popularity
before *Diana of the Crossways* rarely merited a second printing of his novels.
Moreover, and more important, Meredith's interpretation also signifies his
seizure of what he perceives to be commercial property in the name of his
mental property—psychologized "philosophical fiction." In effect, he expropriates melodrama. Diagnosing as speculative mania a behavior that had formerly been accepted as public, inclusive, and appropriate political conduct,
Meredith thereby depicts Diana internalizing melodrama. He therefore pa-
thologizes the melodramatic mode, turning it into a psychic disturbance in
need of a cure. As a psychic disturbance, the melodramatic mode becomes
the gendered figure of difference—a hysterical "illness" or "delusion"—in
contrast to which Meredith develops his masculine model of intellectual subjectivity, the very picture of mental health. In place of a melodrama of telling
incident, discernible emotion, and fortuitous reversals of fortune, Meredith
plots a narrative of psychic development, an "internal history" (p. 15), what

seems to be the necessary precursor to the conceptualization of a history of ideas. He converts the melodramatic and, to him, "yapping" Caroline Norton into the circumspect Diana Warwick of the novel's later chapters; she is meant to represent the intellectual individual that men like Morley and himself were actively representing in their writing and careers. As he confided to Robert Louis Stevenson: "I have had to endow [Norton] with brains."[53]

One must not assume too readily, however, that Meredith is accusing Caroline Norton of stupidity, for in so assuming one accepts as descriptive a phrase that is aggressively prescriptive. In the context of Meredith's project, "brains" signify a specific form of subjectivity characterized by psychological and intellectual depth and individuated by the representation of differential intelligence that his internalization of melodrama allows. By ultimately endowing Diana with a linguistic representation of "brains," Meredith subjects melodrama and Norton to what he variously calls in the novel "philosophy," "the brainstuff of fiction" (p. 15), "internal history," and what Morley calls "speculative intelligence."[54] Such speculation, one need hardly add, is an entirely different sort of speculation from that found in the newspapers or in the market.

Melodramatic situations, heroines, and climaxes exert formative pressure on Meredith's *Diana of the Crossways* to such an extent that the novelist finds it necessary to plot melodrama's expropriation. Such a proprietary strategy of containment is not merely a localized thematic device. Rather, as one of the features of Meredith's distinctive style, it constitutes a portion of the mental property from which the novelist both economically and culturally profits. It is therefore a rhetorical and material manifestation of the intellectual mode that men like Morley and Meredith employed to assert their professional status in English literary culture. The rise of the professional man of letters must in part be examined as a response to the potentially disruptive populism of the melodramatic mode and its perceived production of a feminized public opinion. Only through an examination of the contemporary manipulation of these melodramatic figures can the terms of psychological realism and intellectual culture be thoroughly defined and connected to their wider participation in the cultural politics of the 1880's.

IV

In the texts on prostitution by William Acton and in Josephine Butler's speeches, a preoccupation with female desire frames their dissimilar views of the Contagious Diseases Acts. Changing material conditions for women during these years, especially for women of the upper classes, encouraged rumination on this topic. For example, in addition to Acton and Butler, whose cited texts were written in the 1870's, the Men and Women's Club, founded by the socialist Karl Pearson in 1885, focused on female desire in many of its club meetings.[55] At these mixed-sex gatherings, one of the most frequently discussed books was the recently published *Diana of the Crossways*, a novel whose heroine embodies this new woman of unpredictable desires. Although Meredith sets the novel in the late 1830's and 1840's to provide historical accuracy for the events he borrows from Norton's life, his Diana is a woman of the 1880's. As one critic noticed, for instance, Meredith depicts Diana selling her father's property, "The Crossways," even though, as a married woman of the 1840's, her husband would have been legal owner of the estate.[56] As an estranged wife and a historically anachronistic proprietary woman, Diana most accurately represents an embattled but relatively "independent" lady in search of her desire during the late nineteenth century.

In *Diana of the Crossways* Meredith thematizes this female independence in erotic terms, as Judith Wilt has rightly argued.[57] I do not wish, however, to recapitulate Meredith's own terms, for they tend to result in a feminist reading of the novel that merely revises Whiggish history while keeping its positivism intact. If I accept his terms, I would also inevitably adopt the assumptions of Meredith's liberal bias, as his progressive contemporaries and modern critics have done, through which the 1880's become an advanced stage in the evolution of a reified possessive individualism and, moreover, a privileged period when female "sexual desire" emerged from hidden depths of repression. According to this reasoning, Meredith becomes a protofeminist, as he was and often still is perceived.[58] Rather, the 1880's were a period when older formulations of feminine motivation were losing their cultural dominance and being replaced with newer formulations. Through this framework, "female sexual desire" will not be construed as a biological and ahistorical drive of nature that was in bondage during the height of the Victorian period and only awaited a period of enlightenment for its liberation. Instead, such desire and the individual that is figured as possessing it participate in history; they cannot be isolated from economic and other social pressures that constituted them. In this regard, the "new woman" then taking shape was not simply the result of the spread of democratic principles or the consciousness raising of women themselves, but was the product of complex negotiations among various discourses, including the professionalizing, exclusionary, and ultimately masculine mode of intellectual culture. Seen from this perspective, Meredith's progressive views regarding women become much more complicated.

Despite a long-standing critical celebration of Meredith's feminism, his poetry and prose resemble other contemporary opinions, many of them far less liberal, that register in their representations of women the conflicted status of his and the culture's conception of female subjectivity. Meredith's quintessential depiction of the women in his poetry and novels emphasizes instability, a lack of fixity of character. In one of his earliest lyrics, "Love in the Valley," his speaker pursues an elusive maiden whose features are in a constant flutter, and who ultimately breaks away from her lover's embrace. In one of his later novels, he pays tribute to his heroine's beauty by registering the "flashes" and "commotion" in her face; she, too, ultimately eludes her first lover.[59] In this regard, Meredith, though an outspoken supporter of female suffrage, resembles his contemporary Lord Asquith, who opposed the vote for women because he thought their political views were a "fluid and mobile element."[60]

It is this tantalizing instability perceived in women and most dramatically enacted in the melodramatic mode that elicits the developmental narrative of property and sexual relations in Meredith's *Diana of the Crossways*. In this narrative, Meredith manages the feminine appetites of melodrama and the market and through this exercise carves out a market share of his own that paradoxically effaces its economic and gendered motivations. Such moves, as will be seen below, are characteristic of the process of professionalization.

Like Meredith's other heroines, Diana Warwick draws close to the outstretched hands of her lovers but usually manages to elude permanent possession by men. Like the maiden in Meredith's lyric, the young Diana Merion in the novel is "a spirit leaping and shining like a mountain water" (p. 67). This instability enables Meredith to cast Diana in a variety of roles then under consideration for women: virginal heroine, subsistence laborer, speculative entrepreneur. Diana, as the imperiled virgin of her youth, recalls the melodramatic heroine of Josephine Butler's texts, whose moral purity is endangered by her commodification in the market. As prospective wife or prostitute, she is the victim of male desire, a victim who longs for a rescuing hero. At this point in the novel, Diana expresses the only appropriate desire for a melodramatic heroine—"O for a despot! The cry was for a beneficent despot, naturally: a large-minded benevolent despot" (p. 39). The heroine's first marriage would thus represent the traditional patriarchal union, a union to which she fled when being "in the [marriage] market" (p. 19) threatened to convert her into a mere commodity.

Once Diana separates from Warwick, having recognized the inherent bondage in a hierarchical exchange, she seems to lose her fixity once more, as if she were detached from the motivations that briefly grounded her subjectivity. For a moment in the Italian Alps, Diana considers herself "a girl again," a "quivering sensibility," "an unclaimed self" (p. 39). Having rejected any financial support from her estranged husband, however, Diana must reclaim that "unclaimed self" and become a proprietary self. Thus she takes up writing and selling novels. As a subsistence laborer—"a hanger-on of the market"—she writes to stay alive and, not unlike Acton's desperate prostitutes, provides an "artificial" supply of romance for her hungry buyers. Although critics praise her first novel for its "comprehension of the passion of love," Diana recognizes that she, like a prostitute, is a "stranger" (p. 39) to passion and merely feigns its features for the consumption of her audience.

Diana's climactic affair with Percy Dacier, however, transforms her; she becomes the demanding and consuming woman that troubled Acton. At this point in the narrative, Diana is portrayed as possessing insatiable sexual and economic appetites normally associated with men. Unlike her unequal relationship with Warwick, her relationship with Dacier is ultimately portrayed by Meredith's narrator as a business transaction between two bargaining parties who invest in each other in expectation of windfall profits. Dacier covets Diana's beauty, while Diana covets Dacier's power. Although the parties operate as if in equal bargaining positions, the still-married Diana is at a disadvantage. Before this affair, Diana had been a subsistence novelist; now she is an unlucky speculator who invests large sums of money in order to retain her social standing. In her effort to keep Dacier's admiration, Diana hosts sumptuous dinners that overtax her income. As a result, she sells her beloved Crossways, thereby alienating her familial inheritance and transforming real property into commercial property. Moreover, she rashly invests in mining shares that promise an impossible return of 10 percent. She even panders to the tastes of her reading audience and attempts to write facile romances, just like the women novelists in competition with Meredith. And when she suffers from a lack of inspiration, she considers seeking an advance from her publisher, thus inviting him to speculate on her. At the height of Diana's speculative phase, she seems no different from the mid-Victorian ideal of the free-trading, entrepreneurial male.

These cumulative events immediately precede Diana's midnight visit to the newspaper office and her sale of Dacier's Cabinet secret, the moment when Meredith commandeers melodramatic plotting for his own complicated agenda. Like Butler and Acton before him, Meredith deems it necessary to regulate the content of this female desire, a desire that from his perspective speculates on gossip in the market. As I have outlined, through a restaging of the unconfirmed rumor about Norton's transaction with the *Times,* Meredith conflates the behaviors associated with melodrama—climactic revelations of secrecy and fortuitous reversals in fortune—and those associated with market culture—insatiable greed and unstable economies. In short, he convicts the melodramatic mode for the very crimes it most often opposed. In so doing, Meredith equates one form of speculation with another: the circulation of feminine conversation is at the same time a risky investment in commercial property.[61] Lady Wathin, the epitome of the gossiping woman, has "stock in the moral funds, shares in the sentimental tramways" (p. 341).

Prior to the climactic transaction in the newspaper office, Diana had become a subject of public discussion. In the opening chapter of *Diana of the Crossways*, when Meredith manufactures quotations by and about Diana from published diaries and newspapers, he argues that printing such uncorroborated gossip regarding the qualities and experiences of the subject is a doubled form of speculation, a conjecture about a person that is also an attempt to make a profit. Gossipy publications tattle for profit and "society was largely a purchaser" (p. 69). Publications like these, melodramatic romances, the "new journalism" of the periodicals, all of which eschewed tolerant exchange of opinion, were in fact the popular commodities that, in competing on the market with the works of Meredith and Morley and other literary gentlemen like them, jeopardized their careers. Within months after the serial publication of *Diana of the Crossways* in the *Fortnightly Review*, W. T. Stead achieved incredible popular notoriety with the appearance in the *Pall Mall Gazette* of his "Maiden Tribute of Modern Babylon" in which he narrates the melodramatic story of virtuous heroines sold into sexual slavery by the despotically mercenary drives of pimping villains. This example illustrates the melodramatic mode of the "new journalism" in direct market competition with the rational debate among tolerant people of varied opinion that the *Fortnightly Review* epitomized. It also enacts a public confrontation between two models of exchange and consumption, between the two versions of subjectivity they underwrote, and between the cultures that each model produced.

Despite Meredith's explicit revision of melodramatic scenarios, melodrama's model of exchange, its version of subjectivity and of culture do manage to surface in *Diana of the Crossways*. As is apparent in Meredith's least-loved character, Lady Wathin, society's taste for gossip concerning Diana arises from its melodramatic perspective. For people like Lady Wathin, gossip becomes the ideal version of social exchange. Through these speculations, as in a melodrama on the stage, the public reaffirms its social cohesion by jointly apportioning guilt and innocence, and in so doing, it characterizes the subject of its speculation in terms of socially accepted ethical norms—heroine or villain. For instance, Lady Wathin prefers "innocence under persecution" (p. 129).[62]

Meredith's own cynicism notwithstanding, his account of Lady Wathin's speculation does not obscure the deeper similarities between her conception of public discussion and that initiated by Josephine Butler. The movement to repeal the Contagious Diseases Acts was at its apex during the years Meredith composed *Diana of the Crossways*.[63] Like Meredith, Butler recognized the potential for danger in populist appeals, but she firmly believed that the public discussion Meredith associates with melodrama purified the nation, thereby transforming false public opinion into truth:

> Our public appeal, and our open war against the Government establishment of vice, has been fruitful for social rousing and reform. . . . Our open defiance of governments, and of that false public opinion which made it possible for governments to enact such a law, has done what years—even centuries—of more silent and private work had never done.[64]

In keeping with the logic of the melodramatic mode, Butler mistrusted the bureaucratic disembodiment of the Contagious Diseases Acts—"the Government establishment of vice." Formulated in private and instituted in secret, these acts were, according to Butler, wrongly characterized by their supporters as the public will; they were, instead, "false public opinion," a criticism that comes perilously close to an indictment of parliamentary transactions (debate) that do not include the larger public. In the place of such private deals, she speaks of a "public appeal" and an "open war" that more accurately represent what she constitutes as public opinion—undoubtedly, what critics have been calling the "brawling" opinions of the public. For Butler, public opinion is neither speculative, as Meredith would have it, nor self-serving, but a communal moral sense. "Public opinion is to the community what conscience is to the individual."[65] Her confidence in it connects her polemic to men and women earlier in the nineteenth century who through the melodramatic mode extolled social feelings.

Although Butler frequently emphasizes "the dignity and autonomy of the individual," this should never be mistaken for the private individualism reified by a market culture.[66] Butler's "individual consciences" represent subjects constituted at least in part by their moral exchanges within the family, community, and nation. The operation of public discussion is the broadest example of this melodramatic scene of face-to-face moral exchange, where men and women "in each other's presence, and with each other's help" achieve "[a] deeply-reaching mutual sympathy and common knowledge."[67] She contrasts these exchanges to social relations under what she describes as "Socialism." According to Butler, under this system of governance, human beings are treated in a manner that sounds strikingly like those principles of governance in a class society, for this socialist society is a society "which . . . is too ready to coerce, oppress, or destroy the human being in the supposed interests of an aggregate of human beings which it calls *Society*, or *The State.*" In Butler's ideal world, individuals neither form aggregates nor proprietary free agents; they are "free and responsible before God."[68]

From Meredith's perspective, this melodramatic—and traditionally feminine—discussion, through which character is constituted in terms of public reputation, seems intolerably implicated in market exchange, partly because this public discussion empowered women in the economic and political spheres during the midcentury and well into the 1880's. Diana decides to speculate in a dubious mining venture due to "the prattle of a woman" (p. 263). Furthermore, according to Meredith, the same women who consumed gossip also produced it in the form of best-selling melodramatic romances. Indeed, the sociologist Gaye Tuchman confirms this perception. She has shown that women writers dominated the midcentury novel market, those years when Meredith struggled as a young novelist and occasional journalist.[69]

The fact of women's economic and political empowerment was perhaps less troubling to men like Morley and Meredith than their perception of the content of that empowerment. Moreover, they knew that this new form of social organization implicated them. Apparently unable to see and/or appreciate the communitarian and anticlass bias of populist sentiment, intellectual elites regarded the women who wrote popular novels and the people who read them as common, not communal, as self-seeking, yet not distinctively themselves. Women were becoming proprietary selves, but their personal property was paradoxically seen to be common property—mass produced and purchasable by all. In competition (quite literally) with the mass market, men in search of careers differentiated themselves from populist culture by what should be by now a familiar strategy of containment: private expropriation of common property.

In *Diana of the Crossways*, Meredith takes possession of the melodramatic mode and renders it consistent with his articulation of the intellectual individual that defines both his fiction and his career. In his pivotal interpretation of the Caroline Norton rumor, he privileges Diana's self-revelation—the recognition of her "grossly material, not at all . . . spiritual" desires (p. 263). Rather than the affirmation of popular values and the moral individuals that emerge from the public exchange attendant on melodramatic revelation, this reconfigured scene celebrates psychological growth in the context of a reinvigorated version of private individualism. The novel thus expropriates melodrama to designate an alternative subject—the intellectual individual whose mental property funds a completely different form of speculation, the speculation of abstract thought, logical reasoning, what Morley celebrates as the "highest and most abstract expression."[70] It is this style of abstract expression that Meredith favors for all his later novels.

As Josephine Butler's speeches and letters demonstrate, melodrama's narrative theory represents character in terms of plot; characters display their qualities and form communities as they react to social events. Not unlike the characterization deployed in certain segments of *Oliver Twist*, a character in a typical melodramatic narrative does not possess a three-dimensional psychology—a representation of psychic depth distinct from his or her identity in social configurations. Such narrative theory is flatly denigrated by Meredith. In his novel, *The Amazing Marriage*, one of whose drafts was being composed simultaneously with *Diana of the Crossways*, Meredith satirizes melodramatic narrative theory through a voluble female narrator called, not surprisingly, Dame Gossip: "Character must ever be a mystery, only to be explained in some degree by conduct; and that is very dependent on accident."[71] Despite Meredith's injection of a potent irony into the Dame's formulation, he felt its cultural influence sufficiently to respond to this theory with an alternative narrative method. For its representation of character, melodrama relies on a concept of public reputation that is determined by standards of "conduct," those habitual acts long ago derided by Edwin Chadwick. As Meredith demonstrates in the figure of Dame Gossip, such standards were increasingly seen to be regulated by a feminine and populist voice that mistrusted the private space of selfhood even as it colluded with market culture.

Meredith offers in the place of melodramatic narrative a method that shows plot "growing out of characters" who are therefore represented as masters of their fate, not victims of reversals of fortune.[72] In this refinement of liberal ideology's independent man, Whiggish history takes the shape of a developmental narrative of "internal history," while the public discussion of melodramatic romance is replaced by the private speculation of "philosophical fiction." Indeed, Meredith's psychologized characters take their place within the "realist" tradition that includes George Eliot, whose novels employ free and indirect discourse to represent the thoughts of what formalist critics consider "fully realized" characters. Despite their rigorous efforts to distance themselves from the market, such novelists inevitably reveal the genealogical link between their artistic vision and the larger culture by realizing these characters through the presentation of their "private speculations." Perhaps Meredith's most significant contribution to this tradition is his intensification of private speculation, manifest in his prose's unremitting abstraction, a stylistic feature that becomes thematized in *Diana of the Crossways*. By the end of this developmental novel, seedy speculation in gossip, in mining ventures, and in romantic relationships are heroically superseded by abstract speculation. Even though the "temporary world . . . has not yet been taught to appreciate a quality certifying to sound citizenship as authoritatively as acres of land in fee simple, or coffers of bonds, shares and stocks," Meredith argues that mental possessions, not real or commercial property, are the crucial property requirement for citizenship in the state as well as for characterization in a novel (p. 2). He elaborates this position in the person of Thomas Redworth, Diana's second husband.

Although Redworth possesses many of the trademarks of a melodramatic villain—his speculation in railways, his calculating subjectivity, his erotic desire for Diana—he plays the role of the noble hero. Initially perceived by Diana as the stereotypical calculating self of market culture, Redworth is in fact the model of the intellectual individual. Redworth's truest possessions are mental. His most important trading involves the exchange of ideas; his most "characteristic" speculation is philosophical, and his most prized property is self-possession. Unlike Butler and Norton, who indecorously display their feeling in public, unlike such "feminine, irritable, noisy mind[s], which [are] always clamouring and shrieking for protection," Redworth is "lord of himself." He has a "dungeon-vault for feelings that should not be suffered to cry abroad" (p. 62). This is a psychologized version of self-possession that manifests the "wise suspense," "wise reserve," and "wise tardiness" of Morley's etiquette, what he elsewhere refers to as "coherency of character." Such self-possession is supposed to differ markedly from both the divided and conflicted self-possession of the libertarian subject in a free market and the uncontrollable self-alienation of the gossiping Diana.

As "lord of himself," Redworth is the owner of his private subjectivity. Although he is called "lord of himself" and elsewhere a "Railway King," these regal phrases should not be confused with Butler's description of a woman's "absolute sovereignty" over her being. Butler articulates a relationship to one's self that is undivided, free from the bifurcation implicit in proprietary models of selfhood. Like a sovereign's right to her domain, the woman's body and soul are inalienable and therefore neither can be sold on the market. By definition, Redworth's self-possession is inherently alienable; indeed, the measure of self-possession for any proprietary individual— whether he possesses stocks and bonds or abstract thoughts—is confirmed through exchange (via trade or debate) of his property, an exchange that establishes value. The regal terminology applied to the self simply marks its expropriation from its traditional social setting.

In *Diana of the Crossways*, Meredith confirms the self-possession of the intellectual individual through the exchange of ideas. This exchange of mental property elaborates on Bagehot's liberal ideal of parliamentary debate, taking it to its logical conclusion. Bagehot had described England's government as "a government by discussion . . . where the subjects of that discussion were in some degree abstract, or, as we should say, matters of principle."[73] One can infer from the above that in order to qualify for government service, a person must be able to debate abstract subjects. In Meredith's extended formulation, the exchange of these abstract subjects does not merely signify a person's qualifications for government service, but actually constitutes that person, who is also an abstract subject, otherwise known as the subject of psychological realism, or, in this chapter, the intellectual individual.

Meredith represents his version of the exchange of abstract subjects in the mixed-sex interchanges that take place in Diana's drawing room. In many respects, they resemble the format of the contemporary Men and Women's Club meetings. Going against society's conventions, Diana insists that men forgo the obligatory after-dinner cigars and spirits in the dining room and join the ladies upstairs. Meredith devotes considerable time to dramatizing these scenes, as he implicitly contrasts this exchange of ideas among men and women with the mercenary bargaining between Diana and Dacier.[74] "They rose from table at ten, with the satisfaction of knowing that they had not argued, had not wrangled, had never stagnated, and were digestingly refreshed; as it should be among grown members of the civilized world, who mean to practise philosophy" (p. 301). In contrast to the abstract and three-dimensional characters that are quite literally represented through these exchanges, the flat characters of melodrama seem like cyphers, a contrast that Meredith emphasizes. Through his confrontation with the melodramatic mode, Meredith devised an abstract subject, one of whose most distinguishing features, the feature that renders it an individual, is its difference from melodramatic characterization, now represented as a difference in intelligence. Diana was once "an adventuress without an idea in her head" (p. 311), but Meredith "endow[ed] her with brains."

In arriving at this conception of subjectivity, Meredith had to reformulate the melodramatic mode in terms of this new subject's psychologized economy of self-possession. John Morley had stipulated in *On Compromise* that self-possession, what he calls "coherency of character," involves a "commanding grasp of principles." In imagining the healthy subject in terms of coherence, Morley implies that the subject is made up of disparate parts. More specifically, a healthy subject is one who has "a commanding grasp of principles," who is, in effect, in possession of his thoughts. Morley therefore figures the intellectual subject in terms of a proprietary consciousness of the subject's own ideas. In contrast, purveyors of the melodramatic mode, as Meredith characterizes it in *Diana of the Crossways*, have no firm grasp of principles. As speculators in gossip, these female melodramatists continually vend their knowledge, thereby losing grasp of their possessions and, in keeping with Morley's logic, losing their coherency of character. When Diana sells the Cabinet secret, she thus loses her self-possession, becoming like "Dame Gossip, who keeps the exotic world alive with her fanning whispers" (p. 135). Rather than a villainous husband or, in Caroline Norton's words, a "circle of protected whist-players" or, in Butler's formula, a bureaucratic department of lascivious doctors, the villain in Diana's story turns out to be herself.

Diana of the Crossways thus completes the transformation of melodrama that could be seen in an earlier unfinished form in *East Lynne*. Mrs. Wood's depiction of Lady Isabel generally continues the melodramatic tradition of figuring the heroine's afflictions as objective, not subjective, entities. Sir Francis Levison stalks her; illness and a train accident torture her. And yet the text nearly turns Isabel's physical and social villains into psychic ones; an internalization that becomes explicit in Meredith's novel.[75] In a cryptic passage, Meredith outlines the procedures by which he transforms the traditionally masculine villain of melodrama into a feminine psychological trait. In place of the "magnificent despot" who ordinarily played the estranged villain in melodrama, Meredith evokes "villain whispers," a synonym for gossip. In place of the despot's violent blow, Meredith describes "a whisper as deadly as a blow."[76] By transforming the oriental despot into Dame Gossip's whispers, Meredith suppresses male physical violence, and the appetites it represented, and converts them into a female discourse expressive of a femininized and troubled psyche, what Diana recognizes as a "mania to speculate on herself" (p. 180). Moreover, by transforming the speculation of Dame Gossip, Lady Wathin, Diana, and thus, implicitly, Caroline Norton into a psychological, not physical, act, Meredith subverts the power of the feminine voice of the melodramatic mode in the public sphere; he privatizes it.

This is the point at which the melodramatic mode can be related to the contemporary theorizing of hysteria. Although the relation between melodrama and psychoanalysis deserves extended attention, a full study of it does not fall within the scope of this chapter. Nevertheless, it must be noted that Diana's privatized melodramatic behaviors, such as her extreme emotionalism and her publicizing gestures, correspond to the medical symptoms of hysteria. Moreover, Meredith's structures of characterization startlingly mirror the architecture informing early psychoanalytic diagnosis that evaluated pathological behaviors in terms of a similar model of subjectivity. Meredith's "dungeon-vault for feelings that should not be suffered to cry abroad" prefigures a depth psychology operating according to an economy of displacement, repression, and, of course, the risk of a return of the repressed.

By the last chapters of the novel, the cured Diana and her salutary husband Thomas Redworth become the heroine and hero of a new sort of speculative fiction. Diana ceases to be a writer, subject, and purveyor of melodramatic romance. Instead, Emma Dunstane, a woman whom Meredith notes has a "speculative" turn of mind, is the more frequent outlet in the narrative for the now-reserved Diana's thoughts. By the novel's close, Diana remains the heroine of the novel, but she no longer plays the part of a voracious virgin or speaks in the melodramatic mode; rather, she speaks, we are told, a "language distinct from the mercantile, trafficking in ideas" (p. 371). This exchange of ideas that men like Mill, Morley, Bagehot, and Meredith so valued replaced the face-to-face deferential exchange that was central to hierarchical culture. The psychologized subject responds to and then succeeds the subject of deferential exchange and in this regard elaborates on the romantic subject, an earlier response to the disintegrating dynamics of hierarchical society. Insofar as Meredith relies on a developmental narrative to create the effect of subjectivity in space and time, he represents a continuation of the romantic tradition and its articulation of personhood.[77] Not unlike the romantic subject of Wordsworth's "The Old Cumberland Beggar," the abstract subject of psychological realism seems abstracted from social space, furnished instead with a private space for meditative speculation, a space that is rhetorically and figurally protected from the conflicts of market exchange.

Although Meredith's novels were first and foremost commodities in the market, designed to create a unique consumer base and professional status for the author, they were packaged, represented, and conceived as ideas. In fact, in 1906, Scribner's Sons published *The Meredith Pocket Book*, a compilation of Meredithian epigrams taken out of his novels and poems, which seemed to offer its readers compact wisdom and the opportunity to sparkle at mixed-sex dinner parties. People who read these books did not consider themselves consumers, but thinkers, just as Meredith was seen to be an intellectual or poet, not an entrepreneur. This emphasis on ideas and the mind effaces mental property's participation in market culture and constitutes a mystification of its relation to market economy that was typical of the men who sought to professionalize their literary labors.[78] Intellectual elites did not identify themselves in terms of economic class; professional affiliation seemed to them to transcend class considerations, premised as it was on meritocratic principles of trained expertise. Despite the connotations of market transaction implicit in the term *speculation*, speculation came to represent that activity of all activities most free from market pressures. Paradoxically, it measured the distance between these men and the market's competition, inclusiveness, and uncertain future.

V

In 1877, George Meredith delivered a lecture at the London Institution entitled *An Essay on Comedy and the Uses of the Comic Spirit*.[79] In this essay, Meredith describes the "Comic Spirit" that he imagines infuses his own work. He argues that this spirit eschews the "semi-barbarism of merely giddy communities" and requires an intelligent audience of both men and women. In fact, according to Meredith, the evolving history of literature is also a history of the liberation of women. "[Women] will see that where they have no social freedom, Comedy is absent; where they are household drudges, the form of Comedy is primitive: where they are tolerably independent, but uncultivated, exciting melodrama takes its place and a sentimental version of them."[80] In this Whiggish history, melodramatic heroines, like Butler, Norton, and the youthful Diana, are "tolerably independent, but uncultivated"; they are proprietary selves who lack self-possession. Such heroines, like the young Diana with her desire for a benevolent despot, are "wandering vessels crying for a captain or a pilot."[81] In an era of civilized comedy, however, women's desires are regulated. Even the Comic Spirit herself, whom Meredith figures as a female, once possessed a "satyr's laugh," expressive of unchecked desire, but now exudes "mental richness . . . without any fluttering eagerness."[82] The Comic Spirit's erotic history seems comparable to the narrative of the elusive Diana, who appears to be finally fixed in marriage at the end of *Diana of the Crossways*, when Redworth firmly embraces her: "There . . . now you belong to me! I know you from head to foot" (p. 406).

Like Redworth, Meredith equates possession with knowledge of the female subject—to own her is to know her, and vice versa.[83] Through his exposition of abstract subjectivity, he in fact expropriates his female characters. Meredith marginalizes women and melodrama by pathologizing them in this novel, and through these very procedures of psychological analysis takes possession of them. His third-person rendering of Diana's psyche not only sketches the symptomatic theatricality of melodrama, but also contains his own thoughts—what seem like autobiographical reflections on the writing profession. Unlike the real-life author Caroline Norton, Diana is Meredith's own creation, the author's private mental property.

As a form of exclusive intellectual property, the novel distinguished Meredith from other authors and conferred on him an elite identity within mass culture. This rewritten version of Caroline Norton's life displaces her literary relation to Meredith the novelist. Through its reformulation of melodrama, *Diana of the Crossways* erases its genealogical debt to the romance tradition of Victorian novels and to the women, like Norton, who wrote, read, and lived melodramatic romance. This revisionist technique apparently worked. After reading *Diana of the Crossways*, literary reviewers and critics fully recognized Meredith's efforts to reorient the novelistic project. In his review, even that arch-melodramatic journalist W. T. Stead contrasted Meredith favorably to a "dozen milk-and-water romancers."[84]

Diana of the Crossways thus thematized the more concrete efforts that Meredith was making elsewhere. Throughout his long life, he lobbied for the legal protection of this vital mental property. During the late Victorian period, Meredith was president of the Society of Authors. Because he was chronically ill, he never played an active role, but he did preside as a figurehead over the society's efforts to preserve and extend authorial rights by lobbying for an expanded definition of property that included ideas.[85] For liberal men like Meredith and Morley and members of the Society of Authors, mental property constituted the contents of the intellectual individual, and, specifically, the professional man of letters. In order to establish this profession, they not only needed to convince society that ideas were property from which they could obtain profit, but they also needed to monopolize the possession of that property through various strategies of containment. Although less exclusive than the possession of landed property, the acquisition of mental property required extensive and expensive education and many other intangible and elusive social and sexual qualities. Like property requirements throughout the nineteenth century, mental property was the sole possession of an elite and mostly male population that determined what did and did not constitute mental property. As a reader of manuscripts for Chapman and Hall over the course of thirty years, Meredith contributed to the formation of this definition by rejecting for publication many of the manuscripts submitted to the publishing house. Combined with the exertions of his friend, the Liberal M.P. and reader for Macmillan Books John Morley, Meredith directly influenced the changes in the book market between the years 1866 and 1917, when male novelists came to dominate the bookstore shelves.[86] Gaye Tuchman notes that Morley rejected a novel by Caroline Norton's friend, Fanny Kemble, because he considered it "old ladies' gossip."[87] And Meredith himself twice rejected the classic melodrama *East Lynne*. Meredith disliked Mrs. Henry Wood's novel especially because the melodramatic incidents in it were not shown to be "growing out of the characters."

Meredith also contributed to the institutionalization of elite, male-dominated forms of exchange and consumption by means of his infamously opaque prose, dense with epigram, which demanded educated readers and, apparently, male readers. Diane Elam has observed that Meredith refers to his readers as "he."[88] Although I might be willing to ascribe this to contemporary conventions regarding pronoun usage, Meredith reveals this bias in other ways. In fact, at one point in the essay on comedy, he describes the female Comic Spirit as "the minds of men."[89] Writing to John Morley in the 1870's, Meredith noted that "I write for you and men like you."[90] In writing his "philosophical fiction," Meredith's prose speaks to educated readers only, or, possibly, to educated readers who happen to be his friends, and is thus a discursive analogue to the private cabinet where proprietary men exchange their ideas without interference from the majority of women and where women's public outpourings of emotion and virtue, those "feminine, irritable, noisy mind[s]," are excluded. In order to gain a welcoming admission to this private drawing room, candidates must have "the minds of men"; they must be like the reformed Diana, whose friends, not surprisingly, call her "Tony," who now "knocks at the doors of the mind, and the mind must open to be interested in her" (p. 336). The comic poet, Meredith notes, labors "in the narrow field, or enclosed square, of the society he depicts; and he addresses the still narrower enclosure of men's intellects."[91] Like a villainous lord of the manor, Meredith encloses the commons land once shared between men and women, and expropriates the literary territory once cultivated by both male and female writers; instead of a populist message in the melodramatic mode, he "addresses the still narrower enclosure of men's intellects."

It is from this vantage point that Meredith's loud support of women's suffrage must be seen and discussed. Insofar as women would eventually internalize the prescriptions inherent to intellectual culture and therefore develop "the minds of men," Meredith was more than happy to open the door to their enfranchisement, for the vote was simply a legalized expression of the private opinion of this intellectual individual. He thus favored "freedom" for women within the context of a culture dominated by male-generated notions of the proprietary self and social exchange. Meredith conceded to his friend, Mrs. Leslie Stephen, herself an opponent of the suffrage movement, that he worried about the first few years after the extension of the franchise, when women would first voice their opinions: "It will be a horrible time." Not surprisingly, in this letter he associates what he expects to be the ineptitude of the first female voters with their lack of professional training. "If the avenues of the professions had been thrown open to them, they might have learnt the business of the world, to be competent in governing."[92] Once women adopted the tenets of professional society, however, Meredith was confident that they would relinquish their melodramatic tactics and become more like men. Meredith's implicit bias against women novelists and readers thus comes from his overt prejudices against the principles and practices of the melodramatic mode, a now psychological phenomenon most commonly found in women but soon to be easily cured by the professional ministrations of men, who treat such illnesses with rational talk in their private offices.

In spite of Meredith's expropriation of melodrama and of Norton's personal story in *Diana of the Crossways*, there are indications in the novel that the "fluttering eagerness" of female subjectivity resists ultimate possession, as if Meredith felt some ambivalence when concluding his novel. Although Redworth claims ownership of Diana by literally taking hold of her, his embrace, like that of the lover in Meredith's "Love in the Valley," seems unsure, and hence the satisfying resolution that Meredith seeks may not be within his possessive grasp. At the end of the novel, Diana's hand, throughout the book a synecdoche for her person, is given to Redworth in marriage. When, however, Emma Dunstane expresses her hope for a godchild, "there was an involuntary little twitch of Tony's fingers" (p. 415). The ambiguity of this final sentence inhibits the final familial tableau that Meredith imports from melodramatic romance. Committed to a proprietary model of the self, Meredith finds it difficult to stage a convincing scene of familial communion. Indeed family, whether patriarchal or nuclear, became a deeply problematic notion for both men and women, but especially for women novelists who aspired to the rank of professional author. As Meredith's polemic reveals, entry into professional culture was contingent on the possession of "the minds of men," a price that not only cost women their traditional familial roles and identities, but also the ideological assumptions of the melodramatic mode.[93]

As Meredith draws the curtain on *Diana of the Crossways*, Diana's fingers wander outside the frozen frame of the familial tableau and expose the romantic premise at the heart of the book. As a proprietary individual, Diana cannot be completely possessed, for she is always subject to alienation. Despite his comic denouement, Meredith continues the romantic exploration into consciousness, a wandering journey that is always haunted by memories of home-loving melodrama.

The Curtain Falls

Melodrama's Villains

In the preface to her 1883 novel, *The Story of an African Farm*, Olive Schreiner invokes the by then well-known and widely disseminated ideological assumptions of melodramatic narrative, what she calls "the stage method." Speaking of such a story's cast of characters, Schreiner articulates, with a mixture of scorn and longing, the providential assumptions built into the audience's experience of melodrama: "According to that [stage method] each character is duly marshalled at first, and ticketed; we know with an immutable certainty that at the right crises each one will reappear and act his part, and, when the curtain falls, all will stand before it bowing" (p. 27).

Readers of the first edition of her own novel, Schreiner learned, anticipated these melodramatic plot symmetries; they hoped (without success) for the happy return of one of her male characters, who would, according to melodramatic logic, reveal himself to be a "husband or lover" (p. 27) in a grand theatrical climax. But she, like George Meredith, sharply disassociates herself from melodramatic expectations. In her imaginative world, she instructs her readers: "Men appear, act, and re-act upon each other and pass away. When the crisis comes the man who would fit it does not return. . . .

What the name of the play is no one knows. If there sits a spectator who knows, he sits so high that the players in the gaslight cannot hear his breathing" (p. 27). In place of the fateful coincidences that assert the inherent cohesion of a melodramatic community, Schreiner envisions a world of mischance. In place of the face-to-face connections between audience and players, she imagines radical dispersal that verges on existentialism, for the "players in the gaslight cannot hear [the spectators'] breathing." In place of the presiding spirit of benevolent melodrama, or even Meredith's hovering sprite of comedy, she imagines a panoptic relation that, in its extremity, prefigures the forever-absent godhead of Beckett's *Waiting for Godot*.

Schreiner's envisioned theatrical scenario remotely recalls the volatile situation in 1809, when architectural renovations imposed distance among the diverse members of the Covent Garden Theatre audience and between that audience and the players on the stage. In Schreiner's case, however, the melodramatic tableau that recuperated strangers during the Old Price Wars is never performed, is, indeed, condemned, for Schreiner is committed to the literary tradition of psychological realism and its abstract subjects. Her heroine is in tragic pursuit of Meredith's "minds of men." Instead of the feminized figure of familial tableau, Schreiner seizes for her novel the romantic trope of the questing hero, a stranger who does not return to become a "husband or lover" but in distanced recollection becomes a "mere stimulator of thought" (p. 27)—a piece of mental property. Rather than the return of the prodigal son, she offers us the return of the repressed. Like Wordsworth's wanderers and beggars, like Coleridge's strangers, such stimulators of thought, silent monitors all, roam the perimeter of the proprietary subject, replacing the now-vanished audience. It is this subject who must necessarily expropriate the public spaces once occupied by melodrama's strangers, be they vagrants, actors, or women, to confirm his consciousness of self, his mental property.

As seen throughout the romantic tradition of the nineteenth and twentieth centuries, this proprietary subject is always preoccupied with self-possession—taking stock of and in himself—and yet he remains haunted throughout by the inherent alienation of self-possession. This alienation must have been peculiarly acute for women of Schreiner's era, who had so long been constructed in terms of others. Self-possession costs. Indeed, by the end of Schreiner's novel, the heroine dies unheralded, unmarried, buried by the side of her dead child. These isolated, speculative, self-divided proprietors of the romantic tradition are the villains of the melodramatic mode and, as mental strangers, are an omnipresent challenge to the sort of familiarity offered by melodramatic resolutions.

Perhaps more crucial to the melodrama than even its heroes and heroines, these villains embody all the ills of modernizing Victorian capitalism. By the conclusion of a melodrama, the heroes and heroines of stage melodrama almost always defeat the self-interested plots of these dastardly figures, frequently disinheriting them but not "disowning" them. Eschewing any proprietary interest in people or places, melodrama's heroes and heroines strive for the spectacular familial tableau that ends the play. In the history of the melodramatic mode, however, these villains have usually won, and, as is well known, history belongs to the victors. When casting back to nineteenth-century England, we have also seen with the victors' eyes, and we have seen there a triumphal progress that leaves only remnants of the melodramatic mode, remnants that are most easily read as pieces of the victorious whole. In this interpretation, the melodramatic mode is merely one more artifact of market culture, a tattered bourgeois commodity. Nevertheless, it is an artifact that, when observed closely, manifests conflict, struggle, unmanaged excess, insistent variety in the historical record. Rather than the commanding romantic vision of a wanderer alone in his thoughts, the melodramatic mode fills the stage with heroes, heroines, villains, clowns, and the pleasures of its audience.

Reference Matter

Notes

Introduction

1. Even as late as 1832, there was no consensus regarding the definition of melodrama, even though the term by that time was in general use. During Select Committee hearings on dramatic copyright, John Poole, a dramatist, considered illegitimate drama (melodrama and its variants) to be any comedy or tragedy with musical accompaniment. For Poole, the degree to which nature was "outraged" also distinguished melodrama from legitimate drama. Douglas Jerrold, another dramatist, suggested during his testimony that melodrama "is a piece with what are called a great many telling situations. . . . I would not call a piece like the Hunchback a melodrama, because the interest of the piece is of a mental order." See "Report from the Select Committee Appointed to Inquire," pp. 193, 158.

2. A short list of histories of the nineteenth-century theater: Nicoll, vols. 4 and 5; J. O. Bailey; Booth et al.; and Rowell, *The Victorian Theatre*.

3. One of the few and surely the most widely cited modern book-length studies of the stage genre in its nineteenth-century form, Michael R. Booth's *English Melodrama*, written thirty years ago, helpfully unearthed dozens of melodramas that would otherwise be consigned to oblivion, but his book takes an almost apologetic tone, simultaneously conceding melodrama's ephemerality and arguing for its con-

tinued interest. His approach to the subject is mostly archival in its attempt to classify and catalogue variations on the nineteenth-century melodramatic plot and cast of characters. By concentrating solely on theme within a formalist framework, Booth must inevitably construe melodrama's dramatic disunity and its providential plotting as structural flaws that contaminate the quality of its narratives, especially when contrasted with formalism's more privileged ideals—comedy and tragedy. Booth's few interpretive forays further universalize melodrama's universalizing tendencies rather than locate the motivations for those impulses. Other book-length studies of melodrama and its variants of the nineteenth century are J. L. Smith, and Dye; on American melodrama, Grimsted; and on French melodrama, F. Brown.

4. Dye, p. 12.

5. P. 31.

6. E. H., p. 160. Christopher Prendergast is only one of innumerable modern critics who identify melodrama's effects with what have been generally deemed bargain-basement psychological needs, such as wish fulfillment, moral simplicity, and cheap thrills. See Prendergast, pp. 7–15.

7. Christine Gledhill refers to "melodrama's conflict of polar opposites" that "provided an epistemological and imaginative paradigm across nineteenth-century culture and thought." See p. 20. In 1974, Sennett published *The Fall of Public Man*, in a portion of which he attempted to formulate an alternative approach by treating melodrama as a political rhetoric. Although Sennett mostly concentrates on melodramatic rhetoric of the Dreyfus affair of the 1890's, his sociological method embraces a broader social and historical perspective (1700–1900) than that envisioned by literary historians and critics. Sennett aims to describe melodrama's participation in its social context, and, in this regard, his work anticipates my project, especially in his concern with the changing boundaries between conceptualizations of public life and private existence. Sennett's book, however, lacks a theory of cultural production that would explain the ways in which rhetoric, literary genres, individuals, and bureaucratic systems interact to articulate meaning. Furthermore, lacking a set of interpretive strategies with which to analyze his texts, Sennett provides an account of melodrama that is oddly abstracted from its site of production and therefore appears to be almost arbitrarily connected to its context. Despite his sociological perspective, then, his version of melodrama is merely a gesture of an individual's personality. Such a definition of melodrama minimizes its continual and continuing negotiation with other discourses and transindividual practices.

8. I use here my own criteria, but they are drawn from the salient defining features of melodrama that are generally agreed on by most students of the genre. For a sampling of generic definitions, see Booth, *English Melodrama*; Rahill; Worth, pp. 1–16; Bentley, pp. 217–31; and Heilman, pp. 245–57. Because Booth reveals the greatest breadth of knowledge, I consider him the most reliable scholar of the stage genre, though all of these critics share nearly identical criteria.

9. *Patriarcha* (1630), quoted in Coward, p. 287n.

10. In addition, the melodramatic mode is not reducible to any theme or thematic formula. For instance, although much valuable work has been done on the melodramatic thematic of the deflowering of virginal maidens at the hands of aristocratic

rakes, this represents only one theme among many, and, moreover, this theme represents only one signifying vehicle among the many gestures, signs, languages, etc. of the melodramatic mode. See such thematic discussions in Walkowitz, *Prostitution and Victorian Society*; A. Clark, *Women's Silence* and "Queen Caroline"; Vicinus, pp. 127–43.

11. See p. 282. A concept of constitutive relation is also central to the more specifically literary study of high and low culture cowritten by Stallybrass and White, especially pp. 3–6.

12. For a more thorough exposition of the status of "aesthetic value" in contemporary critical debate, see chap. 5, "The Discourse of Value: From Adam Smith to Barbara Herrnstein Smith," Guillory, pp. 269–340.

13. Brooks's definition of melodrama seems to me not so much erroneous as anachronistic. He takes a basically accurate depiction of melodrama's later manifestations in the novels of high realism and psychological realism and uses it as a timeless literary convention, ultimately reading it backward into early French stage melodrama. He thereby affirms both his formalist starting point and his romantic assumptions about subjectivity, especially the presumption that subjectivity is without a history. See Chap. 1 for a fuller discussion of melodrama's relation to English romanticism.

14. Foucault, *The Order*, *The Archaeology*, and *Discipline*. For a brief and relatively accessible discussion of "discourse" and "discourse networks," see de Bolla, pp. 7–10.

15. P. 81. Through this analysis of the melodramatic mode, I am locating, as Dollimore, p. 87, calls it, "a *discoherence*—an incongruity verging on a meaningful contradiction" in capitalist ideology and practice.

Chapter 1

1. There is, of course, a prevailing distinction amidst these shared interests: melodrama, more often than not, likes to put its Magyars and Michaels in the same play.

2. Habermas, p. 33, for one, tends to idealize the egalitarian interchange of the coffeehouses, as does Sennett, p. 82, while Jarrett tends to overstate the pastoral idyll. For a clear-headed and challenging discussion of this central debate, see E. M. Wood, especially pp. 117–60.

3. P. 146. I agree in detail with much of Newby's argument, though I take issue with his assertion, p. 146, that deference is not a set of behaviors or attitudes, but merely a form of interaction.

4. I do not wish to underestimate the pain and suffering that took place within this society. However, it is important in this instance to refrain from condemning the society even as I am laboring to describe it.

5. E. P. Thompson, "Patrician Society," pp. 382–405; Hay, pp. 17–63; Corrigan and Sayer, pp. 87–113; and Castle.

6. For instance, "political events were invariably described as 'scenes' or 'acts,' and political language was spoken as frequently in the form of dialogues, soliloquies and

panegyrics, as in the simple medium of the pamphlet." See Hindson and Gray, p. 28. Christensen, p. 72, suggests that theatrical convention was congruent with, if not identical to, social convention.

7. P. 87.

8. P. 154.

9. P. 69. Also see Sennett, p. 89, "peculiarities of individual feeling had as yet no social form because, instead, the realm close to the self was ordered by natural, universal human 'sympathies.'"

10. Francis Hutcheson, cited in Radner, p. 195. In formulating this portion of my argument, I was also aided by de Bolla's fine work on the sublime. See especially pp. 283–300.

11. Pp. 210–30. See also Mullan, p. 2, who characterizes the language of sentiment as "a language of feeling for the purpose of representing necessary social bonds."

12. Christensen, p. 77, comments: "One can 'see' into the breast of another in order to determine an ultimate and final relation only by virtue of a sympathy that presupposes that one is simultaneously being seen." Although this seems to me an accurate account of the mutual specularity of sympathetic exchange, I would quibble with the X-ray vision that Christensen describes. True sympathy did not need to pierce through the body, for the body and its costumes spoke.

13. This structural and temporal analysis of cultural change owes much to Raymond Williams's concepts of "emergent" and "residual" cultural formation. See Williams, *Marxism*, pp. 121–27.

14. P. 149. For these criteria, I gratefully rely on E. M. Woods, pp. 148–52, who also notes the decline in politically constituted property, corporate privilege, and fragmented jurisdiction.

15. In *Work, Society*, p. 3, Joyce describes the continuation of deferential culture in the factories of late-nineteenth-century England: "In earlier [late-nineteenth-century] forms of urban industry, above all in textiles, the intimate relationship of work and community produced attitudes of mind often far removed from those of class." Ultimately, his argument corroborates my own regarding the survival of deference.

16. P. 8.

17. Quoted in Hindson and Gray, p. 40. Hindson and Gray's book led me to speculate on the relationship between the textual collision between Burke and Paine and the melodramatic rhetoric of later decades.

18. I would not wish to push this parallel too forcefully, of course. Historians and critics of the nineteenth century far too often underestimate the power of public spectacle and social, collective action, as my account of melodrama will strive to assert. For a ground-breaking—if somewhat rudimentary—study of the distinction between oral and written transmission, see Ong.

19. See More's *Strictures on the Modern System of Female Education* (1799). For a brief discussion of More and early-nineteenth-century attitudes toward theatricality, see Litvak, pp. 6–12.

20. The conviction that many people were "acting" was, of course, becoming

widespread in eighteenth-century England. Mannheim, p. 63, observes that "one of the chief characteristics . . . exemplified by Hume's *History of England* [1754–62], was the presupposition that men were given to 'feigning' and to deceiving their fellows."

21. For more on structural specularity, see de Bolla, pp. 186–222, and Chap. 2.

22. *Making of the English,* especially pp. 711–832.

23. See Wordsworth, "Postscript."

24. Wordsworth, "The Old Cumberland Beggar," p. 54, lines 173–74.

25. Chandler, pp. 81–92, is one notable exception.

26. See Wordsworth's letter to Thomas Poole of April 9, 1801. Speaking of "Michael," the poet mentions, "I have attempted to give a picture of a man, of strong mind and lively sensibility, agitated by two of the most powerful affections of the human heart; the parental affection, and the love of property, *landed* property, including the feelings of inheritance, home, and personal and family independence." Wordsworth, *Early Letters,* p. 266. His final reference to "personal and family independence," however, points, I think, to his views' congruence with various tenets of what we might call "possessive individualism." In regard to this congruence, see below in text.

27. Wordsworth, "Preface," p. 606.

28. Ibid., p. 596.

29. Gordon, p. 23, has written of this subtle transmutation in the conception of sympathy's origins: "The *social duty* of assistance is understood by the economists as *a duty of man in society,* rather than as *a duty of society.*"

30. Pp. 59–71. In regard to romanticism's withdrawal from society, see Levinson, pp. 14–57.

31. It is also necessary, of course, that the romantic subject himself (not herself) remain in nature, secluded from the social. Note Mortimer's description of himself in "The Borderers": "I will wander on/Living by mere intensity of thought." Wordsworth, *The Borderers,* p. 294, lines 2318–19.

32. P. 285.

33. Wordsworth, "'My heart leaps up when I behold,'" p. 246, line 7. Liu first made this clever insight. See *Wordsworth: The Sense,* pp. 225–310. He remarks, p. 305: "The self is the rehabilitated family. It is the family 'transported' to an inner exile." Liu, Siskin, and de Bolla's work have begun to historicize this romantic subject, to place it within its discourse network, and my chapter both relies on and works from their efforts.

34. "Preface," p. 607.

35. McGann, p. 71, notes that "the poetic response to the age's severe political and social dislocations was to reach for solutions in the realm of ideas. The maneuver follows upon a congruent Romantic procedure, which is to define human problems in ideal and spiritual terms. To characterize the Romantic Period as one marked by an 'epistemological crisis' is to follow Romanticism's own definition of its historical problems."

36. I address the relationship between professionalization and the romantic subject in Chap. 5.

37. For an elaboration of this argument, see Chap. 3.

38. Liu also discusses the relationship between the romantic subject and criminality. See Liu, *Wordsworth: The Sense*, pp. 294–99.

39. For a recent, if somewhat breezy, survey of nineteenth-century experiences of subjectivity, see Gagnier.

Chapter 2

1. W. Porter, n.p.

2. P. 7.

3. The composition of the audience is an important feature of my argument in this chapter. I base my conclusions on theater historians' assessments as well as on the newspaper accounts of the court records during the O.P. Wars. Those brought to the magistrate on charges of rioting were often apprentices or skilled journeymen. Although they might have joined the pit once the disturbance began, rather than being a part of its contents prior to the wars, these men are mentioned as pit occupants in contemporary accounts, accounts that are distinct from those partisan articles describing the members of the O.P. faction. The difficulty in characterizing the pit audience is more than a function of limited historical documentation. It is, I would argue, just as much a result of the changes taking place in and out of the theater that began to confuse traditional status criteria. This problem also applies to the inhabitants of the dress boxes, presumably the upper bourgeoisie, though anyone with multiple shillings to spare could purchase a ticket, such as sailors in port, fashionable tradesmen, etc. Many male occupants of the dress boxes would on another night sit in the pit if their wives did not accompany them.

4. I have decided to use the descriptive term *rank* in place of the term *class* for a variety of reasons. *Class* defines one's economic status and thus fails to take into account the lingering—and still powerful—patterns of vertical loyalty (based on traditional deference, geographic identity) that contributed to one's place in society. As McKeon, p. 164, has noted, although "traditional, qualitative criteria of honorific status were being definitively infiltrated by the quantitative criteria of socioeconomic class," this infiltration, even by the early nineteenth century, was far from complete. Consequently, *rank*, which retains the connotations of status criteria, seems most appropriate for my discussion, since the people involved in the O.P. Wars were protesting for the maintenance of these criteria even as they witnessed the development of new forms of social configuration. Some critics, like William Reddy, even suggest that variations on status distinction prevailed throughout the nineteenth century and continued to problematize distinctions based wholly on socioeconomic status.

5. A term such as "the public" can potentially be a blunt analytical tool and requires elaboration. The ahistorical definition of "the public" describes that which is open and inclusive as opposed to that which is closed and exclusive. In Europe, the historical narrative of the term is much more complex. As Habermas has argued in *The Structural Transformation of the Public Sphere*, "the public" was undergoing massive redefinition in the eighteenth and nineteenth centuries as nascent capitalist societies evolved into capitalist systems and experienced the rise of parliamentary gov-

ernment and the dissemination of literacy. By the eighteenth century, Habermas contends, p. 18, the concept of the public had became "'synonymous with state-related,'" while those activities pursued by gentlemen that were not functions of the state, such as business transactions, fell into the category of the private. By the mid–eighteenth century, the "public" realm seemed to shift its parameters once more by separating from the spheres of jurisdiction and coercion and by becoming that entity—public opinion—that authorized the exercise of these powers. Such transformations, I would add, were not cleanly consecutive; ostentatious displays of authority still occurred even as "public opinion" became increasingly influential.

6. Quoted in Hughes, p. 9. In *King v. Leigh* (1775), it was established that hissing was deemed to be a form of expressing disapprobation and was therefore a protected right.

7. In an early essay on the melodrama, the critic describes melodrama's audiences thus: "[Melodrama] is admired by the same class of persons . . . to whom any exertion of the intellect is absolute toil, and carefully to be avoided, who like their other faculties lulled into a slumber." See E.H., pp. 159–60.

8. Rowell, *Victorian Theatre*, p. 3.

9. In a recent book-length study of the Old Price Wars, which, with this contemporaneously researched chapter, marks a renewal of studious interest in these events, the historian Marc Baer independently corroborates my claim that the O.P. riots were not merely a senseless outbreak of anarchic energies. In this respect, his work shares my concern with the intersection of theatricality, society, and politics. Baer's thoroughly researched project ultimately results, however, in a discussion of "themes," as he tellingly labels them, about the theater, local politics, and drama. The book does not develop the ways and means by which these seemingly independent but overlapping spheres of representation mutually produced cultural meaning, nor does it make significant claims about the processes of historical change. This is most evident in his account of the melodramatic content of the riots, in reference to which he relies on a simple concept of contiguous influence and a static framework of context and text: the rioters adopt melodramatic behaviors because they see melodrama on the stage and like it. As a result, melodrama plays only an ornamental, not constitutive, role in his account.

10. Perhaps this representative connotation of the audience explains why theatrical critics of the day quite frequently reviewed the performance of the audience rather than the play on the stage. Seated in a dress box with the lights up, viewing the "classes" of ticket holders in gallery, box, and pit, a member of the audience in an officially licensed theater could convince himself that he was attending a performance of the English nation. In the *Examiner*, December 13, 1830, Hunt gave a rave review of one of these performances: "A large assemblage of human beings . . . enjoying for hours a common sense of pleasure. . . . There the rich learn that the poor are still of account; and the poor, that the rich learn it; there high and low, rich and poor, one with another, smile at the same pleasure, and feel their eyes dimmed with the same sympathy." As befits a sympathizer of the Radical cause, Hunt describes a hierarchical but interactive community based on common responses to shared events. More frequently, reviewers saw in the voluble discord and chaotic intermingling of this com-

munal event a prefigurement of societal conflict and decay. One such writer speaks of the Covent Garden Theatre that is "at all times infested, to a certain degree, with lewdness and indelicacy" so "that no father of a family, who may otherwise be above the prejudices of rank, will venture to expose his wife and daughters to the effects of this abuse." See A Friend to Morality.

11. Unmarked insert in a collector's edition of Boaden, p. 492.

12. Theatrical Examiner, Sept. 24, 1809. The complaints about acoustics and view were wide ranging and pervasive. See, for instance, letters to the editor in the *Morning Chronicle*, Oct. 25, 1809. Many twentieth-century researchers point to the successive enlargements of the theaters in order to account for the rise of spectacle and pantomime in the early nineteenth century. The change in theatrical fare is a more complex occurrence, however, than can be caused by architectural renovations alone. Indeed, these renovations themselves have complex causes related to audience composition, business relationships, and inflation, to name a few.

13. K.H. and Company, p. 8.

14. A.F., Letter, *Constitutional Review*, Oct. 11, 1809, in Stockdale, *Covent Garden*, vol. 2, p. 488. Stockdale's two-volume history and compilation of O.P. Wars documents is difficult to cite with consistency. Included in the two volumes are his own writings as well as newspaper clippings. The clippings in particular are rarely fully documented. Some include dates, others do not; some include author, others do not; some do not carry with them any identifying material. A few of these unidentified pieces may be Stockdale's own work, but it is nearly impossible to determine. With these caveats in mind, I will try to provide as much information as I can when I make reference to this invaluable resource to the "Wars."

15. *Times*, Oct. 11, 1809. Nearly daily accounts of the riots can be found in the *Times* from Sept. 15, 1809 to Dec. 24, 1809.

16. Tegg, p. 20.

17. *Times*, Oct. 11, 1809.

18. Stockdale, "Succinct History," pp. 70–71.

19. Letter to the Editor, *Sunday Advertiser*, n.d., in Stockdale, *Covent Garden*, vol. 2, pp. 610–11.

20. One of the more universal scapegoat populations in London, Jews were especially useful for displacing anxieties related to commerce.

21. J.K., Letter to the Editor, *Constitutional Review*, Nov. 23, 1809, in Stockdale, *Covent Garden*, vol. 2, p. 690.

22. *Times*, Oct. 11, 1809.

23. Attalus, pp. 6–7.

24. In a recent account of the O.P. Wars, Gillian Russell confirms my argument about the heterogeneous membership of the O.P. faction, but she does not examine the protest's content at length or consider its interaction with theatrical genres. Baer, p. 55, also argues that "in 1809 the conflict was between the beau monde and the people, not rich versus poor."

25. Rattenbury, pp. 51–52, argues: "When Covent Garden tried to increase prices in 1809, it organized itself into the Old Price Riots—exactly as elsewhere it organized its Food Price Riots . . . ripping out the boxes as if they were Enclosers' fences." As

will become apparent throughout this book, I will argue, with Rattenbury, that the O.P. Wars were more reactionary than revolutionary, but unlike Rattenbury, I suggest that they were also more than Food Price Riots. For more on classifications of popular uprisings, see Rudé, *Ideology*; and Brewer and Styles.

26. Reddy, p. 192, comments on the problem of using the descriptive term *class*: "Drawing neat class boundaries on a national level or deciding who is and is not a member of the working class in one of the great metropolises, like London . . . is quite a different matter. . . . Relations to the means of production turn out to be diverse and unstable and do not adequately parallel political comportment." For an exposition of Reddy's argument as it applies to nineteenth century protest movements, see 154–96. Also see Weber, vol. 2, p. 932. Weber distinguishes between class and status: "In contrast to the purely economically determined 'class situation,' we wish to designate as *status situation* every typical component of the life of men that is determined by a specific, positive or negative, social estimation of *honor*."

27. John Bull, p. 4.

28. An English Gentleman.

29. Unsigned Letter.

30. Attalus, p. 5.

31. Stockdale, "Succinct History," p. 72.

32. Pp. 1–26.

33. The members were, tellingly, government appointees, merchants, and financiers: John Sylvester, Esq., Recorder of the City; Sir Thomas Plomer, His Majesty's Solicitor; John Whitmore, Esq., Governor of the Bank of England; Sir Charles Price; and John Angerstein, Esq.

34. Stockdale, "Succinct History," p. 71. Colley argues that "it was the dominant landed class which most turned its back on the nation and sought and found refuge in the language of class." Colley, "Whose Nation," p. 117.

35. In "A Bill for Restraining the Number of Houses for Playing of Interludes, and for the better Regulating Common Players of Interludes" (circa 1735), a bill written just before the Licensing Act and never passed, the following is typically stipulated: "That no Person or Persons authorized or to be authorized, shall . . . take or receive from any Person or Persons who shall resort to, or be admitted into any Playhouse, Theatre or other Place . . . any more or greater Price, Hire Or Reward than what hath hitherto been usually and customarily taken and received for the same, upon common and ordinary Occasions." "A Bill for Restraining the Number of Houses for Playing of Interludes, and for the better Regulating Common Players of Interludes," in Liesenfeld, p. 5.

36. Stockdale, "Succinct History," p. 68.

37. Unsigned Letter.

38. The linkage between criminality and capitalism is strikingly pronounced in Charles Dickens's *Oliver Twist*.

39. "Mr. Kemble shall not lay the hands of the law on you, and yet that very law with which he threatens us, declares this mighty and magnanimous John Philip Kemble to be a *vagrant*." *Times*, Sept. 22, 1809.

40. An Englishman. Also, Stockdale argues that "there is not a night on which

this or any of our theatres are open, when the managers are not liable to an indictment for keeping a disorderly house, under its most usual acceptation, viz a brothel." Stockdale, "Succinct History," p. 25.

41. Redhead Yorke, Sept. 16, 1809, in Stockdale, *Covent Garden*, vol. 2, p. 380.

42. Crossick suggests that considerations of rank and status continued to dominate many people's self-perceptions throughout the nineteenth century. Class consciousness was slow to emerge.

43. In a letter signed "NO VOTARY" included in the *Covent Garden Journal*, it is alleged that Colonel Bosville is a dear friend of Cobbett. See NO VOTARY, Dec. 7, 1809, in Stockdale, *Covent Garden*, vol. 2, p. 726.

44. Clifford is reported to have been at a meeting of the Middlesex electors, another election concurrent with the Westminster election for which the Radicals stood a candidate—Sir Francis Burdett. See *Morning Chronicle*, Nov. 17, 1809.

45. Although Stockdale was indeed involved with Radicals, he himself was a Tory. His story is just another indication of the political, but not partisan, content of the O.P. debate.

46. NO VOTARY, in Stockdale, *Covent Garden*, vol. 2, p. 726.

47. Baer provides a measured and detailed assessment of this issue. See especially, pp. 115–29. Hone disagrees, portraying the O.P. riots as part of the Westminster Committee's choreographed activist agenda. The Westminster Committee consisted of the Radical party leaders in the district of Westminster.

48. For a convincing, if partisan, argument on the dominance of immediate economic concerns and the only sporadic interest in the franchise, see J. C. D. Clark, pp. 349–420.

49. Cobbett, *Political Register*, Nov. 22, 1806. The use of theatrical terms to describe political behavior was of course not original with Cobbett and Paull. Edmund Burke called the French Revolution, "the wonderful Spectacle," while Thomas Paine, referring to the parliamentary debates of 1791, commented that "the Comedy of Errors concludes with the Pantomime of HUSH." Both cited in G. Taylor, pp. 109, 113.

50. For a brief discussion of Thomas Paine and theatricality, see Chap. 1.

51. *Times*, Nov. 7, 1806.

52. Paull.

53. Cobbett, *Political Register*, Nov. 29, 1806.

54. Ibid.

55. Paull, quoted in Rhodes, p. 213.

56. Corrigan and Sayer, p. 107.

57. Hay, p. 27; and E. P. Thompson, "Patrician Society," p. 390. Of course, the most influential study of eighteenth-century "spectacles of terror" is Foucault's *Discipline and Punish*, especially pp. 32–73. Also see Corrigan and Sayer, pp. 87–113. Corrigan and Sayer, p. 104, point to theatricality as a "pervasive metaphor in the crucial civic philosophy and sociological theorizing of the Scottish Moral Philosophers." For a discussion of Adam Smith's notion of theatricality see D. Marshall, pp. 167–92.

58. For a fuller discussion of scot-and-lot boroughs and in particular, Westminster, see Porritt, vol. 1, pp. 31–32.

59. There are many instances documenting how the opposition began to view the power of the aristocracy as theatrical, even in its most unpublic manifestations, as if to suggest that the aristocracy themselves were conscious of their reliance on theater. One placard in Covent Garden argued: "No Private Boxes. Let there be no intrigue, nor private Performances in the Anti-rooms behind the Private Boxes!" Cited in *Morning Chronicle*, Oct. 11, 1809.

60. Mayer, p. 21. This is an exhaustive, if somewhat too straightforward, study of early-nineteenth-century pantomime, a genre of great vitality that deserves additional notice. The harsh satire of panto is expressed through a variety of tricks, such as "visual similes," which posit hidden likenesses. These indirect methods of critique can be contrasted to melodrama's urge to bring likenesses, for instance, familial likenesses, out of hiding. My notion of pantomime relies on Mayer's explication and is admittedly schematic.

61. Ibid., p. 60. Cope notes that Joseph Grimaldi's "business" was much more morbid and violent than that of previous clowns. In one of Grimaldi's pantos, *Harlequin and Mother Goose* (1806), the clown gets shot, loses his ear, and suffers more general dismemberment. See Cope, pp. 1–11.

62. Colman, *Blue Beard*, p. 4.

63. Cobbett, *Political Register*, Feb. 7, 1806.

64. Cobbett, *Political Register*, Nov. 22, 1806. Because Sheridan was a comic actor and occasional producer of pantomime, he readily became associated with the licentious clown of the panto and was thus once more implicitly linked with prostitutes, and with their indecent exchanges with the aristocracy. In an issue of *Fraser's Magazine* of 1830, the author recalls Sheridan's offstage behavior as "scheming and shifting trickery." He also sizes up Sheridan's impact in Parliament: "You would as soon have paid serious attention to Joe Grimaldi, or Charles Mathews." [Maginn], pp. 182, 183.

65. It should, however, be noted that Cobbett conceded the proprietors' right to raise profits. Such a split position shows quite explicitly the uneven development of partisan politics at this time. A supporter of property, Cobbett nonetheless balked at some of its incursions, especially when it transformed his ideal of English community.

66. "The Town." "Instruments of torture" and "engines" are used so frequently in a variety of texts that one is encouraged to consider them precise terms. See *Times*, Sept. 20, 1809, Sept. 22, 1809, etc.

67. *Morning Chronicle*, Sept. 19, 1809. See also Stockdale, "Succinct History," vol. 1, p. 151: "However, two or three new *actors* presented themselves in the persons of respectable magistrates, with a dramatic entertainment, called the 'Riot Act.'" Or alternatively, in Tegg, p. 4: "Two magistrates—yes, Nares and Read,/Made their appearance—'tis a fact—/They came to read the *Riot Act*./But all these worthies wish'd to say/Was treated like the farce and play."

68. *Morning Chronicle*, Sept. 22, 1809.

69. *Morning Chronicle*, Sept. 20, 1809.

70. Mad Tom, p. 15. A satirical poem in the *Morning Post*, the print advocate of the N.P. faction, distinguished between the "folks" who like "to *hear* play'rs as well

as see 'em," who "sit quiet," and those who believe that "the best scenes are jumping and stalking" both on stage and in front of it. "The O.P. Garland," in *Morning Post*, in Stockdale, *Covent Garden*, vol. 2, pp. 447–48.

71. Macready, p. 24.

72. "On the nightly Uproar at Covent Garden," in *Public Ledger*, Nov. 25, 1809, in Stockdale, *Covent Garden*, vol. 2, p. 705.

73. A.F., in Stockdale, *Covent Garden*, vol. 2, p. 494. For descriptions of mob violence and an assessment of its prevalence, see E. P. Thompson, "Patrician Society," p. 399.

74. *Morning Post*, Sept. 22, 1809. The Bartholomew Fair simile appears in the *Post* again Sept. 25, 1809.

75. Mad Tom, p. 2.

76. "A Lover of Equity."

77. No Party Man. The *Covent Garden Journal* quotes another placard that explicitly links Kemble's stage performance with his social performance: "Imposture shall not gull the pit." See Stockdale, "Succinct History," p. 120.

78. Baer, p. 163, also raises the possibility that "the riots were, in the end, a species of melodrama." However, a rather loose, unspecified definition of melodrama only enables Baer to suggest that the O.P. Wars were melodrama to the extent "that OPs in the Covent Garden audience turned to this popular genre to give full theatrical form to their beliefs and values." I argue here for a more dialogic and productive interaction between melodrama on stage and off.

79. A Constant Reader, Nov. 8, 1809. Baer, p. 69, links the O.P. polemic with a concept of "populist constitutionalism," which he defines as an aversion for innovation, a hatred of the tyrannical use of power, the limited right of property, and the audience's right to debate. This definition, however, seems more descriptive of the O.P. faction's beliefs than it seems a historically specific formulation of a coherent body of belief regarding the Ancient Constitution, which was the unwritten charter of English governance. Moreover, although some of the texts generated by the O.P. Wars mention constitutional right, I think this was only one of many rhetorical gestures in a large repertoire.

80. Thompson, "Patrician Society," p. 396.

81. Tegg, p. 5.

82. Loraine.

83. *Clifford for ever!*, p. 24. This is a reconstruction of the Clifford trial and closely follows the *Times* account, despite its partisan title.

84. *Times*, Dec. 15, 1809.

85. Stockdale, "Succinct History," p. 28.

86. S.B.E. For a discussion of the way theatrical genre became implicated in the English debate about the French Revolution, see Jacobus. Jacobus, p. 367, notes that "Tragedy becomes the literary manifestation of the *ancien regime*—the genre of tradition or queen of genres."

87. Baer, pp. 149–56, suggests that certain behaviors might actually fall along class lines, with the patrician component of the faction stressing verbal protest and

the plebeian component stressing physical protest. But Baer also notes that very little physical damage was done at all and that plebeian participants often faced off with authorities in the pit.

88. Cited in *Morning Chronicle*, Oct. 11, 1809.

89. For a general survey of the moral and religious "renaissance" of Regency England that was spearheaded by the middle ranks, see Jaeger, and Quinlan.

90. In the 1807 *An Essay on the Stage* by John Styles, p. 45, the typical antitheatrical argument of the day is offered: "The characters and manners [drama] must delineate, are those of the vicious and depraved; or if it pourtray the virtues, it must confine its pictures to the showy and splendid."

91. *Morning Chronicle*, Oct. 16, 1809.

92. The heterogeneous members of the O.P. faction were not all equally powerful, however. By December 12, 1809, when the Covent Garden owners finally consented to meet with the protesters at a dinner in the Crown and Anchor Tavern, the recognized "voice" of the O.P. faction was Henry Clifford, a barrister who chaired the meeting, while tickets for the dinner cost twelve shillings and six pence, a price that inhibited the attendance of anyone beneath the middle and professional classes.

93. A Constant Reader, Oct. 13, 1809.

94. An Old Scene Shifter [Redhead Yorke], Oct. 21 and 28, 1809, in Stockdale, *Covent Garden*, vol. 2, p. 579. Of course, this also derives from the pervasive anxiety of French invasion at this time.

95. Redhead Yorke, Sept. 16, 1809, in Stockdale, *Covent Garden*, vol. 2, p. 378.

96. Mad Tom, p. 31; and An Old Scene Shifter [pseud.], *Political Review*, in Stockdale, *Covent Garden*, vol. 2, p. 392. The *Covent Garden Journal* does not indicate that this "Scene Shifter" is Redhead Yorke. This may be an editor's mistake. A later entry complicates matters further, however, for it indicates that a "Scene Shifter" writes to Yorke.

97. An Old Scene Shifter [pseud.], To Mr. Redhead Yorke, Sept. 21, 1809, in Stockdale, *Covent Garden*, vol. 2, p. 413. This association between hybrid theatrical forms and social subversion is a common theme throughout English literary history. Stallybrass and White's, pp. 80–124, discussion of theatrical genre and social class influences my work on early melodrama.

98. Giddens, p. 26, notes: "Human agents always know what they are doing on the level of discursive consciousness under some description. However what they do may be quite unfamiliar under other descriptions, and they may know little of the ramified consequences of the activities in which they engage."

99. Tetzeli v. Rosador, pp. 92–93. *A Tale of Mystery* was broadly translated from Pixerécourt's *Coelina*.

100. An Old Scene Shifter, Sept. 21, 1809, in Stockdale, *Covent Garden*, vol. 2, p. 416. Smith, p. 73, relates that "it is the misfortunes of kings only which afford the proper subjects for tragedy." He also discusses the pleasures of tragedy, which, I might argue, provide insight into the emotional inequities that contributed to melodrama's radical political valence. "A stranger to human nature, who saw the indifference of men about the misery of their inferiors, and the regret and indignation

which they feel for the misfortunes and sufferings of those above them, would be apt to imagine, that pain must be more agonizing, and the convulsions of death more terrible, to persons of higher rank than to those of meaner stations."

101. An Old Scene Shifter, Sept. 21, 1809, in Stockdale, *Covent Garden*, vol 2, p. 416.

102. See Sypher.

103. Dibdin, n.p.

104. Taylor remarks that aesthetic evaluation and political allegiance were mutually constitutive during this era, as clearly demonstrated in the work and criticism of the romantic poets. Taylor, p. 149, writes: "From 1790 on, the defense of political and social privilege was justified as a defense of the culture of the English people." Also see O. Smith, p. 3, who discusses the period's distinction between the elite and vulgar. The earliest melodramas' ties to Jacobinism were not entirely based on paranoid fantasy. For instance, *A Tale of Mystery* was translated from the French by Thomas Holcroft, who was a member of the Society for Constitutional Information and a disciple of Thomas Paine. At one point, Holcroft was committed to Newgate Prison for fourteen months on a charge of high treason. Moreover, there are many "melodramas" that are lost to the historical record. Perhaps in ramshackle theaters, on stages appended to saloons, within skits performed after illicit political gatherings—all of which were attended almost exclusively by poor working people—unregulated, early melodrama possessed an overtly revolutionary style, "giving voice" to radical political convictions mostly by means of gesture. For a discussion of these theaters, see A. Davies. It should be noted that revolutionaries, like universal suffragists, were not common figures in England in the first decade of the century, even among urban artisans. Fear of a French invasion, the fairly recent regicide in Paris, and traditional English allegiances still tempered most radical opinion. It was not until the teens and twenties and beyond when continued economic hardship, among other events, led to organized calls for alternative social formations.

105. "Melodrama is an effect on an audience, though it can also be a genre." McNeil, p. 73. Davison, p. 158, notes that "the characteristic of melodrama that requires mention is the element of audience participation that was often a part of performances."

106. As Harvey, pp. 4 and 5, notes, "The audience became a participant in the onstage acting."

107. In Book 7 of *The Prelude*, Wordsworth talks at length about his youthful enjoyment of the theater. By the 1850 version, Wordsworth has hastened to distinguish its "allurement" (book 7, line 285; 1805 version) from "mighty Shakespeare's page" read in "solitude" (book 7, lines 484–85; 1850 version). William Hazlitt spoke of Shakespeare: "We do not like to see our author's play acted, and least of all, Hamlet." Quoted in G. Taylor, p. 107. Melodrama itself becomes privatized in print through its appropriation by the novel. For a discussion of Wordsworth and his canonical peers' attitudes toward drama, see Bate, pp. 110–15.

108. Gilliland, p. 12.

109. Quoted in Booth et al., *Revels History*, p. 6.

110. Bentham, *Panopticon; or, The Inspection House*, p. 37.

111. Bentham, *Panopticon: Postscript*, vol. 2, p. 87.

112. For a discussion of the Poor Laws, see Chap. 3.

113. Holcroft, *A Tale of Mystery*, p. 235.

114. Gledhill, p. 22. Gledhill, pp. 14–22, provides a brief discussion of nine-teenth-century melodrama as a prologue to this book on twentieth-century film stud-ies. Although brief, it is an admirable summary of the genre's key features, sensitive to their historical settings. Like most summaries, however, she tends to synthesize her sources' arguments rather than evaluate them; thus there is an uneasy pairing of psychoanalytic and Marxist approaches.

115. Holcroft, *A Tale of Mystery*, p. 231. With melodramatic characters, as Worth, p. 10, observes, "there is never any doubt as to what is on their minds or in their hearts, since they are always quite ready, whether there is anyone else on stage or not, to expose their thoughts and feelings in ornately elevated language."

116. The relationship between the novel and melodrama is certainly more com-plex than this initial formulation. See D. A. Miller, p. 162; and Bender.

117. Holcroft, *Deaf and Dumb*, p. 60.

118. Brooks comments on this feature: "The desire to express all seems a fun-damental characteristic of the melodramatic mode." See *The Melodramatic Imagi-nation*, p. 4. If not already self-evident, this study attempts to define the melodra-matic mode in terms of its contemporary historical context and social role, whereas Brooks's study arrives at a definition of melodrama through literary aesthetics and psychoanalytic concerns. Not surprisingly, there are conjunctions between the two, but where Brooks, p. 75, ultimately points to the imagination of melodrama and the "moral occult," I point to its political and/or institutional structures.

119. Holcroft, *Deaf and Dumb*, p. 57.

120. Holcroft, *A Tale of Mystery*, p. 234.

121. *Times*, Oct. 12, 1809.

122. Harvey, p. 12, mentions *"no one may lie to the audience."*

123. Hook, *Tekeli*, p. 21.

124. The year 1809 was also that of George III's jubilee. In the attendant cele-brations, a familial tableau was often enacted by the monarchy, which thereby em-phasized the patriarchal relationship that was supposedly still inhering between the English people and a delusional, reclusive king. Whether such scenes of familial to-getherness were perceived to be coercive spectacle or melodramatic persuasion prob-ably depended on the eye of the beholder. For more on the jubilee, see Colley, "The Apotheosis of George III."

125. *Deaf and Dumb* is subtitled *The Orphan Protected*. Note also *The Foundling of the Forest*, and *The Two Orphans*, etc.

126. Dimond, *Adrian and Orrila*, p. 75.

127. This was the message of Serjeant Best, counsel for Clifford, as he addressed the jury at Clifford's trial: "The learned Serjeant begged that he might not be under-stood not to recognize distinctions between men; he knew, and looked up with rev-erence to those whose rank in the State place them above him." *Clifford for ever!* p. 7.

128. Mr. Mainwaring, quoted in Stockdale, "Succinct History," p. 96.

129. For a few nights at the beginning of the 1810 season, however, the O.P. War seemed revived. Because the theater had not opened up all of the stipulated boxes, the familiar disturbance in the pit recommenced. Although the proprietors had claimed that these "enclosures" were solely due to ventilation problems, they found it necessary to capitulate and open these boxes, bad air notwithstanding. Stage melodrama also experienced a victory of sorts, for it grew in popularity over the course of the decade.

130. Holcroft, *A Tale of Mystery*, p. 228.

131. Listed in Arnott and Robinson, p. 1293.

Chapter 3

1. The first number of *Oliver Twist; or, The Parish Boy's Progress*, appeared in the February 1837 issue of *Bentley's Miscellany*. Characteristic of monthly periodicals, *Bentley's* appeared on the newsstands a few days prior to its official month of publication, and thus was available for the *Times's* reprint on the last day of January. The *Times* published the passage that begins "the Members of this board were very sage, deep, philosophical men" and concludes with the prophecy of the "white waistcoated man": "That boy will come to be hung."

2. See Roberts. See also Henriques, "How Cruel."

3. See, for instance, Dickens's contemporary, Anthony Trollope, who likens Dickens to the leading playwright of midcentury melodramas, Dion Boucicault: "Nor is the pathos of Dickens human. It is stagey and melodramatic. But it is so expressed that it touches every heart a little. . . . Dickens's novels are like Boucicault's plays. He has known how to draw his lines broadly, so that all should see the colour." Trollope, *An Autobiography*, pp. 248–49. For twentieth-century opinion, see Axton; Eigner; and Worth. Each of these studies defines melodrama with varied emphases, but all agree that Dickens used melodramatic features in his novels.

4. "Address of the Manchester Universal Suffrage Association, to Their Brother Radicals throughout the United Kingdom," *Northern Star*, Nov. 17, 1838. By late 1838, the *Northern Star* was one of the newspapers that was becoming more committed to the Chartist agenda of universal suffrage and class antagonism, as I will discuss later in this chapter.

5. I have encountered very few commentators on the anti–Poor Law Movement who do much more than note, and dismiss, its mode of protest. See Edsall, p. 137, who comments that the "quality" of anti–Poor Law "propaganda" was "abysmal." Sympathetic historians usually avoid an interpretation of this melodramatic discourse; either accepting it unproblematically as a straightforward statement of truth or problematically attributing its features to the limited abilities of its speakers and supporters. Although Knott traces the history of the anti–Poor Law movement in an attempt to argue for its coherence against Edsall's claim that it was disorganized, localized, and reactive, Knott, p. 225, attributes the exaggerations inherent in the protest discourse to rumor and "popular understanding as to what could be expected of those who championed a radical reform of poor relief."

6. Finer, p. 74.

7. There are numerous accounts of the New Poor Law of 1834. See, for instance, Brundage, and Roach.

8. For a succinct, if somewhat cautious, rendering of the working of the Old Poor Laws, see J. D. Marshall. For a more stimulating account, see Dunkley.

9. Quoted in Poynter, p. 33. Jarrett, p. 80, characterizes the eighteenth-century attitude toward the poorer ranks that is in keeping with the assumptions of the old laws: "A dependent peasantry of the old sort was seen as a guarantee of stability, whereas an independent and masterless body of landless labourers seemed to menace the prosperity as well as security of the realm." As will be shown, this contrasts with the New Poor Law's preference for independent laborers.

10. Despite these signs of stress, several historians have recently argued for the continuation well into the Victorian period of so-called eighteenth-century forms of governance, usually headed under the umbrella term "Old Corruption." See for instance, Rubenstein, pp. 265–303.

11. Quoted in Viner, p. 102.

12. See Moore's convincing argument in *The Politics of Deference*, especially pp. 137–89. He uses the phrase "deference communities," a term I shall borrow. In his study, he suggests that the Reform Bill of 1832 was not, as is traditionally assumed, the landmark bill that enfranchised the middle class. Rather, the bill mostly increased the number of voters within already existing deference communities, segregating them from borough politics and thereby strengthening the aristocratic and landed interest. Moore contends that shared interests and personal knowledge were vastly more important than birth and fortune, since even factory operatives would vote in blocks according to their owners' interests if they believed that those particular capitalists had the workers' interests in mind. According to Poynter, p. 24, ranks were a "stratification based only partly on wealth and still influenced by the old mystique of birth and of land, of aristocratic privileges and responsibilities." J. C. D. Clark, p. 93, refers to "the concrete location" necessary for ranks. These concrete locations would be, I imagine, actual geographic regions in which all members of the ranks lived and worked.

13. Dunkley, p. 29, states that " 'deference-entitlement' often requires the attribution of 'goodness' to assure a complete and continuing reconciliation to subordination and obedience."

14. On the theater of authority in the eighteenth century, see Hay.

15. J. D. Marshall, p. 23, states that the poor relief expenditure rose two to three times between 1784 and 1815, but also notes, p. 37, that "in all but the worst parishes, the majority of labouring families were *not*, at most periods, consistently in receipt of any relief."

16. Between the years 1790 and 1830, the documents debating poor relief and poverty geometrically increased, even in proportion to population, or so it seems to a modern researcher. Purported causes and solutions were equally voluminous. Even now, historians rightly find it difficult to trace cause and effect. It is a varied and complicated debate and a varied and complicated historical record, which my chapter does not address but which certainly needs further attention. For a discussion of the contemporary debate, see Himmelfarb.

17. "First Report from His Majesty's Commissioners," p. 55.

18. "Report on the Poor Laws," p. 521. One should note the theme of surveillance that is evident in this quotation. As anxiety increased with increased economic and social upheaval, people chose to emphasize different features of traditional society. In this passage, the emphasis others placed on the shared intimacy of patriarchal communities has given way to an emphasis on the ability of superiors to monitor the lower ranks. The panopticon is a materialized product of this evolution in emphasis.

19. This portion of my argument owes much to Sennett's book, especially pp. 15–255. It is a book concerned with the theatricality of public life and, consequently, has been quite useful to me. It is also, as far as I have discovered, the only book that attempts to study melodrama outside the theater. However, Sennett's study of the public world of the eighteenth and nineteenth centuries does not provide an account of the transition from one century into the other, nor does its brief definition of social melodrama, which he locates in 1890's France, bear much resemblance to my own version of melodrama, whose emergence I locate precisely at the transitional moment between the eighteenth and nineteenth centuries.

20. McKendrick, pp. 53–54.

21. Polanyi, p. 255.

22. Sennett suggests, pp. 57–58, that the costumes worn by the various ranks no longer provided external clues regarding the status, profession, or geographic origins of individuals and thereby contributed to an increasing mistrust of the appearance of strangers.

23. Bray, p. 50. Some critics of the 1834 Poor Law characterized the law as "this robbery of the poor." See J.S.B.

24. Mayhew, p. 161.

25. Martineau, *The Parish*, p. 64.

26. Moore notes that the Utilitarians continually accused the aristocracy of imposture. This widespread and somewhat generic fear of imposture emphasizes the extent to which the ranks had become alien to one another. See "Political Morality," p. 15.

27. "First Report from His Majesty's Commissioners," pp. 148, 359, 136–37.

28. Quoted in Brundage, p. 159.

29. "First Report from His Majesty's Commissioners," p. 171.

30. Ibid., p. 53.

31. Ibid., p. 155.

32. Jones, *Outcast London*, pp. 241–61, has delineated a very similar crisis in the operation of the Poor Law in 1860's London. Thus, thirty years after the melodramatic contest over the New Poor Law of 1834, paupers were still seen to be impostors and the upper ranks were still seen to be retreating from their traditional obligations. Interestingly, however, the reformers at this period favored a return to what looked like parochial forms of social relation combined with utilitarian ideals of industriousness and self-regulation. Utilitarian theory in its pure form had presumably lost its reputation as a remarkable cure for social unrest, thereby enabling the deferential model of "gift giving" to reassert itself as a viable contribution to reform. Because of this relative decline in reputation, certain utilitarian beliefs were able to combine with

a formerly oppositional ideal of kinship. For instance, the self-regulating principles of the market had come into question as a result of economic crises and the appearance of the "speculative mania" of the midcentury. This helped to dissociate personal frugality and self-control from what were once considered "natural" principles of market behavior. Not surprisingly, this resurgence in the popularity of the deference model, albeit somewhat altered in form, coincided with the debate over the extension of the franchise, as it did in the 1830's. For more about the kinship model during the midcentury, see Chap. 4.

33. C. J. Blomfield, bishop of London, was the commission's chairman. Nassau Senior, a commission member, characterized the body's function in this way: "To enquire into the effects of the present system of poor laws in England and Wales, to report the results after enquiries, and to suggest such measures as may appear to them advisable." Quoted in Brundage, p. 21. There were nine members of the committee, the last two, James Traill and Edwin Chadwick, were appointed in 1833.

34. "The New Poor Law," p. 234.

35. For an interesting discussion about the rise in status of arithmetical technique in the eighteenth century, see Brewer, pp. 221–49. Also see Poovey, "Figures of Arithmetic"; and Levy, pp. 20–28.

36. The report is generally considered to be written by two people, Nassau Senior, professor of political economy at Oxford University, and Edwin Chadwick. Senior wrote the first part, which analyzed the operation of the Old Poor Laws, while Chadwick wrote the second part, which outlined the commission's recommendations. The New Poor Law was primarily a direct adoption of these recommendations; only the Bastardy Clause underwent considerable alteration in Parliament. For the details of this clause, see Henriques, "Bastardy"; and Thane.

37. J. D. Marshall, pp. 17–19.

38. Cullen, p. 137.

39. Quoted in T. Porter, p. 57. Statistics were presumed to provide clarity where there had been blindness. Porter, p. 35, quotes the Royal Cornwall Polytechnic Society (1837): "The dry facts have been interpreted; and means have been adopted for carrying the blessings of education, order, and virtue into those dark recesses where ignorance, vice, and misrule appeared to have fortified themselves in impenetrable obscurity."

40. One might argue that an anecdotal methodology had informed the common law. Sir Edward Coke considered the common law to be a multitude of particular decisions. See Pocock, "Burke," p. 214.

41. The confrontation between local anecdote and national knowledge is nicely staged in this dialogue between one of the Poor Law assistant commissioners, John Kay, M.D., and a member of the 1838 House of Lords Select Committee inquiring into the operation of the New Poor Law. The issue under discussion is the appropriateness of the diet established by the Poor Law Board:

Chairman. Do you think that all the Knowledge of the Kingdom is equal to a Knowledge of the Habits of the People in the Parts where the Dietary is to be used?
Kay. I think that all the Knowledge of the Kingdom is much more than equal to the

Knowledge of any particular District, as regards the general Principles upon which a Dietary is to be settled.

Chairman. Is not the whole Knowledge of the Kingdom rather made up of the Aggregate of local Knowledge?

Kay does not directly answer this question; indeed his speech patterns evade agency. His view implies, however, that the "Knowledge of the Kingdom" is not the aggregate of the "Knowledge of any particular District," but something else and something more. "National" knowledge, like nationalized poor laws, exceed the combined experiences of localities. Quoted from "Report from the Select Committee of the House of Lords," vol. 6, p. 485.

42. The 1834 report quotes Chadwick: "The bane of all pauper legislation has been the legislating for extreme cases. Every exception, every violation of the general rule to meet a real case of unusual hardship, lets in a whole class of fraudulent cases, by which that rule must in time be destroyed." "First Report from His Majesty's Commissioners," p. 147.

43. T. Porter, p. 25.

44. Knott, p. 8, for instance, describes the confrontation between the anti–Poor Law movement and the supporters of the new law as that between "two world views . . . moral economy versus political economy." Edsall, p. 1, speaking of the 1834 law, notes: "Many have seen it as a symbol of the ascendancy of the middle class and of middle class views in British public life, as a sort of incarnation in legislative form of the ideas of the Philosophical Radicals, and, specifically, as 'the first victory of the Benthamites.'" The degree to which the commission adopted utilitarian principles is still debated, though Edwin Chadwick certainly considered himself part of the philosophical radical community. To the extent that Himmelfarb recognizes the moral agenda of the Poor Law reforms, she contributes complexity to an otherwise overly simplistic historical debate, but her study of early-nineteenth-century welfare reform, *The Idea of Poverty,* is in other ways devoid of balance, ignoring the valid concerns of social historians while playing for modern political points. For a complex and balanced assessment of Himmelfarb's scholarship, see Malchow.

45. Viner, p. 107, comments on his research of eighteenth-century "sociological" and religious documents: "If there were any theologians who ever explicitly stated that social groups or classes prospered or suffered on earth as groups or classes because of their superior or inferior religious or moral merit, and that there would consequently be special places assigned to them, as members of their temporal groups or classes, in heaven or hell, my search in the literature has failed to turn up any authentic specimens."

46. Himmelfarb, p. 188, refers to this result of classification.

47. Agnew, p. 6, reminds us that "self-interest" is an "ideological solution" to a problem rather than a moral philosophy. The problem is trying to describe the unfamiliar, and unfamilial, behaviors of people engaged in market transactions. This model of self-interested subjectivity constituted by the New Poor Law prefigures but is not identical to economic individualism, as theorized by Weber and described by Lukes. Economic individualism per se emerges much later in the century, when ra-

tional technology and the commercialism of commodity exchange further attenuated patriarchal obligations. See Lukes, pp. 88–89. Weber, vol 2, p. 927, narrowly defines class: "We may speak of a 'class' when (1) a number of people have in common a specific causal component of their life chances, insofar as (2) this component is represented exclusively by economic interests in the possession of goods and opportunities for income, and (3) is represented under the conditions of the commodity or labor markets."

48. [Chadwick], p. 500.

49. "Poor Laws Report," p. 476.

50. Speenhamland came to represent all that was wrong with the Old Poor Laws, but in fact it was not very commonly used by the 1830's, nor had it ever been common in the North. See J. D. Marshall, p. 17. There were other systems of relief used in various parishes throughout the country, such as the "labour rate" and the "roundsman system." The labor rate was a rate levied to cover relief of the able-bodied poor. A ratepayer could pay that rate or hire the pauper. If he paid the pauper less than the rate, he would have to pay the difference in the rate. Surplus laborers would be distributed evenly among ratepayers. The "roundsman system" gave able-bodied men employment one by one, in turn. This eradicated competition for labor. The farmers paid part of the wage; the parish paid the other part. The commission found grave flaws in all three of these systems for similar reasons, but a detailed description of them and the commission's critique of each is not within the scope of this chapter. Suffice it to say that, according to the commission, all these systems tended to favor the worker with a family over the single man and therefore openly ignored so-called natural economic laws.

51. "Poor Laws Report," p. 476. Chadwick, p. 501, writes, "Indigence may be provided for—mendacity may be extirpated; but all attempts to extirpate poverty can have no effects but bad ones."

52. Gurney, p. 13.

53. These provisions were complicated by the laws of settlement. These laws defined the terms under which a person belonged to a certain parish. This parish, then, was responsible for his or her relief, when and if a pauper applied for relief. Ideally, the commission wanted to abolish the laws of settlement so that laborers would be able to go where work was available. For unclear reasons, these laws stayed pretty much in place until the 1860's.

54. J. D. Marshall, p. 30, points out that in 1802 to 1803, records suggest that much less than 20 percent of all paupers were able bodied, so that not much more than 2 percent of the English population were able-bodied relief recipients. Of course, the economy prospered and failed several times in the years between 1802 and 1832, so these statistics are of limited usefulness.

55. F. M. L. Thompson, p. 345, comments that "the idea that the rural destitute were voluntarily unemployed was fanciful enough, for instance in the face of the regular pattern of winter unemployment."

56. "First Report from His Majesty's Commissioners," pp. 359, 95.

57. [Chadwick], p. 503.

58. "First Report from His Majesty's Commissioners," pp. 27–28.

59. Gurney, p. 32. Gurney, p. 6, also glosses the workhouse test: "A separating line being drawn between the parish pauper who loves dependence, and the respectable independent labourer who scorns to beg the bread which he can earn; each will stand before the work in his proper character, and be esteemed according to his *worth.*" Of course, the "characters" to which Gurney refers are those of two classes: "the parish pauper" and the "respectable independent labourer."

60. The case of women under the New Poor Law demands its own study. I have found virtually no interpretive work about the impact of gender on the framing of the Amendment. See Henriques, "Bastardy"; and Thane.

61. "Report from the Select Committee of the House of Lords," vol. 6, pp. 810–11.

62. Of course, the very existence of this old test concedes the difficulty in ascertaining the character of relief applicants, at least some applicants.

63. Quoted in Knott, p. 15.

64. J. P. Barclay, vice-chairman of a Board of Guardians under the new law, also appeared before the Select Committee to defend his union's procedures, which, the committee thought, seemed unreformed. Barclay shares Bowen's assumptions. The committee seemed willing to incorporate into the review process the moral binaries of improvidence and industry:

Barclay. I consider that the Punishment of Vice or the Reward of Virtue is not the Business of a Board of Guardians.

Comm. Would not the Principle upon which you acted be a very great Encouragement to Improvidence on the one Part, and a direct Discouragement to Industry on the other?

"Report from the Select Committee of the House of Lords," vol. 6, p. 288. It should be noted that under the old law each parish could introduce its own system; consequently, some parishes did modify relief according to their assessment of character, as Chadwick, particularly, claims.

65. Workhouses existed prior to 1834. In some parishes, these workhouses did not need to alter many of their practices on the passage of the new law because they had already introduced the idea of the workhouse test and less eligibility, or some variation on that theme. Others were simply asylums for the elderly, insane, sick, and orphaned, and the "work" that took place in them was minimal.

66. The 1834 report observes that "a large proportion of those who become in any way chargeable to the parish, are incapable of self-control, or of altering their habits and making any reservation of money when once it is in their possession." "First Report from His Majesty's Commissioners," p. 189.

67. In *The Parish*, p. 222, Martineau describes her "hero": "He had the good will of all the economical and prudent—that is, of most of the independent laborers of the place."

68. "First Report from His Majesty's Commissioners," p. 29.

69. "Report from the Select Committee of the House of Lords," vol. 6, p. 79. The 1834 report refers to "the absence of the check of shame, owing to the want of a broad

line of distinction between the class of independent labourers and the class of paupers." "First Report from His Majesty's Commissioners," p. 147.

70. Foucault, *Discipline and Punish*, pp. 195–228. I will note here, however, that Foucault's archaeological method obscures the class dynamics of panoptical procedures and the power of local resistances to them. This is especially evidenced in his untheorized use of the term *power*, which seems to take on an anthropomorphic life of its own. One should also note that Foucault, p. 200, has a tendency to depict the panopticon as "so many small theatres, in which each actor is alone." Insofar as the actor and his audience no longer see one another, no longer engage in social exchange, the panopticon is a perversion of the theatrical exchange. For a fuller discussion of this issue, see Chap. 2.

71. "First Report from His Majesty's Commissioners," p. 133.

72. G. S. Bull.

73. For a Marxist historian's critique of poststructuralist method, see Palmer. Although I would argue that the examination of material conditions is my primary concern in this study, I consider language one of two available means, the other being quantitative analysis, through which a historian can "get to" historical meaning.

74. The appearance of the poor before the overseer was called a "representation." One officer wrote: "Weekly, and often daily, I must listen to the tale of wo told by those who are generally my neighbours, whose representations I know to be true, and whose suffering I must have always before me; but I must be bound to refuse relief." "Grievances," p. 637.

75. James Kay, an assistant Poor Law commissioner, furnishes an excellent example of New Poor Law language, especially its disembodied agency: "I apprehend that the Commissioners' Regulations as to Classification do not admit of a Breach of the Classification but as an Exception to the Rule, and for Purposes of Communication with respect to the Affairs of the Family, in which it is desirable that such Communication should occur, but it were permitted out of the Presence of the Master or Matron of the Workhouse, I think that I personally should have deviated from the Views held by the Poor Law Commissioners respecting Workhouse Regulation if I have sanctioned that." "Report from the Select Committee of the House of Lords," vol. 6, p. 521.

76. James Turner, for instance, believes "the parties who concocted such a measure must be void of the milk of human kindness. They cannot—cannot have one social feeling." Quoted in *Northern Star*, Jan. 6, 1838.

77. A careful reading, for instance, of Wordsworth's "The Old Cumberland Beggar" would help to clarify the distinction between romanticism's spontaneous feeling and the social feelings institutionalized by the Old Poor Laws. For more, see Chap. 1. This distinction is an important one, but it is difficult to define since our romantic or postromantic times inhibit our full understanding of the socialized feelings of this more actively public culture. A. Smith, p. 5, observes that social sympathy evolves when "the emotions of the bystander always correspond to what, by bringing the case home to himself, he imagines should be the sentiments of the sufferer." In this scenario, sympathy must be taken home before it can go abroad.

78. [Chadwick], p. 490.

79. For an indication of the instability of melodrama's definition at this time, see the various definitions used throughout the "Report from the Select Committee Appointed to Inquire into the Laws Affecting Dramatic Literature" (1832). Also see Chap. 2.

80. R. Williams, "Social Criticism," p. 227.

81. Knott, p. 79.

82. *Northern Star*, Jan. 13, 1838.

83. Quoted in Brundage, p. 37.

84. *Times*, Feb. 23, 1838.

85. Blakey, p. 24.

86. Quoted in Cross, p. 184. This stance on the part of the New Poor Law administrators, a stance leading inevitably to the accusation of vagrancy, had of course become common in the parish setting during the years leading to and following the new law.

87. Anonymous, introduction to *On the Possibility of Limiting Populousness*, by Marcus, p. 10.

88. Quoted in Gurney, p. 15. E. P. Thompson, *The Making*, p. 223, argues: "The poor-rates, then, were the labourer's last 'inheritance.'"

89. Nicolls, p. 31.

90. Quoted in Edsall, p. 22.

91. Marcus, p. 34.

92. *Times*, Apr. 24, 1840.

93. "First Report from His Majesty's Commissioners," p. 52. A Mr. Hobler, p. 52, considered pauperism a "hereditary" disease.

94. Anonymous, introduction to Marcus, p. 5.

95. On Victorian domesticity see Branca; Cott; Armstrong, *Desire and Domestic Fiction*; and Peterson.

96. The criteria for this domestic morality can now be seen as specifically determined by the bourgeoisie, but class demarcations were only then becoming explicit and consciously held. From the vantage point of the resistance, the bourgeoisie and the Whiggish aristocracy were virtually indistinguishable from one another. Old Corruption, utilitarianism, Prime Minister Melbourne, and Edwin Chadwick formed one group.

97. Mr. John Moore, a governor of the Plomesgate Union, testified that all visitations with inhouse family members as well as with those out of the workhouse were conducted in the presence of workhouse employees. See "Report from the Select Committee of the House of Lords," vol. 6, pp. 511–16.

98. "The 'Milk,'" p. 46.

99. The new law, to borrow the language of one protester, sought to "*make* [the poor] *bad characters*." Baxter, p. 133.

100. *Times*, Dec. 16, 1837.

101. An ethic of visibility and emotional impact, instead of truth and falsity, marks the rules for poor law debate, as is demonstrated by the Marcus controversy of 1838. During that year, two little pamphlets appeared on the shelves of a bookseller generally known for his politically radical merchandise. Entitled *On the Possibility of*

Limiting Populousness and *An Essay on Populousness* and authored by the pseudonymous "Marcus," these pamphlets used arithmetical calculations to arrive at an estimation of England's excess population and then proceeded to outline a "Theory of Painless Extinction," which proposed to eliminate every third baby born to poor families by gently poisoning the newborn in its sleep. The ethical-economic discursive mode used by the author echoed the bureaucratic prose of the commissioners. For example, one of the pamphlets speaks of mothers: "Their honour and virtue may be engaged to economise the space of life so fatally productive of good and evil." Marcus, p. 16. Quite soon after their discovery, and in spite of the pamphlets' radical origin, opponents of the New Poor Law publicly attributed their authorship to the three Poor Law commissioners and suggested that the procedure of "painless extinction" might soon become policy. Although from a late-twentieth-century vantage point these documents seem almost certainly an early Victorian version of Swift's "A Modest Proposal," the opposition found it more productive to read them literally rather than ironically. The Marcus pamphlets were probably a satire, perhaps a hoax, but taken literally, they could become part of the opposition's translation of disembodied, internalized torture into the melodramatic language of public bodily suffering. Opposition sympathizers reissued the pamphlets in a single volume entitled *The Murder-Book*, and provided a melodramatic preface, a sort of translator's gloss, in which, for instance, "painless extinction" is exposed as another painful, visible effect of the invisible forces of the New Poor Law. I would argue that the *Times* never bothered to corroborate the factual accuracy of the workhouse stories it printed for the same reasons that the opposition never bothered to investigate the genesis of the Marcus pamphlets. Whether or not a workhouse master actually beat inmates physically, the workhouse tortured them psychologically.

102. *The Book of the Bastiles* is an invaluable source for the Poor Law debate. The first section of the text consists of Baxter's own letters of protest against the legislation, while the following sections contain an exhaustive catalogue of quotations from New Poor Law supporters and opponents.

103. *Northern Star*, Oct. 13, 1838.

104. Baxter, pp. 43, 72.

105. Melodrama is therefore not "largely a matter of class conflict" as many scholars have contended. See J. O. Bailey, p. 6.

106. See Hollis, p. 248.

107. *Times*, Nov. 29, 1838, and *Northern Star*, Mar. 31, 1838.

108. *Northern Star*, Feb. 23, 1839, records in this way a speech in which the speaker tells the story of a wife who died from overwork trying to avoid the workhouse: "It was the lawfully wedded wife of a hard-working English husband who had been standing in that mill fifteen hours in the day . . . in the last stage of pregnancy, till nature could endure no longer, and had burst the overcharged vessels of her overworked frame; and there the woman was bleeding to death in consequence. (Great emotion.)"

109. B. Taylor, p. 201. Taylor notes that the conjugal freedoms espoused by Owen and others were not materially unlike many contemporary working-class unions that were often formed (and later broken) by verbal agreement, outside the legaliz-

ing circle of the established church. However, simply because such working-class men and women initiated and sustained marriages without legal blessing does not necessarily identify them as radicals and socialists disdainful of melodrama's messages. As B. Taylor, p. 196, remarks of these unions, "This is not to suggest that such a code was any less patriarchal than the highly formalized marital arrangements found in the middle class in the same period; in itself, informality was no guarantee of greater flexibility in social roles." For more on Owenite criticism of capitalism, see N. Thompson.

110. Baxter, p. 87.

111. *Northern Star*, Mar. 26, 1838.

112. In his study of Dickensian melodrama, Worth, p. 23, argues that these scenes of revelation and recognition do not contribute to a definition of melodrama. I disagree.

113. G. S. Bull. *Northern Star*, Jan. 6, 1838, claims, "The people have laid hold of the same rope for a simultaneous pull; they have all embarked in the same boat."

114. Blakey, p. 178.

115. Baxter, p. 44. Baxter, p. 46n, also refers to the "Rural Police-Law" as the "*bastard*" of the New Poor Law and thereby further emphasizes how this amendment was considered a corruption of family lineages. For a discussion of the melodramatic theme in which an aristocrat seduces the virginal daughter of the poor, see A. Clark, "The Politics of Seduction."

116. Anonymous, introduction to Marcus, p. 3. They were also called "Somerset-house Bashaws," which referred to the government building that housed their offices. *Weekly Dispatch*, Nov. 25, 1838. Bashaws, it should be mentioned, were typical villains of orientalized melodramas. This phrase emphasizes their despotic rule. A similar depiction is "three-headed Devil-King," a more theological image. *Northern Star*, Jan. 13, 1838.

117. Anonymous, introduction to Marcus; p. 6. As Baxter, p. 4, exalts: "No *man* of feeling, I am sure, *can* or *will* speak in favour of such inhumanity. No! I know *my* countrymen (for they are men of feeling)."

118. *Spectator*, Nov 24, 1838, pp. 1114–16. Quoted in P. Collins, p. 43.

119. Bumble emphasizes his role by continually referring to his "porochial business." See Dickens, *Oliver Twist*, p. 50.

120. See F. M. L. Thompson, p. 349; and Peter Fairclough, "Appendix A," in *Oliver Twist*, p. 481. The details of Fairclough's argument, though reasonable, are difficult to prove, since Dickens, p. 45, tantalizingly withholds particulars regarding Oliver's day of birth: "A day and date which I need not take upon myself to repeat, inasmuch as it can be of no possible consequence to the reader."

121. J. M. Brown, p. 31. House's influential study, *The Dickens World*, also treats Dickens's social commentary as isolated effects within his novels.

122. P. 146.

123. I think Himmelfarb's comment, p. 459, that "Dickens was more concerned with moral types than with social classes" is particularly true of this novel.

124. Dickens perhaps more than sympathized with the paupers' experience of the

New Poor Law's classificatory procedures, though his personal experience of these specific changes is by no means essential to my argument. Although never consigned to a workhouse per se, Dickens witnessed his father's imprisonment for debt and then experienced his own incarceration when a boy in 1822 at his cousin's place of employment, Warren's Blacking Factory—for Dickens, a place of enforced labor potentially quite similar to the workhouse. Separated from his family, he engaged, like the young paupers who picked oakum, in mechanical and tedious labor. But most important, like the workhouse children under the New Poor Law, Dickens was suddenly measured in terms of a moralized economic function, the working class, rather than as a member of his father's family. And furthermore, like Chadwick's workhouse regimen, this factory work forced the young Dickens to internalize its ethic; Dickens later wrote "of the shame I felt in my position." In his autobiographical fragment, Dickens describes a scenario strikingly like that seen to result from Poor Law reform. Formerly the young boy's cousin, George Lamert suddenly became Dickens's boss, while the utter stranger Bob Fagin, who was of humbler origin, became "related" to him through their common labor. In Dickens's own words, he had become a "poor little drudge." Foreshadowing the institutionalization of the modern principle of classification in the Poor Law Amendment Act twelve years later, a son is forced into a social reclassification defined by his function in the marketplace. As they attached labels to the blacking jars, Dickens and his co-workers were on display in a window facing the street, a setting that was not unlike the publicized existence lived by paupers in the panoptic workhouse. Deprived of patriarchal family relation and its constitution of identity and character, the young Dickens, like Oliver, lived in a monitored public sphere reserved for the working classes. Dickens the boy might have thus experienced class identity as the New Poor Law intended paupers to—as a punitive reconstitution of the self. Before his father's bankruptcy, Dickens had been a son within an immediate family, but he had also been a son within the extended hierarchy of status. Indeed, his "conduct and manners" led his associates, ignoring the laws of economic classification, to "place a space between us" and to call him "the young gentleman." Note Dickens's emphasis here on the traditional visual cues and public acts of deference, what he calls "conduct and manners." Dickens, "Autobiographical Fragment," pp. 26, 25, 30.

125. Notebook, Apr. 7, 1839, quoted in P. Collins, p. 44.

126. Chittick, p. 124, implies that the divided nature of this novel breaks down according to a relation between narrative and its mode of production. In the early stages of its composition, *Oliver Twist* was a serial, a form intended for the lower classes, and hence the narrative's pleasing tale of an orphan and pauper. In the later stages, the story was contracted to become a novel, a form intended for the upper classes, and hence the narrative's appealing romance about a gentleman. In addition to its oversimplified categorization of these forms and their market, this logic also seems to simplify Dickens's own complicated class status.

127. Chittick, p. 181, discusses the consolidation of the category "novel" through an examination of Dickens's early stories, which, she argues, contributed popular forms and formulas to the mix, thereby ineradicably influencing the contours of the

"literary." Guillory, pp. 85–133, discusses the late-eighteenth- and early-nineteenth-century emergence of the category of "Literature," defined as imaginative writing, which necessarily precedes the emergence of the Victorian novel as we know it.

128. Many historians share Dickens's implicit sense that the decline of oral traditions of all kinds, whether theatrical, poetical, or musical, and the concomitant increase in literacy contributed to a more atomized culture. Vincent, p. 274, however, disputes this connection between reading and isolation: "Yet if the registers and memoirs and the other sources are examined carefully, it is possible to detect strong currents running against the expected reduction of orally defined communities to aggregates of private individuals and their families. . . . The claims for the isolating effects of literacy to be found in so many studies of the subject are a function partly of an overestimation of the effects of poverty on the recently trained readers and writers."

129. Knapp and Baldwin, vol. 1, p. iv.

130. In this way, *Oliver Twist* seems to me to be an interesting culmination cum critique of an eighteenth-century narrative trend that has been convincingly elucidated by Bender, who has argued that what he calls "consciousness-centered" novels emerged out of their engagement with panoptic theories of internalization. See *Imagining the Penitentiary*.

131. Foucault, *Discipline and Punish*, pp. 65–67.

132. See D. A. Miller, especially, pp. 1–33. A Marxist-influenced critic has explicitly equated the structure of *Oliver Twist* with the principles of classification, if, in this case, through those of economic, rather than generic, classification. In this reading, Brownlow's adoption of Oliver constitutes a bourgeoisie's version of a suitable reward for goodness: bourgeois domesticity. Raina, pp. 26–27, claims that "there are valid criticisms of Oliver . . . his triumph over evil in the end is denoted eventually by respectable birth and comfortable circumstance—by 'inheritance.'" For a succinct exposition of this type of argument, see Eagleton, pp. 126–27.

133. Interestingly enough, Miller, pp. vii–viii, opens *The Novel and the Police* with an admission of "melodramatizing—even at the risk of seeming to misname—the main concern" of his work. He refers specifically here to his translation of "social control" into "the police." Miller thus uses, as does Dickens, the publicizing symbolism of melodrama to render more visible and palpably threatening the "less visible, less visibly violent modes of 'social control'" that he argues inhabit the novel form. As a result, Miller dramatizes melodrama's power to force the private and invisible into the public realm of debate even as he overlooks its powers within the novel form itself. If, however, melodrama enables him to launch a genuine critique of the reified privacies of the novel, then it should also be allowed to do so within particular novels.

134. For this incident in Dickens's life, see Dickens, "Autobiographical Fragment," p. 32.

135. Axton draws a similar connection between criminality and utilitarianism.

136. The linkages between private subjectivity, criminality, and the crisis in dramatized visual knowledge is not, of course, unique to *Oliver Twist*. For instance, a random look at a contemporary "penny dreadful" entitled *Helen Porter* also estab-

lishes this chain of association. A band of criminals, not unlike Fagin's, makes a "profession" out of breaking and entering. One of the characters, the "president" of this bureaucratized community, likens his immoral life to a series of roles on the stage, thus delineating the criminal's duplicitous, secretive nature that corrupts the visual transmission of character as produced in melodrama. See *Helen Porter*, pp. 30–31.

137. Throughout a sizable portion of Sikes's journey, Dickens writes as a third-person narrator: "He acted upon this impulse without delay, and choosing the least frequented roads began his journey back, resolved to lie concealed within a short distance of the metropolis, and, entering it at dusk by a circuitous route, to proceed straight to that part of it which he had fixed on for his destination." After this passage, however, Dickens suddenly, and momentarily, writes in what appears to be stream-of-consciousness manifested through what verges on first-person voice, "the dog, though." Dickens, *Oliver Twist*, p. 432.

138. Tracy, p. 23. Kettle, pp. 115–19, has also argued that melodramatic tactics in *Oliver Twist* reduce social issues into a superficial conflict between good and evil.

139. Other critics have begun to describe this specific type of private subjectivity. See Armstrong; Belsey; Siskin. These assumptions underwrote a *Bildungsroman* of a different form than *Oliver Twist*. In Martineau's novel of the New Poor Law, *The Parish*, vol. 1, p. 64, the pauperized child Ruth learns to become good through the instruction of Farmer Goldby and his middle-class knowledge of the New Poor Law logic.

140. Literary critics who are uncritical of these assumptions about a psychologized, individualized selfhood immediately notice how, and why, the final characterization of Oliver fails to satisfy the requirements of a well-defined private subjectivity. In his phenomenological essay "The Dark World of *Oliver Twist*," J. H. Miller, p. 69, concludes that Oliver "is willing to accept an identification of himself which does not derive, ultimately, from anything he has done, but *only from what his parents were*. . . . Dickens's single great theme, the search of the outcast for status and authentic identity . . . is essentially based on self-deception" (italics added). Working from a psychoanalytic framework, which defines the Victorian novel as a recasting of "economic and political structures of power . . . in terms of the erotic refinement of the self," Kucich, pp. 31–32, 214, also finds it difficult to classify *Oliver Twist*.

141. Rubenstein, p. 280, suggests that "the other way to look at Old Corruption is that it was quite plainly a system of achieving wealth and status, the system *par excellence* of outdoor relief for the aristocracy and its minions."

142. Dickens's own troubled relationship with his bankrupt father could not of course be so easily recast. Like the Poor Law commissioner considering relief requests from the children of an executed horse stealer, Dickens probably wondered whether he and his siblings should "be supposed to participate in their father's crime." "First Report from His Majesty's Commissioners," vol. 8, p. 155. Perhaps that is why, as Simpson characterizes it, "Dickens's children seem often to have too much parent or not enough." See *Fetishism and Imagination*, p. 58.

143. Frye, p. 47.

144. Baxter, p. 46n.

145. Although they are spectacles of excess, mob scenes, particularly urban mob scenes, are not typical of melodrama. Chase scenes are typical, however. They usually involve individuated participants or, at least, rural participants whose identity is implicit in their local origins.

146. Prendergast, p. 16, suggests that in this scene Dickens is being "deeply ironic" by saying "that it is only through the cruelty of the chase that the barriers of laissez-faire isolation in Victorian London are broken down and some sense of 'community' achieved." I do not detect irony.

147. Some of Dickens's detective fiction includes *Bleak House, Our Mutual Friend,* and, left uncompleted, *The Mystery of Edwin Drood.*

148. Bodenheimer, pp. 119–35, argues, wrongly I think, that Dickens gives priority to nature in an effort to protect what she labels a "natural history of character" from "forms of social interpretation." This misses the social, if rural, content in Dickensian characterization, as I have delineated in this chapter.

149. Bray, p. 114.

150. Ibid., p. 29. Later, p. 108, Bray comments on the *"inequality of wealth in connection with the gradation of classes,* or the division of society into capitalists and producers." Moore, *Politics of Deference,* p. 234, mentions "that, as time went on, many men tended to substitute the distinction between a 'free' and 'unfree' electorate for the earlier distinction between 'legitimate' and 'illegitimate' influence."

Chapter 4

1. For a study of domestic melodrama, see Cross; also see Vicinus.

2. Hence the title for Cross's study of midcentury melodrama, which cites what must have been a common notice on theatrical posters: *Next Week—"East Lynne."*

3. Oxenford, p. 317. *East Lynne's* theatrical popularity was so great that three separate London theaters staged productions of it in 1879—the Olympic, the Standard, and Astley's. The first stage version appeared in 1862 in the United States.

4. Cited in Acland, pp. 213–14. George Eliot, speaking of this confrontation, wrote to John Blackwood: "One feels rather ashamed of authoresses this week after the correspondence in the *Times* between Mrs. Norton and Mrs. Wood. One hardly knows which letter is in the worse taste. However if we are to begin with marvelling at the little wisdom with which the world is governed, we can hardly expect that much wisdom will go to the making of novels." Eliot, "To John Blackwood," Oct. 29, 1871, in *George Eliot Letters,* p. 208.

5. Norton, *Caroline Norton's Defense,* p. 72.

6. See Poovey, *Uneven Developments,* pp. 51–88. My own chapter starts from Poovey's insight, but is also an attempt to elaborate a definition of melodrama, which, ultimately, connects Poovey's observations about law and gender to contemporary structures of perception, theatricality, and the formation of public policy in mid-nineteenth-century culture.

7. Norton, "A Letter to the Queen," p. 58.

8. See Vicinus; see Mitchell, pp. vii–xviii.

9. P. 85.

10. In this regard, melodrama is a response to one of the central conflicts of romanticism, as described here by I. Williams in *The Idea*, pp. 206–7: "In the decades after Rousseau there is widespread throughout Europe an increasing sense of tension between different aspects of personal and social experience and particularly an increasing need to resolve the discrepancy between systems of value which were based on the novel view of the individual human being as the final unit of meaning and social and political systems which embodied different, older, assumptions."

11. See L. Stone's chapter entitled "The Growth of Affective Individualism," pp. 149–80; see also Pollak, *The Poetics*.

12. Liu, "Wordsworth and Subversion," p. 88. According to Liu, and at least thus far I will agree, the test of whether or not some act is subversive in any practical way depends upon an advocate looking back at the act and declaring it so. "Subversion contributes to historical changes that condition us, when we look back from the changed world, to see subversion as part of the way things were established."

13. Kuhn, p. 160.

14. The debate about the extension of the franchise, which gained momentum in the mid 1850's, was not just coincidentally linked to concerns about marital politics. Anthony Trollope, for one, discussed the parliamentary push toward reform by narrating the vicissitudes of courtship and marriage in his series of Palliser novels (1864–80). For a discussion about the relationship between franchise extension and the form of the sensation novel, see Loesberg. Although I agree with Loesberg's argument about the connections between reform and specific narrative effects in contemporary fiction, I obviously disagree with his contention, p. 116, that in sensation novels, *East Lynne* included, "the issue of reform makes virtually no appearance in the content of the novels." Admittedly, the issue of reform receives oblique notice, but I will argue that the melodramatic content of the novel and its stage versions were responding to the various debates surrounding reform. In this regard, I am, of course, more comfortable with identifying certain "sensation" novel features with an older tradition of melodramatic effects. In so doing, I also tease out what I believe to be a more accurate account of the complicated mechanisms involved in various people's response to the onset of an extended franchise.

15. Checkland, p. 139.

16. For more on the rise and fall of George Hudson, see Lambert.

17. Neither this crisis nor the lessons derived from it were unprecedented in English history. Nevertheless, the massive fortunes and widespread wealth acquired through railway speculation heightened this anxiety about the decline in the dominance of landed culture. Pocock discusses the eighteenth-century suspicion of speculation and credit. Trade, and especially financial speculation, were believed to be governed by passion and fantasy, not the sound sense that real land instilled in its owners. See Pocock, *The Machiavellian Moment*, p. 471.

18. C. H. Ellis, p. 159. For an extensive study of the speculation in railways, see Lewin.

19. "Real" property is by definition the land of the family that cannot be circulated for profit, while "commercial" property is that which can be alienated for profit.

20. Concerns about the transformation of the primary forms of exchange among

the aristocracy had been expressed before this time; the railway crisis perpetuated and amplified these concerns. Pocock notes that neo-Harringtonians observed as early as the end of the seventeenth century that lords and landowners were beginning to engage in monetary exchange to the exclusion of land exchange, dowry exchange and the operation of chivalric and benevolent codes. See Pocock, "Machiavelli."

21. See Nicoll, vol. 4, p. 12.

22. Staves, *Players' Sceptres*, p. 116.

23. In addition to Caroline's own texts, see Acland; Poovey, *Uneven Developments*, pp. 51–88; and Perkins.

24. See Pocock, *The Machiavellian Moment*, pp. 462–506.

25. Coward, p. 66, notes the penetration of property law into the patriarchal family: "What is interesting . . . is the extent to which the organization of patriarchal familial relations, 'exclusive possession of wife and children,' is related to ownership of property."

26. Gallagher, "Political Crimes," p. 506. Gallagher speaks of the new roles for women that "civil humanism" in the eighteenth century afforded. Although not politicians per se, women were conceded the skill of conversation that assisted in the constitution of the new civilized public.

27. Others included were Lady Blessington, Miss Laetitia Landon, Mrs. Gore, and Lady Morgan.

28. See Acland, pp. 42–48.

29. These efforts, one of her biographers suggests, created political enemies out of the Duke of Cumberland and Lord Brougham, men who may have later assisted in the criminal conversation case against Caroline. See Acland, p. 74.

30. The term *conversation* has an intriguing etymological history that documents the entangled relationship between trade, marriage, and intimacy. Its first appearance in 1340 suggested variously commerce, society, and intimacy. In the sixteenth century, "conjugal conversation" referred to the married state. By 1740, the Oxford English Dictionary notes a new variant for conversation—a "conversazione"—defined as an "at home." This definition combines a domestic setting with public sociability and is free from connotations of sexual intimacy. Undoubtedly the privatization of women in the eighteenth century contributed to the word's next variation: "criminal conversation."

31. Levy, p. 6, describes the product of this process of classification: "This new individual was composed of an interior self enclosed within a gendered body and anchored to a family radically divided from the political world." As Davidoff and Hall, pp. 198–228, 353–56, indirectly suggest, families within the middle and lower ranks continued to live and work in a social sphere where issues of profession, family, community and local governance overlapped. Wives, for instance, worked alongside their husbands, who were often tradesmen and artisans, and what we might call nuclear families depended on extended kin to sustain their social and economic security.

32. "Custody of Infants Bill," p. 276. Levy, p. 27, usefully notes that the practical relation between these families and the state involved a large amount of regulation and intervention.

33. *Household Words* 9 (Apr. 1, 1854): 160. The reference to "walking hospitals" no doubts refers to Florence Nightingale.

34. The importance attached to female virtue in a postfeudal, landed culture manifested itself at the very beginning of this culture in early-eighteenth-century "she-tragedy." Tumir has argued that static displays of female virtue and vice were then staged as a backdrop to playwrights' meditations on the continued vitality of patriarchy after the Glorious Revolution of 1688 and the emergence of the contract theory of government. By the mid–nineteenth century, because the pressures on patriarchy exerted by contractual ties had become more pronounced, a woman's virtue or vice increased in significance. Static displays of virtue thus gave way to narratives in which the woman would, in effect, work toward this static display as climax. One might argue that the woman's definitional instability now demanded, in place of emblematic display, this representation of moral development.

35. Armstrong, "The Rise of the Domestic Woman," p. 109. Poovey, *Proper Lady*, p. 23, writes that "equating chastity with value . . . required [the woman] to signal her virtue by a physical intactness that is by definition invisible."

36. S. S. Ellis, *The Wives of England*, p. 17. According to Elshtain, p. 14, "[Women's] speech was severed from the name of action."

37. P. 376.

38. P. 376.

39. P. 382.

40. P. 70.

41. Mackay and Thane, p. 191, note that men defined the national characteristics of "Englishness," while women "were not generally perceived as being specifically English. Rather they were those qualities—essentially domestic and maternal—believed to be universal in Woman."

42. For detailed information regarding the status of women under the law in mid-nineteenth-century England, see Holcombe.

43. P. 381.

44. Norton, "Letter to the Queen," p. 67.

45. Within this context, husbands attempted to regain their proprietary rights over this alienated land through criminal conversation trials that aimed to substantiate the act of adultery, albeit in the absence of the alleged adulteress. Adultery was, from society's perspective, "neither palpable or public," but criminal conversation trials sought to be both. "Custody of Infants Bill," p. 336. In Caroline Norton's trial, her husband's attorneys encouraged the servants to describe Caroline's posture as she sat near Melbourne. Indeed, all her "dirty linen" was brought before the jury or, quite literally, reported on by the household's charwoman.

46. Kemble, p. 175.

47. Quoted in Perkins, p. 254.

48. *Times*, Aug. 24, 1853. It should be mentioned that friend and foe alike probably recalled Caroline's theatrical lineage when selecting their metaphors.

49. For studies about Victorian actresses, see Baker; Auerbach, *Ellen Terry* and *Private Theatricals*; and Kent, "Image and Reality."

50. Tracy Davis suggests that this assumption was factually erroneous. See T. C. Davis, "Actresses and Prostitutes." Also see Davis, "The Spectacle."

51. Norton, *The Wife*, vol. 1, p. 160.

52. Psomiades, p. 47, discusses a similar nexus of meanings related to the display of the female body in British aestheticism.

53. See Cominos. For a brief discussion of this issue, see Murray, pp. 10–11. Typical of the belief in the prostitute's awakened desire is Greg's contention, pp. 486–87: "Women's *desires* scarcely ever lead to their fall; for . . . the desire scarcely exists in a definite and conscious form, till they *have* fallen."

54. S., p. 385. W. Thompson, p. 64, speaks of "the engrafted duplicity of character" instilled in women.

55. Herbert, p. 35, has written at length about the dominant conception of human desires in early- and mid-nineteenth-century England, which, he writes, were seen as "uncontrollably self-multiplying individual impulses . . . which in a state of unimpaired freedom, . . . would act without limit." In a chapter entitled "Desire, Wealth, and Value: Anomic Themes in Political Economy," Herbert, pp. 74–150, discusses the intersection of this notion of primitive man with the political economist's notion of economic man, an intersection that resulted in anxieties about insatiable market behavior. The concern that women might also become insatiable speculators continued to influence public debate about roles for women, especially the periodic parliamentary debates about giving women proprietary rights under law. See Holcombe, pp. 148–65.

56. The heroine in Collins's sensation novel *No Name* (1862) helpfully demonstrates the way these theatrical, moral, and epistemological terms interrelated in mid-nineteenth-century England. Stripped of her family name and fortune because her parents had never legally married, the young heroine pledges to regain her inheritance by wedding, under an alias, the unsuspecting heir. As she anguishes over whether she should commit such a deception, she becomes an actress to earn her living. Still somewhat intimidated by her ambition, she portrays in her first public appearance a proper woman; the play is called "A Young Lady at Home." Ultimately, this "humble and sincere" theatrical effort becomes simply one of a series of disguises she puts on to effect her devious plan. This segment of the novel contains an inevitable, and by now familiar, logic. Without a legal birthright, the heroine lacks a domestic identity, in this case the identity she ought to have as the official daughter of her father. Consequently, Collins's heroine loses her lawful surname. Yet Collins does christen her with a first name—Magdalen—as if wanting to suggest that a woman bereft of a domestic existence is always already insincere, a priori a prostitute and actress. Once removed from her domestic setting and the transparent privacy it affords, Magdalen seems capable of playing any number of roles, and her thoughts become a disturbing secret that must be monitored and assessed by the hovering narrator. Much of the remaining novel seeks to reclaim the secretive Magdalen from the public sphere of duplicity, where women inevitably act roles they cannot possibly embody with discretion.

57. Buckstone, *Isabelle*, p. 10. This play was first performed in London in 1834, further demonstrating that concerns about speculative culture predated the railway

mania. This incident serves only as a representative crisis among several that oc-curred throughout this period.

58. It is interesting to note that Napoleon had long represented the decline of deferential culture and its replacement by a mercenary individualism. He was often mentioned during the O.P. Wars, and when, at the Crown and Anchor Tavern, the O.P. faction and John Philip Kemble forged an agreement, the negotiations were fol-lowed by a parody of Napoleon's divorce of Josephine, as if to perform an instructive lesson for the upstart "King John" Kemble.

59. Pocock, *The Machiavellian Moment*, p. 463.

60. At the same time, because of the laws of strict settlement in which fathers were paying more for increased settlements for their daughters, women were, in eco-nomic terms, becoming less valuable. For a more detailed discussion of these laws, see Pollak, pp. 24–76; and Poovey, *The Proper Lady*, pp. 1–44.

61. Pollak, pp. 31–32.

62. Treating women like property was by no means a new observation, but the distinctive character of the mid-nineteenth-century economy encouraged these wor-ries to focus on commodification.

63. Buckstone, *Victorine*, p. 17.

64. Wood, p. 300.

65. In this regard, Isabel's speech is quite similar to Matilda's in *Adrian and Or-rila*: "But now I stood upon creation's verge, a lonely hermit atom—living, yet un-allay'd to kindred life—lo! even as a moment; husband; offspring; friends; with all the heaven-born social charities, endear existence and invite me to a HOME." Dimond, p. 75.

66. Melodramatic syntax is rife with transitive sentences and declarative state-ments that transform the passive, silent sufferer who simply is into the active family member who does. For more on the ideology of rhetorical structures, see Hodge.

67. Melodramatic truth telling is the engine of revelation in *East Lynne*. A typical phrase is: "She read truth in his countenance." Wood, p. 308.

68. These are Isabel's words in Oxenford's 1866 Surrey Theatre version of *East Lynne*. Oxenford, p. 293.

69. Gallagher, "Political Crimes," p. 517.

70. As in all confrontations between these two contending models of social ex-change, the melodramatic response to the secrecy that market culture engendered can look much like the panoptical procedures adopted by many of those whom melodra-matic rhetoric wished to oppose. The anxious desire to reveal what is hidden is com-mon to all who lived at a time when alienation among the ranks had become a no-ticeable concern, but melodramatic rhetoric was distinctive in its consistent attempts to blame this secrecy on the operations of the market. It thus theorized about and located the source of what had become an obsessive anxiety about self-interest. One of the other main differences between melodramatic revelation and panoptic proce-dures lies in melodrama's insistence that all forms of social exchange take place before all eyes, while panoptic procedures shed an authoritative gaze on only those deemed socially abnormal. For a more detailed delineation of this contrast, see the Introduc-tion.

71. S., p. 396.

72. See, for instance, Grant; also Boucicault, in an 1882 speech reproduced in *The Art of Acting*. Although these manuals do not describe their acting style as "melodramatic," melodramatic acting, as we now know it, had become the standard acting method by the 1820's, just as melodramatic attitudes had come to permeate nearly any theatrical production, whether written by Shakespeare or Boucicault.

73. *The Actor*, p. 7.

74. S., p. 396. It must be said at this point, that melodrama's insistence on the sincerity of its acting caused a whole new set of contradictions for actors and, particularly, actresses. Baker, p. 98, notes: "If an actress was capable of performing in a 'pert, flippant manner,' then it went without saying that 'she loses much of her modesty,' but was it any better that she '*act* the best and holiest feelings of her nature?'" Commentators wondered whether particular actresses would in fact be as noble and ethical as the characters they played. Grant, pp. 91–92, comments: "But we conceive there can be no manner of doubt, but that lives and characters of those persons who are vehicles of these instructions, must contribute, in a very material degree, to the impression the fable and moral will make; for to hear virtue, religion, honour, and justice, recommended by an actor of known loose principles, generally provokes a smile from those who would hear the same with awe and respect by actors of known reputation in those particulars." Above all, melodrama wished to avoid farce and the ensuing burlesque of values farce expressed.

75. Staves, "Money for Honor," p. 282.

76. Norton, *Caroline Norton's Defense*, p. 141.

77. Ibid., p. 136. One similar divorce proceeding seemed to contain something very like a melodramatic revelation of the empty spectacle of divorce proceedings. In late 1855 or early 1856, a Mr. Hunt proceeded against the Honourable Maurice Berkeley Portman in a criminal conversation trial in common law court. While Mr. Portman went abroad, a jury awarded Mr. Hunt fifty pounds for the damages he incurred from the alleged affair between his wife and the young man. The case then proceeded to the next stage required to obtain a divorce, the ecclesiastical court. Unlike the common-law courts, the ecclesiastical court did permit testimony from the accused wife. Although Mrs. Hunt had already been presumed guilty because of the criminal conversation trial, her testimony in the Court of Arches showed the failures both of the common-law procedures, which accepted her guilt, and, despite her exceptional testimony, the usual flaws of the ecclesiastical courts. During the trial, the queen's advocate, according to the *Times*, provided evidence, via Mrs. Hunt's testimony, that rather than being an adulteress, Mr. Hunt's wife of several years was still a virgin. By permitting the woman not simply to speak of but to embody her innocence, the ecclesiastical courts enabled Mrs. Hunt to melodramatize. Instead of ferreting out impalpable and secret adultery, this trial discovered tangible and public virginity; instead of characterizing the accused woman's body as a disguise for private desires, this trial declared the woman "*virgo intacta.*" Not divided, but intact, Mrs. Hunt's "body language" confirmed her voice, and both expressed the "sincere" feelings of a publicized woman. The melodramatic discovery of Mrs. Hunt's virginity revealed that the tragic spectacle of the wronged husband was in fact a farce, that such

spectacle took place in public because of backstage machinery. Mr. Hunt had acted (played) a husband but was in fact an adulterer and a mercenary. After hearing the advocate's evidence, Mr. Hunt confessed to committing adultery himself and plotting to encourage his wife to do so in order to divorce her. See "The English Law of Divorce," pp. 338–55.

78. Norton, *Caroline Norton's Defense*, p. 85.

79. George J. Worth notes the importance of reputation in melodrama. See Worth, p. 2. Although George may have struck Norton during their marriage and physically banished her from the home, Norton's frequent and vivid depictions in these texts of George's brutality more specifically represent her efforts to make visible wrongs that were in most respects abstract and impersonal and to embody suffering that was in most respects psychic and therefore invisible.

80. Norton, *Caroline Norton's Defense*, p. 83.

81. Norton, "Letter to the Queen," p. 68.

82. Norton, *Caroline Norton's Defense*, pp. 67–68.

83. Ibid., p. 155. Even the author in the *British and Foreign Review*, who obviously deplores Caroline's actions, agrees: "We ask them [the Peers] to consider whether the notions about the marriage union in the upper classes of society are not already sufficiently lax; whether marriage has not become a matter of mere speculation,—a thing of the money market." "Custody of Infants Bill," p. 386.

84. Norton, "Letter to the Queen," p. 146.

85. Ibid., p. 83.

86. Ibid., p. 128.

87. This combination of what seems to be a call for certain forms of property rights with the continuation of patriarchal obligations was quite common during the years between the first two reform bills. Certainly Dickens's politics could be described in this way—a mixture of commitment to legislative reform and a belief in many traditional forms of social relation. He displays this attitude toward the Norton affair. In *Household Words*, Dickens calls for her protection under law and yet her right to the proceeds of her writing; he combines melodramatic scenarios, some taken from Caroline's own texts, with libertarian claims. See *Household Words* 9 (Apr. 1, 1854): 158–61 and (Apr. 29, 1854): 257–60. Also see Clarke, pp. 337–52. Obviously, I take issue with Clarke's characterization of Norton's efforts as "feminist legal reform."

88. Norton, "Letter to the Queen," p. 124. Norton, *Caroline Norton's Defense*, p. 2, does claim, "What I write, is written in no spirit of rebellion." Later in "Letter to the Queen," however, in apparent contradiction of my argument, she compares herself to rebels. I think the distinction between the two usages is, nonetheless, clear. Rebellion clamors for reform of existing institutions; hence, Caroline "puts forward no absurd claim of equality." Revolution seeks to overturn institutions.

89. Martineau, *Autobiography*, vol. 1, pp. 301–2.

90. Norton, *The Child*, p. xii.

91. Norton, "Letter to the Queen," p. 6.

92. Ibid., p. 112.

93. [Stephen], pp. 348–49.

94. See Chap. 5 for a discussion of the continued dialogue between these two contending ideologies.

95. Norton, *The Wife*, vol. 2, p. 53. "Nineteenth- and twentieth-century life has been full of attempts to divide performing from spectating, street space from play space, education and welfare from recreation, politics from creativity." See Yeo, p. 136.

96. Clarke, p. 342, mentions that the author of the *British and Foreign Review* article insinuated that Caroline had slept with Talfourd in order to obtain from him his preferential support for the Child Custody Act. Apparently, even this exchange of patronage was misconstrued as sexual transaction.

97. P. 4.

98. Debate continues about Queen Victoria's influence and power, especially after the death of Albert. This debate arises in part from the contemporary confusion, shared by Victoria herself, regarding the monarch's role in a constitutional monarchy. The monarch possessed the power to pick a prime minister if the party in majority was split over its leadership or if no single party had the majority in the Commons. In exercising this responsibility, the monarch was presumed to follow the guidance of parliamentary leaders, though at times Victoria bridled at this limitation imposed on her regal judgment. In addition, Queen Victoria believed she could, on her own advice, dissolve the ministry, but most politicians believed that the Crown should move to dissolve only at the request of its ministry. These curbs on her power did not prevent the queen from expressing opinions, which she did frequently and often vehemently. These opinions were never idly received nor were they necessarily considered anything more than her personal view; nevertheless, deferential respect for the English monarchy, even on the part of some radicalized Liberals, should be taken into account in this context. See Hardie; also D. Thompson. Thompson, p. 125, mentions that most people in the Victorian era believed in the queen's neutrality and were unaware, until the posthumous publication of her private letters, that she disliked Gladstone and doted on Disraeli. For what is potentially an intriguing suggestion regarding Victoria's tendency to confuse her role as monarch and her personal life, see Curtis, who notes, p. 263, that "the most tiresome of [the Victorian Prime Minister's] burdens was the Queen's touchiness on all matters which affected the interests of *her* family, *her* people, or *her* Empire." I suspect Victoria's sense of her hereditary identity as queen made it nearly impossible for her to imagine herself as a "private" individual. In this regard, she seems the perfect example of someone whose identity was grounded in familial affiliation, not individual essence.

99. Carlyle, pp. 1–2. Loesberg, p. 121, argues that class chaos is the most troublesome anxiety expressed by opponents of reform. This, I think, is not precisely formulated. Certainly, as was true during the railway crisis in the 1840's, many feared that laborers might become gentry, and vice versa, as both struggled equally in the marketplace. But for many, including Carlyle, the primary fear is the more general spread of market culture itself, an event that led, first, to the formation of class consciousness, then, inexorably, to class conflict and chaos. The 1866–67 collapse of the large London financial house of Overend and Gurney that led to riots in the cities seemed to confirm such suspicions.

100. At this time, it should be noted, the secret ballot was often listed among the desired electoral reforms. The debate over the ballot expressed these tensions between secrecy and disclosure. Although many of its supporters considered it to be a solution to bribery and influence peddling, from what might be called the perspective of melodrama, the secret ballot seemed like just another private box designed to hide what were now the secretive self-interests of the proprietary, alienated individual. The history of the ballot debate in the nineteenth century is a long and complicated one. The Ballot Act, which stipulated the institution of the secret ballot in parliamentary elections, was passed in 1872. For a narrow account of the ballot issue's history, see Kinzer. For an interesting discussion of its knotty significance, see Corrigan and Sayer, pp. 144–49.

101. Wood, p. 63.

102. Ibid.

103. In *Phineas Finn* (1869), Trollope, p. 333, has one of his characters observe: "'Nothing was wrong in the country, but the over-dominant spirit of speculative commerce;—and there was nothing in Reform to check that.'"

104. Bagehot, p. 91.

105. Henry Bleckly, a magistrate in the County of Lancaster, speaking before the Select Committee on Parliamentary and Municipal Elections in 1868–69 noted that "a small percentage of [electors] were inclined to deal with their vote as a marketable commodity." "Report from the Select Committee on Parliamentary and Municipal Elections," p. 85.

106. Bagehot, p. 96.

107. Kuhn, p. 35.

108. Bagehot, p. 64.

109. For pertinent discussions about Bagehot, see Cannadine, p. 107; Kuhn, pp. 19–53; Spring; and Cox.

110. Dilke; and Kuhn, p. 71. In fact, a half million pounds had been transferred since the beginning of Victoria's reign.

111. *Times*, Feb. 28, 1872.

112. See MacKenzie, p. 59; and P. Bailey, "Custom, Capital," p. 196.

113. These are Cannadine's words, p. 104.

114. As Hobsbawm, p. 4, notes, "Insofar as invented traditions reintroduced, as it were, status into a world of contract . . . they could not do so directly."

115. *Illustrated London News*, Mar. 2, 1872.

116. *Saturday Review*, Mar. 2, 1872, p. 259.

117. For pertinent examples, see Cannadine; the varied essays collected in Colls and Dodd; also see Davin.

118. In this regard, I think that D. Thompson, p. 125, is only partly right to argue that "the institution [monarchy] could make national self-definition simpler and less contentious than racial, linguistic or religious forms of identity." The emphasis on familial self-definition in representations of the monarchy could also lead to racial, linguistic, and religious contention if those differences could not somehow be assimilated to the familial model. The imperial thrust, in particular, provoked these contentions. The colonial émigré could be easily cast in a familial drama, but how does

one plausibly cast an Indian potentate as the "son" of the queen? More often, such characters became the villains of melodrama. It should be noted that these two distinct strains of nationalist rhetoric were not necessarily mutually exclusive and can sometimes be seen side by side in expansionist discourses, perhaps moderating the tendencies of each other. Images of the royal family, especially as reproduced in photography, had also dominated the representations of the Windsors prior to Albert's death. See Hayden, p. 66; and Nadel, p. 185.

119. Hugh Cunningham remarks on the English people's resistance to a more expansive notion of patriotic inclusiveness: "It was not easy to wean people away from the specifically English patriotism of landscape and cultural tradition in the direction of 'the greater spiritual content of the wider patriotism.'" Cunningham, "The Conservative Party," p. 298.

120. MacKenzie, p. 49.

121. Cunningham, "The Conservative Party," p. 292, convincingly points out that "the new patriotism which did come into existence, associated with monarchical ceremonial, was available to all parties, or to none." Loyalty to the monarchy, regardless of Victoria's personal partisanship, was experienced as transcendent of party faction. One writer in the *Illustrated London News*, Mar. 2, 1872, p. 205, noted that the queen avoided "party strife," that "pernicious effect against the wholesome union of sentiment that should link all classes of the State together." State-sponsored events throughout this century become subject to these same terms of debate: propaganda or populist sentiment? See Kuhn, whose methodology assumes the "great men" thesis, and Colley, "Whose Nation?" p. 104, who asks this rhetorical question: "Is it really wise therefore to suppose . . . that British national consciousness was never anything more than the creation and the tool of the ruling classes?" Also see Colley, "The Apotheosis." The broader theoretical and methodological ramifications implied in debates of this sort are addressed in Kent, "Presence and Absence."

122. See Kuhn, p. 160, who argues that Gladstone and others believed that the "vulgar and the uneducated, foreigners and Catholics, colonials and black men were more easily impressed with royal melodramas than were cultivated members of the British upper classes."

123. Recalling the days of Victoria and Albert, Gladstone noted that in "a wealthy country, with a large leisured class, in a luxurious age . . . the palaces of England became shrines of domestic happiness" where "vulgar ostentation grew pale in the face of a splendour everywhere associated with duty, and measured by its ends . . . where hospitalities truly regal and unwearied were so organised as not to put disdain upon the homely unattractive duty of living within an appointed income." Cited in Kuhn, p. 120. Gladstone, like Bagehot, appreciated the salutary restraints imposed by the operation of what I have called monarchical melodrama, but unlike Bagehot, Gladstone appears to have participated in the scenes of "intelligible feeling" that only women and poor men were presumed to favor. One might suggest, based on this quotation, that Gladstone's appreciation of melodrama was based less on an attachment to patriarchal culture and its conspicuous expenditure and consumption than on a more bourgeois reading of familial "duty" and frugality. In this regard, Glad-

stone shares with Mrs. Henry Wood a complicated and uneven response to the messages of melodrama. Gladstone's memories can serve as a response to the following more mercenary attitude about the monarchy, characterized by a journalist: "There are tens of thousands of Englishmen who have no prejudice in favour even of a system of government so long and loyally accepted; they would accept any system which insured the highest price of Three per Cents." Arnold, p. 767.

124. One writer in 1884 impatiently describes this lingering respect that even proprietary gentlemen felt for the Crown: "[Practical men] still treat [the House of Commons] as if it were only the representation of the people, and as if the Crown were still the government. When they pass Franchise Bills, the practical effect of which on government they have apparently not forecast, they still talk of uniting the whole nation in a compact body round its ancient throne, though the throne, as they must know, is a pageant." G. Smith, pp. 314.

125. Richards suggests that the Golden Jubilee was primarily a "domestic" display, while the Diamond Jubilee was imperial. This echoes a highly debatable argument that the Golden Jubilee expressed the nationalist patriotism of Liberals like Gladstone and Bagehot, while the Diamond Jubilee represented the empire-building aspirations that Gladstone particularly disliked. See Richards, "The Image of Victoria," p. 32; and Kuhn, pp. 28, 126.

126. These scenes of hierarchical amity between lord and tenant died a slow death, for they, like the royal ceremonies, reappeared as highly theatricalized and frequently "staged" events. After a 1901 fete at Blenheim Palace, the *Primrose League Gazette* noted: "The strength is not always derived from a deep political conviction, but is derived partly, and sometimes wholly, from memories like those which will be handed down from today—a memory of a day spent in a stately park and a historic house, when a champagne luncheon was given to all comers . . . by the prodigal generosity of the Duke . . . when . . . the local merchant's wife met the squire's wife; the parish councillor's wife, whose boy is at the charity school, sat next the Member's wife, whose boy is at Eton; and the parish councillor himself met the Duke." Quoted in Pugh, 148. We find here many of the conditions for melodramatic sentiment— inheritable feeling combined with inheritable status, face-to-face meetings mixed with benevolent "generosity." The Primrose League, the political/social organ of the Conservative party, adopted many of the features characteristic of melodrama's traditionalism.

Chapter 5

1. Pp. 72–73.

2. Accounts like Bagehot's have helped to influence the methodology of much historical writing. Partly because of his persuasive evaluation of party politics and government by the Cabinet, many twentieth-century studies of political and legal change in nineteenth-century England resolve into narratives of parliamentary debates and reconstructions of the secretive conversations among the Cabinet members. Obviously, these narratives of party debate and "great men" cannot easily account for popular movements or offer useful analyses of populist rhetoric, for they reca-

pitulate Bagehot's assumptions about the minimal and modified power of the populace. History becomes a narrative of the prologue before the play.

3. For a thorough study of these melodramatic moments, especially Stead's report of white slavery in his series of articles entitled the "Maiden Tribute of Modern Babylon," see chap. 3, "The Maiden Tribute of Modern Babylon," and chap. 4, "The Maiden Tribute: Cultural Consequences," in Walkowitz, *City of Dreadful Delight*.

4. P. 49.

5. Perkin, among others, argues that class antagonism was at its most acute in the last two decades of the century. See Perkin, *The Rise of Professional Society*, p. 53.

6. Huyssen, pp. 188–207, notes that what a society deems as bad women have often been associated with consumer culture, while its good women are affiliated with high culture.

7. Lee, p. 183, argues that addresses to the public might have only been an effort by the political parties to give the larger public the illusion of influence during an era that was still dominated by an oligarchic government. For my purposes, simply the fact that politicians felt it necessary to address the public—whether for purposes of political illusion or reality—is significant.

8. Ibid., pp. 181–212.

9. F., p. 192.

10. Morley, *On Compromise*, p. 26.

11. Quoted in Showalter, p. 146.

12. [Stephen], pp. 348–49.

13. T. Richards, *Commodity Culture*, p. 113.

14. For instance, in documenting John Morley's long and influential tenure as reader of manuscripts for Macmillan Books, Tuchman, pp. 175–202, cites Morley's assumption that melodramatic plots sold well.

15. H. A. Jones, pp. 4, 12. Jones's attitudes are noticeably influenced by Matthew Arnold's discussions about middle-class Philistines.

16. Lee, p. 194.

17. Morley, *On Compromise*, pp. 3–4.

18. See Wiener; and Perkin, *The Rise of Professional Society*, p. 365.

19. In some sense, real property was also undergoing a diminishment in its privileges. Each successive extension of the franchise further liquidated the property requirement until, by the 1884–85 bill, a man only needed to earn a subsistence wage to qualify for the vote. In one of his earlier drafts of the Third Reform Bill, Gladstone recommended a minimum balance in a savings account as an electoral requirement. Ultimately, however, wage laborers without savings were enfranchised.

20. I rely here on Perkin's more expansive definition of property: "Best conceived not as the ownership of things fixed and immovable but as the right to a flow of income from a scarce resource." *The Rise of Professional Society*, p. 377.

21. Ibid., p. 2.

22. For more on professionalization, see Larson.

23. Morley, *On Compromise*, p. 95.

24. I am indebted to Feltes for this insight into the contradiction inherent in the constitution of profession. See *Modes of Production*, p. 43.

25. I owe the example of Stephenson to Wiener, p. 30.

26. For an admirable exploratory analysis of realism, see Feltes, "Realism."

27. Walkowitz, *Prostitution*; see also Nead. I am indebted to Walkowitz's study for the narrative of the movement and for a summary of the contested issues.

28. Walkowitz, *Prostitution*, pp. 33–35.

29. Stevenson, p. 261.

30. Butler, "An Appeal," p. 146.

31. Walkowitz, *Prostitution*, p. 4. Walkowitz remarks that "the acts were linked to a conscious policy to create a professional bachelor army and navy without family ties or local identities."

32. Butler, "Letter to my Countrywomen," pp. 151–69.

33. Ibid., pp. 151–52. In "An Appeal," p. 119, Butler offers a melodramatic narrative when she describes the effects of state regulation of prostitution in Paris. She tells a familiar tale of outcast daughters whose passive suffering embodies familial as well as national estrangement: "Hunted down, terrified imprisoned, and despairing, the women at last succumbed . . . the effects of which can be truly estimated by one who is thoroughly acquainted with the cold, passionless vice of Paris, the effeminacy of its men, the rapid, steady increase of prostitution, together with the decrease of virtuous marriages since the introduction of the system, the dissolution of family life, the fears of the Emperor lest the population should die out."

34. See Crossick, pp. 101–30.

35. Butler, "Social Purity," pp. 172–73.

36. Butler, "An Appeal," p. 164.

37. Butler, "Social Purity," pp. 172–73.

38. Walkowitz, *Prostitution*, pp. 33–34, notes: "The patriarch whom they idealized was a nostalgic image, more appropriate for the father—head of household of the early modern period—whose authority initially sprang from his crucial role in organizing household production and reproduction among his many dependents, both workers and kin—than for the professional men and industrial employers of 'hands' in Victorian Manchester and Liverpool." Also see Walkowitz, "Male Vice."

39. For instance, see Butler, "An Appeal," p. 129.

40. Ibid., p. 139.

41. Butler, "Social Purity," p. 181.

42. Butler, "Letter to my Countrywomen," p. 160; and "Social Purity," p. 173.

43. Butler, "Letter to my Countrywomen," p. 168.

44. Butler, "An Appeal," p. 116.

45. Butler, "Letter to my Countrywomen," p. 152.

46. Quoted by Nead, p. 97.

47. Acton, "The Functions," p. 60.

48. Ibid., p. 62.

49. These are Lord Penzance's reflections. Quoted in Holcombe, p. 174.

50. These acts of alienation could seem perilously close to prostitution. Through self-proprietorship, such women sold themselves, having relinquished "absolute sovereignty" over their bodies. As one modern critic has noted, the contractual exchange inherent in prostitution "haunted relations between men and women." See Bland, p.

130. Bland, p. 124, comments that "a husband's 'property' rights in his wife's sexuality led to marriage being termed 'legalised prostitution.'" Walkowitz also notes that prostitution became a paradigm of heterosexual relations in the 1880's. See *City of Dreadful Delight*, p. 44. Bailey notes that during the 1880's traditional practices of heterosexual social exchange were indeed changing; they were "pursued in a more fragmented and inchmeal manner, in the individual transactions of a continuously recomposing leisure crowd." See "Parasexuality and Glamour," p. 167.

51. Meredith, "To Robert Louis Stevenson," Mar. 24, 1884, *The Letters*, vol. 2, p. 730.

52. In the 1890's, Lord Dufferin, nephew of Caroline Norton, wrote to the *St. James's Gazette* denying the rumor regarding Caroline's involvement in the Corn Law Repeal incident. According to Alice Acland, Lord Aberdeen leaked the information to the press for purposes of propaganda, as he was wont to do. The family requested and Meredith agreed that he publish a disclaimer in later editions of *Diana of the Crossways*. For more on this dispute, see Acland, pp. 169–73.

53. Meredith, "To Robert Louis Stevenson," Mar. 27, 1884, *The Letters*, vol. 2, p. 731.

54. Morley, *On Compromise*, p. 156. Morley frequently uses variants on "speculation" as a means of describing the type of individual he reifies. Christopher Kent notes that J. S. Mill spoke of a "speculative class" when discussing his concept of minority representation. See Kent, *Brains*, p. 44.

55. See Walkowitz, *City of Dreadful Delight*, pp. 135–70.

56. "If we may be censorious we would object that . . . it would not have been easy for a married woman to sell her landed property without the concurrence of her husband." See Unsigned Review.

57. Wilt, "Meredith's Diana." Also see, Wilt, *The Readable People*. One might note here the title of Wilt's book-length study which invokes the trope of "reading" to describe Meredith's characters, a trope Meredith himself would no doubt accept as accurate. Compare this to the theme of reading in *Oliver Twist*, where reading and characters that need to be read are usually affiliated with deception and criminality.

58. For an example of an essay that adopts such terms, see Fowler, "*Diana of the Crossways*." In the 1980's, influenced by the feminist revision of the canon, Virago Press started its series on works by forgotten female novelists. Included among its first choices was Meredith's *Diana of the Crossways*.

59. Meredith, "Love in the Valley"; and *The Amazing Marriage*, p. 338.

60. Quoted in Harrison, *Separate Spheres*, p. 33.

61. In *Diana of the Crossways*, p. 8, this melodramatic gossip is jokingly figured as a revolutionary threat to the deferential, landed culture that melodramatic content traditionally upheld: "A gouty Diarist, a sheer gossip Diarist, may thus, in the bequest of a trail of reminiscences, explode our temples . . . our treasures, our homesteads, alive with dynamitic stuff; nay, disconcert our inherited veneration, dislocate the intimate connexion between the tugged flaxen forelock and a title."

62. Spacks, pp. 37–46, has alluded to both the communal sociology and policing effect of female gossip.

63. Meredith was working on a draft of *Diana of the Crossways* as early as 1882.

64. Butler, "Social Purity," p. 181.

65. Ibid., p. 174.

66. Ibid., p. 185.

67. Ibid., p. 173.

68. Ibid., p. 185. Oddly, Butler calls this form of governance "socialism." In this passage, she might be referring to the prognostications of class conflict that Marx's works include; more likely, she is referring to contemporary versions of English socialism, many of which did not include theories of community property or utopian egalitarianism as did the beliefs of William Morris, for instance. To modern eyes, many of these socialisms resemble fascism more than Marxism. Whatever her specific reference might be, Butler is opposing statist government and supporting governance by the individual conscience as defined in the text.

69. Tuchman, pp. 1–45.

70. Morley, *On Compromise*, p. 96.

71. P. 551. Throughout this novel, Dame Gossip engages in a struggle with a "philosopher" for control over the narrative.

72. Quoted by Stevenson, p. 101.

73. Quoted in Spring, p. 527.

74. Stead complained: "When [Meredith] gathers all his clever characters round a table, and makes them fire epigrams at one another through eight or ten successive pages, he is excruciatingly tiresome" (*Pall Mall Gazette*).

75. After midcentury, stage melodrama and "sensation" fiction also manifested this psychologizing of the villain. In the melodrama *Gaslight*, one almost sees the actual transformation take place. The heroine's husband, a classic villain of melodrama who is a thief and murderer, attempts to convince the heroine that she is going mad. Only the revelatory powers of melodrama can forestall this internalization of villainy; by the end of the play, the villain is identified as the husband, not the wife's psyche.

76. Meredith, *Diana*, p. 258, links melodramatic villainy and speculation: "Heavy failures and convulsions in the City of London . . . were then beginning cavernously their performance of the part of villain in Diana's history."

77. On this romantic subject and its manifestation through developmental narratives, see Siskin, pp. 94–124.

78. Perkin notes that professional people perceive themselves above the economic system because they provide services, not products. Furthermore, the value of their commodity is seemingly determined by their ability to persuade the client. See *The Rise of Professional Society*, pp. 117–20.

79. Meredith, *An Essay.*

80. Ibid., pp. 54–55.

81. Ibid., p. 23.

82. Ibid., pp. 82–83.

83. Meredith wrote to Lady Ulrica Duncombe: "Even young women have but a confused idea of this masculine sentiment of the complete possession, down to absorption . . . and how it is to pursue them anticipatorily and retrospectively." See "To Lady Ulrica Duncombe," Apr. 19, 1902, in *The Letters*, vol. 3, p. 1438.

84. Stead, *Pall Mall Gazette*. C. Monkhouse in the *Saturday Review* summarized the plot of *Diana of the Crossways*, then commented: "All these are facts, and quite sufficient to form the basis of a very 'sensational' novel. It need scarcely be said that in Mr. Meredith's hands the materials are turned to greater advantage." C. Monkhouse, *Saturday Review*, in I. Williams, *Meredith: The Critical Heritage*, p. 262.

85. In 1902, the Society of Authors released the following statement of purpose: "Pure literature . . . has no society whose aim is to sustain the name, and publicly to represent to foreigners and to the community the power of English intelligence and imagination." Note the evacuation of all economic terms from this statement of mission. Through "philosophy in fiction," Meredith's novels represent "English intelligence and imagination." For the history of the Society, see Bonham-Carter.

86. See Tuchman, especially pp. 65–92, 175–202. I am indebted to Tuchman's sociological research for this portion of my argument. In this chapter, I attempt to isolate some of the historical pressures that contributed to the changes in the book market that Tuchman traces.

87. Ibid., p. 79.

88. Elam, p. 190.

89. Meredith, *An Essay*, p. 82.

90. Meredith, "To John Morley," May 22, 1874, in *The Letters*, vol. 1, p. 484.

91. Meredith, *An Essay*, pp. 79–80. It is interesting to note that during the 1868 elections, E. A. Freeman, one of the intellectual Liberals who sought a seat in Parliament, mentioned in one of his speeches that his candidacy was a contest of "brains against acres." Quoted in Kent, *Brains*, p. 49.

92. Meredith, "To Mrs. Leslie Stephen," June 13, 1889, in *The Letters*, vol. 2, p. 964.

93. For an example of this dilemma for female novelists, see the Epilogue.

Bibliography

Acland, Alice [Anne Marreco (Acland-Troyte)]. *Caroline Norton*. London: Constable, 1948.

Acton, William. "The Functions and Disorders of the Reproductive Organs" [1875]. In Sheila Jeffreys, ed., *Sexuality Debates*, pp. 57–73. New York: Routledge & Kegan Paul, 1987.

———. "Prostitution Considered in Its Social and Sanitary Aspects" [1870]. In Sheila Jeffreys, ed., *Sexuality Debates*, pp. 52–56. New York: Routledge & Kegan Paul, 1987.

The Actor, or Guide to the Stage. New York: Circulating Library and Dramatic Repository, 1823.

Agnew, Jean Christophe. *Worlds Apart: The Market and the Theater in Anglo-American Thought, 1550–1750*. Cambridge, Eng.: Cambridge University Press, 1986.

Altick, Richard D. *The English Common Reader*. Chicago: University of Chicago Press, 1957.

Armstrong, Nancy. *Desire and Domestic Fiction*. New York: Oxford University Press, 1987.

———. "The Rise of the Domestic Woman." In Nancy Armstrong and Leonard Tennenhouse, eds., *The Ideology of Conduct: Essays on Literature and the History of Sexuality*, pp. 96–141. New York: Methuen, 1987.

Arnold, Arthur. "The Queen and Her Family." *Fortnightly Review* 43 (June 1885): 766–71.

Arnott, James F., and John W. Robinson, eds. *English Theatrical Literature, 1559–1900.* London: Society for Theatre Research, 1970.

Attalus [pseud.]. *Justice and Generosity against Malice, Ignorance, and Poverty.* London: Sherwood, Neely and Jones, 1809.

Auerbach, Nina. "Alluring Vacancies in the Victorian Character." *The Kenyon Review* 8 (Summer 1988): 36–48.

———. *Ellen Terry: Player in Her Time.* New York: Norton, 1987.

———. *Private Theatricals: The Lives of the Victorians.* Cambridge, Mass.: Harvard University Press, 1990.

Axton, William F. *Circle of Fire: Dickens' Vision and Style and the Popular Victorian Theater.* Lexington: University of Kentucky Press, 1966.

Baer, Marc. *Theatre and Disorder in Late Georgian London.* Oxford: Clarendon Press, 1992.

Bagehot, Walter. *The English Constitution* [1867]. Ithaca, N.Y.: Cornell University Press, 1963.

Bailey, J. O. *British Plays of the Nineteenth Century.* New York: Odyssey Press, 1966.

Bailey, Peter. "Custom, Capital and Culture in the Victorian Music Hall." In Robert Storch, ed., *Popular Culture and Custom in Nineteenth-Century England*, pp. 180–208. London: Croom Helm, 1982.

———. "Parasexuality and Glamour: The Victorian Barmaid as Cultural Prototype." *Gender & History* 2 (Summer 1990): 148–72.

Baker, Michael. *Rise of the Victorian Actor.* London: Croom Helm, 1978.

Bargainnier, Earl F. "Melodrama as Formula." *Journal of Popular Culture* 9 (Winter 1975): 726–33.

Barker, Clive. "The Chartists, Theatre, Reform and Research." *Theatre Quarterly* 1 (Oct.-Dec. 1971): 3–10.

Bate, Jonathan. *Shakespeare and the English Romantic Imagination.* Oxford: Clarendon Press, 1986.

Baxter, George R. W. *The Book of the Bastiles; or, The History of the Working of the New Poor Law.* London: John Stephens, 1841.

Behagg, Clive. *Politics and Production in the Early Nineteenth Century.* London: Routledge, 1990.

Belsey, Catherine. "The Romantic Construction of the Unconscious." In Francis Barker, Peter Hulme, Margaret Iverson, and Diana Loxley, eds., *Literature, Politics and Theory*, pp. 57–76. London: Methuen, 1986.

Bender, John. *Imagining the Penitentiary: Fiction and the Architecture of Mind in Eighteenth-Century England.* Chicago: University of Chicago Press, 1987.

Bentham, Jeremy. *Panopticon; or, The Inspection House.* London: n.p., 1791.

———. *Panopticon: Postscript.* 2 vols. London: n.p., 1791.

Bentley, Eric. "Melodrama." In Robert W. Corrigan, ed., *Tragedy: Vision and Form*, pp. 217–31. San Francisco: Chandler, 1965.

Blakey, Robert. *Cottage Politics; or, Letters on the New Poor-Law Bill*. London: n.p., 1837.

Bland, Lucy. "Marriage Laid Bare: Middle-Class Women and Marital Sex, 1880–1914." In Jane Lewis, ed., *Labour and Love: Women's Experience of Home and Family, 1850–1940*, pp. 123–46. London: Basil Blackwell, 1986.

Boaden, Joames. *The Life of John Philip Kemble, Esq.* Vol. 7. London: J. Johnston, 1809. Theater Collection, Pusey Library, Harvard University.

Boas, George. *Vox Populi: Essays in the History of an Idea*. Baltimore, Md.: Johns Hopkins University Press, 1969.

Bodenheimer, Rosemarie. *The Politics of Story in Victorian Social Fiction*. Ithaca, N.Y.: Cornell University Press, 1988.

Bogel, Fredric V. "Fables of Knowing: Melodrama and Related Forms." *Genre* 2 (Spring 1978): 83–108.

Bonham-Carter, Victor. *Authors by Profession*. London: Society of Authors, 1978.

Booth, Michael R. *English Melodrama*. London: Herbert Jenkins, 1965.

———. "Introduction." In Michael R. Booth, ed., *English Plays of the Nineteenth Century: Dramas, 1800–50*, vol. 1. Oxford: Clarendon Press, 1969.

———. "The Metropolis on Stage." In H. J. Dyos and Michael Wolff, eds., *The Victorian City: Images and Realities*, pp. 211–24. London: Routledge & Kegan Paul, 1973.

Booth, Michael, Richard Southern, Frederick and Lise-Lone Marker, and Robertson Davies, eds. *The Revels History of Drama in English*. Vol. 6. London: Methuen, 1975.

Boucicault, Dion. *The Art of Acting*. New York: Columbia University Press, 1926.

Bourdieu, Pierre. "The Forms of Capital." In John G. Richardson, ed., *The Handbook of Theory and Research for the Sociology of Education*, pp. 241–58. New York: Greenwood Press, 1983.

Bradby, David, Louis James, and Bernard Sharratt, eds. *Performance and Politics in Popular Drama*. Cambridge, Eng.: Cambridge University Press, 1980.

Branca, Patricia. *Silent Sisterhood: Middle-Class Women in the Victorian Home*. Pittsburgh: Carnegie-Mellon University Press, 1975.

Braudy, Leo. "The Form of the Sentimental Novel." *Novel* 7 (Fall 1973): 5–13.

Bray, J. F. *Labour's Wrongs and Labour's Remedy; or, The Age of Might and the Age of Right*. Leeds, Eng.: David Green, 1839.

Brewer, John. *The Sinews of Power: War, Money and the English State, 1688–1783*. London: Unwin Hyman, 1989.

Brewer, John, and John Styles, eds. *An Ungovernable People*. New Brunswick, N.J.: Rutgers University Press, 1980.

Brooks, Peter. "The Mark of the Beast: Prostitution, Melodrama, and Narrative." In Daniel Gerould, ed., *Melodrama*, pp. 125–38. New York: New York Literary Forum, 1980.

———. *The Melodramatic Imagination: Balzac, Henry James, Melodrama, and the Mode of Excess*. New Haven, Conn.: Yale University Press, 1976.

Brown, Frederick. *Theater and Revolution: The Culture of the French Stage*. New York: Viking Press, 1980.

Bibliography

Brown, James M. *Dickens: Novelist in the Market-Place*. Totowa, N.J.: Barnes & Noble, 1982.

Brundage, Anthony. *The Making of the New Poor Law*. New Brunswick, N.J.: Rutgers University Press, 1978.

Buckstone, J. B. *Isabelle*. In B. Webster, ed., *National Drama*, vol. 8. London: n.p., n.d.

———. *Victorine*. In B. Webster, ed., *National Drama*, vol. 8. London: n.p., n.d.

Bull, Rev. George S. *Times*, Feb. 23, 1837.

Bull, John [pseud.]. *Covent Garden Theatre! Remarks on the Cause of the Dispute*. London: Fairburn, 1809.

Burchell, Graham, Colin Gordon, and Peter Miller, eds. *The Foucault Effect: Studies in Governmentality*. Chicago: University of Chicago Press, 1991.

Burke, Edmund. *Reflections on the Revolution in France* [1790]. Harmondsworth, Middlesex, Eng.: Penguin, 1969.

Butler, Josephine. "An Appeal to the People of England on the Recognition and Superintendence of Prostitution by Governments" [1870]. In Sheila Jeffreys, ed., *The Sexuality Debates*, pp. 111–50. New York: Routledge & Kegan Paul, 1987.

———. "Letter to my Countrywomen, Dwelling in the Farmsteads and Cottages of England" [1871]. In Sheila Jeffreys, ed., *The Sexuality Debates*, pp. 151–69. New York: Routledge & Kegan Paul, 1987.

———. "Social Purity" [n.d.]. In Sheila Jeffreys, ed., *The Sexuality Debates*, pp. 170–89. New York: Routledge & Kegan Paul, 1987.

Cannadine, David. "The Context, Performance and Meaning of Ritual: The British Monarchy and the 'Invention of Tradition,' c. 1820–1977." In Eric Hobsbawm and Terence Ranger, eds., *The Invention of Tradition*, pp. 101–64. Cambridge, Eng.: Cambridge University Press, 1983.

Carlyle, Thomas. "Shooting Niagara: And After?" [1867]. Vol. 5, *Critical and Miscellaneous Essays*. London: Chapman, 1899.

Castle, Terry. *Masquerade and Civilization*. Stanford, Calif.: Stanford University Press, 1986.

[Chadwick, Edwin]. "The New Poor Law." *Edinburgh Review* 63 (July 1836): 487–537.

Chandler, James K. *Wordsworth's Second Nature*. Chicago: University of Chicago Press, 1984.

Checkland, S. G. *The Rise of Industrial Society in England, 1815–1885*. London: Longman, 1964.

Chittick, Kathryn. *Dickens and the 1830s*. Cambridge, Eng.: Cambridge University Press, 1990.

Christensen, Jerome. *Practicing Enlightenment: Hume and the Formation of a Literary Career*. Madison: University of Wisconsin Press, 1987.

Clark, Anna. "The Politics of Seduction in English Popular Culture, 1748–1848." In Jean Radford, ed., *The Progress of Romance*, pp. 46–70. London: Routledge & Kegan Paul, 1986.

———. "Queen Caroline and the Sexual Politics of Popular Culture in London, 1820," *Representations* 31 (Summer 1990): 47–68.

————. *Women's Silences, Men's Violence: Sexual Assault in England, 1770–1845*. London: Pandora, 1987.

Clark, J. C. D. *English Society, 1688–1832*. Cambridge, Eng.: Cambridge University Press, 1985.

Clarke, Micael M. "William Thackeray's Fiction and Caroline Norton's Biography: Narrative Matrix of Feminist Legal Reform." In Michael Timko, Fred Kaplan, and Edward Guiliano, eds., *Dickens Studies Annual*, pp. 337–52. New York: AMS Press, 1989.

Clifford for ever! O.P. and no P.B. London: Fairburn, 1809.

Cobbett, William. *Political Register*. Feb. 7, 1806.

————. *Political Register*. Nov. 22 and 29, 1806.

————. *Rural Rides* [1830]. New York: E. P. Dutton, 1932.

————. "Surplus Population: A Comedy." *Cobbett's Two-Penny Trash* (June 1831): 266–92.

[Coleridge, Hartley]. "Modern English Poetesses." *Quarterly Review* 66 (Sept. 1840): 374–418.

Colley, Linda. "The Apotheosis of George III: Loyalty, Royalty, and the British Nation, 1760–1820." *Past and Present* 102 (Feb. 1984): 94–129.

————. *Britons: Forging the Nation, 1707–1837*. New Haven, Conn.: Yale University Press, 1992.

————. "Whose Nation? Class and National Consciousness in Britain, 1750–1830." *Past and Present* 113 (Nov. 1986): 97–118.

Collini, Stefan. *Public Moralists: Political Thought and Intellectual Life in Britain, 1850–1930*. Oxford: Clarendon Press, 1991.

Collins, Philip, ed. *Dickens: The Critical Heritage*. London: Routledge & Kegan Paul, 1971.

Collins, William Wilkie. *No Name*, ed. Virginia Blain. London, 1862; Oxford: Oxford University Press, 1986.

Colls, Robert. "Englishness and the Political Culture." In Robert Colls and Philip Dodd, eds., *Englishness: Politics and Culture, 1880–1920*, pp. 29–61. London: Croom Helm, 1986.

Colls, Robert, and Philip Dodd. *Englishness: Politics and Culture, 1880–1920*. London: Croom Helm, 1986.

Colman, George. *Blue Beard*. Vol. 21, *New English Drama*. London: W. Simpkin, 1823.

Cominos, Peter T. "Late-Victorian Sexual Respectability and the Social System." *International Review of Social History* 8 (1963): 18–48, 216–50.

Connerton, Paul. *How Societies Remember: Themes in the Social Sciences*. Cambridge, Eng.: Cambridge University Press, 1989.

A Constant Reader [pseud.]. Letter. *Times*, Oct. 13, 1809.

————. Letter. *Times*, Nov. 8, 1809.

Cope, Jackson L. *Dramaturgy of the Daemonic*. Baltimore, Md.: Johns Hopkins University Press, 1984.

Corfield, Penelope J. "Class by Name and Number in Eighteenth-Century Britain."

Bibliography

In Penelope J. Corfield, ed., *Language, History and Class*, pp. 101–30. Oxford: Basil Blackwell, 1991.

Corrigan, Philip, and Derek Sayer. *The Great Arch: English State Formation as Cultural Revolution*. Oxford: Basil Blackwell, 1985.

Cott, Nancy F. *The Bonds of Womanhood: "Woman's Sphere" in New England, 1780–1835*. New Haven, Conn.: Yale University Press, 1977.

Coward, Rosalind. *Patriarchal Precedents: Sexuality and Social Relations*. London: Routledge & Kegan Paul, 1983.

Cowherd, Raymond G. *Political Economists and the English Poor Laws*. Athens: Ohio University Press, 1977.

Cox, Gary. *The Efficient Secret: The Cabinet and the Development of Political Parties in Victorian England*. Cambridge, Eng.: Cambridge University Press, 1987.

Cross, Gilbert B. *Next Week—"East Lynne": Domestic Drama in Performance, 1820–1874*. Lewisburg, Pa.: Bucknell University Press, 1977.

Crossick, Geoffrey. "From Gentlemen to the Residuum: Images of Social Description in Victorian Britain." In Penelope J. Corfield, ed., *Language, History and Class*, pp. 150–78. Oxford: Basil Blackwell, 1991.

Cullen, Michael J. *The Statistical Movement in Early Victorian Britain*. Hassocks, Sussex, Eng.: Harvester Press, 1975.

Cunningham, Hugh. "The Conservative Party and Patriotism." In Robert Colls and Philip Dodd, eds., *Englishness: Politics and Culture, 1880–1920*, pp. 283–307. London: Croom Helm, 1986.

———. *Leisure in the Industrial Revolution*. New York: St. Martin's Press, 1980.

Curtis, L. P., Jr. "The Queen's Two Bonnets." *Victorian Studies* 9 (Mar. 1966): 257–73.

"Custody of Infants Bill," *British and Foreign Review* 7 (July 1838): 269–411.

Davidoff, Leonore, and Catherine Hall. *Family Fortunes: Men and Women of the English Middle Class, 1780–1850*. Chicago: University of Chicago Press, 1987.

Davies, Andrew. *Other Theatres: The Development of Alternative and Experimental Theatre in Britain*. Totowa, N.J.: Barnes & Noble, 1987.

Davies, Robertson. *The Mirror of Nature*. Toronto: University of Toronto Press, 1983.

Davin, Anna. "Imperialism and Motherhood." *History Workshop* 5 (1978): 9–65.

Davis, Richard W. "Deference and Aristocracy in the Time of the Great Reform Act." *American Historical Review* 81 (June 1976): 532–39.

Davis, Tracy C. "Actresses and Prostitutes in Victorian London." *Theatre Research International* 13 (Autumn 1988): 221–33.

———. "The Spectacle of Absent Costume: Nudity on the Victorian Stage." *New Theatre Quarterly* 5 (Nov. 1989): 321–33.

Davison, Peter. *Popular Appeal in English Drama to 1850*. Totowa, N.J.: Barnes & Noble, 1982.

de Bolla, Peter. *The Discourse of the Sublime*. London: Basil Blackwell, 1989.

Dibdin, Thomas John. *Melodrame Mad! or, the Siege of Troy*. London: n.p., 1819.

Dicey, Albert Venn. *Lectures on the Relation Between Law and Public Opinion in England During the Nineteenth Century*. London: Macmillan, 1905; reprint, New Brunswick, N.J.: Transaction Books, 1981.

Dickens, Charles. "Autobiographical Fragment." In John Forster, *Life of Charles Dickens*, vol. 1. London: Chapman & Hall, 1872–74.
———. *Household Words* 9 (Apr. 1, 1854): 158–61.
———. *Household Words* 9 (Apr. 29, 1854): 257–60.
———. *Oliver Twist* [1838]. Harmondsworth, Middlesex, Eng.: Penguin, 1966.
———. *The Pilgrim Edition of the Letters of Charles Dickens*, ed. Madelene House and Graham Storey. 5 vols. Oxford: Clarendon Press, 1965–81.
Dilke, Charles. *Sir Charles Dilke on the Cost of the Crown*. London: n.p., 1871.
Dimond, William. *Adrian and Orrila*. New York: D. Longworth, 1807.
Dollimore, Jonathan. *Sexual Dissidence: Augustine to Wilde, Freud to Foucault*. Oxford: Clarendon Press, 1991.
Donohue, Joseph. "Burletta and the Early Nineteenth-Century English Theatre." *Nineteenth-Century Theatre Research* 1 (Spring 1973): 29–51.
Dunkley, Peter. *The Crisis of the Old Poor Law in England, 1795–1834: An Interpretive Essay*. New York: Garland, 1982.
Dye, William S., Jr. *A Study of Melodrama in England from 1800 to 1840*. State College, Pa.: Nittany Printing, 1919.
E.H. [pseud.]. "On Melo-drama." *Theatrical Inquisitor and Monthly Mirror* 12 (Mar. 1818): 158–64.
Eagleton, Terry. *Criticism and Ideology*. London: Verso, 1978.
Edsall, Nicholas C. *The Anti-Poor Law Movement, 1834–1844*. Manchester, Eng.: Manchester University Press, 1971.
Eigner, Edwin M. *The Dickens Pantomime*. Berkeley: University of California Press, 1989.
Elam, Diane. "'We Pray to Be Defended from Her Cleverness': Conjugating Romance in George Meredith's *Diana of the Crossways*," *Genre* 21 (Summer 1988): 179–202.
Eliot, George. *George Eliot Letters*, ed. Gordon S. Haight. 7 vols. New Haven, Conn.: Yale University Press, 1954–55.
Ellis, C. Hamilton. *British Railway History, 1830–76*. London: Allen & Unwin, 1954.
Ellis, Sarah Stickney. *The Mothers of England*. London: Fisher, Son, 1843.
———. *The Wives of England*. London: Fisher, Son, 1843.
Elshtain, Jean Bethke. *Public Man, Private Woman*. Princeton, N.J.: Princeton University Press, 1981.
An English Gentleman [pseud.]. Letter. *Times*, Nov. 7, 1809.
"The English Law of Divorce." *Westminster Review* 65 (Apr. 1, 1856): 338–55.
An Englishman [pseud.]. Letter. *Times*, Nov. 20, 1809.
Estill, Robin. "The Factory Lad: Melodrama as Propaganda." *Theatre Quarterly* 1 (Oct.-Dec. 1971): 22–26.
F. [pseud.]. "The Redistribution Bill." *Macmillan's Magazine* 51 (Jan. 1885): 190–97.
Fairclough, Peter. Appendix A to *Oliver Twist* [1838], by Charles Dickens. Harmondsworth, Middlesex, Eng.: Penguin, 1966.
Feltes, N. N. *Modes of Production of Victorian Novels*. Chicago: University of Chicago Press, 1986.

Bibliography

―――. "Realism, Consensus and 'Exclusion Itself': Interpellating the Victorian Bourgeoisie." *Textual Practice* 1 (Winter 1987): 297–307.

Findlater, Richard. *Grimaldi: King of Clowns*. London: Macgibbon & Kee, 1955.

Finer, Samuel E. *The Life and Times of Edwin Chadwick*. London: Methuen, 1952.

"First Report from His Majesty's Commissioners on the Administration and Practical Operation of the Poor Laws with Appendix" [1834]. Vol. 8, *British Parliamentary Papers, Poor Laws*. Shannon, Ireland: Irish University Press, 1970.

"First Report of the Commissioners Appointed by Her Majesty to Inquire into the Law of Divorce" [1853]. Vol. 1, *British Parliamentary Papers, Marriage and Divorce*. Shannon, Ireland: Irish University Press, 1969.

Foucault, Michel. *The Archaeology of Knowledge and the Discourse on Language*, trans. A. M. Sheridan Smith. New York: Pantheon Books, 1972.

―――. *Discipline and Punish: The Birth of the Prison*, trans. Alan Sheridan. New York: Vintage Books, 1979.

―――. *The Order of Things*. New York: Vintage Books, 1970.

Fowler, Lois Josephs. "*Diana of the Crossways*: A Prophecy for Feminism." In Joseph Baim, Ann L. Hayes, and Robert Gangewere, eds., *In Honor of Austin Wright*, pp. 30–36. Pittsburgh, Pa.: Carnegie-Mellon University Press, 1972.

Fraser, Derek, ed. *The New Poor Law in the Nineteenth Century*. London: Macmillan, 1976.

A Friend to Morality, But Not a Member of the Society for the Suppression of Vice [pseud.]. Letter. *Morning Chronicle*, Sept. 28, 1809.

Frye, Northrop. *The Anatomy of Criticism*. Princeton, N.J.: Princeton University Press, 1957.

Gagnier, Regenia. *Subjectivities: A History of Self-Representation in Britain, 1832–1920*. New York: Oxford University Press, 1991.

Gallagher, Catherine. "George Eliot and *Daniel Deronda*: The Prostitute and the Jewish Question." In Ruth Bernard Yeazel, ed., *Sex, Politics and Science in the Nineteenth-Century Novel*, pp. 39–62. Baltimore, Md.: Johns Hopkins University Press, 1986.

―――. *The Industrial Reformation of English Fiction: Social Discourse and Narrative Form*. Chicago: University of Chicago Press, 1985.

―――. "Political Crimes and Fictional Alibis: The Case of Delarivier Manley." *Eighteenth-Century Studies* 23 (Summer 1990): 502–21.

A Genuine Collection of O.P. Songs. London: B. Mace, 1809.

Gerould, Daniel, ed. *Melodrama*. New York: New York Literary Forum, 1980.

Giddens, Anthony. *The Constitution of Society: Outline of the Theory of Structuration*. Berkeley: University of California Press, 1984.

Gilliland, Thomas. *Elbow Room*. London: n.p., 1804.

Gillis, John. R. *For Better, For Worse: British Marriages, 1600 to the Present*. New York: Oxford University Press, 1985.

Gledhill, Christine. "The Melodramatic Field: An Investigation." In Christine Gledhill, ed., *Home Is Where the Hearth Is*, pp. 5–42. London: British Film Institute, 1987.

Gordon, Colin. "Governmental Rationality: An Introduction." In Graham Burchell,

Colin Gordon, and Peter Miller, eds., *The Foucault Effect: Studies in Governmentality*, pp. 1–52. Chicago: University of Chicago Press, 1991.

Grant, George. *An Essay on the Science of Acting*. London: Cowie & Strange, 1828.

[Greg, William Rathbone]. "Prostitution." *Westminster Review* 49 (July 1850): 486–87.

"Grievances of a Country Overseer." *Fraser's Magazine* 10 (Dec. 1834): 629–39.

Grimsted, David. *Melodrama Unveiled: American Theater and Culture, 1800–1850*. Chicago: University of Chicago Press, 1968.

Gross, John. *The Rise and Fall of the Man of Letters: Aspects of English Literary Life since 1800*. London: Weidenfeld & Nicolson, 1969; reprint, 1991.

Guillory, John. *Cultural Capital: The Problem of Literary Canon Formation*. Chicago: University of Chicago Press, 1993.

Gurney, Rev. John H. *The New Poor Law the Poor Man's Friend: A Plain Address to the Labouring Classes among his Parishioners*. Leicester, Eng.: T. Combe, 1835.

Habermas, Jürgen. *The Structural Transformation of the Public Sphere*, trans. Thomas Burger. Cambridge, Mass.: MIT Press, 1989.

Hanratty, Jerome. "Melodrama—Then and Now." *Review of English Literature* 4 (Apr. 1963): 108–14.

Hardie, Frank. *The Political Influence of the British Monarchy, 1868–1952*. New York: Harper & Row, 1970.

Harrison, Brian. *Separate Spheres: The Opposition to Women's Suffrage in Britain*. London: Croom Helm, 1978.

Harvey, Michael. "The Actor-Audience in Performance of Nineteenth-Century Melodrama." Paper presented at the Conference on Melodrama, Riverside, Calif., 1990.

Hay, Douglas. "Property, Authority and the Criminal Law." In Douglas Hay, Peter Linebaugh, John G. Rule, E. P. Thompson, and Cal Winslow, eds., *Albion's Fatal Tree*, pp. 17–63. New York: Pantheon Books, 1975.

Hayden, Ilse. *Symbol and Privilege: The Ritual Context of British Royalty*. Tucson: University of Arizona Press, 1987.

Hayes, William A. *The Background and Passage of the Third Reform Act*. New York: Garland, 1982.

Heilman, Robert B. "Tragedy and Melodrama: Speculations on Generic Form." In Robert W. Corrigan, ed., *Tragedy: Vision and Form*, pp. 245–57. San Francisco: Chandler, 1965.

Helen Porter; or, A Wife's Tragedy and A Sister's Trials. London: E. Lloyd, 1840.

Helsinger, Elizabeth K., Robin Lauterbach Sheets, and William Veeder. *The Woman Question: Society and Literature in Britain and America, 1837–1883*. 3 vols. Chicago: University of Chicago Press, 1991.

Henriques, Ursula K. "Bastardy and the New Poor Law." *Past and Present* 37 (July 1967): 103–29.

———. "How Cruel Was the Victorian Poor Law?" *Communications* 11 (1968): 365–71.

Bibliography

Herbert, Christopher. *Culture and Anomie: Ethnographic Imagination in the Nineteenth Century*. Chicago: University of Chicago Press, 1991.

[Hickson, W. E.]. "Fallacies on Poor Laws." *Westminster Review* 26 (Jan. 1837): 357–78.

Himmelfarb, Gertrude. *The Idea of Poverty: England in the Early Industrial Age*. New York: Knopf, 1984.

Hindson, Paul, and Tim Gray. *Burke's Dramatic Theory of Politics*. Avebury Series in Philosophy. Aldershot, Eng.: Gower, 1988.

Hobsbawm, Eric. Introduction in Eric Hobsbawm and Terence Ranger, eds., *The Invention of Tradition*. Cambridge, Eng.: Cambridge University Press, 1983.

Hodge, Bob. "The Ideology of Middle Management." In Roger Fowler, Bob Hodge, Gunther Kress, and Tony Trew, eds., *Language and Control*, pp. 81–93. London: Routledge & Kegan Paul, 1979.

Holcombe, Lee. *Wives and Property: Reform of the Married Women's Property Law in Nineteenth-Century England*. Toronto: University of Toronto Press, 1983.

Holcroft, Thomas. *Deaf and Dumb; or, the Orphan Protected* [1802]. Vol. 33, *Davidson's Shilling Volume of Cumberland's Plays*. London: G. H. Davidson, 1855.

———. *A Tale of Mystery* [1802]. In J. O. Bailey, ed., *British Plays of the Nineteenth Century*, pp. 225–40. New York: Odyssey Press, 1966.

Hollis, Patricia. *The Pauper Press: A Study in Working Class Radicalism of the 1830s*. Oxford: Oxford University Press, 1970.

Hone, J. Ann. *For the Cause of Truth: Radicalism in London, 1796–1821*. Oxford: Oxford University Press, 1982.

Hook, Theodore Edward. *Tekeli; or, The Siege of Montgatz*. Vol. 30, *Cumberland's British Theatre*. London: John Cumberland, n.d.

House, Humphrey. *The Dickens World*. London: Oxford University Press, 1941.

Hughes, Leo. *The Drama's Patrons*. Austin: University of Texas Press, 1971.

Hunt, Leigh. *Examiner*, Dec. 13, 1830.

Hutcheson, Francis. *Inquiry into the Origin of our Ideas of Beauty and Virtue*. London: J. Darby, 1725.

Huyssen, Andreas. "Mass Culture as Woman: Modernism's Other." In Tania Modleski, ed., *Studies in Entertainment*, pp. 188–207. Bloomington: Indiana University Press, 1986.

J.S.B. [pseud.]. Letter to the Editor. *Times*, Feb. 20, 1837.

Jacobus, Mary. "'That Great Stage Where Senators Perform': *Macbeth* and the Politics of Romantic Theatre." *Studies in Romanticism* 22 (Fall 1983): 353–87.

Jaeger, Muriel. *Before Victoria*. London: Chatto & Windus, 1956.

James, Louis. *Fiction for the Working Man, 1830–50*. Harmondsworth, Middlesex, Eng.: Penguin, 1973.

Jarrett, Derek. *England in the Age of Hogarth*. New Haven, Conn.: Yale University Press, 1986.

Johnson, Diane. *The True History of the First Mrs. Meredith and other Lesser Lives*. New York: Knopf, 1972.

Johnson, Samuel. *Prologue at the Opening of the Theatre in Drury Lane* [1747]. New York: Dodd, Mead, 1957.

Jones, Andrew. *The Politics of Reform, 1884*. Cambridge, Eng.: Cambridge University Press, 1972.

Jones, Gareth Steadman. *Languages of Class*. Cambridge, Eng.: Cambridge University Press, 1983.

———. *Outcast London*. New York: Pantheon Books, 1971.

Jones, Henry Arthur. "The Theatre and the Mob" [1883]. In *The Renascence of the English Drama*. London, 1895; reprint, Freeport, N.Y.: Books for Libraries Press, 1971.

Joyce, Patrick. *Visions of the People: Industrial England and the Question of Class*. Cambridge, Eng.: Cambridge University Press, 1991.

———. *Work, Society and Politics: The Culture of the Factory in Later Victorian England*. Hassocks, Sussex, Eng.: Harvester Press, 1980.

K.H. and Company [pseud.]. *A Genuine Collection of O.P. Songs*. London: B. Mace, 1809.

Kaplan, E. Ann. *Motherhood and Representation: The Mother in Popular Culture and Melodrama*. London: Routledge, 1992.

Kaye, J. W. "The 'Non-Existence' of Women." *North British Review* 23 (Aug. 1855): 536–62.

Kemble, Francis Ann. *Records of a Girlhood*. New York: Henry Holt, 1879.

Kent, Christopher. *Brains and Numbers*. Toronto: University of Toronto Press, 1978.

———. "Image and Reality: The Actress and Society." In Martha Vicinus, ed., *A Widening Sphere: Changing Roles of Victorian Women*, pp. 94–116. Bloomington: Indiana University Press, 1977.

———. "Presence and Absence: History, Theory, and the Working Class." *Victorian Studies* 29 (Spring 1986): 437–62.

Kettle, Arnold. *An Introduction to the English Novel*. Vol 2. London: Hutchinson, 1967.

Kinzer, Bruce L. *The Ballot Question in Nineteenth-Century Politics*. New York: Garland, 1982.

Klancher, Jon P. *The Making of English Reading Audiences, 1790–1832*. Madison: University of Wisconsin Press, 1987.

Knapp, Andrew, and William Baldwin. *The Newgate Calendar; Comprising Interesting Memoirs of the Most Notorious Criminals*. 4 vols. London: J. Robins, 1824.

Knott, John. *Popular Opposition to the 1834 Poor Law*. New York: St. Martin's Press, 1986.

Kucich, John. *Repression and the Victorian Novel*. Berkeley: University of California Press, 1987.

Kuhn, William Marshall. "Ceremony and Politics: The Management of British Ceremonial, 1861–1911." Ph.D. diss., Johns Hopkins University, 1989.

Lambert, Richard S. *The Railway King, 1800–71*. London: Allen & Unwin, 1934.

Larson, Magali Sarfatti. *The Rise of Professionalism: A Sociological Analysis*. Berkeley: University of California Press, 1977.

Lee, Alan J. *Origins of the Popular Press, 1855–1914.* London: Croom Helm, 1976.

Leitch, Thomas M. "Closure and Teleology in Dickens." *Studies in the Novel* 18 (Summer 1986): 143–56.

Levinson, Marjorie. "Insight and Oversight: Reading 'Tintern Abbey.'" In *Wordsworth's Great Period Poems: Four Essays,* pp. 14–57. New York: Cambridge University Press, 1986.

Levy, Anita. *Other Women: The Writing of Class, Race, and Gender, 1832–1898.* Princeton, N.J.: Princeton University Press, 1991.

Lewin, Henry Grote. *The Railway Mania and Its Aftermath.* London: Railway Gazette, 1936; reprint, Newton Abbot, Devon, Eng.: David & Charles, 1968.

Liesenfeld, Vincent J., ed. *The Stage and the Licensing Act.* New York: Garland, 1981.

Litvak, Joseph. *Caught in the Act: Theatricality in the Nineteenth-Century Novel.* Berkeley: University of California Press, 1992.

Liu, Alan. *Wordsworth: The Sense of History.* Stanford, Calif.: Stanford University Press, 1989.

———. "Wordsworth and Subversion, 1793–1804: Trying Cultural Criticism." *Yale Journal of Criticism* 2 (Spring 1989): 55–100.

Loesberg, Jonathan. "The Ideology of Narrative Form in Sensation Fiction." *Representations* 13 (Winter 1986): 115–38.

Loraine, J. Letter. *Times,* Oct. 20, 1809.

"A Lover of Equity" [pseud.]. Letter. *Times,* Oct. 4, 1809.

Lowenthal, David. *The Past Is a Foreign Country.* Cambridge, Eng.: Cambridge University Press, 1985.

Lukes, Steven. *Individualism.* Key Concepts in the Social Sciences. New York: Harper & Row, 1973.

McGann, Jerome J. *The Romantic Ideology: A Critical Investigation.* Chicago, Ill.: University of Chicago Press, 1983.

Mackay, Jane, and Pat Thane. "The Englishwoman." In Robert Colls and Philip Dodd, eds., *Englishness: Politics and Culture, 1880–1920,* pp. 191–229. London: Croom Helm, 1986.

McKendrick, Neil. "The Commercialization of Fashion." In Neil McKendrick, John Brewer, and J. H. Plumb, eds., *The Birth of a Consumer Society: The Commercialization of Eighteenth-Century England,* pp. 34–99. Bloomington: Indiana University Press, 1982.

MacKenzie, J. M. *Propaganda and Empire.* Manchester, Eng.: Manchester University Press, 1984.

McKeon, Michael. *The Origins of the English Novel.* Baltimore, Md.: Johns Hopkins University Press, 1987.

McNeil, Helen. "Romance, Research, Melodrama." *Encounter* 53 (July 1979): 72–77.

Macready, William Charles. *Macready's Reminiscences, Selections from His Diaries and Letters.* New York: Macmillan, 1875.

Mad Tom [pseud.]. *A Series of Letters on the Late Theatric Festival, Interspersed with*

Remarks on Some Serio-Comic Pantomimes Fresh in the Memory. London: Sherwood, Neeley and Jones, 1810.

[Maginn, William]. "The Honourable Mrs. Norton's 'Undying One.'" *Fraser's Magazine* 2 (Sept. 1830): 180–89.

Malchow, H. L. "A Victorian Mind: Gertrude Himmelfarb, Poverty, and the Moral Imagination." *Victorian Studies* 35 (Spring 1992): 309–15.

Mannheim, Karl. *Ideology and Utopia*, trans. Louis Wirth and Edward Shils. New York: Harcourt Brace Jovanovich, 1936.

Marcus [pseud]. *On the Possibility of Limiting Populousness [and] An Essay on Populousness, to which is added, The Theory of Painless Extinction* [1838]. 4th ed. London: Dugdale, 1840.

Markley, Robert. "Sentimentality as Performance: Shaftesbury, Sterne, and the Theatrics of Virtue." In Felicity Nussbaum and Laura Brown, eds., *The New Eighteenth Century*, pp. 210–30. New York: Methuen, 1987.

Marshall, David. *The Figure of the Theater*. New York: Columbia University Press, 1986.

Marshall, J. D. *The Old Poor Law, 1795–1834*. London: MacMillan, 1968.

Martineau, Harriet. *Autobiography*, ed. Maria W. Chapman. 2 vols. Boston: James Osgood, 1877.

———. *The Parish*. 2 vols. Poor Laws and Paupers Illustrated. Boston: Leonard C. Bowles, 1833.

Maudsley, Henry. *Sex in Mind and Education*. New York: James Miller, 1874.

Mayer, David III. *Harlequin in His Element*. Cambridge, Mass.: Harvard University Press, 1969.

Mayhew, Henry. *London Labour and the London Poor* [1861–62], ed. Victor Neuburg. Harmondsworth, Middlesex, Eng.: Penguin Books, 1985.

Meisel, Martin. *Realizations: Narrative, Pictorial, and Theatrical Arts in Nineteenth-Century England*. Princeton, N.J.: Princeton University Press, 1983.

Mendilow, Jonathan. *The Romantic Tradition in British Political Thought*. Totowa, N.J.: Barnes & Noble, 1986.

Meredith, George. *The Amazing Marriage*. London: Constable, 1885; reprint, London: Constable, 1900.

———. *Diana of the Crossways*. London: Constable, 1885; reprint, London: Constable, 1901.

———. *An Essay on Comedy and the Uses of the Comic Spirit* [1877]. New York: Scribner's, 1913.

———. *The Letters of George Meredith*, ed. C. L. Cline. 3 vols. Oxford: Clarendon Press, 1970.

———. "Love in the Valley." In Phyllis B. Bartlett, ed., *The Poems of George Meredith*, vol. 1, p. 65. New Haven, Conn.: Yale University Press, 1978.

———. *The Poems of George Meredith*, ed. Phyllis B. Bartlett. 2 vols. New Haven, Conn.: Yale University Press, 1978.

"The 'Milk' of Poor-Law 'Kindness.'" *Punch* 4 (1843): 46.

Mill, John Stuart. *On Liberty* [1859]. New York: Norton, 1975.

Miller, D. A. *The Novel and the Police*. Berkeley: University of California Press, 1988.

Bibliography

Miller, J. Hillis. "The Dark World of *Oliver Twist.*" In Harold Bloom, ed., *Charles Dickens*, Modern Critical Views, pp. 29–70. New York: Chelsea House, 1987.

Mitch, David F. *The Rise of Popular Literacy in Victorian England.* Philadelphia: University of Pennsylvania Press, 1992.

Mitchell, Sally. Introduction to *East Lynne*, by Mrs. Henry Wood. New Brunswick, N.J.: Rutgers University Press, 1984.

Moore, D. C. "Political Morality in Mid–Nineteenth Century England: Concepts, Norms, Violations." *Victorian Studies* 13 (Sept. 1969): 5–36.

———. *The Politics of Deference.* Hassocks, Sussex, Eng.: Harvester Press, 1976.

More, Hannah. *An Estimate of the Religion of the Fashionable World.* London: T. Cadell, 1791.

———. *Strictures on the Modern System of Female Education.* London: Cadell & Davies, 1799.

Morley, John. *Critical Miscellanies.* Second series. London: Chapman & Hall, 1877.

———. *On Compromise.* London: Chapman & Hall, 1874.

Mosse, George L. *Nationalism and Sexuality.* New York: Howard Fertig, 1985.

Mullan, John. *Sentiment and Sociability: The Language of Feeling in the Eighteenth Century.* Oxford: Clarendon Press, 1988.

Murray, Janet Horowitz. Introduction, in Janet Horowitz Murray, *Strong-Minded Women.* Harmondsworth, Middlesex, Eng.: Penguin, 1982.

Nadel, Ira B. "Portraits of the Queen." *Victorian Poetry* 25 (Autumn-Winter 1987): 169–91.

Nead, Lynda. *Myths of Sexuality: Representations of Women in Victorian Britain.* London: Basil Blackwell, 1988.

Newby, Howard. "The Deferential Dialectic." *Comparative Studies in Society and History* 17 (Apr. 1975): 139–64.

"The New Poor Law," *Quarterly Review* 52 (Aug. 1834): 233–61.

Nicoll, Allardyce. *A History of English Drama.* Vols. 4 and 5. Cambridge, Eng.: Cambridge University Press, 1955 and 1959.

Nicholls, S. W. *A Summary View of the Report and Evidence Relative to the Poor Laws.* York, Eng.: n.p., 1818.

Nicolson, Watson. *The Struggle for a Free Stage in London.* Boston, 1906; reissue, New York: Benjamin Blom, 1966.

No Party Man [pseud.]. Letter. *Times*, Sept. 22, 1809.

Norton, Caroline. *Caroline Norton's Defense: English Laws for Women in the Nineteenth Century.* London, 1854; reprint, Chicago: Academy Press, 1982.

———. *The Child of the Islands.* London: Chapman & Hall, 1845.

———. "A Letter to the Queen on Lord Chancellor Cranworth's Marriage and Divorce Bill" [1857]. In James O. Hoge and Jane Marcus, eds., *Selected Writings of Caroline Norton.* Delmar, N.Y.: Scholars' Facsimiles and Reprints, 1978.

———. *The Letters of Caroline Norton to Lord Melbourne*, ed. James O. Hoge and Clark Olney. Athens: Ohio State University Press, 1974.

———. *Selected Writings of Caroline Norton*, ed. James O. Hodge and Jane Marcus. Delmar, N.Y.: Scholars' Fascimiles and Reprints, 1978.

—————. *The Wife and Woman's Reward*. 2 vols. New York: Harper and Brothers, 1835.

Old Prices. London: Gale & Curtis, 1809.

One Who Dares to Think for Himself [pseud.]. *Reason Versus Passion*. London: Wilson, 1809.

Ong, Walter, J. *Orality and Literacy: The Technologizing of the Word*. London: Methuen, 1982.

"An Outline of the Grievances of Women." *Metropolitan Magazine* 22 (May 1838): 16–27.

Oxenford, John. *East Lynne*. In Michael Kilgarriff, ed., *The Golden Age of Melodrama*, pp. 295–320. London: Wolfe, 1974.

Paine, Thomas. *The Rights of Man* [1791], ed. H. Collins. Harmondsworth, Middlesex, Eng.: Penguin, 1969.

Palmer, Bryan D. *Descent into Discourse*. Philadelphia: Temple University Press. 1990.

Paull, James. Letter. *Times*, Nov. 11, 1806.

Perkin, Harold. *Origins of Modern English Society*. London: Arc Paperbacks, 1969.

—————. *The Rise of Professional Society*. London: Routledge, 1989.

Perkins, Jane Gray. *The Life of the Honourable Mrs. Norton*. New York: Henry Holt, 1909.

Peterson, M. Jeanne. *Family, Love and Work in the Lives of Victorian Gentlewomen*. Bloomington: Indiana University Press, 1989.

Pocock, J. G. A. "Burke and the Ancient Constitution: A Problem in the History of Ideas." In *Politics, Language and Time: Essays on Political Thought and History*. New York: Atheneum, 1971.

—————. "Machiavelli, Harrington and English Political Ideologies in the Eighteenth Century." In *Politics, Language and Time: Essays on Political Thought and History*. New York: Atheneum, 1971.

—————. *The Machiavellian Moment: Florentine Political Thought and the Atlantic Republican Tradition*. Princeton, N.J.: Princeton University Press, 1975.

Polanyi, Karl. "The Economy as an Instituted Process." In Karl Polanyi, Conrad M. Arensberg, and Harry W. Pearson, eds. *Trade and Market in Early Empires*. New York and Glencoe, Ill.: Free Press and Falcon's Wing Press, 1957.

A Political Epistle to Henry Clifford, Esq. Edinburgh, Eng.: John Moir, 1810.

Pollak, Ellen. *The Poetics of Sexual Myth: Gender and Ideology in the Verse of Swift and Pope*. Women in Culture and Society Series. Chicago: University of Chicago Press, 1985.

"Poor Laws Report." *Westminster Review* 20 (Apr. 1834): 469–88.

Poovey, Mary. "Figures of Arithmetic, Figures of Speech: The Discourse of Statistics in the 1830's." *Critical Inquiry* 19 (Winter 1993): 256–76.

—————. *The Proper Lady and the Woman Writer: Ideology as Style in the Works of Mary Wollstonecraft, Mary Shelley, and Jane Austen*. Women in Culture and Society Series. Chicago: University of Chicago Press, 1984.

—————. *Uneven Developments: The Ideological Work of Gender in Mid-Victorian England*. Chicago: University of Chicago Press, 1988.

Bibliography

Porritt, Edward. *The Unreformed House of Commons*. 2 vols. Cambridge, Eng.: Cambridge University Press, 1903; reprint, New York: Augustus Kelly, 1963.

Porter, Theodore M. *The Rise of Statistical Thinking, 1820–1900*. Princeton, N.J.: Princeton University Press, 1986.

Porter, Walsh. "Epilogue to *Adrian and Orrila*." In William Dimond, *Adrian and Orrila*. London: Cadell & Davies, 1806.

Poynter, John Riddoch. *Society and Pauperism: English Ideas on Poor Relief, 1795–1854*. London: Routledge & Kegan Paul, 1969.

Prendergast, Christopher. *Balzac: Fiction and Melodrama*. New York: Holmes and Meier, 1978.

"The Present State of the Matrimonial Law." *Law Magazine or Quarterly Review of Jurisprudence* 20 (Feb.-May): 36–50.

Psomiades, Kathy Alexis. "Beauty's Body: Gender Ideology and British Aestheticism." *Victorian Studies* 36 (Fall 1992): 31–52.

Pugh, Martin. *The Tories and the People*. London: Basil Blackwell, 1985.

Quinlan, Maurice J. *Victorian Prelude*. New York: Columbia University Press, 1941; reprint, London: Frank Cass, 1965.

Radner, John B. "The Art of Sympathy in Eighteenth-Century British Moral Thought." In Roseann Runte, ed., *Studies in Eighteenth-Century Culture*, vol. 9. Madison: University of Wisconsin Press, 1979.

Rahill, Frank. *The World of Melodrama*. University Park: Pennsylvania State University Press, 1967.

Raina, Badri. *Dickens and the Dialectic of Growth*. Madison: University of Wisconsin Press, 1986.

Rattenbury, Arnold. "Methodism and Tatterdemalions." In Eileen and Stephen Yeo, eds., *Popular Culture and Class Conflict, 1590–1914*, pp. 28–61. Hassocks, Sussex, Eng.: Harvester Press, 1981.

Reader, W. J. *Professional Men: The Rise of the Professional Classes in Nineteenth-Century England*. London: Weidenfeld & Nicolson, 1966.

Reddy, William. *Money and Liberty in Modern Europe*. Cambridge, Eng.: Cambridge University Press, 1987.

Renter [pseud.]. *A Short Address to the Public Respecting the Raising the Prices at Covent-Garden Theatre*. London: J. M. Richardson, 1809.

"Report from the Select Committee Appointed to Inquire into the Laws Affecting Dramatic Literature" [1832]. Vol. 1, *British Parliamentary Papers, Stage and Theatre*. Shannon, Ireland: Irish University Press, 1968.

"Report from the Select Committee of the House of Lords on the Poor Law Amendment Act with Minutes of Evidence, Part One" [1838]. Vol. 6, *British Parliamentary Papers, Poor Laws*. Shannon, Ireland: Irish University Press, 1968.

"Report from the Select Committee of the House of Lords on the Poor Law Amendment Act with Minutes of Evidence, Part Two" [1838]. Vol. 7, *British Parliamentary Papers, Poor Laws*. Shannon, Ireland: Irish University Press, 1968.

"Report from the Select Committee on Parliamentary and Municipal Elections" [1868–69]. Vol. 4, *British Parliamentary Papers, Elections*. Shannon, Ireland: Irish University Press, 1968.

"Report on the Poor Laws," *Fraser's Magazine* 6 (May 1834): 507–22.

Rhodes, R. Crompton. *Harlequin Sheridan*. Oxford: Basil Blackwell, 1933.

Richards, Kenneth, and Peter Thomson, eds. *Essays on Nineteenth-Century British Theatre*. London: Methuen, 1971.

Richards, Thomas. *The Commodity Culture of Victorian England: Advertising and Spectacle, 1851–1914*. Stanford, Calif.: Stanford University Press, 1990.

———. "The Image of Victoria in the Year of the Jubilee." *Victorian Studies* 31 (Autumn 1987): 7–32.

Roach, John. *Social Reform in England, 1780–1880*. New York: St. Martin's Press, 1978.

Roberts, David. "How Cruel Was the Victorian Poor Law?" *Communications* 6 (1963): 97–107.

Rodgers, Daniel T. "In Search of Progressivism." *Reviews in American History* 10 (Dec. 1982): 113–32.

Rodgers, Silvia. "Women's Space in a Men's House: The British House of Commons." In Shirley Adams, ed., *Women and Space: Ground Rules and Social Maps*, pp. 50–71. New York: St. Martin's Press, 1981.

Rorty, Richard. "The Intellectuals at the End of Socialism." *Yale Review* 80 (Apr. 1992): 1–16.

Rosenberg, Edgar. *From Shylock to Svengali: Jewish Stereotypes in English Fiction*. Stanford, Calif.: Stanford University Press, 1960.

Rosenberg, James L. "Melodrama." In Robert W. Corrigan, ed., *Tragedy: Vision and Form*, pp. 232–44. San Francisco, Calif.: Chandler, 1965.

Rowell, George. *Queen Victoria Goes to the Theatre*. London: Paul Elek, 1978.

———. *The Victorian Theatre*. London: Geoffrey Cumberlege, Oxford University Press, 1956.

Rubenstein, W. D. *Elites and the Wealthy in Modern British History*. Hassocks, Sussex, Eng.: Harvester Press, 1987.

Rudé, George. *The Crowd in History*. London: John Wiley, 1964; reprint, London: Lawrence & Wishart, 1981.

———. *Ideology and Popular Protest*. London: John Wiley, 1964; revised ed., London: Lawrence & Wishart, 1984.

Russell, Gillian. "Playing at Revolution: The Politics of the O.P. Riots of 1809." *Theatre Notebook* 44 (1990): 16–26.

S. [pseud.]. "A Few Words About Actresses and the Profession of the Stage." *Englishwoman's Journal* 2 (Feb. 1859): 385–98.

S.B.E. [pseud.]. Letter. *Times*, Sept. 22, 1809.

Schlicke, Paul. *Dickens and Popular Entertainment*. London: Allen & Unwin, 1985.

Schneewind, Jerome B. "Moral Problems and Moral Philosophy in the Victorian Period." *Victorian Studies* supplement to 9 (1964): 29–46.

Schreiner, Olive. *The Story of an African Farm*. London: Chapman & Hall, 1883; Harmondsworth, Middlesex, Eng.: Penguin, 1939.

Sennett, Richard. *The Fall of Public Man*. Cambridge, Eng.: Cambridge University Press, 1974.

Sheridan, Paul. *Penny Theatres of Victorian London*. London: Dennis Dobson, 1981.

Bibliography

Showalter, Elaine. *The Female Malady: Women, Madness and English Culture, 1830–1980.* New York: Pantheon Books, 1985.

Simpson, David. *Fetishism and Imagination.* Baltimore, Md.: Johns Hopkins University Press, 1982.

———. "Introduction: The Moment of Materialism." In David Simpson, ed., *Subject to History: Ideology, Class, Gender,* pp. 1–33. Ithaca, N.Y.: Cornell University Press, 1991.

Siskin, Clifford. *The Historicity of Romantic Discourse.* New York: Oxford University Press, 1988.

Smith, Adam. *The Theory of Moral Sentiments* [1761]. New York: Arlington House, 1969.

Smith, Goldwin. "The Conflict with the Lords." *Contemporary Review* 46 (Sept. 1884): 313–21.

Smith, James L. *Melodrama.* London: Methuen, 1973.

Smith, Olivia. *The Politics of Language, 1791–1819.* Oxford: Clarendon Press, 1984.

Spacks, Patricia Meyer. *Gossip.* New York: Knopf, 1985.

Spring, David. "Walter Bagehot and Deference." *American Historical Review* 81 (June 1976): 524–31.

Stallybrass, Peter, and Allon White. *The Politics and Poetics of Transgression.* London: Methuen, 1986.

Staves, Susan. "Money for Honor: Damages for Criminal Conversation." In Harry C. Payne, ed., *Studies in Eighteenth-Century Culture,* vol. 11, pp. 279–98. Madison: University of Wisconsin Press, 1982.

———. *Players' Sceptres.* Lincoln: University of Nebraska Press, 1979.

Stead, W. T. *The Maiden Tribute of Modern Babylon (The Report of the "Pall Mall Gazette's" Secret Commission).* London: *Pall Mall Gazette,* 1885.

———. *Pall Mall Gazette,* Mar. 28, 1885.

[Stephen, James Fitzjames]. "Mr. Dickens as a Politician." *Saturday Review.* Mar. 1, 1857. In Philip Collins, ed., *Dickens: The Critical Heritage,* pp. 348–49. London: Routledge & Kegan Paul, 1971.

Stetson, Dorothy M. *A Woman's Issue: The Politics of Family Law Reform in England.* Westport, Conn.: Greenwood Press, 1982.

Stevenson, Lionel. *The Ordeal of George Meredith.* New York: Scribner's, 1953; reprint, New York: Russell & Russell, 1967.

Stockdale, J. J., ed. *The Covent Garden Journal.* 2 vols. London: J. J. Stockdale, 1810.

———. "Succinct History of the Contest." In J. J. Stockdale, ed., *The Covent Garden Journal,* vol. 1. London: J. J. Stockdale, 1810.

Stone, J. S. *George Meredith's Politics.* Ontario: P. D. Meany, 1986.

Stone, Lawrence. *The Family, Sex and Marriage,* abridged edition. New York: Harper & Row, 1977.

Stone, Marjorie. "Dickens, Bentham, and the Fictions of the Law: A Victorian Controversy and Its Consequences." *Victorian Studies* 29 (Autumn 1985): 125–154.

Styles, John. *An Essay on the Stage.* London: Williams & Smith, 1807.

Sypher, Wylie. "Aesthetic of Revolution: The Marxist Melodrama." In Robert W. Corrigan, ed., *Tragedy: Vision and Form*, pp. 258–67. San Francisco: Chandler, 1965.

Tambling, Jeremy. "Prison-bound: Dickens and Foucault." *Essays in Criticism* 36, no. 2 (1986): 11–31.

Taylor, Barbara. *Eve and the New Jerusalem: Socialism and Feminism in the Nineteenth Century*. New York: Pantheon, 1983.

Taylor, Gary. *Reinventing Shakespeare*. New York: Weidenfeld & Nicolson, 1989.

Taylor, Jenny Bourne. *In the Secret Theatre of Home: Wilkie Collins, Sensation Narrative, and Nineteenth-Century Psychology*. London: Routledge, 1988.

Tegg, Thomas. *The Rise, Progress and Termination of the O.P. War, in Poetic Epistles, or Hudibrastic Letters*. London: Tegg, 1810.

Tetzeli v. Rosador, Kurt. "Victorian Theories of Melodrama." *Anglia* 95 (1977): 87–114.

Thane, Pat. "Women and the Poor Law in Victorian and Edwardian England." *History Workshop* 6 (Autumn 1978): 29–51.

Theatrical Examiner [pseud.]. *The Examiner*, Sept. 24, 1809.

———. *The Examiner*, Dec. 13, 1830.

Theatricus [pseud.]. *Theatrical Taxation*. London: G. Hughes, n.d.

Thompson, Dorothy. *Queen Victoria: The Woman, the Monarchy and the People*. New York: Pantheon Books, 1990.

Thompson, E. P. "Eighteenth-Century English Society: Class Struggle Without Class?" *Social History* 3 (May 1978): 133–65.

———. *The Making of the English Working Class*. New York: Vintage Books, 1966.

———. "Patrician Society, Plebeian Culture." *Journal of Social History* 7 (1974): 382–405.

Thompson, F. M. L. *The Rise of Respectable Society*. Cambridge, Mass.: Harvard University Press, 1988.

Thompson, Noel. *The Market and Its Critics: Socialist Political Economy in Nineteenth-Century Britain*. London: Routledge, 1988.

Thompson, William. *Appeal of one Half the Human Race, Women, Against the Pretensions of the Other Half, Men, To Retain Them in Political, and Thence in Civil and Domestic Slavery*. Great Britain: n.p., 1825; reprint, London: Virago Press, 1983.

Thro, A. Brooker. "An Approach to Melodramatic Fiction: Goodness and Energy in the Novels of Dickens, Collins, Reade." *Genre* 2 (Fall 1978): 359–74.

"The Town" [pseud.]. Open Letter to Lord Chamberlain. *Morning Chronicle*, Oct. 28, 1809.

Tracy, Robert. "'The Old Story' and Inside Stories: Modish Fiction and Fictional Modes in *Oliver Twist*." In Michael Timko, Fred Kaplan, and Edward Guiliano, eds., *Dickens Studies Annual*, vol. 17, pp. 1–34. New York: AMS Press, 1988.

Trollope, Anthony. *An Autobiography* [1883]. Oxford: Oxford University Press, 1980.

———. *The Eustace Diamonds* [1873]. Oxford: Oxford University Press, 1983.

————. *Phineas Finn* [1869]. Oxford: Oxford University Press, 1982.

Tuchman, Gaye, with Nina E. Fortin. *Edging Women Out: Victorian Novelists, Publishers and Social Change*. New Haven, Conn.: Yale University Press, 1989.

Tumir, Vaska. "She-Tragedy and Its Men: Conflict and Form in *The Orphan* and *The Fair Penitent*." *Studies in English Literature* 30 (Summer 1990): 411–28.

Unsigned Letter. *Morning Chronicle*, Sept. 28, 1809.

Unsigned Review. *Times*, June 1, 1885.

Verus Amicus [pseud.]. *A Letter to John Kemble, Esq.* London: G. E. Miles, 1809.

Vicinus, Martha. "'Helpless and Unfriended': Nineteenth-Century Domestic Melodrama." *New Literary History* 13 (Autumn 1981): 127–43.

Victory of the O.P.'s. London: Fairburn, 1809.

Vincent, David. *Literacy and Popular Culture, England 1750–1914*. Cambridge, Eng.: Cambridge University Press, 1989.

Viner, Jacob. *The Role of Providence in the Social Order*. Philadelphia: American Philosophical Society, 1972.

Walkowitz, Judith R. *City of Dreadful Delight: Narratives of Sexual Danger in Late-Victorian London*. Chicago: University of Chicago Press, 1992.

————. "Male Vice and Feminist Virtue: Feminism and the Politics of Prostitution in Nineteenth-Century Britain." *History Workshop* 13 (Spring 1982): 79–93.

————. *Prostitution and Victorian Society: Women, Class, and the State*. Cambridge, Eng.: Cambridge University Press, 1980.

————. "Science and the Seance: Transgressions of Gender and Genre in Late Victorian London." *Representations* 22 (Spring 1988): 3–35.

Waller, P. J., ed. *Politics and Social Change in Modern Britain*. Hassocks, Sussex, Eng.: Harvester Press, 1987.

Weber, Max. *Economy and Society: An Outline of Interpretive Sociology*, ed. Guenther Roth and Claus Wittich, trans. Ephraim Fischoff and others. 2 vols. Berkeley: University of California Press, 1978.

Wiener, Martin J. *English Culture and the Decline of the Industrial Spirit, 1850–1980*. Cambridge, Eng.: Cambridge University Press, 1981.

Williams, Ioan, ed. *The Idea of the Novel in Europe, 1600–1800*. New York: New York University Press, 1979.

————. *Meredith: The Critical Heritage*. New York: Barnes & Noble, 1971.

Williams, Raymond. *Marxism and Literature*. Oxford: Oxford University Press, 1977.

————. "Social Criticism in Dickens: Some Problems of Method and Approach." *Critical Inquiry* 6 (Autumn 1964): 214–27.

————. "Social Environment and Theatrical Environment: The Case of English Naturalism." In Marie Axton and Raymond Williams, eds., *English Drama: Forms and Development*, pp. 203–23. Cambridge, Eng.: Cambridge University Press, 1977.

Wilt, Judith. "Meredith's Diana: Freedom, Fiction, and the Female." *Texas Studies in Language and Literature* 18 (Spring 1976): 42–62.

————. *The Readable People of Meredith*. Princeton, N.J.: Princeton University Press, 1975.

Index

Identity: individual, 4, 22–23, 83–84, 145–47; bifurcated, 31–33, 46, 104, 106; national, 176–77, 267n118

Imposture, 85–86, 246n26

Infants and Child Custody Bill, 137

An Inquiry into the Origin of Our Ideas of Beauty and Virtue (Hutcheson), 17

Intellectual individual, 190–92

Isabelle (Buckstone), 151–52, 154, 262n57

James, Henry, 186

Jerrold, Douglas, 229n1

Jews, 42f, 62–63, 236n20

Johnson, Samuel, 34–35

Jones, Henry Arthur, 188, 191, 206

Joyce, Patrick, 167

Kemble, Fanny, 148, 220

Kemble, John Philip, 38–50 *passim*, 57–63 *passim*, 71, 237n39, 263n58

Lee, Alan, 189

Leitch, Thomas, 115

"Letter to My Countrywomen" (Butler), 195

"A Letter to the Queen" (Norton), 5, 138, 158, 163–66

Levinson, Marjorie, 29

Licensing Act of 1737, 66

Liu, Alan, 29–30, 137

Loraine, J., 58

Macbeth (Shakespeare), 56f, 65

McGann, Jerome, 28

MacKenzie, J. M., 183

Maclise, Daniel, 142f

Macready, William, 56

Malthus, Thomas, 82

Market culture, *see under* Culture

Market economy, 46–47, 69, 218, 273n78. *See also* Capitalism

Market exchange, *see under* Exchange

Market practices, 10

Markley, Robert, 17

Married Women's Property Acts, 137, 201

Martineau, Harriet, 85, 162, 166, 169

Matrimonial Causes Act, 137

Mayhew, Henry, 85

Melbourne, Lord William Lamb, 141–47 *passim*

Melodrama, 3, 7, 230n7, 246n19, 259n10; as genre, 1–3, 8, 63–66, 98–99, 229n3; audiences for, 2–3, 67–69, 74, 235n7, 242n105; definitions of, 2, 9, 98–99, 229n1, 230n8, 231n13, 252n79, 258n6; villain in, 67, 73–74, 113–14, 154–55, 196–97, 217–18, 273n75; and novels, 71, 116–19, 244n3, 255nn126–27, 256n133; familial tableau in, 74–75, 76, 154–55, 175, 243n124. *See also specific types*

The Melodramatic Imagination (Brooks), 9

Melodramatic mode, 3–11 *passim*, 30–32, 60–63, 111–14, 194, 230n10, 243n118; of Old Price Wars, 4–5, 38f, 44, 57–60, 65, 76, 194, 240n78; in Caroline Norton's writings, 5–6, 158–66, 168–71; of Butler on Contagious Diseases Acts, 6, 183, 193–202; in Victorian culture, 6, 134–38 *passim*, 166–68, 182–88; of anti–Poor Law movement, 7–8, 77–80, 96–114, 194, 244n5; in Dickens's writings, 77–78, 114–32, 244n3; in Meredith's *Diana of the Crossways*, 202–14 *passim*, 272n61

Mendoza, Daniel, 42

Meredith, George, 9, 181f, 191–92, 201, 223; *Diana of the Crossways*, 6, 31, 192f, 202–20, 222, 272n61; on women, 208–9, 213, 219–22

Middle class, *see under* Class

Middlemarch (Eliot), 31

Mill, John Stuart, 181f, 184, 189, 218

Miller, D. A., 71, 116, 121–22, 128

Mode, 6–7

Monarchical melodrama, *see* Royal melodrama

Monarchy, 172–75, 197–99, 267n118. *See also* Victoria, Queen

Moore, David, 44, 82

"Moral force," 99–100

More, Hannah, 21, 60

Morley, John, 6, 9, 181–85 *passim*, 189–205 *passim*, 216–21 *passim*, 270n14

Napoleon I, 152, 263n58

Newby, Howard, 15

Index

Library of Congress Cataloging-in-Publication Data

Hadley, Elaine.
  Melodramatic tactics : theatricalized dissent in the English
marketplace, 1800–1885 / Elaine Hadley.
    p. cm.
  Includes bibliographical references and index.
  ISBN 0-8047-2403-2
  1. English drama—19th century—History and criticism.
2. Melodrama, English—History and criticism.   3. English
literature—19th century—History and criticism.   4. Literature
and society—England—History—19th century.   5. Theater
and society—England—History—19th century.   6. Social
problems in literature.   I. Title.
PR728.M4H33   1995
822'.052709—dc20
                                        94-42454
                                          CIP

♾ This book is printed on acid-free, recycled paper.